Almighty God,
Father of our Lord Jesus Christ,
grant, we pray,
that we might be grounded and settled
in your truth
by the coming of your Holy Spirit
into our hearts.

What we do not know,
reveal to us;
what is lacking within us,
make complete;
that which we do know,
confirm in us;
and keep us blameless in your service,
through Jesus Christ our Lord.

Amen.

IMMERSE

The Reading **Bible**®

KINGDOMS

Tyndale House Publishers, Inc.
Carol Stream, Illinois

CREATED IN ALLIANCE WITH

INSTITUTE FOR
BIBLE READING

Visit Tyndale online at www.immerseBible.com, www.newlivingtranslation.com, and www.tyndale.com.

Visit the Institute for Bible Reading at www.instituteforbiblereading.org.

Library of Congress Cataloging-in-Publication Data

Title: Kingdoms.
Other titles: Bible. Former Prophets. English. New Living Translation. 2017.
  | Bible. Ruth. English. New Living Translation. 2017.
Description: Carol Stream, Illinois : Tyndale House Publishers, Inc., 2017. |
  Series: Immerse: the reading Bible
Identifiers: LCCN 2017020851 | ISBN 9781496424150 (sc)
Classification: LCC BS1286.5.A3 N495 2017 | DDC 222/.20520834—dc23 LC record
  available at https://lccn.loc.gov/2017020851

Printed in the United States of America

24	23	22	21	20	19	18
8	7	6	5	4	3	2

CONTENTS

———— ✟ ————

These books tell Israel's story from the conquest of Canaan (Joshua) and the struggle to settle the land (Judges, Ruth) to the establishment of a kingdom under David's dynasty. It continues with Israel's division and deepening sin and concludes with Jerusalem's fall and the people's forced exile (Samuel–Kings).

—— *Welcome to* ——

I M M E R S E
The Bible Reading Experience

The Bible is a great gift. The Creator of all things entered into our human story and spoke to us. He inspired people over many centuries to shape words into books that reveal his mind, bringing wisdom into our lives and light to our paths. But God's biggest intention for the Bible is to invite us into its Story. What God wants for us, more than anything else, is that we make the Bible's great drama of restoration and new life the story of our lives, too.

The appropriate way to receive a gift like this is to come to know the Bible deeply, to lose ourselves in it precisely so that we can find ourselves in it. In other words, we need to immerse ourselves in it—to read God's words at length and without distraction, to read with deeper historical and literary perspective, and to read through the Bible with friends in a regular three-year rhythm. *Immerse: The Bible Reading Experience* has been specially designed for this purpose.

Immerse: The Reading Bible presents each book of the Bible without the distractions of chapter and verse markers, subject headers, or footnotes—all later historical additions to the text. The *Holy Bible*, New Living Translation, is presented in a single-column format with easy-to-read type. To provide meaningful perspective, book introductions give historical and literary context, and the books are often reordered chronologically or grouped with books that share similar ancient audiences. Every feature in this unique Bible enhances the opportunity for readers to engage with God's words in simple clarity.

A more complete explanation of this unique Bible presentation can be found in the articles that begin on page 273 at the back of this volume.

——— *Introduction to* ———

KINGDOMS

THE BIBLE'S OPENING BOOKS, Genesis to Samuel–Kings, together constitute Israel's primary history. This opening story covers the events from God's creation of the world and his intentions for humanity to the account of Israel's covenant failure and forced exile from the Promised Land. The first five books—*Beginnings*—take us to the point when God's people have been freed from slavery in Egypt and are about to enter the land promised to their ancestor Abraham.

The story continues in the next four books (Joshua, Judges, Ruth, and Samuel–Kings) as Israel enters the land and is commissioned to be God's light to the nations. It is God's plan for his new people to inhabit a new place, the template for showing all people what it means to follow God and help the world to flourish. These books are written in narrative form and have a prophetic viewpoint, always calling Israel to be faithful to the LORD, their High King.

As these books begin, God's people are living under God's three earlier covenants made with Noah, Abraham, and Moses. The story moves ahead with a description of the events surrounding the fourth covenant. This covenant is with David, Israel's second king, and promises a lasting dynasty of kings descended from him.

Originally, the Israelites didn't have a human king because God himself was their King. Once Abraham's descendants grew into a nation, God sent Moses to be their liberator and leader, freeing them from slavery in Egypt and guiding them to the land of Canaan. But Moses was a prophet, not a king. A new leader named Joshua then leads Israel into the Promised Land. He defeats their enemies and divides the land among the twelve tribes. But Joshua wasn't a king either.

In the years that follow, as described in the book of Judges, God raises up a series of leaders called "judges" to rescue the Israelites whenever their disobedience results in their falling under foreign control. The Israelites see themselves as a nation consisting of twelve tribes, and the tradition of tribal leadership is strong. But still, this period shows that while they have no king, "all the people did whatever seemed right in their own eyes," leading to disastrous consequences for the whole nation.

In the book of Deuteronomy, Moses foresees that the people will want a king. And when they do, the king will be required to make himself a copy of the law and "read it daily as long as he lives," enabling him to lead the people into covenant faithfulness. As the period of the judges comes to a close, the time certainly seems right for a king like this to exert a central authority over Israel and restrain the rampant lawlessness.

So when Samuel, the last of the judges, is growing old, the Israelites ask him to appoint a king for them. God sees this as a rejection of himself as their King, but he relents and tells Samuel to anoint a man named Saul. Saul eventually proves stubborn, self-willed, and disobedient, so the LORD tells Samuel to anoint David to replace Saul as king.

After much intrigue and danger, David finally comes to the throne. He makes grave mistakes himself, but God still knows David as a man after his own heart because he deeply loves and respects God and his covenant.

David's faithfulness to the LORD serves as the standard by which all of his successors are measured in the long book of Samuel–Kings, which begins with the stories of Samuel, Saul, and David and then traces the whole future course of the Israelite kingdom. However, because the kings turn away from the LORD and worship other gods, violence and oppression are introduced and the kingdom splits in two. Both kingdoms are later conquered by foreign empires, and the Israelites are forced into exile.

At this point, God's plan appears to be deeply threatened. His chosen people have failed to fulfill their commitments in the covenant relationship and are therefore losing their Temple, their king, and their land. Just as Adam and Eve were exiled from the garden of God at the beginning of the Story, so now Israel is exiled from God's new Eden, the Promised Land. The tension in the overall Story rises here to fever pitch. Abraham's descendants are supposed to be the means by which God will bless and restore the world. But now, all seems lost.

Only one thread is left: God's new covenant with King David promises that God will not abandon David's family and kingdom. Whatever work God will yet do through Israel for the sake of the world, he will do through this royal line.

THE STORY OF how the tribes of Israel became a kingdom begins with the conquest of the land of Canaan. God promised he would give this land to Abraham's descendants, and Moses brought them right to its border. But Moses' successor, Joshua, actually leads Israel into the land, defeating the city-kingdoms that rule there. The book of Joshua describes how he did this.

Throughout the land there are walled cities, each ruled by its own king. As long as these fortified "royal cities" remain in hostile hands, the Israelites will be under constant threat. The biggest threat of all looms immediately before them as they enter Canaan. Jericho is an imposing fortress that controls the fords of the Jordan River. If the Israelites manage to cross over but then can't defeat Jericho, the river will become a barrier, trapping them where their enemies can destroy them.

The task is daunting, but God promises Joshua, "I will be with you as I was with Moses. I will not fail you or abandon you. Be strong and courageous, for you are the one who will lead these people to possess all the land I swore to their ancestors I would give them."

The book of Joshua has three major sections. Most of it is in the form of a narrative, but at various places there are important lists, including records of defeated cities and kings and of land allotments for Israel's tribes.

The book opens with a description of how God prepares Joshua and the people for entry into the land and then guides them across the Jordan River. It begins with God commissioning and encouraging Joshua in his task, while also urging Joshua and the people to continually meditate on the instructions God has given to Moses. Joshua sends spies into Canaan and then leads the people into the land, crossing the Jordan River on dry ground. In their new land they celebrate their freedom festival—Passover—and, for the first time, eat food from the Land of Promise.

Next Israel invades the central region of Canaan and then spreads out to both the northern and southern regions. Key to this section is the realization that God himself is fighting for Israel, thus keeping his promises to Israel's ancestors. The warfare Joshua conducts is brutal, but in the context of the story, the nations are removed from Canaan because they had become utterly corrupt—just as Israel itself will be brutally removed in the future for its own detestable practices. These events must be read within the context of God's ongoing Story of redemption, especially in light of God's supreme revelation later in Israel's Messiah.

Once the land has been conquered, the second section explains how Joshua divides it among the tribes. We may wonder why there is such a detailed description of the allocation of the land, but this gets at the heart of the covenant. God's intention has always been for his people to thrive in the physical place he set apart for them. Israel's conquest of the Promised Land reflects God's overall objective to reclaim the entire creation as our good home and his glorious Temple.

The final section of the book focuses on Joshua's leading the people in a covenant renewal ceremony. The leaders of the various tribes and clans gather at Shechem and are challenged to serve God alone, obey the Law of Moses, and fully claim their inheritance from the LORD.

"Choose today whom you will serve," Joshua challenges them. "As for me and my family, we will serve the LORD." The people, aware of their story and recognizing that they are to continue living it out, respond, "We would never abandon the LORD and serve other gods. . . . We, too, will serve the LORD, for he alone is our God."

At the end of Joshua's life, the people have received God's gift of land as promised and are poised to fulfill their calling as agents in God's mission to all nations. The LORD has kept his promises to Abraham and Moses. Now Abraham's family must step up to become God's covenant people for the sake of the world.

JOSHUA

✛

After the death of Moses the LORD's servant, the LORD spoke to Joshua son of Nun, Moses' assistant. He said, "Moses my servant is dead. Therefore, the time has come for you to lead these people, the Israelites, across the Jordan River into the land I am giving them. I promise you what I promised Moses: 'Wherever you set foot, you will be on land I have given you—from the Negev wilderness in the south to the Lebanon mountains in the north, from the Euphrates River in the east to the Mediterranean Sea in the west, including all the land of the Hittites.' No one will be able to stand against you as long as you live. For I will be with you as I was with Moses. I will not fail you or abandon you.

"Be strong and courageous, for you are the one who will lead these people to possess all the land I swore to their ancestors I would give them. Be strong and very courageous. Be careful to obey all the instructions Moses gave you. Do not deviate from them, turning either to the right or to the left. Then you will be successful in everything you do. Study this Book of Instruction continually. Meditate on it day and night so you will be sure to obey everything written in it. Only then will you prosper and succeed in all you do. This is my command—be strong and courageous! Do not be afraid or discouraged. For the LORD your God is with you wherever you go."

Joshua then commanded the officers of Israel, "Go through the camp and tell the people to get their provisions ready. In three days you will cross the Jordan River and take possession of the land the LORD your God is giving you."

Then Joshua called together the tribes of Reuben, Gad, and the half-tribe of Manasseh. He told them, "Remember what Moses, the servant of the LORD, commanded you: 'The LORD your God is giving you a place of rest. He has given you this land.' Your wives, children, and livestock may remain here in the land Moses assigned to you on the east side of the Jordan River. But your strong warriors, fully armed, must lead the other tribes across the Jordan to help them conquer their territory. Stay with them until the LORD gives them rest, as he has given you rest, and until they, too, possess the land the LORD your God is giving them. Only then may you return and settle here on the east side of the Jordan River in the land that Moses, the servant of the LORD, assigned to you."

They answered Joshua, "We will do whatever you command us, and we will go wherever you send us. We will obey you just as we obeyed Moses. And may the LORD your God be with you as he was with Moses. Anyone who rebels against your orders and does not obey your words and everything you command will be put to death. So be strong and courageous!"

+

Then Joshua secretly sent out two spies from the Israelite camp at Acacia Grove. He instructed them, "Scout out the land on the other side of the Jordan River, especially around Jericho." So the two men set out and came to the house of a prostitute named Rahab and stayed there that night.

But someone told the king of Jericho, "Some Israelites have come here tonight to spy out the land." So the king of Jericho sent orders to Rahab: "Bring out the men who have come into your house, for they have come here to spy out the whole land."

Rahab had hidden the two men, but she replied, "Yes, the men were here earlier, but I didn't know where they were from. They left the town at dusk, as the gates were about to close. I don't know where they went. If you hurry, you can probably catch up with them." (Actually, she had taken them up to the roof and hidden them beneath bundles of flax she had laid out.) So the king's men went looking for the spies along the road leading to the shallow crossings of the Jordan River. And as soon as the king's men had left, the gate of Jericho was shut.

Before the spies went to sleep that night, Rahab went up on the roof to talk with them. "I know the LORD has given you this land," she told them. "We are all afraid of you. Everyone in the land is living in terror. For we have heard how the LORD made a dry path for you through the Red Sea when you left Egypt. And we know what you did to Sihon and Og, the two Amorite kings east of the Jordan River, whose people you completely destroyed. No wonder our hearts have melted in fear! No one has the courage to fight after hearing such things. For the LORD your God is the supreme God of the heavens above and the earth below.

"Now swear to me by the LORD that you will be kind to me and my family since I have helped you. Give me some guarantee that when Jericho is conquered, you will let me live, along with my father and mother, my brothers and sisters, and all their families."

"We offer our own lives as a guarantee for your safety," the men agreed.

"If you don't betray us, we will keep our promise and be kind to you when the LORD gives us the land."

Then, since Rahab's house was built into the town wall, she let them down by a rope through the window. "Escape to the hill country," she told them. "Hide there for three days from the men searching for you. Then, when they have returned, you can go on your way."

Before they left, the men told her, "We will be bound by the oath we have taken only if you follow these instructions. When we come into the land, you must leave this scarlet rope hanging from the window through which you let us down. And all your family members—your father, mother, brothers, and all your relatives—must be here inside the house. If they go out into the street and are killed, it will not be our fault. But if anyone lays a hand on people inside this house, we will accept the responsibility for their death. If you betray us, however, we are not bound by this oath in any way."

"I accept your terms," she replied. And she sent them on their way, leaving the scarlet rope hanging from the window.

The spies went up into the hill country and stayed there three days. The men who were chasing them searched everywhere along the road, but they finally returned without success.

Then the two spies came down from the hill country, crossed the Jordan River, and reported to Joshua all that had happened to them. "The LORD has given us the whole land," they said, "for all the people in the land are terrified of us."

Early the next morning Joshua and all the Israelites left Acacia Grove and arrived at the banks of the Jordan River, where they camped before crossing. Three days later the Israelite officers went through the camp, giving these instructions to the people: "When you see the Levitical priests carrying the Ark of the Covenant of the LORD your God, move out from your positions and follow them. Since you have never traveled this way before, they will guide you. Stay about half a mile behind them, keeping a clear distance between you and the Ark. Make sure you don't come any closer."

Then Joshua told the people, "Purify yourselves, for tomorrow the LORD will do great wonders among you."

In the morning Joshua said to the priests, "Lift up the Ark of the Covenant and lead the people across the river." And so they started out and went ahead of the people.

The LORD told Joshua, "Today I will begin to make you a great leader in the eyes of all the Israelites. They will know that I am with you, just as I was with Moses. Give this command to the priests who carry the Ark of the Covenant: 'When you reach the banks of the Jordan River, take a few steps into the river and stop there.'"

So Joshua told the Israelites, "Come and listen to what the LORD your God says. Today you will know that the living God is among you. He will surely drive out the Canaanites, Hittites, Hivites, Perizzites, Girgashites, Amorites, and Jebusites ahead of you. Look, the Ark of the Covenant, which belongs to the Lord of the whole earth, will lead you across the Jordan River! Now choose twelve men from the tribes of Israel, one from each tribe. The priests will carry the Ark of the LORD, the Lord of all the earth. As soon as their feet touch the water, the flow of water will be cut off upstream, and the river will stand up like a wall."

So the people left their camp to cross the Jordan, and the priests who were carrying the Ark of the Covenant went ahead of them. It was the harvest season, and the Jordan was overflowing its banks. But as soon as the feet of the priests who were carrying the Ark touched the water at the river's edge, the water above that point began backing up a great distance away at a town called Adam, which is near Zarethan. And the water below that point flowed on to the Dead Sea until the riverbed was dry. Then all the people crossed over near the town of Jericho.

Meanwhile, the priests who were carrying the Ark of the LORD's Covenant stood on dry ground in the middle of the riverbed as the people passed by. They waited there until the whole nation of Israel had crossed the Jordan on dry ground.

When all the people had crossed the Jordan, the LORD said to Joshua, "Now choose twelve men, one from each tribe. Tell them, 'Take twelve stones from the very place where the priests are standing in the middle of the Jordan. Carry them out and pile them up at the place where you will camp tonight.'"

So Joshua called together the twelve men he had chosen—one from each of the tribes of Israel. He told them, "Go into the middle of the Jordan, in front of the Ark of the LORD your God. Each of you must pick up one stone and carry it out on your shoulder—twelve stones in all, one for each of the twelve tribes of Israel. We will use these stones to build a memorial. In the future your children will ask you, 'What do these stones mean?' Then you can tell them, 'They remind us that the Jordan River stopped flowing when the Ark of the LORD's Covenant went across.' These stones will stand as a memorial among the people of Israel forever."

So the men did as Joshua had commanded them. They took twelve stones from the middle of the Jordan River, one for each tribe, just as the LORD had told Joshua. They carried them to the place where they camped for the night and constructed the memorial there.

Joshua also set up another pile of twelve stones in the middle of the Jordan, at the place where the priests who carried the Ark of the Covenant were standing. And they are there to this day.

The priests who were carrying the Ark stood in the middle of the river until all of the LORD's commands that Moses had given to Joshua were carried out. Meanwhile, the people hurried across the riverbed. And when everyone was safely on the other side, the priests crossed over with the Ark of the LORD as the people watched.

The armed warriors from the tribes of Reuben, Gad, and the half-tribe of Manasseh led the Israelites across the Jordan, just as Moses had directed. These armed men—about 40,000 strong—were ready for battle, and the LORD was with them as they crossed over to the plains of Jericho.

That day the LORD made Joshua a great leader in the eyes of all the Israelites, and for the rest of his life they revered him as much as they had revered Moses.

The LORD had said to Joshua, "Command the priests carrying the Ark of the Covenant to come up out of the riverbed." So Joshua gave the command. As soon as the priests carrying the Ark of the LORD's Covenant came up out of the riverbed and their feet were on high ground, the water of the Jordan returned and overflowed its banks as before.

The people crossed the Jordan on the tenth day of the first month. Then they camped at Gilgal, just east of Jericho. It was there at Gilgal that Joshua piled up the twelve stones taken from the Jordan River.

Then Joshua said to the Israelites, "In the future your children will ask, 'What do these stones mean?' Then you can tell them, 'This is where the Israelites crossed the Jordan on dry ground.' For the LORD your God dried up the river right before your eyes, and he kept it dry until you were all across, just as he did at the Red Sea when he dried it up until we had all crossed over. He did this so all the nations of the earth might know that the LORD's hand is powerful, and so you might fear the LORD your God forever."

When all the Amorite kings west of the Jordan and all the Canaanite kings who lived along the Mediterranean coast heard how the LORD had dried up the Jordan River so the people of Israel could cross, they lost heart and were paralyzed with fear because of them.

At that time the LORD told Joshua, "Make flint knives and circumcise this second generation of Israelites." So Joshua made flint knives and circumcised the entire male population of Israel at Gibeath-haaraloth.

Joshua had to circumcise them because all the men who were old enough to fight in battle when they left Egypt had died in the wilderness. Those who left Egypt had all been circumcised, but none of those born after the Exodus, during the years in the wilderness, had been circumcised. The Israelites had traveled in the wilderness for forty years until all the men who were old enough to fight in battle when they left Egypt had died. For they had disobeyed the LORD, and the LORD vowed he would not let them enter the land he had sworn to give us—a land flowing with milk and honey. So Joshua circumcised their sons—those who had grown up to take their fathers' places—for they had not been circumcised on the way to the Promised Land. After all the males had been circumcised, they rested in the camp until they were healed.

Then the LORD said to Joshua, "Today I have rolled away the shame of your slavery in Egypt." So that place has been called Gilgal to this day.

While the Israelites were camped at Gilgal on the plains of Jericho, they celebrated Passover on the evening of the fourteenth day of the first month. The very next day they began to eat unleavened bread and roasted grain harvested from the land. No manna appeared on the day they first ate from the crops of the land, and it was never seen again. So from that time on the Israelites ate from the crops of Canaan.

When Joshua was near the town of Jericho, he looked up and saw a man standing in front of him with sword in hand. Joshua went up to him and demanded, "Are you friend or foe?"

"Neither one," he replied. "I am the commander of the LORD's army."

At this, Joshua fell with his face to the ground in reverence. "I am at your command," Joshua said. "What do you want your servant to do?"

The commander of the LORD's army replied, "Take off your sandals, for the place where you are standing is holy." And Joshua did as he was told.

Now the gates of Jericho were tightly shut because the people were afraid of the Israelites. No one was allowed to go out or in. But the LORD said to Joshua, "I have given you Jericho, its king, and all its strong warriors. You and your fighting men should march around the town once a day for six days. Seven priests will walk ahead of the Ark, each carrying a ram's horn. On the seventh day you are to march around the town seven times, with the priests blowing the horns. When you hear the priests give one long blast on the rams' horns, have all the people shout as loud as they can. Then the walls of the town will collapse, and the people can charge straight into the town."

So Joshua called together the priests and said, "Take up the Ark of the LORD's Covenant, and assign seven priests to walk in front of it, each carrying a ram's horn." Then he gave orders to the people: "March around the town, and the armed men will lead the way in front of the Ark of the LORD."

After Joshua spoke to the people, the seven priests with the rams' horns started marching in the presence of the LORD, blowing the horns as they marched. And the Ark of the LORD's Covenant followed behind them. Some of the armed men marched in front of the priests with the horns and some behind the Ark, with the priests continually blowing the horns. "Do not shout; do not even talk," Joshua commanded. "Not a single word from any of you until I tell you to shout. Then shout!" So the Ark of the LORD was carried around the town once that day, and then everyone returned to spend the night in the camp.

Joshua got up early the next morning, and the priests again carried the Ark of the LORD. The seven priests with the rams' horns marched in front of the Ark of the LORD, blowing their horns. Again the armed men marched both in front of the priests with the horns and behind the Ark of the LORD. All this time the priests were blowing their horns. On the second day they again marched around the town once and returned to the camp. They followed this pattern for six days.

On the seventh day the Israelites got up at dawn and marched around the town as they had done before. But this time they went around the town seven times. The seventh time around, as the priests sounded the long blast on their horns, Joshua commanded the people, "Shout! For the LORD has given you the town! Jericho and everything in it must be completely destroyed as an offering to the LORD. Only Rahab the prostitute and the others in her house will be spared, for she protected our spies.

"Do not take any of the things set apart for destruction, or you yourselves will be completely destroyed, and you will bring trouble on the camp of Israel. Everything made from silver, gold, bronze, or iron is sacred to the LORD and must be brought into his treasury."

When the people heard the sound of the rams' horns, they shouted as loud as they could. Suddenly, the walls of Jericho collapsed, and the Israelites charged straight into the town and captured it. They completely destroyed everything in it with their swords—men and women, young and old, cattle, sheep, goats, and donkeys.

Meanwhile, Joshua said to the two spies, "Keep your promise. Go to the prostitute's house and bring her out, along with all her family."

The men who had been spies went in and brought out Rahab, her father, mother, brothers, and all the other relatives who were with her. They moved her whole family to a safe place near the camp of Israel.

Then the Israelites burned the town and everything in it. Only the things made from silver, gold, bronze, or iron were kept for the treasury of the LORD's house. So Joshua spared Rahab the prostitute and her relatives who were with her in the house, because she had hidden the spies Joshua sent to Jericho. And she lives among the Israelites to this day.

At that time Joshua invoked this curse:

"May the curse of the Lord fall on anyone
   who tries to rebuild the town of Jericho.
At the cost of his firstborn son,
   he will lay its foundation.
At the cost of his youngest son,
   he will set up its gates."

So the Lord was with Joshua, and his reputation spread throughout the land.

+

But Israel violated the instructions about the things set apart for the Lord. A man named Achan had stolen some of these dedicated things, so the Lord was very angry with the Israelites. Achan was the son of Carmi, a descendant of Zimri son of Zerah, of the tribe of Judah.

Joshua sent some of his men from Jericho to spy out the town of Ai, east of Bethel, near Beth-aven. When they returned, they told Joshua, "There's no need for all of us to go up there; it won't take more than two or three thousand men to attack Ai. Since there are so few of them, don't make all our people struggle to go up there."

So approximately 3,000 warriors were sent, but they were soundly defeated. The men of Ai chased the Israelites from the town gate as far as the quarries, and they killed about thirty-six who were retreating down the slope. The Israelites were paralyzed with fear at this turn of events, and their courage melted away.

Joshua and the elders of Israel tore their clothing in dismay, threw dust on their heads, and bowed face down to the ground before the Ark of the Lord until evening. Then Joshua cried out, "Oh, Sovereign Lord, why did you bring us across the Jordan River if you are going to let the Amorites kill us? If only we had been content to stay on the other side! Lord, what can I say now that Israel has fled from its enemies? For when the Canaanites and all the other people living in the land hear about it, they will surround us and wipe our name off the face of the earth. And then what will happen to the honor of your great name?"

But the Lord said to Joshua, "Get up! Why are you lying on your face like this? Israel has sinned and broken my covenant! They have stolen some of the things that I commanded must be set apart for me. And they have not only stolen them but have lied about it and hidden the things among their own belongings. That is why the Israelites are running from their enemies in defeat. For now Israel itself has been set apart for destruction. I will not remain with you any longer unless you destroy the things among you that were set apart for destruction.

"Get up! Command the people to purify themselves in preparation for tomorrow. For this is what the LORD, the God of Israel, says: Hidden among you, O Israel, are things set apart for the LORD. You will never defeat your enemies until you remove these things from among you.

"In the morning you must present yourselves by tribes, and the LORD will point out the tribe to which the guilty man belongs. That tribe must come forward with its clans, and the LORD will point out the guilty clan. That clan will then come forward, and the LORD will point out the guilty family. Finally, each member of the guilty family must come forward one by one. The one who has stolen what was set apart for destruction will himself be burned with fire, along with everything he has, for he has broken the covenant of the LORD and has done a horrible thing in Israel."

Early the next morning Joshua brought the tribes of Israel before the LORD, and the tribe of Judah was singled out. Then the clans of Judah came forward, and the clan of Zerah was singled out. Then the families of Zerah came forward, and the family of Zimri was singled out. Every member of Zimri's family was brought forward person by person, and Achan was singled out.

Then Joshua said to Achan, "My son, give glory to the LORD, the God of Israel, by telling the truth. Make your confession and tell me what you have done. Don't hide it from me."

Achan replied, "It is true! I have sinned against the LORD, the God of Israel. Among the plunder I saw a beautiful robe from Babylon, 200 silver coins, and a bar of gold weighing more than a pound. I wanted them so much that I took them. They are hidden in the ground beneath my tent, with the silver buried deeper than the rest."

So Joshua sent some men to make a search. They ran to the tent and found the stolen goods hidden there, just as Achan had said, with the silver buried beneath the rest. They took the things from the tent and brought them to Joshua and all the Israelites. Then they laid them on the ground in the presence of the LORD.

Then Joshua and all the Israelites took Achan, the silver, the robe, the bar of gold, his sons, daughters, cattle, donkeys, sheep, goats, tent, and everything he had, and they brought them to the valley of Achor. Then Joshua said to Achan, "Why have you brought trouble on us? The LORD will now bring trouble on you." And all the Israelites stoned Achan and his family and burned their bodies. They piled a great heap of stones over Achan, which remains to this day. That is why the place has been called the Valley of Trouble ever since. So the LORD was no longer angry.

Then the LORD said to Joshua, "Do not be afraid or discouraged. Take all your fighting men and attack Ai, for I have given you the king of Ai, his people, his town, and his land. You will destroy them as you destroyed Jericho and its king. But this time you may keep the plunder and the livestock for yourselves. Set an ambush behind the town."

So Joshua and all the fighting men set out to attack Ai. Joshua chose 30,000 of his best warriors and sent them out at night with these orders: "Hide in ambush close behind the town and be ready for action. When our main army attacks, the men of Ai will come out to fight as they did before, and we will run away from them. We will let them chase us until we have drawn them away from the town. For they will say, 'The Israelites are running away from us as they did before.' Then, while we are running from them, you will jump up from your ambush and take possession of the town, for the LORD your God will give it to you. Set the town on fire, as the LORD has commanded. You have your orders."

So they left and went to the place of ambush between Bethel and the west side of Ai. But Joshua remained among the people in the camp that night. Early the next morning Joshua roused his men and started toward Ai, accompanied by the elders of Israel. All the fighting men who were with Joshua marched in front of the town and camped on the north side of Ai, with a valley between them and the town. That night Joshua sent about 5,000 men to lie in ambush between Bethel and Ai, on the west side of the town. So they stationed the main army north of the town and the ambush west of the town. Joshua himself spent that night in the valley.

When the king of Ai saw the Israelites across the valley, he and all his army hurried out early in the morning and attacked the Israelites at a place overlooking the Jordan Valley. But he didn't realize there was an ambush behind the town. Joshua and the Israelite army fled toward the wilderness as though they were badly beaten. Then all the men in the town were called out to chase after them. In this way, they were lured away from the town. There was not a man left in Ai or Bethel who did not chase after the Israelites, and the town was left wide open.

Then the LORD said to Joshua, "Point the spear in your hand toward Ai, for I will hand the town over to you." Joshua did as he was commanded. As soon as Joshua gave this signal, all the men in ambush jumped up from their position and poured into the town. They quickly captured it and set it on fire.

When the men of Ai looked behind them, smoke from the town was filling the sky, and they had nowhere to go. For the Israelites who had fled in the direction of the wilderness now turned on their pursuers. When Joshua and all the other Israelites saw that the ambush had succeeded and that smoke was rising from the town, they turned and attacked the men of Ai. Meanwhile, the Israelites who were inside the town came out and attacked the enemy from the rear. So the men of Ai were caught in the middle, with Israelite fighters on both sides. Israel attacked them, and not a single person survived or escaped. Only the king of Ai was taken alive and brought to Joshua.

When the Israelite army finished chasing and killing all the men of Ai in the open fields, they went back and finished off everyone inside. So the entire population of Ai, including men and women, was wiped out that day—12,000 in all. For Joshua kept holding out his spear until everyone who had lived in Ai was completely destroyed. Only the livestock and the treasures of the town were not destroyed, for the Israelites kept these as plunder for themselves, as the LORD had commanded Joshua. So Joshua burned the town of Ai, and it became a permanent mound of ruins, desolate to this very day.

Joshua impaled the king of Ai on a sharpened pole and left him there until evening. At sunset the Israelites took down the body, as Joshua commanded, and threw it in front of the town gate. They piled a great heap of stones over him that can still be seen today.

+

Then Joshua built an altar to the LORD, the God of Israel, on Mount Ebal. He followed the commands that Moses the LORD's servant had written in the Book of Instruction: "Make me an altar from stones that are uncut and have not been shaped with iron tools." Then on the altar they presented burnt offerings and peace offerings to the LORD. And as the Israelites watched, Joshua copied onto the stones of the altar the instructions Moses had given them.

Then all the Israelites—foreigners and native-born alike—along with the elders, officers, and judges, were divided into two groups. One group stood in front of Mount Gerizim, the other in front of Mount Ebal. Each group faced the other, and between them stood the Levitical priests carrying the Ark of the LORD's Covenant. This was all done according to the commands that Moses, the servant of the LORD, had previously given for blessing the people of Israel.

Joshua then read to them all the blessings and curses Moses had written in the Book of Instruction. Every word of every command that Moses had ever given was read to the entire assembly of Israel, including the women and children and the foreigners who lived among them.

+

Now all the kings west of the Jordan River heard about what had happened. These were the kings of the Hittites, Amorites, Canaanites, Perizzites, Hivites, and Jebusites, who lived in the hill country, in the western foothills, and along the coast of the Mediterranean Sea as far north as the Lebanon mountains. These kings combined their armies to fight as one against Joshua and the Israelites.

But when the people of Gibeon heard what Joshua had done to Jericho and Ai, they resorted to deception to save themselves. They sent ambassadors to Joshua, loading their donkeys with weathered saddlebags and old, patched wineskins. They put on worn-out, patched sandals and ragged clothes. And the bread they took with them was dry and moldy. When they arrived at the camp of Israel at Gilgal, they told Joshua and the men of Israel, "We have come from a distant land to ask you to make a peace treaty with us."

The Israelites replied to these Hivites, "How do we know you don't live nearby? For if you do, we cannot make a treaty with you."

They replied, "We are your servants."

"But who are you?" Joshua demanded. "Where do you come from?"

They answered, "Your servants have come from a very distant country. We have heard of the might of the Lord your God and of all he did in Egypt. We have also heard what he did to the two Amorite kings east of the Jordan River—King Sihon of Heshbon and King Og of Bashan (who lived in Ashtaroth). So our elders and all our people instructed us, 'Take supplies for a long journey. Go meet with the people of Israel and tell them, "We are your servants; please make a treaty with us."'

"This bread was hot from the ovens when we left our homes. But now, as you can see, it is dry and moldy. These wineskins were new when we filled them, but now they are old and split open. And our clothing and sandals are worn out from our very long journey."

So the Israelites examined their food, but they did not consult the Lord. Then Joshua made a peace treaty with them and guaranteed their safety, and the leaders of the community ratified their agreement with a binding oath.

Three days after making the treaty, they learned that these people actually lived nearby! The Israelites set out at once to investigate and reached their towns in three days. The names of these towns were Gibeon, Kephirah, Beeroth, and Kiriath-jearim. But the Israelites did not attack the towns, for the Israelite leaders had made a vow to them in the name of the Lord, the God of Israel.

The people of Israel grumbled against their leaders because of the treaty. But the leaders replied, "Since we have sworn an oath in the presence of the Lord, the God of Israel, we cannot touch them. This is what we must do.

We must let them live, for divine anger would come upon us if we broke our oath. Let them live." So they made them woodcutters and water carriers for the entire community, as the Israelite leaders directed.

Joshua called together the Gibeonites and said, "Why did you lie to us? Why did you say that you live in a distant land when you live right here among us? May you be cursed! From now on you will always be servants who cut wood and carry water for the house of my God."

They replied, "We did it because we—your servants—were clearly told that the LORD your God commanded his servant Moses to give you this entire land and to destroy all the people living in it. So we feared greatly for our lives because of you. That is why we have done this. Now we are at your mercy—do to us whatever you think is right."

So Joshua did not allow the people of Israel to kill them. But that day he made the Gibeonites the woodcutters and water carriers for the community of Israel and for the altar of the LORD—wherever the LORD would choose to build it. And that is what they do to this day.

Adoni-zedek, king of Jerusalem, heard that Joshua had captured and completely destroyed Ai and killed its king, just as he had destroyed the town of Jericho and killed its king. He also learned that the Gibeonites had made peace with Israel and were now their allies. He and his people became very afraid when they heard all this because Gibeon was a large town—as large as the royal cities and larger than Ai. And the Gibeonite men were strong warriors.

So King Adoni-zedek of Jerusalem sent messengers to several other kings: Hoham of Hebron, Piram of Jarmuth, Japhia of Lachish, and Debir of Eglon. "Come and help me destroy Gibeon," he urged them, "for they have made peace with Joshua and the people of Israel." So these five Amorite kings combined their armies for a united attack. They moved all their troops into place and attacked Gibeon.

The men of Gibeon quickly sent messengers to Joshua at his camp in Gilgal. "Don't abandon your servants now!" they pleaded. "Come at once! Save us! Help us! For all the Amorite kings who live in the hill country have joined forces to attack us."

So Joshua and his entire army, including his best warriors, left Gilgal and set out for Gibeon. "Do not be afraid of them," the LORD said to Joshua, "for I have given you victory over them. Not a single one of them will be able to stand up to you."

Joshua traveled all night from Gilgal and took the Amorite armies by surprise. The LORD threw them into a panic, and the Israelites slaughtered great numbers of them at Gibeon. Then the Israelites chased the enemy along the road to Beth-horon, killing them all along the way to Azekah and

Makkedah. As the Amorites retreated down the road from Beth-horon, the LORD destroyed them with a terrible hailstorm from heaven that continued until they reached Azekah. The hail killed more of the enemy than the Israelites killed with the sword.

On the day the LORD gave the Israelites victory over the Amorites, Joshua prayed to the LORD in front of all the people of Israel. He said,

> "Let the sun stand still over Gibeon,
>   and the moon over the valley of Aijalon."

So the sun stood still and the moon stayed in place until the nation of Israel had defeated its enemies.

Is this event not recorded in *The Book of Jashar?* The sun stayed in the middle of the sky, and it did not set as on a normal day. There has never been a day like this one before or since, when the LORD answered such a prayer. Surely the LORD fought for Israel that day!

Then Joshua and the Israelite army returned to their camp at Gilgal.

During the battle the five kings escaped and hid in a cave at Makkedah. When Joshua heard that they had been found, he issued this command: "Cover the opening of the cave with large rocks, and place guards at the entrance to keep the kings inside. The rest of you continue chasing the enemy and cut them down from the rear. Don't give them a chance to get back to their towns, for the LORD your God has given you victory over them."

So Joshua and the Israelite army continued the slaughter and completely crushed the enemy. They totally wiped out the five armies except for a tiny remnant that managed to reach their fortified towns. Then the Israelites returned safely to Joshua in the camp at Makkedah. After that, no one dared to speak even a word against Israel.

Then Joshua said, "Remove the rocks covering the opening of the cave, and bring the five kings to me." So they brought the five kings out of the cave—the kings of Jerusalem, Hebron, Jarmuth, Lachish, and Eglon. When they brought them out, Joshua told the commanders of his army, "Come and put your feet on the kings' necks." And they did as they were told.

"Don't ever be afraid or discouraged," Joshua told his men. "Be strong and courageous, for the LORD is going to do this to all of your enemies." Then Joshua killed each of the five kings and impaled them on five sharpened poles, where they hung until evening.

As the sun was going down, Joshua gave instructions for the bodies of the kings to be taken down from the poles and thrown into the cave where they had been hiding. Then they covered the opening of the cave with a pile of large rocks, which remains to this very day.

That same day Joshua captured and destroyed the town of Makkedah. He killed everyone in it, including the king, leaving no survivors. He destroyed them all, and he killed the king of Makkedah as he had killed the king of Jericho.

Then Joshua and the Israelites went to Libnah and attacked it. There, too, the LORD gave them the town and its king. He killed everyone in it, leaving no survivors. Then Joshua killed the king of Libnah as he had killed the king of Jericho.

From Libnah, Joshua and the Israelites went to Lachish and attacked it. Here again, the LORD gave them Lachish. Joshua took it on the second day and killed everyone in it, just as he had done at Libnah. During the attack on Lachish, King Horam of Gezer arrived with his army to help defend the town. But Joshua's men killed him and his army, leaving no survivors.

Then Joshua and the Israelite army went on to Eglon and attacked it. They captured it that day and killed everyone in it. He completely destroyed everyone, just as he had done at Lachish.

From Eglon, Joshua and the Israelite army went up to Hebron and attacked it. They captured the town and killed everyone in it, including its king, leaving no survivors. They did the same thing to all of its surrounding villages. And just as he had done at Eglon, he completely destroyed the entire population.

Then Joshua and the Israelites turned back and attacked Debir. He captured the town, its king, and all of its surrounding villages. He completely destroyed everyone in it, leaving no survivors. He did to Debir and its king just what he had done to Hebron and to Libnah and its king.

So Joshua conquered the whole region—the kings and people of the hill country, the Negev, the western foothills, and the mountain slopes. He completely destroyed everyone in the land, leaving no survivors, just as the LORD, the God of Israel, had commanded. Joshua slaughtered them from Kadesh-barnea to Gaza and from the region around the town of Goshen up to Gibeon. Joshua conquered all these kings and their land in a single campaign, for the LORD, the God of Israel, was fighting for his people.

Then Joshua and the Israelite army returned to their camp at Gilgal.

+

When King Jabin of Hazor heard what had happened, he sent messages to the following kings: King Jobab of Madon; the king of Shimron; the king of Acshaph; all the kings of the northern hill country; the kings in the Jordan Valley south of Galilee; the kings in the Galilean foothills; the kings of Naphoth-dor on the west; the kings of Canaan, both east and west; the kings of the Amorites, the Hittites, the Perizzites, the Jebusites in the hill country, and the Hivites in the towns on the slopes of Mount Hermon in the land of Mizpah.

All these kings came out to fight. Their combined armies formed a vast horde. And with all their horses and chariots, they covered the landscape like the sand on the seashore. The kings joined forces and established their camp around the water near Merom to fight against Israel.

Then the LORD said to Joshua, "Do not be afraid of them. By this time tomorrow I will hand all of them over to Israel as dead men. Then you must cripple their horses and burn their chariots."

So Joshua and all his fighting men traveled to the water near Merom and attacked suddenly. And the LORD gave them victory over their enemies. The Israelites chased them as far as Greater Sidon and Misrephoth-maim, and eastward into the valley of Mizpah, until not one enemy warrior was left alive. Then Joshua crippled the horses and burned all the chariots, as the LORD had instructed.

Joshua then turned back and captured Hazor and killed its king. (Hazor had at one time been the capital of all these kingdoms.) The Israelites completely destroyed every living thing in the city, leaving no survivors. Not a single person was spared. And then Joshua burned the city.

Joshua slaughtered all the other kings and their people, completely destroying them, just as Moses, the servant of the LORD, had commanded. But the Israelites did not burn any of the towns built on mounds except Hazor, which Joshua burned. And the Israelites took all the plunder and livestock of the ravaged towns for themselves. But they killed all the people, leaving no survivors. As the LORD had commanded his servant Moses, so Moses commanded Joshua. And Joshua did as he was told, carefully obeying all the commands that the LORD had given to Moses.

+

So Joshua conquered the entire region—the hill country, the entire Negev, the whole area around the town of Goshen, the western foothills, the Jordan Valley, the mountains of Israel, and the Galilean foothills. The Israelite territory now extended all the way from Mount Halak, which leads up to Seir in the south, as far north as Baal-gad at the foot of Mount Hermon in the valley of Lebanon. Joshua killed all the kings of those territories, waging war for a long time to accomplish this. No one in this region made peace with the Israelites except the Hivites of Gibeon. All the others were defeated. For the LORD hardened their hearts and caused them to fight the Israelites. So they were completely destroyed without mercy, as the LORD had commanded Moses.

During this period Joshua destroyed all the descendants of Anak, who lived in the hill country of Hebron, Debir, Anab, and the entire hill country of Judah and Israel. He killed them all and completely destroyed their towns. None of the descendants of Anak were left in all the land of Israel, though some still remained in Gaza, Gath, and Ashdod.

So Joshua took control of the entire land, just as the LORD had instructed Moses. He gave it to the people of Israel as their special possession, dividing the land among the tribes. So the land finally had rest from war.

+ + +

These are the kings east of the Jordan River who had been killed by the Israelites and whose land was taken. Their territory extended from the Arnon Gorge to Mount Hermon and included all the land east of the Jordan Valley.

King Sihon of the Amorites, who lived in Heshbon, was defeated. His kingdom included Aroer, on the edge of the Arnon Gorge, and extended from the middle of the Arnon Gorge to the Jabbok River, which serves as a border for the Ammonites. This territory included the southern half of the territory of Gilead. Sihon also controlled the Jordan Valley and regions to the east—from as far north as the Sea of Galilee to as far south as the Dead Sea, including the road to Beth-jeshimoth and southward to the slopes of Pisgah.

King Og of Bashan, the last of the Rephaites, lived at Ashtaroth and Edrei. He ruled a territory stretching from Mount Hermon to Salecah in the north and to all of Bashan in the east, and westward to the borders of the kingdoms of Geshur and Maacah. This territory included the northern half of Gilead, as far as the boundary of King Sihon of Heshbon.

Moses, the servant of the LORD, and the Israelites had destroyed the people of King Sihon and King Og. And Moses gave their land as a possession to the tribes of Reuben, Gad, and the half-tribe of Manasseh.

The following is a list of the kings that Joshua and the Israelite armies defeated on the west side of the Jordan, from Baal-gad in the valley of Lebanon to Mount Halak, which leads up to Seir. (Joshua gave this land to the tribes of Israel as their possession, including the hill country, the western foothills, the Jordan Valley, the mountain slopes, the Judean wilderness, and the Negev. The people who lived in this region were the Hittites, the Amorites, the Canaanites, the Perizzites, the Hivites, and the Jebusites.) These are the kings Israel defeated:

The king of Jericho
The king of Ai, near Bethel
The king of Jerusalem
The king of Hebron
The king of Jarmuth
The king of Lachish
The king of Eglon
The king of Gezer
The king of Debir
The king of Geder
The king of Hormah
The king of Arad
The king of Libnah
The king of Adullam
The king of Makkedah
The king of Bethel
The king of Tappuah
The king of Hepher
The king of Aphek
The king of Lasharon
The king of Madon
The king of Hazor
The king of Shimron-meron
The king of Acshaph
The king of Taanach
The king of Megiddo
The king of Kedesh
The king of Jokneam in Carmel
The king of Dor in the town of Naphoth-dor
The king of Goyim in Gilgal
The king of Tirzah.

In all, thirty-one kings were defeated.

When Joshua was an old man, the Lord said to him, "You are growing old, and much land remains to be conquered. This is the territory that remains: all the regions of the Philistines and the Geshurites, and the larger territory of the Canaanites, extending from the stream of Shihor on the border of Egypt, northward to the boundary of Ekron. It includes the territory of the five Philistine rulers of Gaza, Ashdod, Ashkelon, Gath, and Ekron. The land of the Avvites in the south also remains to be conquered. In the north, the following area has not yet been conquered: all the land of the Canaanites, including Mearah (which belongs to the Sidonians), stretching northward to Aphek on the border of the Amorites; the land of the Gebalites and all of the Lebanon mountain area to the east, from Baal-gad below Mount Hermon to Lebo-hamath; and all the hill country from Lebanon to Misrephoth-maim, including all the land of the Sidonians.

"I myself will drive these people out of the land ahead of the Israelites. So be sure to give this land to Israel as a special possession, just as I have commanded you. Include all this territory as Israel's possession when you divide this land among the nine tribes and the half-tribe of Manasseh."

✛

Half the tribe of Manasseh and the tribes of Reuben and Gad had already received their grants of land on the east side of the Jordan, for Moses, the servant of the LORD, had previously assigned this land to them.

> Their territory extended from Aroer on the edge of the Arnon Gorge (including the town in the middle of the gorge) to the plain beyond Medeba, as far as Dibon. It also included all the towns of King Sihon of the Amorites, who had reigned in Heshbon, and extended as far as the borders of Ammon. It included Gilead, the territory of the kingdoms of Geshur and Maacah, all of Mount Hermon, all of Bashan as far as Salecah, and all the territory of King Og of Bashan, who had reigned in Ashtaroth and Edrei. King Og was the last of the Rephaites, for Moses had attacked them and driven them out. But the Israelites failed to drive out the people of Geshur and Maacah, so they continue to live among the Israelites to this day.

> Moses did not assign any allotment of land to the tribe of Levi. Instead, as the LORD had promised them, their allotment came from the offerings burned on the altar to the LORD, the God of Israel.

Moses had assigned the following area to the clans of the tribe of Reuben.

> Their territory extended from Aroer on the edge of the Arnon Gorge (including the town in the middle of the gorge) to the plain beyond Medeba. It included Heshbon and the other towns on the plain— Dibon, Bamoth-baal, Beth-baal-meon, Jahaz, Kedemoth, Mephaath, Kiriathaim, Sibmah, Zereth-shahar on the hill above the valley, Beth-peor, the slopes of Pisgah, and Beth-jeshimoth.

The land of Reuben also included all the towns of the plain and the entire kingdom of Sihon. Sihon was the Amorite king who had reigned in Heshbon and was killed by Moses along with the leaders of Midian—Evi, Rekem, Zur, Hur, and Reba—princes living in the region who were allied with Sihon. The Israelites had also killed Balaam son of Beor, who used magic to tell the future. The Jordan River marked the western boundary for the tribe of Reuben. The towns and their surrounding villages in this area were given as a homeland to the clans of the tribe of Reuben.

Moses had assigned the following area to the clans of the tribe of Gad.

Their territory included Jazer, all the towns of Gilead, and half of the land of Ammon, as far as the town of Aroer just west of Rabbah. It extended from Heshbon to Ramath-mizpeh and Betonim, and from Mahanaim to the territory of Lo-debar. In the valley were Beth-haram, Beth-nimrah, Succoth, Zaphon, and the rest of the kingdom of King Sihon of Heshbon. The western boundary ran along the Jordan River, extended as far north as the tip of the Sea of Galilee, and then turned eastward. The towns and their surrounding villages in this area were given as a homeland to the clans of the tribe of Gad.

Moses had assigned the following area to the clans of the half-tribe of Manasseh.

Their territory extended from Mahanaim, including all of Bashan, all the former kingdom of King Og, and the sixty towns of Jair in Bashan. It also included half of Gilead and King Og's royal cities of Ashtaroth and Edrei. All this was given to the clans of the descendants of Makir, who was Manasseh's son.

These are the allotments Moses had made while he was on the plains of Moab, across the Jordan River, east of Jericho. But Moses gave no allotment of land to the tribe of Levi, for the LORD, the God of Israel, had promised that he himself would be their allotment.

+

The remaining tribes of Israel received land in Canaan as allotted by Eleazar the priest, Joshua son of Nun, and the tribal leaders. These nine and a half tribes received their grants of land by means of sacred lots, in accordance with the LORD's command through Moses. Moses had already given a grant of land to the two and a half tribes on the east side of the Jordan River, but he had given the Levites no such allotment. The descendants of Joseph had become two separate tribes—Manasseh and Ephraim. And the Levites were given no land at all, only towns to live in with surrounding pasturelands for their livestock and all their possessions. So the land was distributed in strict accordance with the LORD's commands to Moses.

A delegation from the tribe of Judah, led by Caleb son of Jephunneh the Kenizzite, came to Joshua at Gilgal. Caleb said to Joshua, "Remember what the LORD said to Moses, the man of God, about you and me when we were at Kadesh-barnea. I was forty years old when Moses, the servant of the LORD, sent me from Kadesh-barnea to explore the land of Canaan. I returned and gave an honest report, but my brothers who went with me frightened the people from entering the Promised Land. For my part, I wholeheartedly followed the LORD my God. So that day Moses solemnly promised me, 'The land of Canaan on which you were just walking will be your grant of land and that of your descendants forever, because you wholeheartedly followed the LORD my God.'

"Now, as you can see, the LORD has kept me alive and well as he promised for all these forty-five years since Moses made this promise—even while Israel wandered in the wilderness. Today I am eighty-five years old. I am as strong now as I was when Moses sent me on that journey, and I can still travel and fight as well as I could then. So give me the hill country that the LORD promised me. You will remember that as scouts we found the descendants of Anak living there in great, walled towns. But if the LORD is with me, I will drive them out of the land, just as the LORD said."

So Joshua blessed Caleb son of Jephunneh and gave Hebron to him as his portion of land. Hebron still belongs to the descendants of Caleb son of Jephunneh the Kenizzite because he wholeheartedly followed the LORD, the God of Israel. (Previously Hebron had been called Kiriath-arba. It had been named after Arba, a great hero of the descendants of Anak.)

And the land had rest from war.

The allotment for the clans of the tribe of Judah reached southward to the border of Edom, as far south as the wilderness of Zin.

The southern boundary began at the south bay of the Dead Sea, ran south of Scorpion Pass into the wilderness of Zin, and then went south of Kadesh-barnea to Hezron. Then it went up to Addar, where it turned toward Karka. From there it passed to Azmon until it finally reached the Brook of Egypt, which it followed to the Mediterranean Sea. This was their southern boundary.

The eastern boundary extended along the Dead Sea to the mouth of the Jordan River.

The northern boundary began at the bay where the Jordan River empties into the Dead Sea, went up from there to Beth-hoglah, then proceeded north of Beth-arabah to the Stone of Bohan. (Bohan was Reuben's son.) From that point it went through the valley of Achor to Debir, turning north toward Gilgal, which is across from the slopes of Adummim on the south side of the valley. From there the boundary extended to the springs at En-shemesh and on to En-rogel. The boundary then passed through the valley of Ben-Hinnom, along the southern slopes of the Jebusites, where the city of Jerusalem is located. Then it went west to the top of the mountain above the valley of Hinnom, and on up to the northern end of the valley of Rephaim. From there the boundary extended from the top of the mountain to the spring at the waters of Nephtoah, and from there to the towns on Mount Ephron. Then it turned toward Baalah (that is, Kiriath-jearim). The boundary circled west of Baalah to Mount Seir, passed along to the town of Kesalon on the northern slope of Mount Jearim, and went down to Beth-shemesh and on to Timnah. The boundary then proceeded to the slope of the hill north of Ekron, where it turned toward Shikkeron and Mount Baalah. It passed Jabneel and ended at the Mediterranean Sea.

The western boundary was the shoreline of the Mediterranean Sea.

These are the boundaries for the clans of the tribe of Judah.

The LORD commanded Joshua to assign some of Judah's territory to Caleb son of Jephunneh. So Caleb was given the town of Kiriath-arba (that is, Hebron), which had been named after Anak's ancestor. Caleb drove out the three groups of Anakites—the descendants of Sheshai, Ahiman, and Talmai, the sons of Anak.

From there he went to fight against the people living in the town of Debir (formerly called Kiriath-sepher). Caleb said, "I will give my daughter Acsah in marriage to the one who attacks and captures Kiriath-sepher." Othniel, the son of Caleb's brother Kenaz, was the one who conquered it, so Acsah became Othniel's wife.

When Acsah married Othniel, she urged him to ask her father for a field. As she got down off her donkey, Caleb asked her, "What's the matter?"

She said, "Give me another gift. You have already given me land in the Negev; now please give me springs of water, too." So Caleb gave her the upper and lower springs.

This was the homeland allocated to the clans of the tribe of Judah.

The towns of Judah situated along the borders of Edom in the extreme south were Kabzeel, Eder, Jagur, Kinah, Dimonah, Adadah, Kedesh, Hazor, Ithnan, Ziph, Telem, Bealoth, Hazor-hadattah, Kerioth-hezron (that is, Hazor), Amam, Shema, Moladah, Hazar-gaddah, Heshmon, Beth-pelet, Hazar-shual, Beersheba, Biziothiah, Baalah, Iim, Ezem, Eltolad, Kesil, Hormah, Ziklag, Madmannah, Sansannah, Lebaoth, Shilhim, Ain, and Rimmon—twenty-nine towns with their surrounding villages.

The following towns situated in the western foothills were also given to Judah: Eshtaol, Zorah, Ashnah, Zanoah, En-gannim, Tappuah, Enam, Jarmuth, Adullam, Socoh, Azekah, Shaaraim, Adithaim, Gederah, and Gederothaim—fourteen towns with their surrounding villages.

Also included were Zenan, Hadashah, Migdal-gad, Dilean, Mizpeh, Joktheel, Lachish, Bozkath, Eglon, Cabbon, Lahmam, Kitlish, Gederoth, Beth-dagon, Naamah, and Makkedah—sixteen towns with their surrounding villages.

Besides these, there were Libnah, Ether, Ashan, Iphtah, Ashnah, Nezib, Keilah, Aczib, and Mareshah—nine towns with their surrounding villages.

The territory of the tribe of Judah also included Ekron and its surrounding settlements and villages. From Ekron the boundary extended west and included the towns near Ashdod with their surrounding villages. It also included Ashdod with its surrounding settlements and villages and Gaza with its settlements and villages, as far as the Brook of Egypt and along the coast of the Mediterranean Sea.

Judah also received the following towns in the hill country: Shamir, Jattir, Socoh, Dannah, Kiriath-sannah (that is, Debir), Anab, Eshtemoh, Anim, Goshen, Holon, and Giloh—eleven towns with their surrounding villages.

Also included were the towns of Arab, Dumah, Eshan, Janim, Beth-tappuah, Aphekah, Humtah, Kiriath-arba (that is, Hebron), and Zior—nine towns with their surrounding villages.

Besides these, there were Maon, Carmel, Ziph, Juttah, Jezreel, Jokdeam, Zanoah, Kain, Gibeah, and Timnah—ten towns with their surrounding villages.

In addition, there were Halhul, Beth-zur, Gedor, Maarath, Beth-anoth, and Eltekon—six towns with their surrounding villages.

There were also Kiriath-baal (that is, Kiriath-jearim) and Rabbah—two towns with their surrounding villages.

In the wilderness there were the towns of Beth-arabah, Middin, Secacah, Nibshan, the City of Salt, and En-gedi—six towns with their surrounding villages.

But the tribe of Judah could not drive out the Jebusites, who lived in the city of Jerusalem, so the Jebusites live there among the people of Judah to this day.

+

The allotment for the descendants of Joseph extended from the Jordan River near Jericho, east of the springs of Jericho, through the wilderness and into the hill country of Bethel. From Bethel (that is, Luz) it ran over to Ataroth in the territory of the Arkites. Then it descended westward to the territory of the Japhletites as far as Lower Beth-horon, then to Gezer and over to the Mediterranean Sea.

This was the homeland allocated to the families of Joseph's sons, Manasseh and Ephraim.

The following territory was given to the clans of the tribe of Ephraim.

The boundary of their homeland began at Ataroth-addar in the east. From there it ran to Upper Beth-horon, then on to the Mediterranean Sea. From Micmethath on the north, the boundary curved eastward past Taanath-shiloh to the east of Janoah. From Janoah it turned southward to Ataroth and Naarah, touched Jericho, and ended at the Jordan River. From Tappuah the boundary extended westward, following the Kanah Ravine to the Mediterranean Sea. This is the homeland allocated to the clans of the tribe of Ephraim.

In addition, some towns with their surrounding villages in the territory allocated to the half-tribe of Manasseh were set aside for the tribe of Ephraim. They did not drive the Canaanites out of Gezer, however, so the people of Gezer live as slaves among the people of Ephraim to this day.

The next allotment of land was given to the half-tribe of Manasseh, the descendants of Joseph's older son. Makir, the firstborn son of Manasseh, was the father of Gilead. Because his descendants were experienced soldiers, the regions of Gilead and Bashan on the east side of the Jordan had already been given to them. So the allotment on the west side of the Jordan was for the remaining families within the clans of the tribe of Manasseh: Abiezer, Helek, Asriel, Shechem, Hepher, and Shemida. These clans represent the male descendants of Manasseh son of Joseph.

However, Zelophehad, a descendant of Hepher son of Gilead, son of Makir, son of Manasseh, had no sons. He had only daughters, whose names were Mahlah, Noah, Hoglah, Milcah, and Tirzah. These women came to Eleazar the priest, Joshua son of Nun, and the Israelite leaders and said, "The LORD commanded Moses to give us a grant of land along with the men of our tribe."

So Joshua gave them a grant of land along with their uncles, as the LORD had commanded. As a result, Manasseh's total allocation came to ten parcels of land, in addition to the land of Gilead and Bashan across the Jordan River, because the female descendants of Manasseh received a grant of land along with the male descendants. (The land of Gilead was given to the rest of the male descendants of Manasseh.)

The boundary of the tribe of Manasseh extended from the border of Asher to Micmethath, near Shechem. Then the boundary went south from Micmethath to the settlement near the spring of Tappuah. The land surrounding Tappuah belonged to Manasseh, but the town of Tappuah itself, on the border of Manasseh's territory, belonged to the tribe of Ephraim. From the spring of Tappuah, the boundary of Manasseh followed the Kanah Ravine to the Mediterranean Sea. Several towns south of the ravine were inside Manasseh's territory, but they actually belonged to the tribe of Ephraim. In general, however, the land south of the ravine belonged to Ephraim, and the land north of the ravine belonged to Manasseh. Manasseh's boundary ran along the northern side of the ravine and ended at the Mediterranean Sea. North of Manasseh was the territory of Asher, and to the east was the territory of Issachar.

The following towns within the territory of Issachar and Asher, however, were given to Manasseh: Beth-shan, Ibleam, Dor (that is, Naphoth-dor), Endor, Taanach, and Megiddo, each with their surrounding settlements.

But the descendants of Manasseh were unable to occupy these towns because the Canaanites were determined to stay in that region. Later, however, when the Israelites became strong enough, they forced the Canaanites to work as slaves. But they did not drive them out of the land.

The descendants of Joseph came to Joshua and asked, "Why have you given us only one portion of land as our homeland when the LORD has blessed us with so many people?"

Joshua replied, "If there are so many of you, and if the hill country of Ephraim is not large enough for you, clear out land for yourselves in the forest where the Perizzites and Rephaites live."

The descendants of Joseph responded, "It's true that the hill country is not large enough for us. But all the Canaanites in the lowlands have iron chariots, both those in Beth-shan and its surrounding settlements and those in the valley of Jezreel. They are too strong for us."

Then Joshua said to the tribes of Ephraim and Manasseh, the descendants of Joseph, "Since you are so large and strong, you will be given more than one portion. The forests of the hill country will be yours as well. Clear as much of the land as you wish, and take possession of its farthest corners. And you will drive out the Canaanites from the valleys, too, even though they are strong and have iron chariots."

+

Now that the land was under Israelite control, the entire community of Israel gathered at Shiloh and set up the Tabernacle. But there remained seven tribes who had not yet been allotted their grants of land.

Then Joshua asked them, "How long are you going to wait before taking possession of the remaining land the LORD, the God of your ancestors, has given to you? Select three men from each tribe, and I will send them out to explore the land and map it out. They will then return to me with a written report of their proposed divisions of their new homeland. Let them divide the land into seven sections, excluding Judah's territory in the south and Joseph's territory in the north. And when you record the seven divisions of the land and bring them to me, I will cast sacred lots in the presence of the LORD our God to assign land to each tribe.

"The Levites, however, will not receive any allotment of land. Their role as priests of the LORD is their allotment. And the tribes of Gad, Reuben, and the half-tribe of Manasseh won't receive any more land, for they have already received their grant of land, which Moses, the servant of the LORD, gave them on the east side of the Jordan River."

As the men started on their way to map out the land, Joshua commanded them, "Go and explore the land and write a description of it. Then return to me, and I will assign the land to the tribes by casting sacred lots here in the presence of the LORD at Shiloh." The men did as they were told and mapped the entire territory into seven sections, listing the towns in each section. They made a written record and then returned to Joshua in the camp at Shiloh. And there at Shiloh, Joshua cast sacred lots in the presence of the LORD to determine which tribe should have each section.

The first allotment of land went to the clans of the tribe of Benjamin. It lay between the territory assigned to the tribes of Judah and Joseph.

The northern boundary of Benjamin's land began at the Jordan River, went north of the slope of Jericho, then west through the hill country and the wilderness of Beth-aven. From there the boundary went south to Luz (that is, Bethel) and proceeded down to Ataroth-addar on the hill that lies south of Lower Beth-horon.

The boundary then made a turn and swung south along the western edge of the hill facing Beth-horon, ending at the village of Kiriath-baal (that is, Kiriath-jearim), a town belonging to the tribe of Judah. This was the western boundary.

The southern boundary began at the outskirts of Kiriath-jearim. From that western point it ran to the spring at the waters of Nephtoah, and down to the base of the mountain beside the valley of Ben-Hinnom, at the northern end of the valley of Rephaim. From there it went down the valley of Hinnom, crossing south of the slope where the Jebusites lived, and continued down to En-rogel. From En-rogel the boundary proceeded in a northerly direction and came to En-shemesh and on to Geliloth (which is across from the slopes of Adummim). Then it went down to the Stone of Bohan. (Bohan was Reuben's son.) From there it passed along the north side of the slope overlooking the Jordan Valley. The border then went down into the valley, ran past the north slope of Beth-hoglah, and ended at the north bay of the Dead Sea, which is the southern end of the Jordan River. This was the southern boundary.

The eastern boundary was the Jordan River.

These were the boundaries of the homeland allocated to the clans of the tribe of Benjamin.

These were the towns given to the clans of the tribe of Benjamin.

Jericho, Beth-hoglah, Emek-keziz, Beth-arabah, Zemaraim, Bethel, Avvim, Parah, Ophrah, Kephar-ammoni, Ophni, and Geba—twelve towns with their surrounding villages. Also Gibeon, Ramah, Beeroth, Mizpah, Kephirah, Mozah, Rekem, Irpeel, Taralah, Zela, Haeleph, the Jebusite town (that is, Jerusalem), Gibeah, and Kiriath-jearim—fourteen towns with their surrounding villages.

This was the homeland allocated to the clans of the tribe of Benjamin.

The second allotment of land went to the clans of the tribe of Simeon. Their homeland was surrounded by Judah's territory.

Simeon's homeland included Beersheba, Sheba, Moladah, Hazar-shual, Balah, Ezem, Eltolad, Bethul, Hormah, Ziklag, Beth-marcaboth,

Hazar-susah, Beth-lebaoth, and Sharuhen—thirteen towns with their surrounding villages. It also included Ain, Rimmon, Ether, and Ashan— four towns with their villages, including all the surrounding villages as far south as Baalath-beer (also known as Ramah of the Negev).

This was the homeland allocated to the clans of the tribe of Simeon. Their allocation of land came from part of what had been given to Judah because Judah's territory was too large for them. So the tribe of Simeon received an allocation within the territory of Judah.

The third allotment of land went to the clans of the tribe of Zebulun.

The boundary of Zebulun's homeland started at Sarid. From there it went west, going past Maralah, touching Dabbesheth, and proceeding to the brook east of Jokneam. In the other direction, the boundary went east from Sarid to the border of Kisloth-tabor, and from there to Daberath and up to Japhia. Then it continued east to Gath-hepher, Eth-kazin, and Rimmon and turned toward Neah. The northern boundary of Zebulun passed Hannathon and ended at the valley of Iphtah-el. The towns in these areas included Kattath, Nahalal, Shimron, Idalah, and Bethlehem—twelve towns with their surrounding villages.

The homeland allocated to the clans of the tribe of Zebulun included these towns and their surrounding villages.

The fourth allotment of land went to the clans of the tribe of Issachar.

Its boundaries included the following towns: Jezreel, Kesulloth, Shunem, Hapharaim, Shion, Anaharath, Rabbith, Kishion, Ebez, Remeth, En-gannim, En-haddah, and Beth-pazzez. The boundary also touched Tabor, Shahazumah, and Beth-shemesh, ending at the Jordan River—sixteen towns with their surrounding villages.

The homeland allocated to the clans of the tribe of Issachar included these towns and their surrounding villages.

The fifth allotment of land went to the clans of the tribe of Asher.

Its boundaries included these towns: Helkath, Hali, Beten, Acshaph, Allammelech, Amad, and Mishal. The boundary on the west touched Carmel and Shihor-libnath, then it turned east toward Beth-dagon, and ran as far as Zebulun in the valley of Iphtah-el, going north to Beth-emek and Neiel. It then continued north to Cabul, Abdon, Rehob, Hammon, Kanah, and as far as Greater Sidon. Then the

boundary turned toward Ramah and the fortress of Tyre, where
it turned toward Hosah and came to the Mediterranean Sea. The
territory also included Mehebel, Aczib, Ummah, Aphek, and
Rehob—twenty-two towns with their surrounding villages.

The homeland allocated to the clans of the tribe of Asher included these
towns and their surrounding villages.

The sixth allotment of land went to the clans of the tribe of Naphtali.

Its boundary ran from Heleph, from the oak at Zaanannim, and
extended across to Adami-nekeb, Jabneel, and as far as Lakkum,
ending at the Jordan River. The western boundary ran past Aznoth-
tabor, then to Hukkok, and touched the border of Zebulun in the
south, the border of Asher on the west, and the Jordan River on the
east. The fortified towns included in this territory were Ziddim, Zer,
Hammath, Rakkath, Kinnereth, Adamah, Ramah, Hazor, Kedesh,
Edrei, En-hazor, Yiron, Migdal-el, Horem, Beth-anath, and Beth-
shemesh—nineteen towns with their surrounding villages.

The homeland allocated to the clans of the tribe of Naphtali included
these towns and their surrounding villages.

The seventh allotment of land went to the clans of the tribe of Dan.

The land allocated as their homeland included the following
towns: Zorah, Eshtaol, Ir-shemesh, Shaalabbin, Aijalon, Ithlah,
Elon, Timnah, Ekron, Eltekeh, Gibbethon, Baalath, Jehud, Bene-
berak, Gath-rimmon, Me-jarkon, Rakkon, and the territory across
from Joppa.
　　But the tribe of Dan had trouble taking possession of their land,
so they attacked the town of Laish. They captured it, slaughtered its
people, and settled there. They renamed the town Dan after their
ancestor.

The homeland allocated to the clans of the tribe of Dan included these
towns and their surrounding villages.

After all the land was divided among the tribes, the Israelites gave a piece
of land to Joshua as his allocation. For the LORD had said he could have any
town he wanted. He chose Timnath-serah in the hill country of Ephraim.
He rebuilt the town and lived there.

These are the territories that Eleazar the priest, Joshua son of Nun, and the
tribal leaders allocated as grants of land to the tribes of Israel by casting

sacred lots in the presence of the LORD at the entrance of the Tabernacle at Shiloh. So the division of the land was completed.

+

The LORD said to Joshua, "Now tell the Israelites to designate the cities of refuge, as I instructed Moses. Anyone who kills another person accidentally and unintentionally can run to one of these cities; they will be places of refuge from relatives seeking revenge for the person who was killed.

"Upon reaching one of these cities, the one who caused the death will appear before the elders at the city gate and present his case. They must allow him to enter the city and give him a place to live among them. If the relatives of the victim come to avenge the killing, the leaders must not release the slayer to them, for he killed the other person unintentionally and without previous hostility. But the slayer must stay in that city and be tried by the local assembly, which will render a judgment. And he must continue to live in that city until the death of the high priest who was in office at the time of the accident. After that, he is free to return to his own home in the town from which he fled."

The following cities were designated as cities of refuge: Kedesh of Galilee, in the hill country of Naphtali; Shechem, in the hill country of Ephraim; and Kiriath-arba (that is, Hebron), in the hill country of Judah. On the east side of the Jordan River, across from Jericho, the following cities were designated: Bezer, in the wilderness plain of the tribe of Reuben; Ramoth in Gilead, in the territory of the tribe of Gad; and Golan in Bashan, in the land of the tribe of Manasseh. These cities were set apart for all the Israelites as well as the foreigners living among them. Anyone who accidentally killed another person could take refuge in one of these cities. In this way, they could escape being killed in revenge prior to standing trial before the local assembly.

+

Then the leaders of the tribe of Levi came to consult with Eleazar the priest, Joshua son of Nun, and the leaders of the other tribes of Israel. They came to them at Shiloh in the land of Canaan and said, "The LORD commanded Moses to give us towns to live in and pasturelands for our livestock." So by the command of the LORD the people of Israel gave the Levites the following towns and pasturelands out of their own grants of land.

The descendants of Aaron, who were members of the Kohathite clan within the tribe of Levi, were allotted thirteen towns that were originally assigned to the tribes of Judah, Simeon, and Benjamin. The other families of the Kohathite clan were allotted ten towns from the tribes of Ephraim, Dan, and the half-tribe of Manasseh.

The clan of Gershon was allotted thirteen towns from the tribes of Issachar, Asher, Naphtali, and the half-tribe of Manasseh in Bashan.

The clan of Merari was allotted twelve towns from the tribes of Reuben, Gad, and Zebulun.

So the Israelites obeyed the Lord's command to Moses and assigned these towns and pasturelands to the Levites by casting sacred lots.

The Israelites gave the following towns from the tribes of Judah and Simeon to the descendants of Aaron, who were members of the Kohathite clan within the tribe of Levi, since the sacred lot fell to them first: Kiriath-arba (that is, Hebron), in the hill country of Judah, along with its surrounding pasturelands. (Arba was an ancestor of Anak.) But the open fields beyond the town and the surrounding villages were given to Caleb son of Jephunneh as his possession.

The following towns with their pasturelands were given to the descendants of Aaron the priest: Hebron (a city of refuge for those who accidentally killed someone), Libnah, Jattir, Eshtemoa, Holon, Debir, Ain, Juttah, and Beth-shemesh—nine towns from these two tribes.

From the tribe of Benjamin the priests were given the following towns with their pasturelands: Gibeon, Geba, Anathoth, and Almon—four towns. So in all, thirteen towns with their pasturelands were given to the priests, the descendants of Aaron.

The rest of the Kohathite clan from the tribe of Levi was allotted the following towns and pasturelands from the tribe of Ephraim: Shechem in the hill country of Ephraim (a city of refuge for those who accidentally killed someone), Gezer, Kibzaim, and Beth-horon—four towns.

The following towns and pasturelands were allotted to the priests from the tribe of Dan: Eltekeh, Gibbethon, Aijalon, and Gath-rimmon—four towns.

The half-tribe of Manasseh allotted the following towns with their pasturelands to the priests: Taanach and Gath-rimmon—two towns. So in all, ten towns with their pasturelands were given to the rest of the Kohathite clan.

The descendants of Gershon, another clan within the tribe of Levi, received the following towns with their pasturelands from the half-tribe of Manasseh: Golan in Bashan (a city of refuge for those who accidentally killed someone) and Be-eshterah—two towns.

From the tribe of Issachar they received the following towns with their pasturelands: Kishion, Daberath, Jarmuth, and En-gannim—four towns.

From the tribe of Asher they received the following towns with their pasturelands: Mishal, Abdon, Helkath, and Rehob—four towns.

From the tribe of Naphtali they received the following towns with their pasturelands: Kedesh in Galilee (a city of refuge for those who accidentally killed someone), Hammoth-dor, and Kartan—three towns. So in all, thirteen towns with their pasturelands were allotted to the clan of Gershon.

The rest of the Levites—the Merari clan—were given the following towns with their pasturelands from the tribe of Zebulun: Jokneam, Kartah, Dimnah, and Nahalal—four towns.

From the tribe of Reuben they received the following towns with their pasturelands: Bezer, Jahaz, Kedemoth, and Mephaath—four towns.

From the tribe of Gad they received the following towns with their pasturelands: Ramoth in Gilead (a city of refuge for those who accidentally killed someone), Mahanaim, Heshbon, and Jazer—four towns. So in all, twelve towns were allotted to the clan of Merari.

The total number of towns and pasturelands within Israelite territory given to the Levites came to forty-eight. Every one of these towns had pasturelands surrounding it.

+

So the LORD gave to Israel all the land he had sworn to give their ancestors, and they took possession of it and settled there. And the LORD gave them rest on every side, just as he had solemnly promised their ancestors. None of their enemies could stand against them, for the LORD helped them conquer all their enemies. Not a single one of all the good promises the LORD had given to the family of Israel was left unfulfilled; everything he had spoken came true.

+ + +

Then Joshua called together the tribes of Reuben, Gad, and the half-tribe of Manasseh. He told them, "You have done as Moses, the servant of the LORD, commanded you, and you have obeyed every order I have given you. During all this time you have not deserted the other tribes. You have been careful to obey the commands of the LORD your God right up to the present day. And now the LORD your God has given the other tribes rest, as he promised them. So go back home to the land that Moses, the servant of the LORD, gave you as your possession on the east side of the Jordan River. But be very careful to obey all the commands and the instructions that Moses gave to you. Love the LORD your God, walk in all his ways, obey his commands, hold firmly to him, and serve him with all your heart and all your soul." So Joshua blessed them and sent them away, and they went home.

Moses had given the land of Bashan, east of the Jordan River, to the half-tribe of Manasseh. (The other half of the tribe was given land west of the Jordan.) As Joshua sent them away and blessed them, he said to them, "Go back to your homes with the great wealth you have taken from your enemies—the vast herds of livestock, the silver, gold, bronze, and iron, and the large supply of clothing. Share the plunder with your relatives."

So the men of Reuben, Gad, and the half-tribe of Manasseh left the rest of Israel at Shiloh in the land of Canaan. They started the journey back to their own land of Gilead, the territory that belonged to them according to the LORD's command through Moses.

But while they were still in Canaan, and when they came to a place called Geliloth near the Jordan River, the men of Reuben, Gad, and the half-tribe of Manasseh stopped to build a large and imposing altar.

The rest of Israel heard that the people of Reuben, Gad, and the half-tribe of Manasseh had built an altar at Geliloth at the edge of the land of Canaan, on the west side of the Jordan River. So the whole community of Israel gathered at Shiloh and prepared to go to war against them. First, however, they sent a delegation led by Phinehas son of Eleazar, the priest, to talk with the tribes of Reuben, Gad, and the half-tribe of Manasseh. In this delegation were ten leaders of Israel, one from each of the ten tribes, and each the head of his family within the clans of Israel.

When they arrived in the land of Gilead, they said to the tribes of Reuben, Gad, and the half-tribe of Manasseh, "The whole community of the LORD demands to know why you are betraying the God of Israel. How could you turn away from the LORD and build an altar for yourselves in rebellion against him? Was our sin at Peor not enough? To this day we are not fully cleansed of it, even after the plague that struck the entire community of the LORD. And yet today you are turning away from following the LORD. If you rebel against the LORD today, he will be angry with all of us tomorrow.

"If you need the altar because the land you possess is defiled, then join us in the LORD's land, where the Tabernacle of the LORD is situated, and share our land with us. But do not rebel against the LORD or against us by building an altar other than the one true altar of the LORD our God. Didn't divine anger fall on the entire community of Israel when Achan, a member of the clan of Zerah, sinned by stealing the things set apart for the LORD? He was not the only one who died because of his sin."

Then the people of Reuben, Gad, and the half-tribe of Manasseh answered the heads of the clans of Israel: "The LORD, the Mighty One, is God! The LORD, the Mighty One, is God! He knows the truth, and may Israel know it, too! We have not built the altar in treacherous rebellion against the LORD. If we have done so, do not spare our lives this day. If we have built an altar for ourselves to turn away from the LORD or to offer burnt offerings or grain offerings or peace offerings, may the LORD himself punish us.

"The truth is, we have built this altar because we fear that in the future your descendants will say to ours, 'What right do you have to worship the LORD, the God of Israel? The LORD has placed the Jordan River as a barrier between our people and you people of Reuben and Gad. You have no claim to the LORD.' So your descendants may prevent our descendants from worshiping the LORD.

"So we decided to build the altar, not for burnt offerings or sacrifices, but as a memorial. It will remind our descendants and your descendants that we, too, have the right to worship the LORD at his sanctuary with our burnt offerings, sacrifices, and peace offerings. Then your descendants will not be able to say to ours, 'You have no claim to the LORD.'

"If they say this, our descendants can reply, 'Look at this copy of the LORD's altar that our ancestors made. It is not for burnt offerings or sacrifices; it is a reminder of the relationship both of us have with the LORD.' Far be it from us to rebel against the LORD or turn away from him by building our own altar for burnt offerings, grain offerings, or sacrifices. Only the altar of the LORD our God that stands in front of the Tabernacle may be used for that purpose."

When Phinehas the priest and the leaders of the community—the heads of the clans of Israel—heard this from the tribes of Reuben, Gad, and the half-tribe of Manasseh, they were satisfied. Phinehas son of Eleazar, the priest, replied to them, "Today we know the LORD is among us because you have not committed this treachery against the LORD as we thought. Instead, you have rescued Israel from being destroyed by the hand of the LORD."

Then Phinehas son of Eleazar, the priest, and the other leaders left the tribes of Reuben and Gad in Gilead and returned to the land of Canaan to tell the Israelites what had happened. And all the Israelites were satisfied and praised God and spoke no more of war against Reuben and Gad.

The people of Reuben and Gad named the altar "Witness," for they said, "It is a witness between us and them that the LORD is our God, too."

+

The years passed, and the LORD had given the people of Israel rest from all their enemies. Joshua, who was now very old, called together all the elders, leaders, judges, and officers of Israel. He said to them, "I am now a very old man. You have seen everything the LORD your God has done for you during my lifetime. The LORD your God has fought for you against your enemies. I have allotted to you as your homeland all the land of the nations yet unconquered, as well as the land of those we have already conquered—from the Jordan River to the Mediterranean Sea in the west. This land will be yours, for the LORD your God will himself drive out all the people living there now. You will take possession of their land, just as the LORD your God promised you.

"So be very careful to follow everything Moses wrote in the Book of Instruction. Do not deviate from it, turning either to the right or to the left. Make sure you do not associate with the other people still remaining in the land. Do not even mention the names of their gods, much less swear by them or serve them or worship them. Rather, cling tightly to the LORD your God as you have done until now.

"For the LORD has driven out great and powerful nations for you, and no one has yet been able to defeat you. Each one of you will put to flight a thousand of the enemy, for the LORD your God fights for you, just as he has promised. So be very careful to love the LORD your God.

"But if you turn away from him and cling to the customs of the survivors of these nations remaining among you, and if you intermarry with them, then know for certain that the LORD your God will no longer drive them out of your land. Instead, they will be a snare and a trap to you, a whip for your backs and thorny brambles in your eyes, and you will vanish from this good land the LORD your God has given you.

"Soon I will die, going the way of everything on earth. Deep in your hearts you know that every promise of the LORD your God has come true. Not a single one has failed! But as surely as the LORD your God has given you the good things he promised, he will also bring disaster on you if you disobey him. He will completely destroy you from this good land he has given you. If you break the covenant of the LORD your God by worshiping and serving other gods, his anger will burn against you, and you will quickly vanish from the good land he has given you."

Then Joshua summoned all the tribes of Israel to Shechem, including their elders, leaders, judges, and officers. So they came and presented themselves to God.

Joshua said to the people, "This is what the LORD, the God of Israel, says: Long ago your ancestors, including Terah, the father of Abraham and Nahor, lived beyond the Euphrates River, and they worshiped other gods. But I took your ancestor Abraham from the land beyond the Euphrates and led him into the land of Canaan. I gave him many descendants through his son Isaac. To Isaac I gave Jacob and Esau. To Esau I gave the mountains of Seir, while Jacob and his children went down into Egypt.

"Then I sent Moses and Aaron, and I brought terrible plagues on Egypt; and afterward I brought you out as a free people. But when your ancestors arrived at the Red Sea, the Egyptians chased after you with chariots and charioteers. When your ancestors cried out to the LORD, I put darkness between you and the Egyptians. I brought the sea crashing down on the Egyptians, drowning them. With your very own eyes you saw what I did. Then you lived in the wilderness for many years.

"Finally, I brought you into the land of the Amorites on the east side of the Jordan. They fought against you, but I destroyed them before you. I gave you victory over them, and you took possession of their land. Then Balak son of Zippor, king of Moab, started a war against Israel. He summoned Balaam son of Beor to curse you, but I would not listen to him. Instead, I made Balaam bless you, and so I rescued you from Balak.

"When you crossed the Jordan River and came to Jericho, the men of Jericho fought against you, as did the Amorites, the Perizzites, the Canaanites, the Hittites, the Girgashites, the Hivites, and the Jebusites. But I gave you victory over them. And I sent terror ahead of you to drive out the two kings of the Amorites. It was not your swords or bows that brought you victory. I gave you land you had not worked on, and I gave you towns you did not build—the towns where you are now living. I gave you vineyards and olive groves for food, though you did not plant them.

"So fear the LORD and serve him wholeheartedly. Put away forever the idols your ancestors worshiped when they lived beyond the Euphrates River and in Egypt. Serve the LORD alone. But if you refuse to serve the LORD, then choose today whom you will serve. Would you prefer the gods your ancestors served beyond the Euphrates? Or will it be the gods of the Amorites in whose land you now live? But as for me and my family, we will serve the LORD."

The people replied, "We would never abandon the LORD and serve other gods. For the LORD our God is the one who rescued us and our ancestors from slavery in the land of Egypt. He performed mighty miracles before our very eyes. As we traveled through the wilderness among our enemies, he preserved us. It was the LORD who drove out the Amorites and the other nations living here in the land. So we, too, will serve the LORD, for he alone is our God."

Then Joshua warned the people, "You are not able to serve the LORD, for he is a holy and jealous God. He will not forgive your rebellion and your sins. If you abandon the LORD and serve other gods, he will turn against you and destroy you, even though he has been so good to you."

But the people answered Joshua, "No, we will serve the LORD!"

"You are a witness to your own decision," Joshua said. "You have chosen to serve the LORD."

"Yes," they replied, "we are witnesses to what we have said."

"All right then," Joshua said, "destroy the idols among you, and turn your hearts to the LORD, the God of Israel."

The people said to Joshua, "We will serve the LORD our God. We will obey him alone."

So Joshua made a covenant with the people that day at Shechem, committing them to follow the decrees and regulations of the LORD. Joshua recorded these things in the Book of God's Instructions. As a reminder of their agreement, he took a huge stone and rolled it beneath the terebinth tree beside the Tabernacle of the LORD.

Joshua said to all the people, "This stone has heard everything the LORD said to us. It will be a witness to testify against you if you go back on your word to God."

Then Joshua sent all the people away to their own homelands.

After this, Joshua son of Nun, the servant of the LORD, died at the age of 110. They buried him in the land he had been allocated, at Timnath-serah in the hill country of Ephraim, north of Mount Gaash.

The people of Israel served the LORD throughout the lifetime of Joshua and of the elders who outlived him—those who had personally experienced all that the LORD had done for Israel.

The bones of Joseph, which the Israelites had brought along with them when they left Egypt, were buried at Shechem, in the plot of land Jacob had bought from the sons of Hamor for 100 pieces of silver. This land was located in the territory allotted to the descendants of Joseph.

Eleazar son of Aaron also died. He was buried in the hill country of Ephraim, in the town of Gibeah, which had been given to his son Phinehas.

IMMERSED IN JUDGES

THE BOOK OF JUDGES DESCRIBES the period in Israel's history between its conquest of the Promised Land and the anointing of the nation's first king. With each new generation, one question keeps appearing: Will Israel remain committed to its covenant relationship with God? In answering this crucial question, the book of Judges expresses two themes. It shows that Israel has a recurring problem with idolatry and turning away from God, and it makes the case that the nation would benefit from having a single, strong leader—particularly one from the tribe of Judah.

The status of God's covenant bond with his people is a central concern throughout the Bible. At this point in the Story, the book of Judges seems to suggest that Israel could be led into more faithful covenant-keeping by a strong and worthy king.

The three major sections in the book's literary structure help to make a case for a monarchy in Israel. The brief opening part of the book centers on the question of Israel's loyalty to God and to the covenant after Joshua's death. Will the people follow God's instructions? Will they take full possession of the land? In a pattern that repeats throughout the book, Israel falls short of God's plan and then suffers the inevitable consequences.

The second and largest part of the book tells the story of twelve judges (or rescuers) chosen by God to rescue Israel from its enemies. The number matches the number of Israel's tribes and seems designed to show that the nation will remain in disunity and confusion if it relies on temporary leaders who only arise to deal with an immediate crisis.

There is a pronounced pattern in the accounts of the judges, a dismal cycle in which Israel fails to keep its covenant with God, falls under God's judgment, and cries out in distress, after which God raises up a rescuer to save them. The cycle repeats again and again, showing that Israel's present status as a tribal confederation is not helping it fulfill its covenant calling in the world. The people continually forget their identity as God's chosen people and fail to demonstrate through their lives that God is their King.

The individual stories of Israel's judges are interesting in their own right. In the accounts of leaders like Gideon, Deborah, Samson, and others, we read stories of doubt, military cunning, decisive action, and God's sovereignty—as he works for his people in spite of their compromises and moral failures. But it has become clear that Israel needs a new kind of leader to unify the tribes in faithful covenant obedience to God.

The third and final section of Judges focuses on two stories of unimaginable moral failure and disaster, demonstrating the desperate need for change in Israel. It is noted at both the beginning and end of these stories that "In those days Israel had no king; all the people did whatever seemed right in their own eyes."

Thus the overall argument of the book of Judges proposes that the nation needs not merely *individuals* but an *institution*—the kingship—to protect it and help it to remain faithful to the LORD. Specifically, the book has David's royal line in mind.

At both the beginning and the end of Judges, the Israelites ask God which tribe should lead them into battle. God answers, "Judah is to go first." The placement of these episodes is designed to confirm that God's choice to rule over Israel is the line of David from the tribe of Judah. In contrast, the tribe of Israel's first king, Saul—the tribe of Benjamin—is frequently shown in a negative light.

Israel is to have a king, but not just any king. Since Israel has rejected the LORD as King, an adequate human king will have to lead the people to faithfully worship and honor God. This brings the story of Israel to the point where God is ready to make his fourth covenant, establishing David as king of Israel and founder of a royal dynasty.

JUDGES

———— ✦ ————

After the death of Joshua, the Israelites asked the LORD, "Which tribe should go first to attack the Canaanites?"

The LORD answered, "Judah, for I have given them victory over the land."

The men of Judah said to their relatives from the tribe of Simeon, "Join with us to fight against the Canaanites living in the territory allotted to us. Then we will help you conquer your territory." So the men of Simeon went with Judah.

When the men of Judah attacked, the LORD gave them victory over the Canaanites and Perizzites, and they killed 10,000 enemy warriors at the town of Bezek. While at Bezek they encountered King Adoni-bezek and fought against him, and the Canaanites and Perizzites were defeated. Adoni-bezek escaped, but the Israelites soon captured him and cut off his thumbs and big toes.

Adoni-bezek said, "I once had seventy kings with their thumbs and big toes cut off, eating scraps from under my table. Now God has paid me back for what I did to them." They took him to Jerusalem, and he died there.

The men of Judah attacked Jerusalem and captured it, killing all its people and setting the city on fire. Then they went down to fight the Canaanites living in the hill country, the Negev, and the western foothills. Judah marched against the Canaanites in Hebron (formerly called Kiriath-arba), defeating the forces of Sheshai, Ahiman, and Talmai.

From there they went to fight against the people living in the town of Debir (formerly called Kiriath-sepher). Caleb said, "I will give my daughter Acsah in marriage to the one who attacks and captures Kiriath-sepher." Othniel, the son of Caleb's younger brother, Kenaz, was the one who conquered it, so Acsah became Othniel's wife.

When Acsah married Othniel, she urged him to ask her father for a field. As she got down off her donkey, Caleb asked her, "What's the matter?"

She said, "Let me have another gift. You have already given me land in the Negev; now please give me springs of water, too." So Caleb gave her the upper and lower springs.

When the tribe of Judah left Jericho—the city of palms—the Kenites, who were descendants of Moses' father-in-law, traveled with them into the wilderness of Judah. They settled among the people there, near the town of Arad in the Negev.

Then Judah joined with Simeon to fight against the Canaanites living in Zephath, and they completely destroyed the town. So the town was named Hormah. In addition, Judah captured the towns of Gaza, Ashkelon, and Ekron, along with their surrounding territories.

The LORD was with the people of Judah, and they took possession of the hill country. But they failed to drive out the people living in the plains, who had iron chariots. The town of Hebron was given to Caleb as Moses had promised. And Caleb drove out the people living there, who were descendants of the three sons of Anak.

The tribe of Benjamin, however, failed to drive out the Jebusites, who were living in Jerusalem. So to this day the Jebusites live in Jerusalem among the people of Benjamin.

The descendants of Joseph attacked the town of Bethel, and the LORD was with them. They sent men to scout out Bethel (formerly known as Luz). They confronted a man coming out of the town and said to him, "Show us a way into the town, and we will have mercy on you." So he showed them a way in, and they killed everyone in the town except that man and his family. Later the man moved to the land of the Hittites, where he built a town. He named it Luz, which is its name to this day.

The tribe of Manasseh failed to drive out the people living in Beth-shan, Taanach, Dor, Ibleam, Megiddo, and all their surrounding settlements, because the Canaanites were determined to stay in that region. When the Israelites grew stronger, they forced the Canaanites to work as slaves, but they never did drive them completely out of the land.

The tribe of Ephraim failed to drive out the Canaanites living in Gezer, so the Canaanites continued to live there among them.

The tribe of Zebulun failed to drive out the residents of Kitron and Nahalol, so the Canaanites continued to live among them. But the Canaanites were forced to work as slaves for the people of Zebulun.

The tribe of Asher failed to drive out the residents of Acco, Sidon, Ahlab, Aczib, Helbah, Aphik, and Rehob. Instead, the people of Asher moved in among the Canaanites, who controlled the land, for they failed to drive them out.

Likewise, the tribe of Naphtali failed to drive out the residents of Beth-shemesh and Beth-anath. Instead, they moved in among the Canaanites, who controlled the land. Nevertheless, the people of Beth-shemesh and Beth-anath were forced to work as slaves for the people of Naphtali.

As for the tribe of Dan, the Amorites forced them back into the hill country and would not let them come down into the plains. The Amorites were determined to stay in Mount Heres, Aijalon, and Shaalbim, but when the descendants of Joseph became stronger, they forced the Amorites to work as slaves. The boundary of the Amorites ran from Scorpion Pass to Sela and continued upward from there.

The angel of the LORD went up from Gilgal to Bokim and said to the Israelites, "I brought you out of Egypt into this land that I swore to give your ancestors, and I said I would never break my covenant with you. For your part, you were not to make any covenants with the people living in this land; instead, you were to destroy their altars. But you disobeyed my command. Why did you do this? So now I declare that I will no longer drive out the people living in your land. They will be thorns in your sides, and their gods will be a constant temptation to you."

When the angel of the LORD finished speaking to all the Israelites, the people wept loudly. So they called the place Bokim (which means "weeping"), and they offered sacrifices there to the LORD.

+ + +

After Joshua sent the people away, each of the tribes left to take possession of the land allotted to them. And the Israelites served the LORD throughout the lifetime of Joshua and the leaders who outlived him—those who had seen all the great things the LORD had done for Israel.

Joshua son of Nun, the servant of the LORD, died at the age of 110. They buried him in the land he had been allocated, at Timnath-serah in the hill country of Ephraim, north of Mount Gaash.

After that generation died, another generation grew up who did not acknowledge the LORD or remember the mighty things he had done for Israel.

The Israelites did evil in the LORD's sight and served the images of Baal. They abandoned the LORD, the God of their ancestors, who had brought them out of Egypt. They went after other gods, worshiping the gods of the people around them. And they angered the LORD. They abandoned the LORD to serve Baal and the images of Ashtoreth. This made the LORD burn with anger against Israel, so he handed them over to raiders who stole their possessions. He turned them over to their enemies all around, and they were no longer able to resist them. Every time Israel went out to battle, the LORD fought against them, causing them to be defeated, just as he had warned. And the people were in great distress.

Then the LORD raised up judges to rescue the Israelites from their attackers. Yet Israel did not listen to the judges but prostituted themselves by worshiping other gods. How quickly they turned away from the path of their ancestors, who had walked in obedience to the LORD's commands.

Whenever the LORD raised up a judge over Israel, he was with that judge and rescued the people from their enemies throughout the judge's lifetime. For the LORD took pity on his people, who were burdened by oppression and suffering. But when the judge died, the people returned to their corrupt ways, behaving worse than those who had lived before them. They went after other gods, serving and worshiping them. And they refused to give up their evil practices and stubborn ways.

So the LORD burned with anger against Israel. He said, "Because these people have violated my covenant, which I made with their ancestors, and have ignored my commands, I will no longer drive out the nations that Joshua left unconquered when he died. I did this to test Israel—to see whether or not they would follow the ways of the LORD as their ancestors did." That is why the LORD left those nations in place. He did not quickly drive them out or allow Joshua to conquer them all.

These are the nations that the LORD left in the land to test those Israelites who had not experienced the wars of Canaan. He did this to teach warfare to generations of Israelites who had no experience in battle. These are the nations: the Philistines (those living under the five Philistine rulers), all the Canaanites, the Sidonians, and the Hivites living in the mountains of Lebanon from Mount Baal-hermon to Lebo-hamath. These people were left to test the Israelites—to see whether they would obey the commands the LORD had given to their ancestors through Moses.

So the people of Israel lived among the Canaanites, Hittites, Amorites, Perizzites, Hivites, and Jebusites, and they intermarried with them. Israelite sons married their daughters, and Israelite daughters were given in marriage to their sons. And the Israelites served their gods.

+

The Israelites did evil in the LORD's sight. They forgot about the LORD their God, and they served the images of Baal and the Asherah poles. Then the LORD burned with anger against Israel, and he turned them over to King Cushan-rishathaim of Aram-naharaim. And the Israelites served Cushan-rishathaim for eight years.

But when the people of Israel cried out to the LORD for help, the LORD raised up a rescuer to save them. His name was Othniel, the son of Caleb's younger brother, Kenaz. The Spirit of the LORD came upon him, and he became Israel's judge. He went to war against King Cushan-rishathaim of Aram, and the LORD gave Othniel victory over him. So there was peace in the land for forty years. Then Othniel son of Kenaz died.

+

Once again the Israelites did evil in the LORD's sight, and the LORD gave King Eglon of Moab control over Israel because of their evil. Eglon enlisted the Ammonites and Amalekites as allies, and then he went out and defeated Israel, taking possession of Jericho, the city of palms. And the Israelites served Eglon of Moab for eighteen years.

But when the people of Israel cried out to the LORD for help, the LORD again raised up a rescuer to save them. His name was Ehud son of Gera, a left-handed man of the tribe of Benjamin. The Israelites sent Ehud to deliver their tribute money to King Eglon of Moab. So Ehud made a double-edged dagger that was about a foot long, and he strapped it to his right thigh, keeping it hidden under his clothing. He brought the tribute money to Eglon, who was very fat.

After delivering the payment, Ehud started home with those who had helped carry the tribute. But when Ehud reached the stone idols near Gilgal, he turned back. He came to Eglon and said, "I have a secret message for you."

So the king commanded his servants, "Be quiet!" and he sent them all out of the room.

Ehud walked over to Eglon, who was sitting alone in a cool upstairs room. And Ehud said, "I have a message from God for you!" As King Eglon rose from his seat, Ehud reached with his left hand, pulled out the dagger strapped to his right thigh, and plunged it into the king's belly. The dagger went so deep that the handle disappeared beneath the king's fat. So Ehud did not pull out the dagger, and the king's bowels emptied. Then Ehud closed and locked the doors of the room and escaped down the latrine.

After Ehud was gone, the king's servants returned and found the doors to the upstairs room locked. They thought he might be using the latrine in the room, so they waited. But when the king didn't come out after a long delay, they became concerned and got a key. And when they opened the doors, they found their master dead on the floor.

While the servants were waiting, Ehud escaped, passing the stone idols on his way to Seirah. When he arrived in the hill country of Ephraim, Ehud sounded a call to arms. Then he led a band of Israelites down from the hills.

"Follow me," he said, "for the LORD has given you victory over Moab your enemy." So they followed him. And the Israelites took control of the shallow crossings of the Jordan River across from Moab, preventing anyone from crossing.

They attacked the Moabites and killed about 10,000 of their strongest and most able-bodied warriors. Not one of them escaped. So Moab was conquered by Israel that day, and there was peace in the land for eighty years.

+

After Ehud, Shamgar son of Anath rescued Israel. He once killed 600 Philistines with an ox goad.

+

After Ehud's death, the Israelites again did evil in the LORD's sight. So the LORD turned them over to King Jabin of Hazor, a Canaanite king. The commander of his army was Sisera, who lived in Harosheth-haggoyim. Sisera, who had 900 iron chariots, ruthlessly oppressed the Israelites for twenty years. Then the people of Israel cried out to the LORD for help.

Deborah, the wife of Lappidoth, was a prophet who was judging Israel at that time. She would sit under the Palm of Deborah, between Ramah and Bethel in the hill country of Ephraim, and the Israelites would go to her for judgment. One day she sent for Barak son of Abinoam, who lived in Kedesh in the land of Naphtali. She said to him, "This is what the LORD, the God of Israel, commands you: Call out 10,000 warriors from the tribes of Naphtali and Zebulun at Mount Tabor. And I will call out Sisera, commander of Jabin's army, along with his chariots and warriors, to the Kishon River. There I will give you victory over him."

Barak told her, "I will go, but only if you go with me."

"Very well," she replied, "I will go with you. But you will receive no honor in this venture, for the LORD's victory over Sisera will be at the hands of a woman." So Deborah went with Barak to Kedesh. At Kedesh, Barak called together the tribes of Zebulun and Naphtali, and 10,000 warriors went up with him. Deborah also went with him.

Now Heber the Kenite, a descendant of Moses' brother-in-law Hobab, had moved away from the other members of his tribe and pitched his tent by the oak of Zaanannim near Kedesh.

When Sisera was told that Barak son of Abinoam had gone up to Mount Tabor, he called for all 900 of his iron chariots and all of his warriors, and they marched from Harosheth-haggoyim to the Kishon River.

Then Deborah said to Barak, "Get ready! This is the day the LORD will give you victory over Sisera, for the LORD is marching ahead of you." So Barak led his 10,000 warriors down the slopes of Mount Tabor into battle. When Barak attacked, the LORD threw Sisera and all his chariots and warriors into a panic. Sisera leaped down from his chariot and escaped on foot. Then Barak chased the chariots and the enemy army all the way to Harosheth-haggoyim, killing all of Sisera's warriors. Not a single one was left alive.

Meanwhile, Sisera ran to the tent of Jael, the wife of Heber the Kenite, because Heber's family was on friendly terms with King Jabin of Hazor. Jael went out to meet Sisera and said to him, "Come into my tent, sir. Come in. Don't be afraid." So he went into her tent, and she covered him with a blanket.

"Please give me some water," he said. "I'm thirsty." So she gave him some milk from a leather bag and covered him again.

"Stand at the door of the tent," he told her. "If anybody comes and asks you if there is anyone here, say no."

But when Sisera fell asleep from exhaustion, Jael quietly crept up to him with a hammer and tent peg in her hand. Then she drove the tent peg through his temple and into the ground, and so he died.

When Barak came looking for Sisera, Jael went out to meet him. She said, "Come, and I will show you the man you are looking for." So he followed her into the tent and found Sisera lying there dead, with the tent peg through his temple.

So on that day Israel saw God defeat Jabin, the Canaanite king. And from that time on Israel became stronger and stronger against King Jabin until they finally destroyed him.

On that day Deborah and Barak son of Abinoam sang this song:

"Israel's leaders took charge,
    and the people gladly followed.
Praise the LORD!

"Listen, you kings!
    Pay attention, you mighty rulers!
For I will sing to the LORD.
    I will make music to the LORD, the God of Israel.

"LORD, when you set out from Seir
    and marched across the fields of Edom,
the earth trembled,
    and the cloudy skies poured down rain.
The mountains quaked in the presence of the LORD,
    the God of Mount Sinai—
in the presence of the LORD,
    the God of Israel.

"In the days of Shamgar son of Anath,
and in the days of Jael,
people avoided the main roads,
and travelers stayed on winding pathways.
There were few people left in the villages of Israel—
until Deborah arose as a mother for Israel.
When Israel chose new gods,
war erupted at the city gates.
Yet not a shield or spear could be seen
among forty thousand warriors in Israel!
My heart is with the commanders of Israel,
with those who volunteered for war.
Praise the LORD!

"Consider this, you who ride on fine donkeys,
you who sit on fancy saddle blankets,
and you who walk along the road.
Listen to the village musicians
gathered at the watering holes.
They recount the righteous victories of the LORD
and the victories of his villagers in Israel.
Then the people of the LORD
marched down to the city gates.

"Wake up, Deborah, wake up!
Wake up, wake up, and sing a song!
Arise, Barak!
Lead your captives away, son of Abinoam!

"Down from Tabor marched the few against the nobles.
The people of the LORD marched down against mighty warriors.
They came down from Ephraim—
a land that once belonged to the Amalekites;
they followed you, Benjamin, with your troops.
From Makir the commanders marched down;
from Zebulun came those who carry a commander's staff.
The princes of Issachar were with Deborah and Barak.
They followed Barak, rushing into the valley.
But in the tribe of Reuben
there was great indecision.
Why did you sit at home among the sheepfolds—
to hear the shepherds whistle for their flocks?
Yes, in the tribe of Reuben
there was great indecision.

Gilead remained east of the Jordan.
  And why did Dan stay home?
Asher sat unmoved at the seashore,
  remaining in his harbors.
But Zebulun risked his life,
  as did Naphtali, on the heights of the battlefield.

"The kings of Canaan came and fought,
  at Taanach near Megiddo's springs,
  but they carried off no silver treasures.
The stars fought from heaven.
  The stars in their orbits fought against Sisera.
The Kishon River swept them away—
  that ancient torrent, the Kishon.
March on with courage, my soul!
Then the horses' hooves hammered the ground,
  the galloping, galloping of Sisera's mighty steeds.
'Let the people of Meroz be cursed,' said the angel of
    the Lord.
  'Let them be utterly cursed,
because they did not come to help the Lord—
  to help the Lord against the mighty warriors.'

"Most blessed among women is Jael,
  the wife of Heber the Kenite.
  May she be blessed above all women who live in tents.
Sisera asked for water,
  and she gave him milk.
In a bowl fit for nobles,
  she brought him yogurt.
Then with her left hand she reached for a tent peg,
  and with her right hand for the workman's hammer.
She struck Sisera with the hammer, crushing his head.
  With a shattering blow, she pierced his temples.
He sank, he fell,
  he lay still at her feet.
And where he sank,
  there he died.

"From the window Sisera's mother looked out.
  Through the window she watched for his return, saying,
'Why is his chariot so long in coming?
  Why don't we hear the sound of chariot wheels?'

"Her wise women answer,
　and she repeats these words to herself:
'They must be dividing the captured plunder—
　with a woman or two for every man.
There will be colorful robes for Sisera,
　and colorful, embroidered robes for me.
Yes, the plunder will include
　colorful robes embroidered on both sides.'

"LORD, may all your enemies die like Sisera!
　But may those who love you rise like the sun in all its power!"

Then there was peace in the land for forty years.

+

The Israelites did evil in the LORD's sight. So the LORD handed them over to the Midianites for seven years. The Midianites were so cruel that the Israelites made hiding places for themselves in the mountains, caves, and strongholds. Whenever the Israelites planted their crops, marauders from Midian, Amalek, and the people of the east would attack Israel, camping in the land and destroying crops as far away as Gaza. They left the Israelites with nothing to eat, taking all the sheep, goats, cattle, and donkeys. These enemy hordes, coming with their livestock and tents, were as thick as locusts; they arrived on droves of camels too numerous to count. And they stayed until the land was stripped bare. So Israel was reduced to starvation by the Midianites. Then the Israelites cried out to the LORD for help.

When they cried out to the LORD because of Midian, the LORD sent a prophet to the Israelites. He said, "This is what the LORD, the God of Israel, says: I brought you up out of slavery in Egypt. I rescued you from the Egyptians and from all who oppressed you. I drove out your enemies and gave you their land. I told you, 'I am the LORD your God. You must not worship the gods of the Amorites, in whose land you now live.' But you have not listened to me."

Then the angel of the LORD came and sat beneath the great tree at Ophrah, which belonged to Joash of the clan of Abiezer. Gideon son of Joash was threshing wheat at the bottom of a winepress to hide the grain from the Midianites. The angel of the LORD appeared to him and said, "Mighty hero, the LORD is with you!"

"Sir," Gideon replied, "if the LORD is with us, why has all this happened to us? And where are all the miracles our ancestors told us about? Didn't they say, 'The LORD brought us up out of Egypt'? But now the LORD has abandoned us and handed us over to the Midianites."

Then the LORD turned to him and said, "Go with the strength you have, and rescue Israel from the Midianites. I am sending you!"

"But Lord," Gideon replied, "how can I rescue Israel? My clan is the weakest in the whole tribe of Manasseh, and I am the least in my entire family!"

The LORD said to him, "I will be with you. And you will destroy the Midianites as if you were fighting against one man."

Gideon replied, "If you are truly going to help me, show me a sign to prove that it is really the LORD speaking to me. Don't go away until I come back and bring my offering to you."

He answered, "I will stay here until you return."

Gideon hurried home. He cooked a young goat, and with a basket of flour he baked some bread without yeast. Then, carrying the meat in a basket and the broth in a pot, he brought them out and presented them to the angel, who was under the great tree.

The angel of God said to him, "Place the meat and the unleavened bread on this rock, and pour the broth over it." And Gideon did as he was told. Then the angel of the LORD touched the meat and bread with the tip of the staff in his hand, and fire flamed up from the rock and consumed all he had brought. And the angel of the LORD disappeared.

When Gideon realized that it was the angel of the LORD, he cried out, "Oh, Sovereign LORD, I'm doomed! I have seen the angel of the LORD face to face!"

"It is all right," the LORD replied. "Do not be afraid. You will not die." And Gideon built an altar to the LORD there and named it Yahweh-Shalom (which means "the LORD is peace"). The altar remains in Ophrah in the land of the clan of Abiezer to this day.

That night the LORD said to Gideon, "Take the second bull from your father's herd, the one that is seven years old. Pull down your father's altar to Baal, and cut down the Asherah pole standing beside it. Then build an altar to the LORD your God here on this hilltop sanctuary, laying the stones carefully. Sacrifice the bull as a burnt offering on the altar, using as fuel the wood of the Asherah pole you cut down."

So Gideon took ten of his servants and did as the LORD had commanded. But he did it at night because he was afraid of the other members of his father's household and the people of the town.

Early the next morning, as the people of the town began to stir, someone discovered that the altar of Baal had been broken down and that the Asherah pole beside it had been cut down. In their place a new altar had been built, and on it were the remains of the bull that had been sacrificed. The people said to each other, "Who did this?" And after asking around and making a careful search, they learned that it was Gideon, the son of Joash.

"Bring out your son," the men of the town demanded of Joash. "He must die for destroying the altar of Baal and for cutting down the Asherah pole."

But Joash shouted to the mob that confronted him, "Why are you defending Baal? Will you argue his case? Whoever pleads his case will be put to death by morning! If Baal truly is a god, let him defend himself and destroy the one who broke down his altar!" From then on Gideon was called Jerub-baal, which means "Let Baal defend himself," because he broke down Baal's altar.

Soon afterward the armies of Midian, Amalek, and the people of the east formed an alliance against Israel and crossed the Jordan, camping in the valley of Jezreel. Then the Spirit of the LORD clothed Gideon with power. He blew a ram's horn as a call to arms, and the men of the clan of Abiezer came to him. He also sent messengers throughout Manasseh, Asher, Zebulun, and Naphtali, summoning their warriors, and all of them responded.

Then Gideon said to God, "If you are truly going to use me to rescue Israel as you promised, prove it to me in this way. I will put a wool fleece on the threshing floor tonight. If the fleece is wet with dew in the morning but the ground is dry, then I will know that you are going to help me rescue Israel as you promised." And that is just what happened. When Gideon got up early the next morning, he squeezed the fleece and wrung out a whole bowlful of water.

Then Gideon said to God, "Please don't be angry with me, but let me make one more request. Let me use the fleece for one more test. This time let the fleece remain dry while the ground around it is wet with dew." So that night God did as Gideon asked. The fleece was dry in the morning, but the ground was covered with dew.

So Jerub-baal (that is, Gideon) and his army got up early and went as far as the spring of Harod. The armies of Midian were camped north of them in the valley near the hill of Moreh. The LORD said to Gideon, "You have too many warriors with you. If I let all of you fight the Midianites, the Israelites will boast to me that they saved themselves by their own strength. Therefore, tell the people, 'Whoever is timid or afraid may leave this mountain and go home.'" So 22,000 of them went home, leaving only 10,000 who were willing to fight.

But the LORD told Gideon, "There are still too many! Bring them down to the spring, and I will test them to determine who will go with you and who will not." When Gideon took his warriors down to the water, the

LORD told him, "Divide the men into two groups. In one group put all those who cup water in their hands and lap it up with their tongues like dogs. In the other group put all those who kneel down and drink with their mouths in the stream." Only 300 of the men drank from their hands. All the others got down on their knees and drank with their mouths in the stream.

The LORD told Gideon, "With these 300 men I will rescue you and give you victory over the Midianites. Send all the others home." So Gideon collected the provisions and rams' horns of the other warriors and sent them home. But he kept the 300 men with him.

The Midianite camp was in the valley just below Gideon. That night the LORD said, "Get up! Go down into the Midianite camp, for I have given you victory over them! But if you are afraid to attack, go down to the camp with your servant Purah. Listen to what the Midianites are saying, and you will be greatly encouraged. Then you will be eager to attack."

So Gideon took Purah and went down to the edge of the enemy camp. The armies of Midian, Amalek, and the people of the east had settled in the valley like a swarm of locusts. Their camels were like grains of sand on the seashore—too many to count! Gideon crept up just as a man was telling his companion about a dream. The man said, "I had this dream, and in my dream a loaf of barley bread came tumbling down into the Midianite camp. It hit a tent, turned it over, and knocked it flat!"

His companion answered, "Your dream can mean only one thing—God has given Gideon son of Joash, the Israelite, victory over Midian and all its allies!"

When Gideon heard the dream and its interpretation, he bowed in worship before the LORD. Then he returned to the Israelite camp and shouted, "Get up! For the LORD has given you victory over the Midianite hordes!" He divided the 300 men into three groups and gave each man a ram's horn and a clay jar with a torch in it.

Then he said to them, "Keep your eyes on me. When I come to the edge of the camp, do just as I do. As soon as I and those with me blow the rams' horns, blow your horns, too, all around the entire camp, and shout, 'For the LORD and for Gideon!'"

It was just after midnight, after the changing of the guard, when Gideon and the 100 men with him reached the edge of the Midianite camp. Suddenly, they blew the rams' horns and broke their clay jars. Then all three groups blew their horns and broke their jars. They held the blazing torches in their left hands and the horns in their right hands, and they all shouted, "A sword for the LORD and for Gideon!"

Each man stood at his position around the camp and watched as all the

Midianites rushed around in a panic, shouting as they ran to escape. When the 300 Israelites blew their rams' horns, the LORD caused the warriors in the camp to fight against each other with their swords. Those who were not killed fled to places as far away as Beth-shittah near Zererah and to the border of Abel-meholah near Tabbath.

Then Gideon sent for the warriors of Naphtali, Asher, and Manasseh, who joined in chasing the army of Midian. Gideon also sent messengers throughout the hill country of Ephraim, saying, "Come down to attack the Midianites. Cut them off at the shallow crossings of the Jordan River at Beth-barah."

So all the men of Ephraim did as they were told. They captured Oreb and Zeeb, the two Midianite commanders, killing Oreb at the rock of Oreb, and Zeeb at the winepress of Zeeb. And they continued to chase the Midianites. Afterward the Israelites brought the heads of Oreb and Zeeb to Gideon, who was by the Jordan River.

Then the people of Ephraim asked Gideon, "Why have you treated us this way? Why didn't you send for us when you first went out to fight the Midianites?" And they argued heatedly with Gideon.

But Gideon replied, "What have I accomplished compared to you? Aren't even the leftover grapes of Ephraim's harvest better than the entire crop of my little clan of Abiezer? God gave you victory over Oreb and Zeeb, the commanders of the Midianite army. What have I accomplished compared to that?" When the men of Ephraim heard Gideon's answer, their anger subsided.

Gideon then crossed the Jordan River with his 300 men, and though exhausted, they continued to chase the enemy. When they reached Succoth, Gideon asked the leaders of the town, "Please give my warriors some food. They are very tired. I am chasing Zebah and Zalmunna, the kings of Midian."

But the officials of Succoth replied, "Catch Zebah and Zalmunna first, and then we will feed your army."

So Gideon said, "After the LORD gives me victory over Zebah and Zalmunna, I will return and tear your flesh with the thorns and briers from the wilderness."

From there Gideon went up to Peniel and again asked for food, but he got the same answer. So he said to the people of Peniel, "After I return in victory, I will tear down this tower."

By this time Zebah and Zalmunna were in Karkor with about 15,000 warriors—all that remained of the allied armies of the east, for 120,000 had already been killed. Gideon circled around by the caravan route east of Nobah and Jogbehah, taking the Midianite army by surprise. Zebah and

Zalmunna, the two Midianite kings, fled, but Gideon chased them down and captured all their warriors.

After this, Gideon returned from the battle by way of Heres Pass. There he captured a young man from Succoth and demanded that he write down the names of all the seventy-seven officials and elders in the town. Gideon then returned to Succoth and said to the leaders, "Here are Zebah and Zalmunna. When we were here before, you taunted me, saying, 'Catch Zebah and Zalmunna first, and then we will feed your exhausted army.'" Then Gideon took the elders of the town and taught them a lesson, punishing them with thorns and briers from the wilderness. He also tore down the tower of Peniel and killed all the men in the town.

Then Gideon asked Zebah and Zalmunna, "The men you killed at Tabor—what were they like?"

"Like you," they replied. "They all had the look of a king's son."

"They were my brothers, the sons of my own mother!" Gideon exclaimed. "As surely as the LORD lives, I wouldn't kill you if you hadn't killed them."

Turning to Jether, his oldest son, he said, "Kill them!" But Jether did not draw his sword, for he was only a boy and was afraid.

Then Zebah and Zalmunna said to Gideon, "Be a man! Kill us yourself!" So Gideon killed them both and took the royal ornaments from the necks of their camels.

Then the Israelites said to Gideon, "Be our ruler! You and your son and your grandson will be our rulers, for you have rescued us from Midian."

But Gideon replied, "I will not rule over you, nor will my son. The LORD will rule over you! However, I do have one request—that each of you give me an earring from the plunder you collected from your fallen enemies." (The enemies, being Ishmaelites, all wore gold earrings.)

"Gladly!" they replied. They spread out a cloak, and each one threw in a gold earring he had gathered from the plunder. The weight of the gold earrings was forty-three pounds, not including the royal ornaments and pendants, the purple clothing worn by the kings of Midian, or the chains around the necks of their camels.

Gideon made a sacred ephod from the gold and put it in Ophrah, his hometown. But soon all the Israelites prostituted themselves by worshiping it, and it became a trap for Gideon and his family.

That is the story of how the people of Israel defeated Midian, which never recovered. Throughout the rest of Gideon's lifetime—about forty years—there was peace in the land.

Then Gideon son of Joash returned home. He had seventy sons born to him, for he had many wives. He also had a concubine in Shechem, who gave birth to a son, whom he named Abimelech. Gideon died when he was very old, and he was buried in the grave of his father, Joash, at Ophrah in the land of the clan of Abiezer.

+

As soon as Gideon died, the Israelites prostituted themselves by worshiping the images of Baal, making Baal-berith their god. They forgot the LORD their God, who had rescued them from all their enemies surrounding them. Nor did they show any loyalty to the family of Jerub-baal (that is, Gideon), despite all the good he had done for Israel.

One day Gideon's son Abimelech went to Shechem to visit his uncles—his mother's brothers. He said to them and to the rest of his mother's family, "Ask the leading citizens of Shechem whether they want to be ruled by all seventy of Gideon's sons or by one man. And remember that I am your own flesh and blood!"

So Abimelech's uncles gave his message to all the citizens of Shechem on his behalf. And after listening to this proposal, the people of Shechem decided in favor of Abimelech because he was their relative. They gave him seventy silver coins from the temple of Baal-berith, which he used to hire some reckless troublemakers who agreed to follow him. He went to his father's home at Ophrah, and there, on one stone, they killed all seventy of his half brothers, the sons of Gideon. But the youngest brother, Jotham, escaped and hid.

Then all the leading citizens of Shechem and Beth-millo called a meeting under the oak beside the pillar at Shechem and made Abimelech their king.

When Jotham heard about this, he climbed to the top of Mount Gerizim and shouted,

"Listen to me, citizens of Shechem!
  Listen to me if you want God to listen to you!
Once upon a time the trees decided to choose a king.
  First they said to the olive tree,
  'Be our king!'
But the olive tree refused, saying,
'Should I quit producing the olive oil
  that blesses both God and people,
  just to wave back and forth over the trees?'

"Then they said to the fig tree,
  'You be our king!'

But the fig tree also refused, saying,
'Should I quit producing my sweet fruit
    just to wave back and forth over the trees?'

"Then they said to the grapevine,
    'You be our king!'
But the grapevine also refused, saying,
'Should I quit producing the wine
    that cheers both God and people,
    just to wave back and forth over the trees?'

"Then all the trees finally turned to the thornbush and said,
    'Come, you be our king!'
And the thornbush replied to the trees,
'If you truly want to make me your king,
    come and take shelter in my shade.
If not, let fire come out from me
    and devour the cedars of Lebanon.'"

Jotham continued, "Now make sure you have acted honorably and in good faith by making Abimelech your king, and that you have done right by Gideon and all of his descendants. Have you treated him with the honor he deserves for all he accomplished? For he fought for you and risked his life when he rescued you from the Midianites. But today you have revolted against my father and his descendants, killing his seventy sons on one stone. And you have chosen his slave woman's son, Abimelech, to be your king just because he is your relative.

"If you have acted honorably and in good faith toward Gideon and his descendants today, then may you find joy in Abimelech, and may he find joy in you. But if you have not acted in good faith, then may fire come out from Abimelech and devour the leading citizens of Shechem and Beth-millo; and may fire come out from the citizens of Shechem and Beth-millo and devour Abimelech!"

Then Jotham escaped and lived in Beer because he was afraid of his brother Abimelech.

After Abimelech had ruled over Israel for three years, God sent a spirit that stirred up trouble between Abimelech and the leading citizens of Shechem, and they revolted. God was punishing Abimelech for murdering Gideon's seventy sons, and the citizens of Shechem for supporting him in this treachery of murdering his brothers. The citizens of Shechem set an ambush for Abimelech on the hilltops and robbed everyone who passed that way. But someone warned Abimelech about their plot.

One day Gaal son of Ebed moved to Shechem with his brothers and gained the confidence of the leading citizens of Shechem. During the annual harvest festival at Shechem, held in the temple of the local god, the wine flowed freely, and everyone began cursing Abimelech. "Who is Abimelech?" Gaal shouted. "He's not a true son of Shechem, so why should we be his servants? He's merely the son of Gideon, and this Zebul is merely his deputy. Serve the true sons of Hamor, the founder of Shechem. Why should we serve Abimelech? If I were in charge here, I would get rid of Abimelech. I would say to him, 'Get some soldiers, and come out and fight!'"

But when Zebul, the leader of the city, heard what Gaal was saying, he was furious. He sent messengers to Abimelech in Arumah, telling him, "Gaal son of Ebed and his brothers have come to live in Shechem, and now they are inciting the city to rebel against you. Come by night with an army and hide out in the fields. In the morning, as soon as it is daylight, attack the city. When Gaal and those who are with him come out against you, you can do with them as you wish."

So Abimelech and all his men went by night and split into four groups, stationing themselves around Shechem. Gaal was standing at the city gates when Abimelech and his army came out of hiding. When Gaal saw them, he said to Zebul, "Look, there are people coming down from the hilltops!"

Zebul replied, "It's just the shadows on the hills that look like men."

But again Gaal said, "No, people are coming down from the hills. And another group is coming down the road past the Diviners' Oak."

Then Zebul turned on him and asked, "Now where is that big mouth of yours? Wasn't it you that said, 'Who is Abimelech, and why should we be his servants?' The men you mocked are right outside the city! Go out and fight them!"

So Gaal led the leading citizens of Shechem into battle against Abimelech. But Abimelech chased him, and many of Shechem's men were wounded and fell along the road as they retreated to the city gate. Abimelech returned to Arumah, and Zebul drove Gaal and his brothers out of Shechem.

The next day the people of Shechem went out into the fields to battle. When Abimelech heard about it, he divided his men into three groups and set an ambush in the fields. When Abimelech saw the people coming out of the city, he and his men jumped up from their hiding places and attacked them. Abimelech and his group stormed the city gate to keep the men of Shechem from getting back in, while Abimelech's other two groups cut them down in the fields. The battle went on all day before Abimelech finally captured the city. He killed the people, leveled the city, and scattered salt all over the ground.

When the leading citizens who lived in the tower of Shechem heard what had happened, they ran and hid in the temple of Baal-berith. Someone reported to Abimelech that the citizens had gathered in the temple, so he led his forces to Mount Zalmon. He took an ax and chopped some branches from a tree, then put them on his shoulder. "Quick, do as I have done!" he told his men. So each of them cut down some branches, following Abimelech's example. They piled the branches against the walls of the temple and set them on fire. So all the people who had lived in the tower of Shechem died—about 1,000 men and women.

Then Abimelech attacked the town of Thebez and captured it. But there was a strong tower inside the town, and all the men and women—the entire population—fled to it. They barricaded themselves in and climbed up to the roof of the tower. Abimelech followed them to attack the tower. But as he prepared to set fire to the entrance, a woman on the roof dropped a millstone that landed on Abimelech's head and crushed his skull.

He quickly said to his young armor bearer, "Draw your sword and kill me! Don't let it be said that a woman killed Abimelech!" So the young man ran him through with his sword, and he died. When Abimelech's men saw that he was dead, they disbanded and returned to their homes.

In this way, God punished Abimelech for the evil he had done against his father by murdering his seventy brothers. God also punished the men of Shechem for all their evil. So the curse of Jotham son of Gideon was fulfilled.

+

After Abimelech died, Tola son of Puah, son of Dodo, was the next person to rescue Israel. He was from the tribe of Issachar but lived in the town of Shamir in the hill country of Ephraim. He judged Israel for twenty-three years. When he died, he was buried in Shamir.

+

After Tola died, Jair from Gilead judged Israel for twenty-two years. His thirty sons rode around on thirty donkeys, and they owned thirty towns in the land of Gilead, which are still called the Towns of Jair. When Jair died, he was buried in Kamon.

+

Again the Israelites did evil in the LORD's sight. They served the images of Baal and Ashtoreth, and the gods of Aram, Sidon, Moab, Ammon, and Philistia. They abandoned the LORD and no longer served him at all. So the LORD burned with anger against Israel, and he turned them over to the Philistines and the Ammonites, who began to oppress them that year. For eighteen years they oppressed all the Israelites east of the Jordan River in the land of the Amorites (that is, in Gilead). The Ammonites also crossed to the west side of the Jordan and attacked Judah, Benjamin, and Ephraim.

The Israelites were in great distress. Finally, they cried out to the LORD for help, saying, "We have sinned against you because we have abandoned you as our God and have served the images of Baal."

The LORD replied, "Did I not rescue you from the Egyptians, the Amorites, the Ammonites, the Philistines, the Sidonians, the Amalekites, and the Maonites? When they oppressed you, you cried out to me for help, and I rescued you. Yet you have abandoned me and served other gods. So I will not rescue you anymore. Go and cry out to the gods you have chosen! Let them rescue you in your hour of distress!"

But the Israelites pleaded with the LORD and said, "We have sinned. Punish us as you see fit, only rescue us today from our enemies." Then the Israelites put aside their foreign gods and served the LORD. And he was grieved by their misery.

At that time the armies of Ammon had gathered for war and were camped in Gilead, and the people of Israel assembled and camped at Mizpah. The leaders of Gilead said to each other, "Whoever attacks the Ammonites first will become ruler over all the people of Gilead."

Now Jephthah of Gilead was a great warrior. He was the son of Gilead, but his mother was a prostitute. Gilead's wife also had several sons, and when these half brothers grew up, they chased Jephthah off the land. "You will not get any of our father's inheritance," they said, "for you are the son of a prostitute." So Jephthah fled from his brothers and lived in the land of Tob. Soon he had a band of worthless rebels following him.

At about this time, the Ammonites began their war against Israel. When the Ammonites attacked, the elders of Gilead sent for Jephthah in the land of Tob. The elders said, "Come and be our commander! Help us fight the Ammonites!"

But Jephthah said to them, "Aren't you the ones who hated me and drove me from my father's house? Why do you come to me now when you're in trouble?"

"Because we need you," the elders replied. "If you lead us in battle against the Ammonites, we will make you ruler over all the people of Gilead."

Jephthah said to the elders, "Let me get this straight. If I come with you and if the LORD gives me victory over the Ammonites, will you really make me ruler over all the people?"

"The LORD is our witness," the elders replied. "We promise to do whatever you say."

So Jephthah went with the elders of Gilead, and the people made him their ruler and commander of the army. At Mizpah, in the presence of the LORD, Jephthah repeated what he had said to the elders.

Then Jephthah sent messengers to the king of Ammon, asking, "Why have you come out to fight against my land?"

The king of Ammon answered Jephthah's messengers, "When the Israelites came out of Egypt, they stole my land from the Arnon River to the Jabbok River and all the way to the Jordan. Now then, give back the land peaceably."

Jephthah sent this message back to the Ammonite king:

"This is what Jephthah says: Israel did not steal any land from Moab or Ammon. When the people of Israel arrived at Kadesh on their journey from Egypt after crossing the Red Sea, they sent messengers to the king of Edom asking for permission to pass through his land. But their request was denied. Then they asked the king of Moab for similar permission, but he wouldn't let them pass through either. So the people of Israel stayed in Kadesh.

"Finally, they went around Edom and Moab through the wilderness. They traveled along Moab's eastern border and camped on the other side of the Arnon River. But they never once crossed the Arnon River into Moab, for the Arnon was the border of Moab.

"Then Israel sent messengers to King Sihon of the Amorites, who ruled from Heshbon, asking for permission to cross through his land to get to their destination. But King Sihon didn't trust Israel to pass through his land. Instead, he mobilized his army at Jahaz and attacked them. But the LORD, the God of Israel, gave his people victory over King Sihon. So Israel took control of all the land of the Amorites, who lived in that region, from the Arnon River to the Jabbok River, and from the eastern wilderness to the Jordan.

"So you see, it was the LORD, the God of Israel, who took away the land from the Amorites and gave it to Israel. Why, then, should we give it back to you? You keep whatever your god Chemosh gives you, and we will keep whatever the LORD our God gives us. Are you any better than Balak son of Zippor, king of Moab? Did he try to make a case against Israel for disputed land? Did he go to war against them?

"Israel has been living here for 300 years, inhabiting Heshbon and its surrounding settlements, all the way to Aroer and its settlements, and in all the towns along the Arnon River. Why have you made no effort to recover it before now? Therefore, I have not sinned against you. Rather, you have wronged me by attacking me. Let the LORD, who is judge, decide today which of us is right—Israel or Ammon."

But the king of Ammon paid no attention to Jephthah's message.

At that time the Spirit of the LORD came upon Jephthah, and he went throughout the land of Gilead and Manasseh, including Mizpah in Gilead, and from there he led an army against the Ammonites. And Jephthah made a vow to the LORD. He said, "If you give me victory over the Ammonites, I will give to the LORD whatever comes out of my house to meet me when I return in triumph. I will sacrifice it as a burnt offering."

So Jephthah led his army against the Ammonites, and the LORD gave him victory. He crushed the Ammonites, devastating about twenty towns from Aroer to an area near Minnith and as far away as Abel-keramim. In this way Israel defeated the Ammonites.

When Jephthah returned home to Mizpah, his daughter came out to meet him, playing on a tambourine and dancing for joy. She was his one and only child; he had no other sons or daughters. When he saw her, he tore his clothes in anguish. "Oh, my daughter!" he cried out. "You have completely destroyed me! You've brought disaster on me! For I have made a vow to the LORD, and I cannot take it back."

And she said, "Father, if you have made a vow to the LORD, you must do to me what you have vowed, for the LORD has given you a great victory over your enemies, the Ammonites. But first let me do this one thing: Let me go up and roam in the hills and weep with my friends for two months, because I will die a virgin."

"You may go," Jephthah said. And he sent her away for two months. She and her friends went into the hills and wept because she would never have children. When she returned home, her father kept the vow he had made, and she died a virgin.

So it has become a custom in Israel for young Israelite women to go away for four days each year to lament the fate of Jephthah's daughter.

Then the people of Ephraim mobilized an army and crossed over the Jordan River to Zaphon. They sent this message to Jephthah: "Why didn't you call for us to help you fight against the Ammonites? We are going to burn down your house with you in it!"

Jephthah replied, "I summoned you at the beginning of the dispute, but you refused to come! You failed to help us in our struggle against Ammon. So when I realized you weren't coming, I risked my life and went to battle without you, and the LORD gave me victory over the Ammonites. So why have you now come to fight me?"

The people of Ephraim responded, "You men of Gilead are nothing more than fugitives from Ephraim and Manasseh." So Jephthah gathered all the men of Gilead and attacked the men of Ephraim and defeated them.

Jephthah captured the shallow crossings of the Jordan River, and whenever a fugitive from Ephraim tried to go back across, the men of Gilead would challenge him. "Are you a member of the tribe of Ephraim?" they would ask. If the man said, "No, I'm not," they would tell him to say "Shibboleth." If he was from Ephraim, he would say "Sibboleth," because people from Ephraim cannot pronounce the word correctly. Then they would take him and kill him at the shallow crossings of the Jordan. In all, 42,000 Ephraimites were killed at that time.

Jephthah judged Israel for six years. When he died, he was buried in one of the towns of Gilead.

+

After Jephthah died, Ibzan from Bethlehem judged Israel. He had thirty sons and thirty daughters. He sent his daughters to marry men outside his clan, and he brought in thirty young women from outside his clan to marry his sons. Ibzan judged Israel for seven years. When he died, he was buried at Bethlehem.

+

After Ibzan died, Elon from the tribe of Zebulun judged Israel for ten years. When he died, he was buried at Aijalon in Zebulun.

+

After Elon died, Abdon son of Hillel, from Pirathon, judged Israel. He had forty sons and thirty grandsons, who rode on seventy donkeys. He judged Israel for eight years. When he died, he was buried at Pirathon in Ephraim, in the hill country of the Amalekites.

+

Again the Israelites did evil in the LORD's sight, so the LORD handed them over to the Philistines, who oppressed them for forty years.

In those days a man named Manoah from the tribe of Dan lived in the town of Zorah. His wife was unable to become pregnant, and they had no children. The angel of the LORD appeared to Manoah's wife and said, "Even though you have been unable to have children, you will soon become pregnant and give birth to a son. So be careful; you must not drink wine or any other alcoholic drink nor eat any forbidden food. You will become pregnant and give birth to a son, and his hair must never be cut. For he will be dedicated to God as a Nazirite from birth. He will begin to rescue Israel from the Philistines."

The woman ran and told her husband, "A man of God appeared to me! He looked like one of God's angels, terrifying to see. I didn't ask where he was from, and he didn't tell me his name. But he told me, 'You will become pregnant and give birth to a son. You must not drink wine or any other alcoholic drink nor eat any forbidden food. For your son will be dedicated to God as a Nazirite from the moment of his birth until the day of his death.'"

Then Manoah prayed to the LORD, saying, "Lord, please let the man of God come back to us again and give us more instructions about this son who is to be born."

God answered Manoah's prayer, and the angel of God appeared once again to his wife as she was sitting in the field. But her husband, Manoah, was not with her. So she quickly ran and told her husband, "The man who appeared to me the other day is here again!"

Manoah ran back with his wife and asked, "Are you the man who spoke to my wife the other day?"

"Yes," he replied, "I am."

So Manoah asked him, "When your words come true, what kind of rules should govern the boy's life and work?"

The angel of the LORD replied, "Be sure your wife follows the instructions I gave her. She must not eat grapes or raisins, drink wine or any other alcoholic drink, or eat any forbidden food."

Then Manoah said to the angel of the LORD, "Please stay here until we can prepare a young goat for you to eat."

"I will stay," the angel of the LORD replied, "but I will not eat anything. However, you may prepare a burnt offering as a sacrifice to the LORD." (Manoah didn't realize it was the angel of the LORD.)

Then Manoah asked the angel of the LORD, "What is your name? For when all this comes true, we want to honor you."

"Why do you ask my name?" the angel of the LORD replied. "It is too wonderful for you to understand."

Then Manoah took a young goat and a grain offering and offered it on a rock as a sacrifice to the LORD. And as Manoah and his wife watched, the LORD did an amazing thing. As the flames from the altar shot up toward the sky, the angel of the LORD ascended in the fire. When Manoah and his wife saw this, they fell with their faces to the ground.

The angel did not appear again to Manoah and his wife. Manoah finally realized it was the angel of the Lord, and he said to his wife, "We will certainly die, for we have seen God!"

But his wife said, "If the Lord were going to kill us, he wouldn't have accepted our burnt offering and grain offering. He wouldn't have appeared to us and told us this wonderful thing and done these miracles."

When her son was born, she named him Samson. And the Lord blessed him as he grew up. And the Spirit of the Lord began to stir him while he lived in Mahaneh-dan, which is located between the towns of Zorah and Eshtaol.

One day when Samson was in Timnah, one of the Philistine women caught his eye. When he returned home, he told his father and mother, "A young Philistine woman in Timnah caught my eye. I want to marry her. Get her for me."

His father and mother objected. "Isn't there even one woman in our tribe or among all the Israelites you could marry?" they asked. "Why must you go to the pagan Philistines to find a wife?"

But Samson told his father, "Get her for me! She looks good to me." His father and mother didn't realize the Lord was at work in this, creating an opportunity to work against the Philistines, who ruled over Israel at that time.

As Samson and his parents were going down to Timnah, a young lion suddenly attacked Samson near the vineyards of Timnah. At that moment the Spirit of the Lord came powerfully upon him, and he ripped the lion's jaws apart with his bare hands. He did it as easily as if it were a young goat. But he didn't tell his father or mother about it. When Samson arrived in Timnah, he talked with the woman and was very pleased with her.

Later, when he returned to Timnah for the wedding, he turned off the path to look at the carcass of the lion. And he found that a swarm of bees had made some honey in the carcass. He scooped some of the honey into his hands and ate it along the way. He also gave some to his father and mother, and they ate it. But he didn't tell them he had taken the honey from the carcass of the lion.

As his father was making final arrangements for the marriage, Samson threw a party at Timnah, as was the custom for elite young men. When the bride's parents saw him, they selected thirty young men from the town to be his companions.

Samson said to them, "Let me tell you a riddle. If you solve my riddle during these seven days of the celebration, I will give you thirty fine linen robes and thirty sets of festive clothing. But if you can't solve it, then you must give me thirty fine linen robes and thirty sets of festive clothing."

"All right," they agreed, "let's hear your riddle."

So he said:

"Out of the one who eats came something to eat;
  out of the strong came something sweet."

Three days later they were still trying to figure it out. On the fourth day
they said to Samson's wife, "Entice your husband to explain the riddle for
us, or we will burn down your father's house with you in it. Did you invite
us to this party just to make us poor?"

So Samson's wife came to him in tears and said, "You don't love me;
you hate me! You have given my people a riddle, but you haven't told me
the answer."

"I haven't even given the answer to my father or mother," he replied.
"Why should I tell you?" So she cried whenever she was with him and kept
it up for the rest of the celebration. At last, on the seventh day he told her
the answer because she was tormenting him with her nagging. Then she
explained the riddle to the young men.

So before sunset of the seventh day, the men of the town came to Samson with their answer:

"What is sweeter than honey?
  What is stronger than a lion?"

Samson replied, "If you hadn't plowed with my heifer, you wouldn't have
solved my riddle!"

Then the Spirit of the LORD came powerfully upon him. He went down
to the town of Ashkelon, killed thirty men, took their belongings, and
gave their clothing to the men who had solved his riddle. But Samson was
furious about what had happened, and he went back home to live with his
father and mother. So his wife was given in marriage to the man who had
been Samson's best man at the wedding.

Later on, during the wheat harvest, Samson took a young goat as a present
to his wife. He said, "I'm going into my wife's room to sleep with her," but
her father wouldn't let him in.

"I truly thought you must hate her," her father explained, "so I gave her
in marriage to your best man. But look, her younger sister is even more
beautiful than she is. Marry her instead."

Samson said, "This time I cannot be blamed for everything I am going
to do to you Philistines." Then he went out and caught 300 foxes. He tied
their tails together in pairs, and he fastened a torch to each pair of tails.
Then he lit the torches and let the foxes run through the grain fields of the
Philistines. He burned all their grain to the ground, including the sheaves
and the uncut grain. He also destroyed their vineyards and olive groves.

"Who did this?" the Philistines demanded.

"Samson," was the reply, "because his father-in-law from Timnah gave Samson's wife to be married to his best man." So the Philistines went and got the woman and her father and burned them to death.

"Because you did this," Samson vowed, "I won't rest until I take my revenge on you!" So he attacked the Philistines with great fury and killed many of them. Then he went to live in a cave in the rock of Etam.

The Philistines retaliated by setting up camp in Judah and spreading out near the town of Lehi. The men of Judah asked the Philistines, "Why are you attacking us?"

The Philistines replied, "We've come to capture Samson. We've come to pay him back for what he did to us."

So 3,000 men of Judah went down to get Samson at the cave in the rock of Etam. They said to Samson, "Don't you realize the Philistines rule over us? What are you doing to us?"

But Samson replied, "I only did to them what they did to me."

But the men of Judah told him, "We have come to tie you up and hand you over to the Philistines."

"All right," Samson said. "But promise that you won't kill me yourselves."

"We will only tie you up and hand you over to the Philistines," they replied. "We won't kill you." So they tied him up with two new ropes and brought him up from the rock.

As Samson arrived at Lehi, the Philistines came shouting in triumph. But the Spirit of the LORD came powerfully upon Samson, and he snapped the ropes on his arms as if they were burnt strands of flax, and they fell from his wrists. Then he found the jawbone of a recently killed donkey. He picked it up and killed 1,000 Philistines with it. Then Samson said,

"With the jawbone of a donkey,
　I've piled them in heaps!
With the jawbone of a donkey,
　I've killed a thousand men!"

When he finished his boasting, he threw away the jawbone; and the place was named Jawbone Hill.

Samson was now very thirsty, and he cried out to the LORD, "You have accomplished this great victory by the strength of your servant. Must I now die of thirst and fall into the hands of these pagans?" So God caused water to gush out of a hollow in the ground at Lehi, and Samson was revived as he drank. Then he named that place "The Spring of the One Who Cried Out," and it is still in Lehi to this day.

Samson judged Israel for twenty years during the period when the Philistines dominated the land.

One day Samson went to the Philistine town of Gaza and spent the night with a prostitute. Word soon spread that Samson was there, so the men of Gaza gathered together and waited all night at the town gates. They kept quiet during the night, saying to themselves, "When the light of morning comes, we will kill him."

But Samson stayed in bed only until midnight. Then he got up, took hold of the doors of the town gate, including the two posts, and lifted them up, bar and all. He put them on his shoulders and carried them all the way to the top of the hill across from Hebron.

Some time later Samson fell in love with a woman named Delilah, who lived in the valley of Sorek. The rulers of the Philistines went to her and said, "Entice Samson to tell you what makes him so strong and how he can be overpowered and tied up securely. Then each of us will give you 1,100 pieces of silver."

So Delilah said to Samson, "Please tell me what makes you so strong and what it would take to tie you up securely."

Samson replied, "If I were tied up with seven new bowstrings that have not yet been dried, I would become as weak as anyone else."

So the Philistine rulers brought Delilah seven new bowstrings, and she tied Samson up with them. She had hidden some men in one of the inner rooms of her house, and she cried out, "Samson! The Philistines have come to capture you!" But Samson snapped the bowstrings as a piece of string snaps when it is burned by a fire. So the secret of his strength was not discovered.

Afterward Delilah said to him, "You've been making fun of me and telling me lies! Now please tell me how you can be tied up securely."

Samson replied, "If I were tied up with brand-new ropes that had never been used, I would become as weak as anyone else."

So Delilah took new ropes and tied him up with them. The men were hiding in the inner room as before, and again Delilah cried out, "Samson! The Philistines have come to capture you!" But again Samson snapped the ropes from his arms as if they were thread.

Then Delilah said, "You've been making fun of me and telling me lies! Now tell me how you can be tied up securely."

Samson replied, "If you were to weave the seven braids of my hair into the fabric on your loom and tighten it with the loom shuttle, I would become as weak as anyone else."

So while he slept, Delilah wove the seven braids of his hair into the fabric. Then she tightened it with the loom shuttle. Again she cried out, "Samson! The Philistines have come to capture you!" But Samson woke up, pulled back the loom shuttle, and yanked his hair away from the loom and the fabric.

Then Delilah pouted, "How can you tell me, 'I love you,' when you don't share your secrets with me? You've made fun of me three times now, and you still haven't told me what makes you so strong!" She tormented him with her nagging day after day until he was sick to death of it.

Finally, Samson shared his secret with her. "My hair has never been cut," he confessed, "for I was dedicated to God as a Nazirite from birth. If my head were shaved, my strength would leave me, and I would become as weak as anyone else."

Delilah realized he had finally told her the truth, so she sent for the Philistine rulers. "Come back one more time," she said, "for he has finally told me his secret." So the Philistine rulers returned with the money in their hands. Delilah lulled Samson to sleep with his head in her lap, and then she called in a man to shave off the seven locks of his hair. In this way she began to bring him down, and his strength left him.

Then she cried out, "Samson! The Philistines have come to capture you!"

When he woke up, he thought, "I will do as before and shake myself free." But he didn't realize the LORD had left him.

So the Philistines captured him and gouged out his eyes. They took him to Gaza, where he was bound with bronze chains and forced to grind grain in the prison.

But before long, his hair began to grow back.

The Philistine rulers held a great festival, offering sacrifices and praising their god, Dagon. They said, "Our god has given us victory over our enemy Samson!"

When the people saw him, they praised their god, saying, "Our god has delivered our enemy to us! The one who killed so many of us is now in our power!"

Half drunk by now, the people demanded, "Bring out Samson so he can amuse us!" So he was brought from the prison to amuse them, and they had him stand between the pillars supporting the roof.

Samson said to the young servant who was leading him by the hand, "Place my hands against the pillars that hold up the temple. I want to rest against them." Now the temple was completely filled with people. All the Philistine rulers were there, and there were about 3,000 men and women on the roof who were watching as Samson amused them.

Then Samson prayed to the LORD, "Sovereign LORD, remember me again. O God, please strengthen me just one more time. With one blow let me pay back the Philistines for the loss of my two eyes." Then Samson put his hands on the two center pillars that held up the temple. Pushing against them with both hands, he prayed, "Let me die with the Philistines." And the temple crashed down on the Philistine rulers and all the people. So he killed more people when he died than he had during his entire lifetime.

Later his brothers and other relatives went down to get his body. They took him back home and buried him between Zorah and Eshtaol, where his father, Manoah, was buried. Samson had judged Israel for twenty years.

+ + +

There was a man named Micah, who lived in the hill country of Ephraim. One day he said to his mother, "I heard you place a curse on the person who stole 1,100 pieces of silver from you. Well, I have the money. I was the one who took it."

"The LORD bless you for admitting it," his mother replied. He returned the money to her, and she said, "I now dedicate these silver coins to the LORD. In honor of my son, I will have an image carved and an idol cast."

So when he returned the money to his mother, she took 200 silver coins and gave them to a silversmith, who made them into an image and an idol. And these were placed in Micah's house. Micah set up a shrine for the idol, and he made a sacred ephod and some household idols. Then he installed one of his sons as his personal priest.

In those days Israel had no king; all the people did whatever seemed right in their own eyes.

One day a young Levite, who had been living in Bethlehem in Judah, arrived in that area. He had left Bethlehem in search of another place to live, and as he traveled, he came to the hill country of Ephraim. He happened to stop at Micah's house as he was traveling through. "Where are you from?" Micah asked him.

He replied, "I am a Levite from Bethlehem in Judah, and I am looking for a place to live."

"Stay here with me," Micah said, "and you can be a father and priest to me. I will give you ten pieces of silver a year, plus a change of clothes and your food." The Levite agreed to this, and the young man became like one of Micah's sons.

So Micah installed the Levite as his personal priest, and he lived in Micah's house. "I know the LORD will bless me now," Micah said, "because I have a Levite serving as my priest."

Now in those days Israel had no king. And the tribe of Dan was trying to find a place where they could settle, for they had not yet moved into the land assigned to them when the land was divided among the tribes of Israel. So the men of Dan chose from their clans five capable warriors from the towns of Zorah and Eshtaol to scout out a land for them to settle in.

When these warriors arrived in the hill country of Ephraim, they came to Micah's house and spent the night there. While at Micah's house, they recognized the young Levite's accent, so they went over and asked him, "Who brought you here, and what are you doing in this place? Why are you here?" He told them about his agreement with Micah and that he had been hired as Micah's personal priest.

Then they said, "Ask God whether or not our journey will be successful."

"Go in peace," the priest replied. "For the LORD is watching over your journey."

So the five men went on to the town of Laish, where they noticed the people living carefree lives, like the Sidonians; they were peaceful and secure. The people were also wealthy because their land was very fertile. And they lived a great distance from Sidon and had no allies nearby.

When the men returned to Zorah and Eshtaol, their relatives asked them, "What did you find?"

The men replied, "Come on, let's attack them! We have seen the land, and it is very good. What are you waiting for? Don't hesitate to go and take possession of it. When you get there, you will find the people living care-free lives. God has given us a spacious and fertile land, lacking in nothing!"

So 600 men from the tribe of Dan, armed with weapons of war, set out from Zorah and Eshtaol. They camped at a place west of Kiriath-jearim in Judah, which is called Mahaneh-dan to this day. Then they went on from there into the hill country of Ephraim and came to the house of Micah.

The five men who had scouted out the land around Laish explained to the others, "These buildings contain a sacred ephod, as well as some household idols, a carved image, and a cast idol. What do you think you should do?" Then the five men turned off the road and went over to Micah's house, where the young Levite lived, and greeted him kindly. As the 600 armed warriors from the tribe of Dan stood at the entrance of the gate, the five scouts entered the shrine and removed the carved image, the sacred ephod, the household idols, and the cast idol. Meanwhile, the priest was standing at the gate with the 600 armed warriors.

When the priest saw the men carrying all the sacred objects out of Micah's shrine, he said, "What are you doing?"

"Be quiet and come with us," they said. "Be a father and priest to all of us. Isn't it better to be a priest for an entire tribe and clan of Israel than for the household of just one man?"

The young priest was quite happy to go with them, so he took along the sacred ephod, the household idols, and the carved image. They turned and started on their way again, placing their children, livestock, and possessions in front of them.

When the people from the tribe of Dan were quite a distance from Micah's house, the people who lived near Micah came chasing after them. They were shouting as they caught up with them. The men of Dan turned around and said to Micah, "What's the matter? Why have you called these men together and chased after us like this?"

"What do you mean, 'What's the matter?'" Micah replied. "You've taken away all the gods I have made, and my priest, and I have nothing left!"

The men of Dan said, "Watch what you say! There are some short-tempered men around here who might get angry and kill you and your family." So the men of Dan continued on their way. When Micah saw that there were too many of them for him to attack, he turned around and went home.

Then, with Micah's idols and his priest, the men of Dan came to the town of Laish, whose people were peaceful and secure. They attacked with swords and burned the town to the ground. There was no one to rescue the people, for they lived a great distance from Sidon and had no allies nearby. This happened in the valley near Beth-rehob.

Then the people of the tribe of Dan rebuilt the town and lived there. They renamed the town Dan after their ancestor, Israel's son, but it had originally been called Laish.

Then they set up the carved image, and they appointed Jonathan son of Gershom, son of Moses, as their priest. This family continued as priests for the tribe of Dan until the Exile. So Micah's carved image was worshiped by the tribe of Dan as long as the Tabernacle of God remained at Shiloh.

+

Now in those days Israel had no king. There was a man from the tribe of Levi living in a remote area of the hill country of Ephraim. One day he brought home a woman from Bethlehem in Judah to be his concubine. But she became angry with him and returned to her father's home in Bethlehem.

After about four months, her husband set out for Bethlehem to speak personally to her and persuade her to come back. He took with him a servant and a pair of donkeys. When he arrived at her father's house, her father saw him and welcomed him. Her father urged him to stay awhile, so he stayed three days, eating, drinking, and sleeping there.

On the fourth day the man was up early, ready to leave, but the woman's father said to his son-in-law, "Have something to eat before you go."

So the two men sat down together and had something to eat and drink. Then the woman's father said, "Please stay another night and enjoy yourself." The man got up to leave, but his father-in-law kept urging him to stay, so he finally gave in and stayed the night.

On the morning of the fifth day he was up early again, ready to leave, and again the woman's father said, "Have something to eat; then you can leave later this afternoon." So they had another day of feasting. Later, as the man and his concubine and servant were preparing to leave, his father-in-law said, "Look, it's almost evening. Stay the night and enjoy yourself. Tomorrow you can get up early and be on your way."

But this time the man was determined to leave. So he took his two saddled donkeys and his concubine and headed in the direction of Jebus (that is, Jerusalem). It was late in the day when they neared Jebus, and the man's servant said to him, "Let's stop at this Jebusite town and spend the night there."

"No," his master said, "we can't stay in this foreign town where there are no Israelites. Instead, we will go on to Gibeah. Come on, let's try to get as far as Gibeah or Ramah, and we'll spend the night in one of those towns." So they went on. The sun was setting as they came to Gibeah, a town in the land of Benjamin, so they stopped there to spend the night. They rested in the town square, but no one took them in for the night.

That evening an old man came home from his work in the fields. He was from the hill country of Ephraim, but he was living in Gibeah, where the people were from the tribe of Benjamin. When he saw the travelers sitting in the town square, he asked them where they were from and where they were going.

"We have been in Bethlehem in Judah," the man replied. "We are on our way to a remote area in the hill country of Ephraim, which is my home. I traveled to Bethlehem, and now I'm returning home. But no one has taken us in for the night, even though we have everything we need. We have straw and feed for our donkeys and plenty of bread and wine for ourselves."

"You are welcome to stay with me," the old man said. "I will give you anything you might need. But whatever you do, don't spend the night in the square." So he took them home with him and fed the donkeys. After they washed their feet, they ate and drank together.

While they were enjoying themselves, a crowd of troublemakers from the town surrounded the house. They began beating at the door and shouting to the old man, "Bring out the man who is staying with you so we can have sex with him."

The old man stepped outside to talk to them. "No, my brothers, don't do such an evil thing. For this man is a guest in my house, and such a thing would be shameful. Here, take my virgin daughter and this man's concubine. I will bring them out to you, and you can abuse them and do whatever you like. But don't do such a shameful thing to this man."

But they wouldn't listen to him. So the Levite took hold of his concubine and pushed her out the door. The men of the town abused her all night, taking turns raping her until morning. Finally, at dawn they let her go. At daybreak the woman returned to the house where her husband was staying. She collapsed at the door of the house and lay there until it was light.

When her husband opened the door to leave, there lay his concubine with her hands on the threshold. He said, "Get up! Let's go!" But there was no answer. So he put her body on his donkey and took her home.

When he got home, he took a knife and cut his concubine's body into twelve pieces. Then he sent one piece to each tribe throughout all the territory of Israel.

Everyone who saw it said, "Such a horrible crime has not been committed in all the time since Israel left Egypt. Think about it! What are we going to do? Who's going to speak up?"

Then all the Israelites were united as one man, from Dan in the north to Beersheba in the south, including those from across the Jordan in the land of Gilead. The entire community assembled in the presence of the LORD at Mizpah. The leaders of all the people and all the tribes of Israel—400,000 warriors armed with swords—took their positions in the assembly of the people of God. (Word soon reached the land of Benjamin that the other tribes had gone up to Mizpah.) The Israelites then asked how this terrible crime had happened.

The Levite, the husband of the woman who had been murdered, said, "My concubine and I came to spend the night in Gibeah, a town that belongs to the people of Benjamin. That night some of the leading citizens of Gibeah surrounded the house, planning to kill me, and they raped my concubine until she was dead. So I cut her body into twelve pieces and sent the pieces throughout the territory assigned to Israel, for these men have committed a terrible and shameful crime. Now then, all of you—the entire community of Israel—must decide here and now what should be done about this!"

And all the people rose to their feet in unison and declared, "None of us will return home! No, not even one of us! Instead, this is what we will do to Gibeah; we will draw lots to decide who will attack it. One-tenth of the men from each tribe will be chosen to supply the warriors with food, and the rest of us will take revenge on Gibeah of Benjamin for this shameful thing they have done in Israel." So all the Israelites were completely united, and they gathered together to attack the town.

The Israelites sent messengers to the tribe of Benjamin, saying, "What a terrible thing has been done among you! Give up those evil men, those troublemakers from Gibeah, so we can execute them and purge Israel of this evil."

But the people of Benjamin would not listen. Instead, they came from their towns and gathered at Gibeah to fight the Israelites. In all, 26,000 of their warriors armed with swords arrived in Gibeah to join the 700 elite troops who lived there. Among Benjamin's elite troops, 700 were left-handed, and each of them could sling a rock and hit a target within a hairs-breadth without missing. Israel had 400,000 experienced soldiers armed with swords, not counting Benjamin's warriors.

Before the battle the Israelites went to Bethel and asked God, "Which tribe should go first to attack the people of Benjamin?"

The LORD answered, "Judah is to go first."

So the Israelites left early the next morning and camped near Gibeah. Then they advanced toward Gibeah to attack the men of Benjamin. But Benjamin's warriors, who were defending the town, came out and killed 22,000 Israelites on the battlefield that day.

But the Israelites encouraged each other and took their positions again at the same place they had fought the previous day. For they had gone up to Bethel and wept in the presence of the LORD until evening. They had asked the LORD, "Should we fight against our relatives from Benjamin again?"

And the LORD had said, "Go out and fight against them."

So the next day they went out again to fight against the men of Benjamin, but the men of Benjamin killed another 18,000 Israelites, all of whom were experienced with the sword.

Then all the Israelites went up to Bethel and wept in the presence of the LORD and fasted until evening. They also brought burnt offerings and peace offerings to the LORD. The Israelites went up seeking direction from the LORD. (In those days the Ark of the Covenant of God was in Bethel, and Phinehas son of Eleazar and grandson of Aaron was the priest.) The Israelites asked the LORD, "Should we fight against our relatives from Benjamin again, or should we stop?"

The LORD said, "Go! Tomorrow I will hand them over to you."

So the Israelites set an ambush all around Gibeah. They went out on the third day and took their positions at the same place as before. When the men of Benjamin came out to attack, they were drawn away from the town. And as they had done before, they began to kill the Israelites. About thirty Israelites died in the open fields and along the roads, one leading to Bethel and the other leading back to Gibeah.

Then the warriors of Benjamin shouted, "We're defeating them as we did before!" But the Israelites had planned in advance to run away so that the men of Benjamin would chase them along the roads and be drawn away from the town.

When the main group of Israelite warriors reached Baal-tamar, they turned and took up their positions. Meanwhile, the Israelites hiding in ambush to the west of Gibeah jumped up to fight. There were 10,000 elite Israelite troops who advanced against Gibeah. The fighting was so heavy that Benjamin didn't realize the impending disaster. So the LORD helped Israel defeat Benjamin, and that day the Israelites killed 25,100 of Benjamin's warriors, all of whom were experienced swordsmen. Then the men of Benjamin saw that they were beaten.

The Israelites had retreated from Benjamin's warriors in order to give those hiding in ambush more room to maneuver against Gibeah. Then those who were hiding rushed in from all sides and killed everyone in the town. They had arranged to send up a large cloud of smoke from the town as a signal. When the Israelites saw the smoke, they turned and attacked Benjamin's warriors.

By that time Benjamin's warriors had killed about thirty Israelites, and they shouted, "We're defeating them as we did in the first battle!" But when the warriors of Benjamin looked behind them and saw the smoke rising into the sky from every part of the town, the men of Israel turned and attacked. At this point the men of Benjamin became terrified, because they realized disaster was close at hand. So they turned around and fled before the Israelites toward the wilderness. But they couldn't escape the battle, and the people who came out of the nearby towns were also killed. The Israelites surrounded the men of Benjamin and chased them relentlessly, finally overtaking them east of Gibeah. That day 18,000 of Benjamin's strongest warriors died in battle. The survivors fled into the wilderness toward the rock of Rimmon, but Israel killed 5,000 of them along the road. They continued the chase until they had killed another 2,000 near Gidom.

So that day the tribe of Benjamin lost 25,000 strong warriors armed with swords, leaving only 600 men who escaped to the rock of Rimmon, where they lived for four months. And the Israelites returned and slaughtered every living thing in all the towns—the people, the livestock, and everything they found. They also burned down all the towns they came to.

The Israelites had vowed at Mizpah, "We will never give our daughters in marriage to a man from the tribe of Benjamin." Now the people went to Bethel and sat in the presence of God until evening, weeping loudly and bitterly. "O LORD, God of Israel," they cried out, "why has this happened in Israel? Now one of our tribes is missing from Israel!"

Early the next morning the people built an altar and presented their burnt offerings and peace offerings on it. Then they said, "Who among the tribes of Israel did not join us at Mizpah when we held our assembly in the presence of the LORD?" At that time they had taken a solemn oath in the LORD's presence, vowing that anyone who refused to come would be put to death.

The Israelites felt sorry for their brother Benjamin and said, "Today one of the tribes of Israel has been cut off. How can we find wives for the few who remain, since we have sworn by the LORD not to give them our daughters in marriage?"

So they asked, "Who among the tribes of Israel did not join us at Mizpah when we assembled in the presence of the LORD?" And they discovered that no one from Jabesh-gilead had attended the assembly. For after they counted all the people, no one from Jabesh-gilead was present.

So the assembly sent 12,000 of their best warriors to Jabesh-gilead with orders to kill everyone there, including women and children. "This is what you are to do," they said. "Completely destroy all the males and every woman who is not a virgin." Among the residents of Jabesh-gilead they found 400 young virgins who had never slept with a man, and they brought them to the camp at Shiloh in the land of Canaan.

The Israelite assembly sent a peace delegation to the remaining people of Benjamin who were living at the rock of Rimmon. Then the men of Benjamin returned to their homes, and the 400 women of Jabesh-gilead who had been spared were given to them as wives. But there were not enough women for all of them.

The people felt sorry for Benjamin because the LORD had made this gap among the tribes of Israel. So the elders of the assembly asked, "How can we find wives for the few who remain, since the women of the tribe of Benjamin are dead? There must be heirs for the survivors so that an entire tribe of Israel is not wiped out. But we cannot give them our own daughters in marriage because we have sworn with a solemn oath that anyone who does this will fall under God's curse."

Then they thought of the annual festival of the LORD held in Shiloh, south of Lebonah and north of Bethel, along the east side of the road that goes from Bethel to Shechem. They told the men of Benjamin who still needed wives, "Go and hide in the vineyards. When you see the young women of Shiloh come out for their dances, rush out from the vineyards, and each of you can take one of them home to the land of Benjamin to be your wife! And when their fathers and brothers come to us in protest, we will tell them, 'Please be sympathetic. Let them have your daughters, for we didn't find wives for all of them when we destroyed Jabesh-gilead. And you are not guilty of breaking the vow since you did not actually give your daughters to them in marriage.'"

So the men of Benjamin did as they were told. Each man caught one of the women as she danced in the celebration and carried her off to be his wife. They returned to their own land, and they rebuilt their towns and lived in them.

Then the people of Israel departed by tribes and families, and they returned to their own homes.

In those days Israel had no king; all the people did whatever seemed right in their own eyes.

IMMERSED IN RUTH

THE BOOK OF JUDGES ENDS with a disturbing depiction of how bad things had gotten: "In those days Israel had no king; all the people did whatever seemed right in their own eyes." But the book of Ruth shows that Israel wasn't universally corrupt—some Israelites actually did follow God's merciful and compassionate ways "in the days when the judges ruled."

In telling this remarkable story of Ruth, the book reveals a crucial link from the period of the judges to the stories of Israel's kings that follow in the book of Samuel–Kings. It concludes with a surprising connection to the future appearance of Israel's famous King David.

The book of Ruth tells a single story and is written like a short drama or play. First the narrative stage is set, and then a series of brief dramatic scenes appear. Because of a famine in the land, an Israelite woman named Naomi moves to the neighboring country of Moab with her husband and sons to find food. They settle there, and her sons marry Moabite women. The story's conflict arises through the multiple tragedies that Naomi endures and her subsequent struggle to survive.

As the story unfolds, Naomi decides to return home to Israel. "I went away full," she sadly tells her friends, "but the LORD has brought me home empty." Naomi, now joined by her Moabite daughter-in-law Ruth, faces the considerable hardship of being a single woman with no male heir in an ancient patriarchal culture.

We discover that Naomi and Ruth both have deep reservoirs of inner strength and resourcefulness. They face the significant challenges in their lives together with courage, daring, and hard work. Along the way they encounter Boaz—a faithful and compassionate Israelite who proves to be a refuge to the women by following the provisions in Israel's law to help the poor. We see that God is at work throughout the story from the way that people keep showing up in the right place at the right time.

We can learn much from this brief but richly crafted story of Ruth and Naomi. God is directly involved in our own human dramas, working in ways we cannot always see and understand. So we must faithfully press on and play our own parts in the story well, creatively using all the resources and gifts he provides, including the help of other people living in God's Story.

This book also plays a part in the story of God's covenant faithfulness. Simply stated, like Judges, the book of Ruth supports the right of David's house to rule in Israel. But there's a problem. As the genealogy at the end of the book reveals, David is the great-grandson of Ruth the Moabite. Because the Moabites refused to provide the Israelites with food and water when they escaped from Egypt, a declaration was made in the Law of Moses that none of their descendants should be accepted into the Israelite community for ten generations. David was a fourth-generation descendant of a Moabite. So how could he legitimately be Israel's king?

The book of Ruth shows that David's Moabite ancestor was a woman of true faith in the God of Israel. Beyond this, she *did* provide a desperate Israelite (Naomi) with the help she needed, and in this way Ruth effectively redressed the wrongs of her ancestors. At the end of the book, the women of Bethlehem accept Ruth and pray that she will be another great ancestor for the community "like Rachel and Leah, from whom all the nation of Israel descended!" Those prayers are answered when she becomes a mother in the royal line of David. Significantly, the genealogy at the end of the book lists ten generations leading up to King David, showing the old prohibition regarding the Moabites to be overcome in the wider purposes of God to bring blessing to all the nations of earth.

RUTH

✟

In the days when the judges ruled in Israel, a severe famine came upon the land. So a man from Bethlehem in Judah left his home and went to live in the country of Moab, taking his wife and two sons with him. The man's name was Elimelech, and his wife was Naomi. Their two sons were Mahlon and Kilion. They were Ephrathites from Bethlehem in the land of Judah. And when they reached Moab, they settled there.

Then Elimelech died, and Naomi was left with her two sons. The two sons married Moabite women. One married a woman named Orpah, and the other a woman named Ruth. But about ten years later, both Mahlon and Kilion died. This left Naomi alone, without her two sons or her husband.

Then Naomi heard in Moab that the LORD had blessed his people in Judah by giving them good crops again. So Naomi and her daughters-in-law got ready to leave Moab to return to her homeland. With her two daughters-in-law she set out from the place where she had been living, and they took the road that would lead them back to Judah.

But on the way, Naomi said to her two daughters-in-law, "Go back to your mothers' homes. And may the LORD reward you for your kindness to your husbands and to me. May the LORD bless you with the security of another marriage." Then she kissed them good-bye, and they all broke down and wept.

"No," they said. "We want to go with you to your people."

But Naomi replied, "Why should you go on with me? Can I still give birth to other sons who could grow up to be your husbands? No, my daughters, return to your parents' homes, for I am too old to marry again. And even if it were possible, and I were to get married tonight and bear sons, then what? Would you wait for them to grow up and refuse to marry someone else? No, of course not, my daughters! Things are far more bitter for me than for you, because the LORD himself has raised his fist against me."

And again they wept together, and Orpah kissed her mother-in-law good-bye. But Ruth clung tightly to Naomi. "Look," Naomi said to her, "your sister-in-law has gone back to her people and to her gods. You should do the same."

But Ruth replied, "Don't ask me to leave you and turn back. Wherever you go, I will go; wherever you live, I will live. Your people will be my people, and your God will be my God. Wherever you die, I will die, and there I will be buried. May the LORD punish me severely if I allow anything but death to separate us!" When Naomi saw that Ruth was determined to go with her, she said nothing more.

So the two of them continued on their journey. When they came to Bethlehem, the entire town was excited by their arrival. "Is it really Naomi?" the women asked.

"Don't call me Naomi," she responded. "Instead, call me Mara, for the Almighty has made life very bitter for me. I went away full, but the LORD has brought me home empty. Why call me Naomi when the LORD has caused me to suffer and the Almighty has sent such tragedy upon me?"

So Naomi returned from Moab, accompanied by her daughter-in-law Ruth, the young Moabite woman. They arrived in Bethlehem in late spring, at the beginning of the barley harvest.

Now there was a wealthy and influential man in Bethlehem named Boaz, who was a relative of Naomi's husband, Elimelech.

One day Ruth the Moabite said to Naomi, "Let me go out into the harvest fields to pick up the stalks of grain left behind by anyone who is kind enough to let me do it."

Naomi replied, "All right, my daughter, go ahead." So Ruth went out to gather grain behind the harvesters. And as it happened, she found herself working in a field that belonged to Boaz, the relative of her father-in-law, Elimelech.

While she was there, Boaz arrived from Bethlehem and greeted the harvesters. "The LORD be with you!" he said.

"The LORD bless you!" the harvesters replied.

Then Boaz asked his foreman, "Who is that young woman over there? Who does she belong to?"

And the foreman replied, "She is the young woman from Moab who came back with Naomi. She asked me this morning if she could gather grain behind the harvesters. She has been hard at work ever since, except for a few minutes' rest in the shelter."

Boaz went over and said to Ruth, "Listen, my daughter. Stay right here with us when you gather grain; don't go to any other fields. Stay right behind the young women working in my field. See which part of the field they are harvesting, and then follow them. I have warned the young men not to treat you roughly. And when you are thirsty, help yourself to the water they have drawn from the well."

Ruth fell at his feet and thanked him warmly. "What have I done to deserve such kindness?" she asked. "I am only a foreigner."

"Yes, I know," Boaz replied. "But I also know about everything you have done for your mother-in-law since the death of your husband. I have heard how you left your father and mother and your own land to live here among complete strangers. May the LORD, the God of Israel, under whose wings you have come to take refuge, reward you fully for what you have done."

"I hope I continue to please you, sir," she replied. "You have comforted me by speaking so kindly to me, even though I am not one of your workers."

At mealtime Boaz called to her, "Come over here, and help yourself to some food. You can dip your bread in the sour wine." So she sat with his harvesters, and Boaz gave her some roasted grain to eat. She ate all she wanted and still had some left over.

When Ruth went back to work again, Boaz ordered his young men, "Let her gather grain right among the sheaves without stopping her. And pull out some heads of barley from the bundles and drop them on purpose for her. Let her pick them up, and don't give her a hard time!"

So Ruth gathered barley there all day, and when she beat out the grain that evening, it filled an entire basket. She carried it back into town and showed it to her mother-in-law. Ruth also gave her the roasted grain that was left over from her meal.

"Where did you gather all this grain today?" Naomi asked. "Where did you work? May the LORD bless the one who helped you!"

So Ruth told her mother-in-law about the man in whose field she had worked. She said, "The man I worked with today is named Boaz."

"May the LORD bless him!" Naomi told her daughter-in-law. "He is showing his kindness to us as well as to your dead husband. That man is one of our closest relatives, one of our family redeemers."

Then Ruth said, "What's more, Boaz even told me to come back and stay with his harvesters until the entire harvest is completed."

"Good!" Naomi exclaimed. "Do as he said, my daughter. Stay with his young women right through the whole harvest. You might be harassed in other fields, but you'll be safe with him."

So Ruth worked alongside the women in Boaz's fields and gathered grain with them until the end of the barley harvest. Then she continued working with them through the wheat harvest in early summer. And all the while she lived with her mother-in-law.

One day Naomi said to Ruth, "My daughter, it's time that I found a permanent home for you, so that you will be provided for. Boaz is a close relative of ours, and he's been very kind by letting you gather grain with his young women. Tonight he will be winnowing barley at the threshing floor. Now do as I tell you—take a bath and put on perfume and dress in your nicest clothes. Then go to the threshing floor, but don't let Boaz see you until he has finished eating and drinking. Be sure to notice where he lies down; then go and uncover his feet and lie down there. He will tell you what to do."

"I will do everything you say," Ruth replied. So she went down to the threshing floor that night and followed the instructions of her mother-in-law.

After Boaz had finished eating and drinking and was in good spirits, he lay down at the far end of the pile of grain and went to sleep. Then Ruth came quietly, uncovered his feet, and lay down. Around midnight Boaz suddenly woke up and turned over. He was surprised to find a woman lying at his feet! "Who are you?" he asked.

"I am your servant Ruth," she replied. "Spread the corner of your covering over me, for you are my family redeemer."

"The LORD bless you, my daughter!" Boaz exclaimed. "You are showing even more family loyalty now than you did before, for you have not gone after a younger man, whether rich or poor. Now don't worry about a thing, my daughter. I will do what is necessary, for everyone in town knows you are a virtuous woman. But while it's true that I am one of your family redeemers, there is another man who is more closely related to you than I am. Stay here tonight, and in the morning I will talk to him. If he is willing to redeem you, very well. Let him marry you. But if he is not willing, then as surely as the LORD lives, I will redeem you myself! Now lie down here until morning."

So Ruth lay at Boaz's feet until the morning, but she got up before it was light enough for people to recognize each other. For Boaz had said, "No one must know that a woman was here at the threshing floor." Then Boaz said to her, "Bring your cloak and spread it out." He measured six scoops of barley into the cloak and placed it on her back. Then he returned to the town.

When Ruth went back to her mother-in-law, Naomi asked, "What happened, my daughter?"

Ruth told Naomi everything Boaz had done for her, and she added, "He gave me these six scoops of barley and said, 'Don't go back to your mother-in-law empty-handed.'"

Then Naomi said to her, "Just be patient, my daughter, until we hear what happens. The man won't rest until he has settled things today."

Boaz went to the town gate and took a seat there. Just then the family redeemer he had mentioned came by, so Boaz called out to him, "Come over here and sit down, friend. I want to talk to you." So they sat down together. Then Boaz called ten leaders from the town and asked them to sit as witnesses. And Boaz said to the family redeemer, "You know Naomi, who came back from Moab. She is selling the land that belonged to our relative Elimelech. I thought I should speak to you about it so that you can redeem it if you wish. If you want the land, then buy it here in the presence of these witnesses. But if you don't want it, let me know right away, because I am next in line to redeem it after you."

The man replied, "All right, I'll redeem it."

Then Boaz told him, "Of course, your purchase of the land from Naomi also requires that you marry Ruth, the Moabite widow. That way she can have children who will carry on her husband's name and keep the land in the family."

"Then I can't redeem it," the family redeemer replied, "because this might endanger my own estate. You redeem the land; I cannot do it."

Now in those days it was the custom in Israel for anyone transferring a right of purchase to remove his sandal and hand it to the other party. This publicly validated the transaction. So the other family redeemer drew off his sandal as he said to Boaz, "You buy the land."

Then Boaz said to the elders and to the crowd standing around, "You are witnesses that today I have bought from Naomi all the property of Elimelech, Kilion, and Mahlon. And with the land I have acquired Ruth, the Moabite widow of Mahlon, to be my wife. This way she can have a son to carry on the family name of her dead husband and to inherit the family property here in his hometown. You are all witnesses today."

Then the elders and all the people standing in the gate replied, "We are witnesses! May the LORD make this woman who is coming into your home like Rachel and Leah, from whom all the nation of Israel descended! May you prosper in Ephrathah and be famous in Bethlehem. And may the LORD give you descendants by this young woman who will be like those of our ancestor Perez, the son of Tamar and Judah."

So Boaz took Ruth into his home, and she became his wife. When he slept with her, the LORD enabled her to become pregnant, and she gave birth to a son. Then the women of the town said to Naomi, "Praise the LORD, who has now provided a redeemer for your family! May this child be famous in Israel. May he restore your youth and care for you in your old age. For he is the son of your daughter-in-law who loves you and has been better to you than seven sons!"

Naomi took the baby and cuddled him to her breast. And she cared for him as if he were her own. The neighbor women said, "Now at last Naomi has a son again!" And they named him Obed. He became the father of Jesse and the grandfather of David.

+

This is the genealogical record of their ancestor Perez:

> Perez was the father of Hezron.
> Hezron was the father of Ram.
> Ram was the father of Amminadab.
> Amminadab was the father of Nahshon.
> Nahshon was the father of Salmon.
> Salmon was the father of Boaz.
> Boaz was the father of Obed.
> Obed was the father of Jesse.
> Jesse was the father of David.

IMMERSED IN SAMUEL–KINGS

THE BOOKS KNOWN TODAY as 1 and 2 Samuel and 1 and 2 Kings were originally a single work later divided due to the size limitations of ancient scrolls. In its original unity, Samuel–Kings tells the story of the Israelite monarchy from beginning to end.

Hebrew tradition tells us that this grand work was put together over time from the records kept by prophets—such as Samuel, Nathan, and Gad—who were God's messengers to the people of Israel. They observed crucial moments in the life of the nation, interpreted events in light of God's covenants, and recorded their insights for posterity. The royal history of Samuel–Kings, therefore, is also the story of the word of the LORD, spoken through his prophets in response to the deeds of Israel's rulers.

While Samuel–Kings is drawn from the records of various prophets and collected to address the concerns of different historical periods, a single literary structural pattern runs all the way through the work. A repeated formula describes how long the kings reigned, where they reigned, and how old they were when their reigns began.

But the two halves of Samuel–Kings also have separate concerns. We can understand the intent of the first half by recalling one of the purposes of the preceding books—to predict and defend the monarchy in Israel. The book of Deuteronomy made provision for the requirements of a future king. The book of Judges reminded Israel how bad things were before they had their first king. The story of Ruth revealed how the descendant of a Moabite could still be "God's anointed."

The first half of Samuel–Kings is similarly *a defense of the monarchy*. It reminds the people that they asked for a king, even though the prophet Samuel warned them that a king would burden them with taxes and labor. Specifically, it describes the establishment of the monarchy and then explains why God ultimately rejected Saul, the first king.

But far more importantly, the first half of Samuel–Kings describes the fourth covenant, which gives structure to the ongoing story of the Bible. Israel's second king, David, is a man after God's own heart, and God promises that a lasting dynasty of kings will come from David. Israel's future thus comes to be tied up with the destiny of King David and his descendants.

The second half of Samuel–Kings returns to a focus on the earlier covenant God made with Israel through Moses. That covenant promised them blessings or curses based on whether or not they were faithful to his instructions. The stories of Israel's successive kings demonstrate an increasing failure of the monarchy to lead the people into wholehearted allegiance to God. So the prophets build an extended "covenant lawsuit"—an indictment of the kings and people—because the people haven't kept their part of the covenant. The nation first splits in two, then the territory of each remaining kingdom diminishes. Both kingdoms—now called Israel and Judah—are eventually conquered by foreign empires. Jerusalem itself is sacked, its walls torn down, and the Temple burned to the ground. The people are carried away from the land. In other words, the second half of Samuel–Kings is *a defense of the exile.*

Samuel–Kings seemingly ends on this note of failure—the failure of Israel, of God's plans for Israel, and indeed, of God's plans for the world through Israel. But at the end of the whole work, Jehoiachin, the surviving heir to David's throne, is released from prison and treated as an honored vassal by the king of the Babylonian Empire. A thin sliver of hope remains.

The Bible portrays the LORD as the Creator of the earth, the true King of all nations. With Israel now in shambles, the question returns to God himself. How will he keep his promise to redeem and restore the world now that his chosen instrument has fallen?

SAMUEL-KINGS

✢

There was a man named Elkanah who lived in Ramah in the region of Zuph in the hill country of Ephraim. He was the son of Jeroham, son of Elihu, son of Tohu, son of Zuph, of Ephraim. Elkanah had two wives, Hannah and Peninnah. Peninnah had children, but Hannah did not.

Each year Elkanah would travel to Shiloh to worship and sacrifice to the LORD of Heaven's Armies at the Tabernacle. The priests of the LORD at that time were the two sons of Eli—Hophni and Phinehas. On the days Elkanah presented his sacrifice, he would give portions of the meat to Peninnah and each of her children. And though he loved Hannah, he would give her only one choice portion because the LORD had given her no children. So Peninnah would taunt Hannah and make fun of her because the LORD had kept her from having children. Year after year it was the same—Peninnah would taunt Hannah as they went to the Tabernacle. Each time, Hannah would be reduced to tears and would not even eat.

"Why are you crying, Hannah?" Elkanah would ask. "Why aren't you eating? Why be downhearted just because you have no children? You have me—isn't that better than having ten sons?"

Once after a sacrificial meal at Shiloh, Hannah got up and went to pray. Eli the priest was sitting at his customary place beside the entrance of the Tabernacle. Hannah was in deep anguish, crying bitterly as she prayed to the LORD. And she made this vow: "O LORD of Heaven's Armies, if you will look upon my sorrow and answer my prayer and give me a son, then I will give him back to you. He will be yours for his entire lifetime, and as a sign that he has been dedicated to the LORD, his hair will never be cut."

As she was praying to the LORD, Eli watched her. Seeing her lips moving but hearing no sound, he thought she had been drinking. "Must you come here drunk?" he demanded. "Throw away your wine!"

"Oh no, sir!" she replied. "I haven't been drinking wine or anything stronger. But I am very discouraged, and I was pouring out my heart to the LORD. Don't think I am a wicked woman! For I have been praying out of great anguish and sorrow."

"In that case," Eli said, "go in peace! May the God of Israel grant the request you have asked of him."

"Oh, thank you, sir!" she exclaimed. Then she went back and began to eat again, and she was no longer sad.

The entire family got up early the next morning and went to worship the LORD once more. Then they returned home to Ramah. When Elkanah slept with Hannah, the LORD remembered her plea, and in due time she gave birth to a son. She named him Samuel, for she said, "I asked the LORD for him."

The next year Elkanah and his family went on their annual trip to offer a sacrifice to the LORD and to keep his vow. But Hannah did not go. She told her husband, "Wait until the boy is weaned. Then I will take him to the Tabernacle and leave him there with the LORD permanently."

"Whatever you think is best," Elkanah agreed. "Stay here for now, and may the LORD help you keep your promise." So she stayed home and nursed the boy until he was weaned.

When the child was weaned, Hannah took him to the Tabernacle in Shiloh. They brought along a three-year-old bull for the sacrifice and a basket of flour and some wine. After sacrificing the bull, they brought the boy to Eli. "Sir, do you remember me?" Hannah asked. "I am the very woman who stood here several years ago praying to the LORD. I asked the LORD to give me this boy, and he has granted my request. Now I am giving him to the LORD, and he will belong to the LORD his whole life." And they worshiped the LORD there.

Then Hannah prayed:

"My heart rejoices in the LORD!
    The LORD has made me strong.
Now I have an answer for my enemies;
    I rejoice because you rescued me.
No one is holy like the LORD!
    There is no one besides you;
    there is no Rock like our God.

"Stop acting so proud and haughty!
    Don't speak with such arrogance!
For the LORD is a God who knows what you have done;
    he will judge your actions.
The bow of the mighty is now broken,
    and those who stumbled are now strong.
Those who were well fed are now starving,
    and those who were starving are now full.

The childless woman now has seven children,
  and the woman with many children wastes away.
The LORD gives both death and life;
  he brings some down to the grave but raises others up.
The LORD makes some poor and others rich;
  he brings some down and lifts others up.
He lifts the poor from the dust
  and the needy from the garbage dump.
He sets them among princes,
  placing them in seats of honor.
For all the earth is the LORD's,
  and he has set the world in order.

"He will protect his faithful ones,
  but the wicked will disappear in darkness.
No one will succeed by strength alone.
  Those who fight against the LORD will be shattered.
He thunders against them from heaven;
  the LORD judges throughout the earth.
He gives power to his king;
  he increases the strength of his anointed one."

Then Elkanah returned home to Ramah without Samuel. And the boy served the LORD by assisting Eli the priest.

Now the sons of Eli were scoundrels who had no respect for the LORD or for their duties as priests. Whenever anyone offered a sacrifice, Eli's sons would send over a servant with a three-pronged fork. While the meat of the sacrificed animal was still boiling, the servant would stick the fork into the pot and demand that whatever it brought up be given to Eli's sons. All the Israelites who came to worship at Shiloh were treated this way. Sometimes the servant would come even before the animal's fat had been burned on the altar. He would demand raw meat before it had been boiled so that it could be used for roasting.

The man offering the sacrifice might reply, "Take as much as you want, but the fat must be burned first." Then the servant would demand, "No, give it to me now, or I'll take it by force." So the sin of these young men was very serious in the LORD's sight, for they treated the LORD's offerings with contempt.

But Samuel, though he was only a boy, served the LORD. He wore a linen garment like that of a priest. Each year his mother made a small coat for him and brought it to him when she came with her husband for the sacrifice. Before they returned home, Eli would bless Elkanah and his wife and say, "May the LORD give you other children to take the place of this one she gave to the LORD." And the LORD blessed Hannah, and she conceived and gave birth to three sons and two daughters. Meanwhile, Samuel grew up in the presence of the LORD.

Now Eli was very old, but he was aware of what his sons were doing to the people of Israel. He knew, for instance, that his sons were seducing the young women who assisted at the entrance of the Tabernacle. Eli said to them, "I have been hearing reports from all the people about the wicked things you are doing. Why do you keep sinning? You must stop, my sons! The reports I hear among the LORD's people are not good. If someone sins against another person, God can mediate for the guilty party. But if someone sins against the LORD, who can intercede?" But Eli's sons wouldn't listen to their father, for the LORD was already planning to put them to death.

Meanwhile, the boy Samuel grew taller and grew in favor with the LORD and with the people.

One day a man of God came to Eli and gave him this message from the LORD: "I revealed myself to your ancestors when they were Pharaoh's slaves in Egypt. I chose your ancestor Aaron from among all the tribes of Israel to be my priest, to offer sacrifices on my altar, to burn incense, and to wear the priestly vest as he served me. And I assigned the sacrificial offerings to you priests. So why do you scorn my sacrifices and offerings? Why do you give your sons more honor than you give me—for you and they have become fat from the best offerings of my people Israel!

"Therefore, the LORD, the God of Israel, says: I promised that your branch of the tribe of Levi would always be my priests. But I will honor those who honor me, and I will despise those who think lightly of me. The time is coming when I will put an end to your family, so it will no longer serve as my priests. All the members of your family will die before their time. None will reach old age. You will watch with envy as I pour out prosperity on the people of Israel. But no members of your family will ever live out their days. The few not cut off from serving at my altar will survive, but only so their eyes can go blind and their hearts break, and their children will die a violent death. And to prove that what I have said will come true, I will cause your two sons, Hophni and Phinehas, to die on the same day!

"Then I will raise up a faithful priest who will serve me and do what I desire. I will establish his family, and they will be priests to my anointed kings forever. Then all of your surviving family will bow before him, begging for money and food. 'Please,' they will say, 'give us jobs among the priests so we will have enough to eat.'"

Meanwhile, the boy Samuel served the LORD by assisting Eli. Now in those days messages from the LORD were very rare, and visions were quite uncommon.

One night Eli, who was almost blind by now, had gone to bed. The lamp of God had not yet gone out, and Samuel was sleeping in the Tabernacle near the Ark of God. Suddenly the LORD called out, "Samuel!"

"Yes?" Samuel replied. "What is it?" He got up and ran to Eli. "Here I am. Did you call me?"

"I didn't call you," Eli replied. "Go back to bed." So he did.

Then the LORD called out again, "Samuel!"

Again Samuel got up and went to Eli. "Here I am. Did you call me?"

"I didn't call you, my son," Eli said. "Go back to bed."

Samuel did not yet know the LORD because he had never had a message from the LORD before. So the LORD called a third time, and once more Samuel got up and went to Eli. "Here I am. Did you call me?"

Then Eli realized it was the LORD who was calling the boy. So he said to Samuel, "Go and lie down again, and if someone calls again, say, 'Speak, LORD, your servant is listening.'" So Samuel went back to bed.

And the LORD came and called as before, "Samuel! Samuel!"

And Samuel replied, "Speak, your servant is listening."

Then the LORD said to Samuel, "I am about to do a shocking thing in Israel. I am going to carry out all my threats against Eli and his family, from beginning to end. I have warned him that judgment is coming upon his family forever, because his sons are blaspheming God and he hasn't disciplined them. So I have vowed that the sins of Eli and his sons will never be forgiven by sacrifices or offerings."

Samuel stayed in bed until morning, then got up and opened the doors of the Tabernacle as usual. He was afraid to tell Eli what the LORD had said to him. But Eli called out to him, "Samuel, my son."

"Here I am," Samuel replied.

"What did the LORD say to you? Tell me everything. And may God strike you and even kill you if you hide anything from me!" So Samuel told Eli everything; he didn't hold anything back. "It is the LORD's will," Eli replied. "Let him do what he thinks best."

As Samuel grew up, the LORD was with him, and everything Samuel said proved to be reliable. And all Israel, from Dan in the north to Beersheba in the south, knew that Samuel was confirmed as a prophet of the LORD. The LORD continued to appear at Shiloh and gave messages to Samuel there at the Tabernacle. And Samuel's words went out to all the people of Israel.

+

At that time Israel was at war with the Philistines. The Israelite army was camped near Ebenezer, and the Philistines were at Aphek. The Philistines attacked and defeated the army of Israel, killing 4,000 men. After the battle was over, the troops retreated to their camp, and the elders of Israel asked, "Why did the LORD allow us to be defeated by the Philistines?" Then they said, "Let's bring the Ark of the Covenant of the LORD from Shiloh. If we carry it into battle with us, it will save us from our enemies."

So they sent men to Shiloh to bring the Ark of the Covenant of the LORD of Heaven's Armies, who is enthroned between the cherubim. Hophni and Phinehas, the sons of Eli, were also there with the Ark of the Covenant of God. When all the Israelites saw the Ark of the Covenant of the LORD coming into the camp, their shout of joy was so loud it made the ground shake!

"What's going on?" the Philistines asked. "What's all the shouting about in the Hebrew camp?" When they were told it was because the Ark of the LORD had arrived, they panicked. "The gods have come into their camp!" they cried. "This is a disaster! We have never had to face anything like this before! Help! Who can save us from these mighty gods of Israel? They are the same gods who destroyed the Egyptians with plagues when Israel was in the wilderness. Fight as never before, Philistines! If you don't, we will become the Hebrews' slaves just as they have been ours! Stand up like men and fight!"

So the Philistines fought desperately, and Israel was defeated again. The slaughter was great; 30,000 Israelite soldiers died that day. The survivors turned and fled to their tents. The Ark of God was captured, and Hophni and Phinehas, the two sons of Eli, were killed.

A man from the tribe of Benjamin ran from the battlefield and arrived at Shiloh later that same day. He had torn his clothes and put dust on his head to show his grief. Eli was waiting beside the road to hear the news of the battle, for his heart trembled for the safety of the Ark of God. When the messenger arrived and told what had happened, an outcry resounded throughout the town.

"What is all the noise about?" Eli asked.

The messenger rushed over to Eli, who was ninety-eight years old and blind. He said to Eli, "I have just come from the battlefield—I was there this very day."

"What happened, my son?" Eli demanded.

"Israel has been defeated by the Philistines," the messenger replied. "The people have been slaughtered, and your two sons, Hophni and Phinehas, were also killed. And the Ark of God has been captured."

When the messenger mentioned what had happened to the Ark of

God, Eli fell backward from his seat beside the gate. He broke his neck and died, for he was old and overweight. He had been Israel's judge for forty years.

Eli's daughter-in-law, the wife of Phinehas, was pregnant and near her time of delivery. When she heard that the Ark of God had been captured and that her father-in-law and husband were dead, she went into labor and gave birth. She died in childbirth, but before she passed away the midwives tried to encourage her. "Don't be afraid," they said. "You have a baby boy!" But she did not answer or pay attention to them.

She named the child Ichabod (which means "Where is the glory?"), for she said, "Israel's glory is gone." She named him this because the Ark of God had been captured and because her father-in-law and husband were dead. Then she said, "The glory has departed from Israel, for the Ark of God has been captured."

After the Philistines captured the Ark of God, they took it from the battle-ground at Ebenezer to the town of Ashdod. They carried the Ark of God into the temple of Dagon and placed it beside an idol of Dagon. But when the citizens of Ashdod went to see it the next morning, Dagon had fallen with his face to the ground in front of the Ark of the LORD! So they took Dagon and put him in his place again. But the next morning the same thing happened—Dagon had fallen face down before the Ark of the LORD again. This time his head and hands had broken off and were lying in the doorway. Only the trunk of his body was left intact. That is why to this day neither the priests of Dagon nor anyone who enters the temple of Dagon in Ashdod will step on its threshold.

Then the LORD's heavy hand struck the people of Ashdod and the nearby villages with a plague of tumors. When the people realized what was happening, they cried out, "We can't keep the Ark of the God of Israel here any longer! He is against us! We will all be destroyed along with Dagon, our god." So they called together the rulers of the Philistine towns and asked, "What should we do with the Ark of the God of Israel?"

The rulers discussed it and replied, "Move it to the town of Gath." So they moved the Ark of the God of Israel to Gath. But when the Ark arrived at Gath, the LORD's heavy hand fell on its men, young and old; he struck them with a plague of tumors, and there was a great panic.

So they sent the Ark of God to the town of Ekron, but when the people of Ekron saw it coming they cried out, "They are bringing the Ark of the God of Israel here to kill us, too!" The people summoned the Philistine rulers again and begged them, "Please send the Ark of the God of Israel back to its own country, or it will kill us all." For the deadly plague from God had already begun, and great fear was sweeping across the town.

Those who didn't die were afflicted with tumors; and the cry from the town rose to heaven.

The Ark of the LORD remained in Philistine territory seven months in all. Then the Philistines called in their priests and diviners and asked them, "What should we do about the Ark of the LORD? Tell us how to return it to its own country."

"Send the Ark of the God of Israel back with a gift," they were told. "Send a guilt offering so the plague will stop. Then, if you are healed, you will know it was his hand that caused the plague."

"What sort of guilt offering should we send?" they asked.

And they were told, "Since the plague has struck both you and your five rulers, make five gold tumors and five gold rats, just like those that have ravaged your land. Make these things to show honor to the God of Israel. Perhaps then he will stop afflicting you, your gods, and your land. Don't be stubborn and rebellious as Pharaoh and the Egyptians were. By the time God was finished with them, they were eager to let Israel go.

"Now build a new cart, and find two cows that have just given birth to calves. Make sure the cows have never been yoked to a cart. Hitch the cows to the cart, but shut their calves away from them in a pen. Put the Ark of the LORD on the cart, and beside it place a chest containing the gold rats and gold tumors you are sending as a guilt offering. Then let the cows go wherever they want. If they cross the border of our land and go to Beth-shemesh, we will know it was the LORD who brought this great disaster upon us. If they don't, we will know it was not his hand that caused the plague. It came simply by chance."

So these instructions were carried out. Two cows were hitched to the cart, and their newborn calves were shut up in a pen. Then the Ark of the LORD and the chest containing the gold rats and gold tumors were placed on the cart. And sure enough, without veering off in other directions, the cows went straight along the road toward Beth-shemesh, lowing as they went. The Philistine rulers followed them as far as the border of Beth-shemesh.

The people of Beth-shemesh were harvesting wheat in the valley, and when they saw the Ark, they were overjoyed! The cart came into the field of a man named Joshua and stopped beside a large rock. So the people broke up the wood of the cart for a fire and killed the cows and sacrificed them to the LORD as a burnt offering. Several men of the tribe of Levi lifted the Ark of the LORD and the chest containing the gold rats and gold tumors from the cart and placed them on the large rock. Many sacrifices and burnt offerings were offered to the LORD that day by the people of Beth-shemesh. The five Philistine rulers watched all this and then returned to Ekron that same day.

The five gold tumors sent by the Philistines as a guilt offering to the LORD were gifts from the rulers of Ashdod, Gaza, Ashkelon, Gath, and Ekron. The five gold rats represented the five Philistine towns and their surrounding villages, which were controlled by the five rulers. The large rock at Beth-shemesh, where they set the Ark of the LORD, still stands in the field of Joshua as a witness to what happened there.

But the LORD killed seventy men from Beth-shemesh because they looked into the Ark of the LORD. And the people mourned greatly because of what the LORD had done. "Who is able to stand in the presence of the LORD, this holy God?" they cried out. "Where can we send the Ark from here?"

So they sent messengers to the people at Kiriath-jearim and told them, "The Philistines have returned the Ark of the LORD. Come here and get it!"

So the men of Kiriath-jearim came to get the Ark of the LORD. They took it to the hillside home of Abinadab and ordained Eleazar, his son, to be in charge of it. The Ark remained in Kiriath-jearim for a long time—twenty years in all. During that time all Israel mourned because it seemed the LORD had abandoned them.

Then Samuel said to all the people of Israel, "If you want to return to the LORD with all your hearts, get rid of your foreign gods and your images of Ashtoreth. Turn your hearts to the LORD and obey him alone; then he will rescue you from the Philistines." So the Israelites got rid of their images of Baal and Ashtoreth and worshiped only the LORD.

Then Samuel told them, "Gather all of Israel to Mizpah, and I will pray to the LORD for you." So they gathered at Mizpah and, in a great ceremony, drew water from a well and poured it out before the LORD. They also went without food all day and confessed that they had sinned against the LORD. (It was at Mizpah that Samuel became Israel's judge.)

When the Philistine rulers heard that Israel had gathered at Mizpah, they mobilized their army and advanced. The Israelites were badly frightened when they learned that the Philistines were approaching. "Don't stop pleading with the LORD our God to save us from the Philistines!" they begged Samuel. So Samuel took a young lamb and offered it to the LORD as a whole burnt offering. He pleaded with the LORD to help Israel, and the LORD answered him.

Just as Samuel was sacrificing the burnt offering, the Philistines arrived to attack Israel. But the LORD spoke with a mighty voice of thunder from heaven that day, and the Philistines were thrown into such confusion that the Israelites defeated them. The men of Israel chased them from Mizpah to a place below Beth-car, slaughtering them all along the way.

Samuel then took a large stone and placed it between the towns of

Mizpah and Jeshanah. He named it Ebenezer (which means "the stone of help"), for he said, "Up to this point the LORD has helped us!"

So the Philistines were subdued and didn't invade Israel again for some time. And throughout Samuel's lifetime, the LORD's powerful hand was raised against the Philistines. The Israelite villages near Ekron and Gath that the Philistines had captured were restored to Israel, along with the rest of the territory that the Philistines had taken. And there was peace between Israel and the Amorites in those days.

Samuel continued as Israel's judge for the rest of his life. Each year he traveled around, setting up his court first at Bethel, then at Gilgal, and then at Mizpah. He judged the people of Israel at each of these places. Then he would return to his home at Ramah, and he would hear cases there, too. And Samuel built an altar to the LORD at Ramah.

+

As Samuel grew old, he appointed his sons to be judges over Israel. Joel and Abijah, his oldest sons, held court in Beersheba. But they were not like their father, for they were greedy for money. They accepted bribes and perverted justice.

Finally, all the elders of Israel met at Ramah to discuss the matter with Samuel. "Look," they told him, "you are now old, and your sons are not like you. Give us a king to judge us like all the other nations have."

Samuel was displeased with their request and went to the LORD for guidance. "Do everything they say to you," the LORD replied, "for they are rejecting me, not you. They don't want me to be their king any longer. Ever since I brought them from Egypt they have continually abandoned me and followed other gods. And now they are giving you the same treatment. Do as they ask, but solemnly warn them about the way a king will reign over them."

So Samuel passed on the LORD's warning to the people who were asking him for a king. "This is how a king will reign over you," Samuel said. "The king will draft your sons and assign them to his chariots and his charioteers, making them run before his chariots. Some will be generals and captains in his army, some will be forced to plow in his fields and harvest his crops, and some will make his weapons and chariot equipment. The king will take your daughters from you and force them to cook and bake and make perfumes for him. He will take away the best of your fields and vineyards and olive groves and give them to his own officials. He will take a tenth of your grain and your grape harvest and distribute it among his officers and attendants. He will take your male and female slaves and

demand the finest of your cattle and donkeys for his own use. He will
demand a tenth of your flocks, and you will be his slaves. When that day
comes, you will beg for relief from this king you are demanding, but then
the LORD will not help you."

But the people refused to listen to Samuel's warning. "Even so, we still
want a king," they said. "We want to be like the nations around us. Our
king will judge us and lead us into battle."

So Samuel repeated to the LORD what the people had said, and the
LORD replied, "Do as they say, and give them a king." Then Samuel agreed
and sent the people home.

There was a wealthy, influential man named Kish from the tribe of Benjamin. He was the son of Abiel, son of Zeror, son of Becorath, son of Aphiah,
of the tribe of Benjamin. His son Saul was the most handsome man in Israel—head and shoulders taller than anyone else in the land.

One day Kish's donkeys strayed away, and he told Saul, "Take a servant
with you, and go look for the donkeys." So Saul took one of the servants
and traveled through the hill country of Ephraim, the land of Shalishah,
the Shaalim area, and the entire land of Benjamin, but they couldn't find
the donkeys anywhere.

Finally, they entered the region of Zuph, and Saul said to his servant,
"Let's go home. By now my father will be more worried about us than
about the donkeys!"

But the servant said, "I've just thought of something! There is a man of
God who lives here in this town. He is held in high honor by all the people
because everything he says comes true. Let's go find him. Perhaps he can
tell us which way to go."

"But we don't have anything to offer him," Saul replied. "Even our food
is gone, and we don't have a thing to give him."

"Well," the servant said, "I have one small silver piece. We can at least
offer it to the man of God and see what happens!" (In those days if people
wanted a message from God, they would say, "Let's go and ask the seer,"
for prophets used to be called seers.)

"All right," Saul agreed, "let's try it!" So they started into the town where
the man of God lived.

As they were climbing the hill to the town, they met some young women
coming out to draw water. So Saul and his servant asked, "Is the seer here
today?"

"Yes," they replied. "Stay right on this road. He is at the town gates. He
has just arrived to take part in a public sacrifice up at the place of worship.
Hurry and catch him before he goes up there to eat. The guests won't
begin eating until he arrives to bless the food."

So they entered the town, and as they passed through the gates, Samuel was coming out toward them to go up to the place of worship.

Now the LORD had told Samuel the previous day, "About this time tomorrow I will send you a man from the land of Benjamin. Anoint him to be the leader of my people, Israel. He will rescue them from the Philistines, for I have looked down on my people in mercy and have heard their cry."

When Samuel saw Saul, the LORD said, "That's the man I told you about! He will rule my people."

Just then Saul approached Samuel at the gateway and asked, "Can you please tell me where the seer's house is?"

"I am the seer!" Samuel replied. "Go up to the place of worship ahead of me. We will eat there together, and in the morning I'll tell you what you want to know and send you on your way. And don't worry about those donkeys that were lost three days ago, for they have been found. And I am here to tell you that you and your family are the focus of all Israel's hopes."

Saul replied, "But I'm only from the tribe of Benjamin, the smallest tribe in Israel, and my family is the least important of all the families of that tribe! Why are you talking like this to me?"

Then Samuel brought Saul and his servant into the hall and placed them at the head of the table, honoring them above the thirty special guests. Samuel then instructed the cook to bring Saul the finest cut of meat, the piece that had been set aside for the guest of honor. So the cook brought in the meat and placed it before Saul. "Go ahead and eat it," Samuel said. "I was saving it for you even before I invited these others!" So Saul ate with Samuel that day.

When they came down from the place of worship and returned to town, Samuel took Saul up to the roof of the house and prepared a bed for him there. At daybreak the next morning, Samuel called to Saul, "Get up! It's time you were on your way." So Saul got ready, and he and Samuel left the house together. When they reached the edge of town, Samuel told Saul to send his servant on ahead. After the servant was gone, Samuel said, "Stay here, for I have received a special message for you from God."

Then Samuel took a flask of olive oil and poured it over Saul's head. He kissed Saul and said, "I am doing this because the LORD has appointed you to be the ruler over Israel, his special possession. When you leave me today, you will see two men beside Rachel's tomb at Zelzah, on the border of Benjamin. They will tell you that the donkeys have been found and that your father has stopped worrying about them and is now worried about you. He is asking, 'Have you seen my son?'

"When you get to the oak of Tabor, you will see three men coming toward you who are on their way to worship God at Bethel. One will be bringing three young goats, another will have three loaves of bread, and the third will be carrying a wineskin full of wine. They will greet you and offer you two of the loaves, which you are to accept.

"When you arrive at Gibeah of God, where the garrison of the Philistines is located, you will meet a band of prophets coming down from the place of worship. They will be playing a harp, a tambourine, a flute, and a lyre, and they will be prophesying. At that time the Spirit of the LORD will come powerfully upon you, and you will prophesy with them. You will be changed into a different person. After these signs take place, do what must be done, for God is with you. Then go down to Gilgal ahead of me. I will join you there to sacrifice burnt offerings and peace offerings. You must wait for seven days until I arrive and give you further instructions."

As Saul turned and started to leave, God gave him a new heart, and all Samuel's signs were fulfilled that day. When Saul and his servant arrived at Gibeah, they saw a group of prophets coming toward them. Then the Spirit of God came powerfully upon Saul, and he, too, began to prophesy. When those who knew Saul heard about it, they exclaimed, "What? Is even Saul a prophet? How did the son of Kish become a prophet?"

And one of those standing there said, "Can anyone become a prophet, no matter who his father is?" So that is the origin of the saying "Is even Saul a prophet?"

When Saul had finished prophesying, he went up to the place of worship. "Where have you been?" Saul's uncle asked him and his servant.

"We were looking for the donkeys," Saul replied, "but we couldn't find them. So we went to Samuel to ask him where they were."

"Oh? And what did he say?" his uncle asked.

"He told us that the donkeys had already been found," Saul replied. But Saul didn't tell his uncle what Samuel said about the kingdom.

Later Samuel called all the people of Israel to meet before the LORD at Mizpah. And he said, "This is what the LORD, the God of Israel, has declared: I brought you from Egypt and rescued you from the Egyptians and from all of the nations that were oppressing you. But though I have rescued you from your misery and distress, you have rejected your God today and have said, 'No, we want a king instead!' Now, therefore, present yourselves before the LORD by tribes and clans."

So Samuel brought all the tribes of Israel before the LORD, and the tribe of Benjamin was chosen by lot. Then he brought each family of the tribe of Benjamin before the LORD, and the family of the Matrites was chosen. And finally Saul son of Kish was chosen from among them. But when they looked for him, he had disappeared! So they asked the LORD, "Where is he?"

And the LORD replied, "He is hiding among the baggage." So they found him and brought him out, and he stood head and shoulders above anyone else.

Then Samuel said to all the people, "This is the man the LORD has chosen as your king. No one in all Israel is like him!"

And all the people shouted, "Long live the king!"

Then Samuel told the people what the rights and duties of a king were. He wrote them down on a scroll and placed it before the LORD. Then Samuel sent the people home again.

When Saul returned to his home at Gibeah, a group of men whose hearts God had touched went with him. But there were some scoundrels who complained, "How can this man save us?" And they scorned him and refused to bring him gifts. But Saul ignored them.

[Nahash, king of the Ammonites, had been grievously oppressing the people of Gad and Reuben who lived east of the Jordan River. He gouged out the right eye of each of the Israelites living there, and he didn't allow anyone to come and rescue them. In fact, of all the Israelites east of the Jordan, there wasn't a single one whose right eye Nahash had not gouged out. But there were 7,000 men who had escaped from the Ammonites, and they had settled in Jabesh-gilead.]

About a month later, King Nahash of Ammon led his army against the Israelite town of Jabesh-gilead. But all the citizens of Jabesh asked for peace. "Make a treaty with us, and we will be your servants," they pleaded.

"All right," Nahash said, "but only on one condition. I will gouge out the right eye of every one of you as a disgrace to all Israel!"

"Give us seven days to send messengers throughout Israel!" replied the elders of Jabesh. "If no one comes to save us, we will agree to your terms."

When the messengers came to Gibeah of Saul and told the people about their plight, everyone broke into tears. Saul had been plowing a field with his oxen, and when he returned to town, he asked, "What's the matter? Why is everyone crying?" So they told him about the message from Jabesh.

Then the Spirit of God came powerfully upon Saul, and he became very angry. He took two oxen and cut them into pieces and sent the messengers to carry them throughout Israel with this message: "This is what will happen to the oxen of anyone who refuses to follow Saul and Samuel into battle!" And the LORD made the people afraid of Saul's anger, and all of them came out together as one. When Saul mobilized them at Bezek, he found that there were 300,000 men from Israel and 30,000 men from Judah.

So Saul sent the messengers back to Jabesh-gilead to say, "We will rescue you by noontime tomorrow!" There was great joy throughout the town when that message arrived!

The men of Jabesh then told their enemies, "Tomorrow we will come out to you, and you can do to us whatever you wish." But before dawn the next morning, Saul arrived, having divided his army into three detachments. He launched a surprise attack against the Ammonites and slaughtered them the whole morning. The remnant of their army was so badly scattered that no two of them were left together.

Then the people exclaimed to Samuel, "Now where are those men who said, 'Why should Saul rule over us?' Bring them here, and we will kill them!"

But Saul replied, "No one will be executed today, for today the LORD has rescued Israel!"

Then Samuel said to the people, "Come, let us all go to Gilgal to renew the kingdom." So they all went to Gilgal, and in a solemn ceremony before the LORD they made Saul king. Then they offered peace offerings to the LORD, and Saul and all the Israelites were filled with joy.

Then Samuel addressed all Israel: "I have done as you asked and given you a king. Your king is now your leader. I stand here before you—an old, gray-haired man—and my sons serve you. I have served as your leader from the time I was a boy to this very day. Now testify against me in the presence of the LORD and before his anointed one. Whose ox or donkey have I stolen? Have I ever cheated any of you? Have I ever oppressed you? Have I ever taken a bribe and perverted justice? Tell me and I will make right whatever I have done wrong."

"No," they replied, "you have never cheated or oppressed us, and you have never taken even a single bribe."

"The LORD and his anointed one are my witnesses today," Samuel declared, "that my hands are clean."

"Yes, he is a witness," they replied.

"It was the LORD who appointed Moses and Aaron," Samuel continued. "He brought your ancestors out of the land of Egypt. Now stand here quietly before the LORD as I remind you of all the great things the LORD has done for you and your ancestors.

"When the Israelites were in Egypt and cried out to the LORD, he sent Moses and Aaron to rescue them from Egypt and to bring them into this land. But the people soon forgot about the LORD their God, so he handed them over to Sisera, the commander of Hazor's army, and also to the Philistines and to the king of Moab, who fought against them.

"Then they cried to the LORD again and confessed, 'We have sinned by turning away from the LORD and worshiping the images of Baal and Ashtoreth. But we will worship you and you alone if you will rescue us from our enemies.' Then the LORD sent Gideon, Bedan, Jephthah, and Samuel to save you, and you lived in safety.

"But when you were afraid of Nahash, the king of Ammon, you came to me and said that you wanted a king to reign over you, even though the LORD your God was already your king. All right, here is the king you have chosen. You asked for him, and the LORD has granted your request.

"Now if you fear and worship the LORD and listen to his voice, and if you do not rebel against the LORD's commands, then both you and your king will show that you recognize the LORD as your God. But if you rebel against the LORD's commands and refuse to listen to him, then his hand will be as heavy upon you as it was upon your ancestors.

"Now stand here and see the great thing the LORD is about to do. You know that it does not rain at this time of the year during the wheat harvest. I will ask the LORD to send thunder and rain today. Then you will realize how wicked you have been in asking the LORD for a king!"

So Samuel called to the LORD, and the LORD sent thunder and rain that day. And all the people were terrified of the LORD and of Samuel. "Pray to the LORD your God for us, or we will die!" they all said to Samuel. "For now we have added to our sins by asking for a king."

"Don't be afraid," Samuel reassured them. "You have certainly done wrong, but make sure now that you worship the LORD with all your heart, and don't turn your back on him. Don't go back to worshiping worthless idols that cannot help or rescue you—they are totally useless! The LORD will not abandon his people, because that would dishonor his great name. For it has pleased the LORD to make you his very own people.

"As for me, I will certainly not sin against the LORD by ending my prayers for you. And I will continue to teach you what is good and right. But be sure to fear the LORD and faithfully serve him. Think of all the wonderful things he has done for you. But if you continue to sin, you and your king will be swept away."

+ + +

Saul was thirty years old when he became king, and he reigned for forty-two years.

Saul selected 3,000 special troops from the army of Israel and sent the rest of the men home. He took 2,000 of the chosen men with him to Micmash and the hill country of Bethel. The other 1,000 went with Saul's son Jonathan to Gibeah in the land of Benjamin.

Soon after this, Jonathan attacked and defeated the garrison of Philistines at Geba. The news spread quickly among the Philistines. So Saul blew the ram's horn throughout the land, saying, "Hebrews, hear this! Rise up in revolt!" All Israel heard the news that Saul had destroyed the Philistine garrison at Geba and that the Philistines now hated the Israelites more than ever. So the entire Israelite army was summoned to join Saul at Gilgal.

The Philistines mustered a mighty army of 3,000 chariots, 6,000 charioteers, and as many warriors as the grains of sand on the seashore! They camped at Micmash east of Beth-aven. The men of Israel saw what a tight spot they were in; and because they were hard pressed by the enemy, they tried to hide in caves, thickets, rocks, holes, and cisterns. Some of them crossed the Jordan River and escaped into the land of Gad and Gilead.

Meanwhile, Saul stayed at Gilgal, and his men were trembling with fear. Saul waited there seven days for Samuel, as Samuel had instructed him earlier, but Samuel still didn't come. Saul realized that his troops were rapidly slipping away. So he demanded, "Bring me the burnt offering and the peace offerings!" And Saul sacrificed the burnt offering himself.

Just as Saul was finishing with the burnt offering, Samuel arrived. Saul went out to meet and welcome him, but Samuel said, "What is this you have done?"

Saul replied, "I saw my men scattering from me, and you didn't arrive when you said you would, and the Philistines are at Micmash ready for battle. So I said, 'The Philistines are ready to march against us at Gilgal, and I haven't even asked for the LORD's help!' So I felt compelled to offer the burnt offering myself before you came."

"How foolish!" Samuel exclaimed. "You have not kept the command the LORD your God gave you. Had you kept it, the LORD would have established your kingdom over Israel forever. But now your kingdom must end, for the LORD has sought out a man after his own heart. The LORD has already appointed him to be the leader of his people, because you have not kept the LORD's command."

Samuel then left Gilgal and went on his way, but the rest of the troops went with Saul to meet the army. They went up from Gilgal to Gibeah in the land of Benjamin. When Saul counted the men who were still with him, he found only 600 were left! Saul and Jonathan and the troops with them were staying at Geba in the land of Benjamin. The Philistines set up their camp at Micmash. Three raiding parties soon left the camp of the Philistines. One went north toward Ophrah in the land of Shual, another went west to Beth-horon, and the third moved toward the border above the valley of Zeboim near the wilderness.

There were no blacksmiths in the land of Israel in those days. The Philistines wouldn't allow them for fear they would make swords and spears for the Hebrews. So whenever the Israelites needed to sharpen their plowshares, picks, axes, or sickles, they had to take them to a Philistine blacksmith. The charges were as follows: a quarter of an ounce of silver for sharpening a plowshare or a pick, and an eighth of an ounce for sharpening an ax or making the point of an ox goad. So on the day of the battle none of the people of Israel had a sword or spear, except for Saul and Jonathan.

The pass at Micmash had meanwhile been secured by a contingent of the Philistine army.

One day Jonathan said to his armor bearer, "Come on, let's go over to where the Philistines have their outpost." But Jonathan did not tell his father what he was doing.

Meanwhile, Saul and his 600 men were camped on the outskirts of Gibeah, around the pomegranate tree at Migron. Among Saul's men was Ahijah the priest, who was wearing the ephod, the priestly vest. Ahijah was the son of Ichabod's brother Ahitub, son of Phinehas, son of Eli, the priest of the LORD who had served at Shiloh.

No one realized that Jonathan had left the Israelite camp. To reach the Philistine outpost, Jonathan had to go down between two rocky cliffs that were called Bozez and Seneh. The cliff on the north was in front of Micmash, and the one on the south was in front of Geba. "Let's go across to the outpost of those pagans," Jonathan said to his armor bearer. "Perhaps the LORD will help us, for nothing can hinder the LORD. He can win a battle whether he has many warriors or only a few!"

"Do what you think is best," the armor bearer replied. "I'm with you completely, whatever you decide."

"All right, then," Jonathan told him. "We will cross over and let them see us. If they say to us, 'Stay where you are or we'll kill you,' then we will stop and not go up to them. But if they say, 'Come on up and fight,' then we will go up. That will be the LORD's sign that he will help us defeat them."

When the Philistines saw them coming, they shouted, "Look! The Hebrews are crawling out of their holes!" Then the men from the outpost shouted to Jonathan, "Come on up here, and we'll teach you a lesson!"

"Come on, climb right behind me," Jonathan said to his armor bearer, "for the LORD will help us defeat them!"

So they climbed up using both hands and feet, and the Philistines fell before Jonathan, and his armor bearer killed those who came behind them. They killed some twenty men in all, and their bodies were scattered over about half an acre.

Suddenly, panic broke out in the Philistine army, both in the camp and in the field, including even the outposts and raiding parties. And just then an earthquake struck, and everyone was terrified.

Saul's lookouts in Gibeah of Benjamin saw a strange sight—the vast army of Philistines began to melt away in every direction. "Call the roll and find out who's missing," Saul ordered. And when they checked, they found that Jonathan and his armor bearer were gone.

Then Saul shouted to Ahijah, "Bring the ephod here!" For at that time Ahijah was wearing the ephod in front of the Israelites. But while Saul was talking to the priest, the confusion in the Philistine camp grew louder and louder. So Saul said to the priest, "Never mind; let's get going!"

Then Saul and all his men rushed out to the battle and found the Philistines killing each other. There was terrible confusion everywhere. Even the Hebrews who had previously gone over to the Philistine army revolted and joined in with Saul, Jonathan, and the rest of the Israelites. Likewise, the men of Israel who were hiding in the hill country of Ephraim joined the chase when they saw the Philistines running away. So the LORD saved Israel that day, and the battle continued to rage even beyond Beth-aven.

Now the men of Israel were pressed to exhaustion that day, because Saul had placed them under an oath, saying, "Let a curse fall on anyone who eats before evening—before I have full revenge on my enemies." So no one ate anything all day, even though they had all found honeycomb on the ground in the forest. They didn't dare touch the honey because they all feared the oath they had taken.

But Jonathan had not heard his father's command, and he dipped the end of his stick into a piece of honeycomb and ate the honey. After he had eaten it, he felt refreshed. But one of the men saw him and said, "Your father made the army take a strict oath that anyone who eats food today will be cursed. That is why everyone is weary and faint."

"My father has made trouble for us all!" Jonathan exclaimed. "A command like that only hurts us. See how refreshed I am now that I have eaten this little bit of honey. If the men had been allowed to eat freely from the food they found among our enemies, think how many more Philistines we could have killed!"

They chased and killed the Philistines all day from Micmash to Aijalon, growing more and more faint. That evening they rushed for the battle plunder and butchered the sheep, goats, cattle, and calves, but they ate them without draining the blood. Someone reported to Saul, "Look, the men are sinning against the LORD by eating meat that still has blood in it."

"That is very wrong," Saul said. "Find a large stone and roll it over here. Then go out among the troops and tell them, 'Bring the cattle, sheep, and goats here to me. Kill them here, and drain the blood before you eat them. Do not sin against the LORD by eating meat with the blood still in it.'"

So that night all the troops brought their animals and slaughtered them there. Then Saul built an altar to the LORD; it was the first of the altars he built to the LORD.

Then Saul said, "Let's chase the Philistines all night and plunder them until sunrise. Let's destroy every last one of them."

His men replied, "We'll do whatever you think is best."

But the priest said, "Let's ask God first."

So Saul asked God, "Should we go after the Philistines? Will you help us defeat them?" But God made no reply that day.

Then Saul said to the leaders, "Something's wrong! I want all my army commanders to come here. We must find out what sin was committed today. I vow by the name of the LORD who rescued Israel that the sinner will surely die, even if it is my own son Jonathan!" But no one would tell him what the trouble was.

Then Saul said, "Jonathan and I will stand over here, and all of you stand over there."

And the people responded to Saul, "Whatever you think is best."

Then Saul prayed, "O LORD, God of Israel, please show us who is guilty and who is innocent." Then they cast sacred lots, and Jonathan and Saul were chosen as the guilty ones, and the people were declared innocent.

Then Saul said, "Now cast lots again and choose between me and Jonathan." And Jonathan was shown to be the guilty one.

"Tell me what you have done," Saul demanded of Jonathan.

"I tasted a little honey," Jonathan admitted. "It was only a little bit on the end of my stick. Does that deserve death?"

"Yes, Jonathan," Saul said, "you must die! May God strike me and even kill me if you do not die for this."

But the people broke in and said to Saul, "Jonathan has won this great victory for Israel. Should he die? Far from it! As surely as the LORD lives, not one hair on his head will be touched, for God helped him do a great deed today." So the people rescued Jonathan, and he was not put to death.

Then Saul called back the army from chasing the Philistines, and the Philistines returned home.

Now when Saul had secured his grasp on Israel's throne, he fought against his enemies in every direction—against Moab, Ammon, Edom, the kings of Zobah, and the Philistines. And wherever he turned, he was victorious. He performed great deeds and conquered the Amalekites, saving Israel from all those who had plundered them.

Saul's sons included Jonathan, Ishbosheth, and Malkishua. He also had two daughters: Merab, who was older, and Michal. Saul's wife was Ahinoam, the daughter of Ahimaaz. The commander of Saul's army was Abner, the son of Saul's uncle Ner. Saul's father, Kish, and Abner's father, Ner, were both sons of Abiel.

The Israelites fought constantly with the Philistines throughout Saul's lifetime. So whenever Saul observed a young man who was brave and strong, he drafted him into his army.

+

One day Samuel said to Saul, "It was the LORD who told me to anoint you as king of his people, Israel. Now listen to this message from the LORD! This is what the LORD of Heaven's Armies has declared: I have decided to settle accounts with the nation of Amalek for opposing Israel when they came from Egypt. Now go and completely destroy the entire Amalekite nation—men, women, children, babies, cattle, sheep, goats, camels, and donkeys."

So Saul mobilized his army at Telaim. There were 200,000 soldiers from Israel and 10,000 men from Judah. Then Saul and his army went to a town of the Amalekites and lay in wait in the valley. Saul sent this warning to the Kenites: "Move away from where the Amalekites live, or you will die with them. For you showed kindness to all the people of Israel when they came up from Egypt." So the Kenites packed up and left.

Then Saul slaughtered the Amalekites from Havilah all the way to Shur, east of Egypt. He captured Agag, the Amalekite king, but completely destroyed everyone else. Saul and his men spared Agag's life and kept the best of the sheep and goats, the cattle, the fat calves, and the lambs— everything, in fact, that appealed to them. They destroyed only what was worthless or of poor quality.

Then the LORD said to Samuel, "I am sorry that I ever made Saul king, for he has not been loyal to me and has refused to obey my command." Samuel was so deeply moved when he heard this that he cried out to the LORD all night.

Early the next morning Samuel went to find Saul. Someone told him, "Saul went to the town of Carmel to set up a monument to himself; then he went on to Gilgal."

When Samuel finally found him, Saul greeted him cheerfully. "May the LORD bless you," he said. "I have carried out the LORD's command!"

"Then what is all the bleating of sheep and goats and the lowing of cattle I hear?" Samuel demanded.

"It's true that the army spared the best of the sheep, goats, and cattle," Saul admitted. "But they are going to sacrifice them to the LORD your God. We have destroyed everything else."

Then Samuel said to Saul, "Stop! Listen to what the LORD told me last night!"

"What did he tell you?" Saul asked.

And Samuel told him, "Although you may think little of yourself, are you not the leader of the tribes of Israel? The LORD has anointed you king of Israel. And the LORD sent you on a mission and told you, 'Go and completely destroy the sinners, the Amalekites, until they are all dead.' Why haven't you obeyed the LORD? Why did you rush for the plunder and do what was evil in the LORD's sight?"

"But I did obey the LORD," Saul insisted. "I carried out the mission he gave me. I brought back King Agag, but I destroyed everyone else. Then my troops brought in the best of the sheep, goats, cattle, and plunder to sacrifice to the LORD your God in Gilgal."

But Samuel replied,

"What is more pleasing to the LORD:
   your burnt offerings and sacrifices
   or your obedience to his voice?
Listen! Obedience is better than sacrifice,
   and submission is better than offering the fat of rams.
Rebellion is as sinful as witchcraft,
   and stubbornness as bad as worshiping idols.
So because you have rejected the command of the LORD,
   he has rejected you as king."

Then Saul admitted to Samuel, "Yes, I have sinned. I have disobeyed your instructions and the LORD's command, for I was afraid of the people and did what they demanded. But now, please forgive my sin and come back with me so that I may worship the LORD."

But Samuel replied, "I will not go back with you! Since you have rejected the LORD's command, he has rejected you as king of Israel."

As Samuel turned to go, Saul tried to hold him back and tore the hem of his robe. And Samuel said to him, "The LORD has torn the kingdom of Israel from you today and has given it to someone else—one who is better than you. And he who is the Glory of Israel will not lie, nor will he change his mind, for he is not human that he should change his mind!"

Then Saul pleaded again, "I know I have sinned. But please, at least honor me before the elders of my people and before Israel by coming back with me so that I may worship the LORD your God." So Samuel finally agreed and went back with him, and Saul worshiped the LORD.

Then Samuel said, "Bring King Agag to me." Agag arrived full of hope, for he thought, "Surely the worst is over, and I have been spared!" But Samuel said, "As your sword has killed the sons of many mothers, now your mother will be childless." And Samuel cut Agag to pieces before the LORD at Gilgal.

Then Samuel went home to Ramah, and Saul returned to his house at Gibeah of Saul. Samuel never went to meet with Saul again, but he mourned constantly for him. And the LORD was sorry he had ever made Saul king of Israel.

Now the LORD said to Samuel, "You have mourned long enough for Saul. I have rejected him as king of Israel, so fill your flask with olive oil and go to Bethlehem. Find a man named Jesse who lives there, for I have selected one of his sons to be my king."

But Samuel asked, "How can I do that? If Saul hears about it, he will kill me."

"Take a heifer with you," the LORD replied, "and say that you have come to make a sacrifice to the LORD. Invite Jesse to the sacrifice, and I will show you which of his sons to anoint for me."

So Samuel did as the LORD instructed. When he arrived at Bethlehem, the elders of the town came trembling to meet him. "What's wrong?" they asked. "Do you come in peace?"

"Yes," Samuel replied. "I have come to sacrifice to the LORD. Purify yourselves and come with me to the sacrifice." Then Samuel performed the purification rite for Jesse and his sons and invited them to the sacrifice, too.

When they arrived, Samuel took one look at Eliab and thought, "Surely this is the LORD's anointed!"

But the LORD said to Samuel, "Don't judge by his appearance or height, for I have rejected him. The LORD doesn't see things the way you see them. People judge by outward appearance, but the LORD looks at the heart."

Then Jesse told his son Abinadab to step forward and walk in front of Samuel. But Samuel said, "This is not the one the LORD has chosen." Next Jesse summoned Shimea, but Samuel said, "Neither is this the one the LORD has chosen." In the same way all seven of Jesse's sons were presented to Samuel. But Samuel said to Jesse, "The LORD has not chosen any of these." Then Samuel asked, "Are these all the sons you have?"

"There is still the youngest," Jesse replied. "But he's out in the fields watching the sheep and goats."

"Send for him at once," Samuel said. "We will not sit down to eat until he arrives."

So Jesse sent for him. He was dark and handsome, with beautiful eyes. And the LORD said, "This is the one; anoint him."

So as David stood there among his brothers, Samuel took the flask of olive oil he had brought and anointed David with the oil. And the Spirit of the LORD came powerfully upon David from that day on. Then Samuel returned to Ramah.

Now the Spirit of the LORD had left Saul, and the LORD sent a tormenting spirit that filled him with depression and fear.

Some of Saul's servants said to him, "A tormenting spirit from God is troubling you. Let us find a good musician to play the harp whenever the tormenting spirit troubles you. He will play soothing music, and you will soon be well again."

"All right," Saul said. "Find me someone who plays well, and bring him here."

One of the servants said to Saul, "One of Jesse's sons from Bethlehem is a talented harp player. Not only that—he is a brave warrior, a man of war, and has good judgment. He is also a fine-looking young man, and the LORD is with him."

So Saul sent messengers to Jesse to say, "Send me your son David, the shepherd." Jesse responded by sending David to Saul, along with a young goat, a donkey loaded with bread, and a wineskin full of wine.

So David went to Saul and began serving him. Saul loved David very much, and David became his armor bearer.

Then Saul sent word to Jesse asking, "Please let David remain in my service, for I am very pleased with him."

And whenever the tormenting spirit from God troubled Saul, David would play the harp. Then Saul would feel better, and the tormenting spirit would go away.

The Philistines now mustered their army for battle and camped between Socoh in Judah and Azekah at Ephes-dammim. Saul countered by gathering his Israelite troops near the valley of Elah. So the Philistines and Israelites faced each other on opposite hills, with the valley between them.

Then Goliath, a Philistine champion from Gath, came out of the Philistine ranks to face the forces of Israel. He was over nine feet tall! He wore a bronze helmet, and his bronze coat of mail weighed 125 pounds. He also wore bronze leg armor, and he carried a bronze javelin on his shoulder. The shaft of his spear was as heavy and thick as a weaver's beam, tipped with an iron spearhead that weighed 15 pounds. His armor bearer walked ahead of him carrying a shield.

Goliath stood and shouted a taunt across to the Israelites. "Why are you all coming out to fight?" he called. "I am the Philistine champion, but you are only the servants of Saul. Choose one man to come down here and fight me! If he kills me, then we will be your slaves. But if I kill him, you will be our slaves! I defy the armies of Israel today! Send me a man who will fight me!" When Saul and the Israelites heard this, they were terrified and deeply shaken.

Now David was the son of a man named Jesse, an Ephrathite from

Bethlehem in the land of Judah. Jesse was an old man at that time, and he had eight sons. Jesse's three oldest sons—Eliab, Abinadab, and Shimea—had already joined Saul's army to fight the Philistines. David was the youngest son. David's three oldest brothers stayed with Saul's army, but David went back and forth so he could help his father with the sheep in Bethlehem.

For forty days, every morning and evening, the Philistine champion strutted in front of the Israelite army.

One day Jesse said to David, "Take this basket of roasted grain and these ten loaves of bread, and carry them quickly to your brothers. And give these ten cuts of cheese to their captain. See how your brothers are getting along, and bring back a report on how they are doing." David's brothers were with Saul and the Israelite army at the valley of Elah, fighting against the Philistines.

So David left the sheep with another shepherd and set out early the next morning with the gifts, as Jesse had directed him. He arrived at the camp just as the Israelite army was leaving for the battlefield with shouts and battle cries. Soon the Israelite and Philistine forces stood facing each other, army against army. David left his things with the keeper of supplies and hurried out to the ranks to greet his brothers. As he was talking with them, Goliath, the Philistine champion from Gath, came out from the Philistine ranks. Then David heard him shout his usual taunt to the army of Israel.

As soon as the Israelite army saw him, they began to run away in fright. "Have you seen the giant?" the men asked. "He comes out each day to defy Israel. The king has offered a huge reward to anyone who kills him. He will give that man one of his daughters for a wife, and the man's entire family will be exempted from paying taxes!"

David asked the soldiers standing nearby, "What will a man get for killing this Philistine and ending his defiance of Israel? Who is this pagan Philistine anyway, that he is allowed to defy the armies of the living God?"

And these men gave David the same reply. They said, "Yes, that is the reward for killing him."

But when David's oldest brother, Eliab, heard David talking to the men, he was angry. "What are you doing around here anyway?" he demanded. "What about those few sheep you're supposed to be taking care of? I know about your pride and deceit. You just want to see the battle!"

"What have I done now?" David replied. "I was only asking a question!" He walked over to some others and asked them the same thing and received the same answer. Then David's question was reported to King Saul, and the king sent for him.

"Don't worry about this Philistine," David told Saul. "I'll go fight him!"

"Don't be ridiculous!" Saul replied. "There's no way you can fight this

Philistine and possibly win! You're only a boy, and he's been a man of war since his youth."

But David persisted. "I have been taking care of my father's sheep and goats," he said. "When a lion or a bear comes to steal a lamb from the flock, I go after it with a club and rescue the lamb from its mouth. If the animal turns on me, I catch it by the jaw and club it to death. I have done this to both lions and bears, and I'll do it to this pagan Philistine, too, for he has defied the armies of the living God! The LORD who rescued me from the claws of the lion and the bear will rescue me from this Philistine!"

Saul finally consented. "All right, go ahead," he said. "And may the LORD be with you!"

Then Saul gave David his own armor—a bronze helmet and a coat of mail. David put it on, strapped the sword over it, and took a step or two to see what it was like, for he had never worn such things before.

"I can't go in these," he protested to Saul. "I'm not used to them." So David took them off again. He picked up five smooth stones from a stream and put them into his shepherd's bag. Then, armed only with his shepherd's staff and sling, he started across the valley to fight the Philistine.

Goliath walked out toward David with his shield bearer ahead of him, sneering in contempt at this ruddy-faced boy. "Am I a dog," he roared at David, "that you come at me with a stick?" And he cursed David by the names of his gods. "Come over here, and I'll give your flesh to the birds and wild animals!" Goliath yelled.

David replied to the Philistine, "You come to me with sword, spear, and javelin, but I come to you in the name of the LORD of Heaven's Armies— the God of the armies of Israel, whom you have defied. Today the LORD will conquer you, and I will kill you and cut off your head. And then I will give the dead bodies of your men to the birds and wild animals, and the whole world will know that there is a God in Israel! And everyone assembled here will know that the LORD rescues his people, but not with sword and spear. This is the LORD's battle, and he will give you to us!"

As Goliath moved closer to attack, David quickly ran out to meet him. Reaching into his shepherd's bag and taking out a stone, he hurled it with his sling and hit the Philistine in the forehead. The stone sank in, and Goliath stumbled and fell face down on the ground.

So David triumphed over the Philistine with only a sling and a stone, for he had no sword. Then David ran over and pulled Goliath's sword from its sheath. David used it to kill him and cut off his head.

When the Philistines saw that their champion was dead, they turned and ran. Then the men of Israel and Judah gave a great shout of triumph and rushed after the Philistines, chasing them as far as Gath and the gates of Ekron. The bodies of the dead and wounded Philistines were strewn all along the road from Shaaraim, as far as Gath and Ekron. Then the Israelite army returned and plundered the deserted Philistine camp. (David took the Philistine's head to Jerusalem, but he stored the man's armor in his own tent.)

As Saul watched David go out to fight the Philistine, he asked Abner, the commander of his army, "Abner, whose son is this young man?"

"I really don't know," Abner declared.

"Well, find out who he is!" the king told him.

As soon as David returned from killing Goliath, Abner brought him to Saul with the Philistine's head still in his hand. "Tell me about your father, young man," Saul said.

And David replied, "His name is Jesse, and we live in Bethlehem."

After David had finished talking with Saul, he met Jonathan, the king's son. There was an immediate bond between them, for Jonathan loved David. From that day on Saul kept David with him and wouldn't let him return home. And Jonathan made a solemn pact with David, because he loved him as he loved himself. Jonathan sealed the pact by taking off his robe and giving it to David, together with his tunic, sword, bow, and belt.

Whatever Saul asked David to do, David did it successfully. So Saul made him a commander over the men of war, an appointment that was welcomed by the people and Saul's officers alike.

+

When the victorious Israelite army was returning home after David had killed the Philistine, women from all the towns of Israel came out to meet King Saul. They sang and danced for joy with tambourines and cymbals. This was their song:

"Saul has killed his thousands,
   and David his ten thousands!"

This made Saul very angry. "What's this?" he said. "They credit David with ten thousands and me with only thousands. Next they'll be making him their king!" So from that time on Saul kept a jealous eye on David.

The very next day a tormenting spirit from God overwhelmed Saul, and he began to rave in his house like a madman. David was playing the harp, as he did each day. But Saul had a spear in his hand, and he suddenly hurled it at David, intending to pin him to the wall. But David escaped him twice.

Saul was then afraid of David, for the LORD was with David and had turned away from Saul. Finally, Saul sent him away and appointed him commander over 1,000 men, and David faithfully led his troops into battle.

David continued to succeed in everything he did, for the LORD was with him. When Saul recognized this, he became even more afraid of him. But all Israel and Judah loved David because he was so successful at leading his troops into battle.

One day Saul said to David, "I am ready to give you my older daughter, Merab, as your wife. But first you must prove yourself to be a real warrior by fighting the LORD's battles." For Saul thought, "I'll send him out against the Philistines and let them kill him rather than doing it myself."

"Who am I, and what is my family in Israel that I should be the king's son-in-law?" David exclaimed. "My father's family is nothing!" So when the time came for Saul to give his daughter Merab in marriage to David, he gave her instead to Adriel, a man from Meholah.

In the meantime, Saul's daughter Michal had fallen in love with David, and Saul was delighted when he heard about it. "Here's another chance to see him killed by the Philistines!" Saul said to himself. But to David he said, "Today you have a second chance to become my son-in-law!"

Then Saul told his men to say to David, "The king really likes you, and so do we. Why don't you accept the king's offer and become his son-in-law?"

When Saul's men said these things to David, he replied, "How can a poor man from a humble family afford the bride price for the daughter of a king?"

When Saul's men reported this back to the king, he told them, "Tell David that all I want for the bride price is 100 Philistine foreskins! Vengeance on my enemies is all I really want." But what Saul had in mind was that David would be killed in the fight.

David was delighted to accept the offer. Before the time limit expired, he and his men went out and killed 200 Philistines. Then David fulfilled the king's requirement by presenting all their foreskins to him. So Saul gave his daughter Michal to David to be his wife.

When Saul realized that the LORD was with David and how much his daughter Michal loved him, Saul became even more afraid of him, and he remained David's enemy for the rest of his life.

Every time the commanders of the Philistines attacked, David was more successful against them than all the rest of Saul's officers. So David's name became very famous.

Saul now urged his servants and his son Jonathan to assassinate David. But Jonathan, because of his strong affection for David, told him what his father was planning. "Tomorrow morning," he warned him, "you must find a hiding place out in the fields. I'll ask my father to go out there with me, and I'll talk to him about you. Then I'll tell you everything I can find out."

The next morning Jonathan spoke with his father about David, saying many good things about him. "The king must not sin against his servant David," Jonathan said. "He's never done anything to harm you. He has always helped you in any way he could. Have you forgotten about the time he risked his life to kill the Philistine giant and how the LORD brought a great victory to all Israel as a result? You were certainly happy about it then. Why should you murder an innocent man like David? There is no reason for it at all!"

So Saul listened to Jonathan and vowed, "As surely as the LORD lives, David will not be killed."

Afterward Jonathan called David and told him what had happened. Then he brought David to Saul, and David served in the court as before.

War broke out again after that, and David led his troops against the Philistines. He attacked them with such fury that they all ran away.

But one day when Saul was sitting at home, with spear in hand, the tormenting spirit from the LORD suddenly came upon him again. As David played his harp, Saul hurled his spear at David. But David dodged out of the way, and leaving the spear stuck in the wall, he fled and escaped into the night.

Then Saul sent troops to watch David's house. They were told to kill David when he came out the next morning. But Michal, David's wife, warned him, "If you don't escape tonight, you will be dead by morning." So she helped him climb out through a window, and he fled and escaped. Then she took an idol and put it in his bed, covered it with blankets, and put a cushion of goat's hair at its head.

When the troops came to arrest David, she told them he was sick and couldn't get out of bed.

But Saul sent the troops back to get David. He ordered, "Bring him to me in his bed so I can kill him!" But when they came to carry David out, they discovered that it was only an idol in the bed with a cushion of goat's hair at its head.

"Why have you betrayed me like this and let my enemy escape?" Saul demanded of Michal.

"I had to," Michal replied. "He threatened to kill me if I didn't help him."

So David escaped and went to Ramah to see Samuel, and he told him all that Saul had done to him. Then Samuel took David with him to live at Naioth. When the report reached Saul that David was at Naioth in Ramah, he sent troops to capture him. But when they arrived and saw Samuel leading a group of prophets who were prophesying, the Spirit of God came upon Saul's men, and they also began to prophesy. When Saul heard what had happened, he sent other troops, but they, too, prophesied! The same thing happened a third time. Finally, Saul himself went to Ramah and arrived at the great well in Secu. "Where are Samuel and David?" he demanded.

"They are at Naioth in Ramah," someone told him.

But on the way to Naioth in Ramah the Spirit of God came even upon Saul, and he, too, began to prophesy all the way to Naioth! He tore off his clothes and lay naked on the ground all day and all night, prophesying in the presence of Samuel. The people who were watching exclaimed, "What? Is even Saul a prophet?"

David now fled from Naioth in Ramah and found Jonathan. "What have I done?" he exclaimed. "What is my crime? How have I offended your father that he is so determined to kill me?"

"That's not true!" Jonathan protested. "You're not going to die. He always tells me everything he's going to do, even the little things. I know my father wouldn't hide something like this from me. It just isn't so!"

Then David took an oath before Jonathan and said, "Your father knows perfectly well about our friendship, so he has said to himself, 'I won't tell Jonathan—why should I hurt him?' But I swear to you that I am only a step away from death! I swear it by the LORD and by your own soul!"

"Tell me what I can do to help you," Jonathan exclaimed.

David replied, "Tomorrow we celebrate the new moon festival. I've always eaten with the king on this occasion, but tomorrow I'll hide in the field and stay there until the evening of the third day. If your father asks where I am, tell him I asked permission to go home to Bethlehem for an annual family sacrifice. If he says, 'Fine!' you will know all is well. But if he is angry and loses his temper, you will know he is determined to kill me. Show me this loyalty as my sworn friend—for we made a solemn pact before the LORD—or kill me yourself if I have sinned against your father. But please don't betray me to him!"

"Never!" Jonathan exclaimed. "You know that if I had the slightest notion my father was planning to kill you, I would tell you at once."

Then David asked, "How will I know whether or not your father is angry?"

"Come out to the field with me," Jonathan replied. And they went out there together. Then Jonathan told David, "I promise by the LORD, the God of Israel, that by this time tomorrow, or the next day at the latest, I will talk to my father and let you know at once how he feels about you. If he speaks favorably about you, I will let you know. But if he is angry and wants you killed, may the LORD strike me and even kill me if I don't warn you so you can escape and live. May the LORD be with you as he used to be with my father. And may you treat me with the faithful love of the LORD as long as I live. But if I die, treat my family with this faithful love, even when the LORD destroys all your enemies from the face of the earth."

So Jonathan made a solemn pact with David, saying, "May the LORD destroy all your enemies!" And Jonathan made David reaffirm his vow of friendship again, for Jonathan loved David as he loved himself.

Then Jonathan said, "Tomorrow we celebrate the new moon festival. You will be missed when your place at the table is empty. The day after tomorrow, toward evening, go to the place where you hid before, and wait there by the stone pile. I will come out and shoot three arrows to the side of the stone pile as though I were shooting at a target. Then I will send a boy to bring the arrows back. If you hear me tell him, 'They're on this side,' then you will know, as surely as the LORD lives, that all is well, and there is no trouble. But if I tell him, 'Go farther—the arrows are still ahead of you,' then it will mean that you must leave immediately, for the LORD is sending you away. And may the LORD make us keep our promises to each other, for he has witnessed them."

So David hid himself in the field, and when the new moon festival began, the king sat down to eat. He sat at his usual place against the wall, with Jonathan sitting opposite him and Abner beside him. But David's place was empty. Saul didn't say anything about it that day, for he said to himself, "Something must have made David ceremonially unclean." But when David's place was empty again the next day, Saul asked Jonathan, "Why hasn't the son of Jesse been here for the meal either yesterday or today?"

Jonathan replied, "David earnestly asked me if he could go to Bethlehem. He said, 'Please let me go, for we are having a family sacrifice. My brother demanded that I be there. So please let me get away to see my brothers.' That's why he isn't here at the king's table."

Saul boiled with rage at Jonathan. "You stupid son of a whore!" he swore at him. "Do you think I don't know that you want him to be king in your place, shaming yourself and your mother? As long as that son of Jesse is alive, you'll never be king. Now go and get him so I can kill him!"

"But why should he be put to death?" Jonathan asked his father. "What has he done?" Then Saul hurled his spear at Jonathan, intending to kill him. So at last Jonathan realized that his father was really determined to kill David.

Jonathan left the table in fierce anger and refused to eat on that second day of the festival, for he was crushed by his father's shameful behavior toward David.

The next morning, as agreed, Jonathan went out into the field and took a young boy with him to gather his arrows. "Start running," he told the boy, "so you can find the arrows as I shoot them." So the boy ran, and Jonathan shot an arrow beyond him. When the boy had almost reached the arrow, Jonathan shouted, "The arrow is still ahead of you. Hurry, hurry, don't wait." So the boy quickly gathered up the arrows and ran back to his master. He, of course, suspected nothing; only Jonathan and David understood the signal. Then Jonathan gave his bow and arrows to the boy and told him to take them back to town.

As soon as the boy was gone, David came out from where he had been hiding near the stone pile. Then David bowed three times to Jonathan with his face to the ground. Both of them were in tears as they embraced each other and said good-bye, especially David.

At last Jonathan said to David, "Go in peace, for we have sworn loyalty to each other in the LORD's name. The LORD is the witness of a bond between us and our children forever." Then David left, and Jonathan returned to the town.

David went to the town of Nob to see Ahimelech the priest. Ahimelech trembled when he saw him. "Why are you alone?" he asked. "Why is no one with you?"

"The king has sent me on a private matter," David said. "He told me not to tell anyone why I am here. I have told my men where to meet me later. Now, what is there to eat? Give me five loaves of bread or anything else you have."

"We don't have any regular bread," the priest replied. "But there is the holy bread, which you can have if your young men have not slept with any women recently."

"Don't worry," David replied. "I never allow my men to be with women when we are on a campaign. And since they stay clean even on ordinary trips, how much more on this one!"

Since there was no other food available, the priest gave him the holy bread—the Bread of the Presence that was placed before the LORD in the Tabernacle. It had just been replaced that day with fresh bread.

Now Doeg the Edomite, Saul's chief herdsman, was there that day, having been detained before the LORD.

David asked Ahimelech, "Do you have a spear or sword? The king's business was so urgent that I didn't even have time to grab a weapon!"

"I only have the sword of Goliath the Philistine, whom you killed in the valley of Elah," the priest replied. "It is wrapped in a cloth behind the ephod. Take that if you want it, for there is nothing else here."

"There is nothing like it!" David replied. "Give it to me!"

So David escaped from Saul and went to King Achish of Gath. But the officers of Achish were unhappy about his being there. "Isn't this David, the king of the land?" they asked. "Isn't he the one the people honor with dances, singing,

'Saul has killed his thousands,
  and David his ten thousands'?"

David heard these comments and was very afraid of what King Achish of Gath might do to him. So he pretended to be insane, scratching on doors and drooling down his beard.

Finally, King Achish said to his men, "Must you bring me a madman? We already have enough of them around here! Why should I let someone like this be my guest?"

So David left Gath and escaped to the cave of Adullam. Soon his brothers and all his other relatives joined him there. Then others began coming—men who were in trouble or in debt or who were just discontented—until David was the captain of about 400 men.

Later David went to Mizpeh in Moab, where he asked the king, "Please allow my father and mother to live here with you until I know what God is going to do for me." So David's parents stayed in Moab with the king during the entire time David was living in his stronghold.

One day the prophet Gad told David, "Leave the stronghold and return to the land of Judah." So David went to the forest of Hereth.

The news of his arrival in Judah soon reached Saul. At the time, the king was sitting beneath the tamarisk tree on the hill at Gibeah, holding his spear and surrounded by his officers.

"Listen here, you men of Benjamin!" Saul shouted to his officers when he heard the news. "Has that son of Jesse promised every one of you fields and vineyards? Has he promised to make you all generals and captains in his army? Is that why you have conspired against me? For not one of you told me when my own son made a solemn pact with the son of Jesse. You're not even sorry for me. Think of it! My own son—encouraging him to kill me, as he is trying to do this very day!"

Then Doeg the Edomite, who was standing there with Saul's men, spoke up. "When I was at Nob," he said, "I saw the son of Jesse talking to the priest, Ahimelech son of Ahitub. Ahimelech consulted the LORD for him. Then he gave him food and the sword of Goliath the Philistine."

King Saul immediately sent for Ahimelech and all his family, who served as priests at Nob. When they arrived, Saul shouted at him, "Listen to me, you son of Ahitub!"

"What is it, my king?" Ahimelech asked.

"Why have you and the son of Jesse conspired against me?" Saul demanded. "Why did you give him food and a sword? Why have you consulted God for him? Why have you encouraged him to kill me, as he is trying to do this very day?"

"But sir," Ahimelech replied, "is anyone among all your servants as faithful as David, your son-in-law? Why, he is the captain of your bodyguard and a highly honored member of your household! This was certainly not the first time I had consulted God for him! May the king not accuse me and my family in this matter, for I knew nothing at all of any plot against you."

"You will surely die, Ahimelech, along with your entire family!" the king shouted. And he ordered his bodyguards, "Kill these priests of the LORD, for they are allies and conspirators with David! They knew he was running away from me, but they didn't tell me!" But Saul's men refused to kill the LORD's priests.

Then the king said to Doeg, "You do it." So Doeg the Edomite turned on them and killed them that day, eighty-five priests in all, still wearing their priestly garments. Then he went to Nob, the town of the priests, and killed the priests' families—men and women, children and babies—and all the cattle, donkeys, sheep, and goats.

Only Abiathar, one of the sons of Ahimelech, escaped and fled to David. When he told David that Saul had killed the priests of the LORD, David exclaimed, "I knew it! When I saw Doeg the Edomite there that day, I knew he was sure to tell Saul. Now I have caused the death of all your father's family. Stay here with me, and don't be afraid. I will protect you with my own life, for the same person wants to kill us both."

One day news came to David that the Philistines were at Keilah stealing grain from the threshing floors. David asked the LORD, "Should I go and attack them?"

"Yes, go and save Keilah," the LORD told him.

But David's men said, "We're afraid even here in Judah. We certainly don't want to go to Keilah to fight the whole Philistine army!"

So David asked the LORD again, and again the LORD replied, "Go down to Keilah, for I will help you conquer the Philistines."

So David and his men went to Keilah. They slaughtered the Philistines and took all their livestock and rescued the people of Keilah. Now when Abiathar son of Ahimelech fled to David at Keilah, he brought the ephod with him.

Saul soon learned that David was at Keilah. "Good!" he exclaimed. "We've got him now! God has handed him over to me, for he has trapped himself in a walled town!" So Saul mobilized his entire army to march to Keilah and besiege David and his men.

But David learned of Saul's plan and told Abiathar the priest to bring the ephod and ask the LORD what he should do. Then David prayed, "O LORD, God of Israel, I have heard that Saul is planning to come and destroy Keilah because I am here. Will the leaders of Keilah betray me to him? And will Saul actually come as I have heard? O LORD, God of Israel, please tell me."

And the LORD said, "He will come."

Again David asked, "Will the leaders of Keilah betray me and my men to Saul?"

And the LORD replied, "Yes, they will betray you."

So David and his men—about 600 of them now—left Keilah and began roaming the countryside. Word soon reached Saul that David had escaped, so he didn't go to Keilah after all.

David now stayed in the strongholds of the wilderness and in the hill country of Ziph. Saul hunted him day after day, but God didn't let Saul find him.

✢

One day near Horesh, David received the news that Saul was on the way to Ziph to search for him and kill him. Jonathan went to find David and encouraged him to stay strong in his faith in God. "Don't be afraid," Jonathan reassured him. "My father will never find you! You are going to be the king of Israel, and I will be next to you, as my father, Saul, is well aware." So the two of them renewed their solemn pact before the LORD. Then Jonathan returned home, while David stayed at Horesh.

But now the men of Ziph went to Saul in Gibeah and betrayed David to him. "We know where David is hiding," they said. "He is in the strongholds of Horesh on the hill of Hakilah, which is in the southern part of Jeshimon. Come down whenever you're ready, O king, and we will catch him and hand him over to you!"

"The LORD bless you," Saul said. "At last someone is concerned about me! Go and check again to be sure of where he is staying and who has seen him there, for I know that he is very crafty. Discover his hiding places, and come back when you are sure. Then I'll go with you. And if he is in the area at all, I'll track him down, even if I have to search every hiding place in Judah!" So the men of Ziph returned home ahead of Saul.

Meanwhile, David and his men had moved into the wilderness of Maon in the Arabah Valley south of Jeshimon. When David heard that Saul and his men were searching for him, he went even farther into the wilderness to the great rock, and he remained there in the wilderness of Maon. But Saul kept after him in the wilderness.

Saul and David were now on opposite sides of a mountain. Just as Saul

and his men began to close in on David and his men, an urgent message
reached Saul that the Philistines were raiding Israel again. So Saul quit
chasing David and returned to fight the Philistines. Ever since that time,
the place where David was camped has been called the Rock of Escape.
David then went to live in the strongholds of En-gedi.

After Saul returned from fighting the Philistines, he was told that David
had gone into the wilderness of En-gedi. So Saul chose 3,000 elite troops
from all Israel and went to search for David and his men near the rocks of
the wild goats.

At the place where the road passes some sheepfolds, Saul went into a
cave to relieve himself. But as it happened, David and his men were hiding
farther back in that very cave!

"Now's your opportunity!" David's men whispered to him. "Today the
LORD is telling you, 'I will certainly put your enemy into your power, to
do with as you wish.'" So David crept forward and cut off a piece of the
hem of Saul's robe.

But then David's conscience began bothering him because he had cut
Saul's robe. He said to his men, "The LORD forbid that I should do this
to my lord the king. I shouldn't attack the LORD's anointed one, for the
LORD himself has chosen him." So David restrained his men and did not
let them kill Saul.

After Saul had left the cave and gone on his way, David came out and
shouted after him, "My lord the king!" And when Saul looked around,
David bowed low before him.

Then he shouted to Saul, "Why do you listen to the people who say I
am trying to harm you? This very day you can see with your own eyes it
isn't true. For the LORD placed you at my mercy back there in the cave.
Some of my men told me to kill you, but I spared you. For I said, 'I will
never harm the king—he is the LORD's anointed one.' Look, my father, at
what I have in my hand. It is a piece of the hem of your robe! I cut it off,
but I didn't kill you. This proves that I am not trying to harm you and
that I have not sinned against you, even though you have been hunting
for me to kill me.

"May the LORD judge between us. Perhaps the LORD will punish you
for what you are trying to do to me, but I will never harm you. As that
old proverb says, 'From evil people come evil deeds.' So you can be sure
I will never harm you. Who is the king of Israel trying to catch anyway?
Should he spend his time chasing one who is as worthless as a dead dog
or a single flea? May the LORD therefore judge which of us is right and
punish the guilty one. He is my advocate, and he will rescue me from
your power!"

When David had finished speaking, Saul called back, "Is that really you, my son David?" Then he began to cry. And he said to David, "You are a better man than I am, for you have repaid me good for evil. Yes, you have been amazingly kind to me today, for when the LORD put me in a place where you could have killed me, you didn't do it. Who else would let his enemy get away when he had him in his power? May the LORD reward you well for the kindness you have shown me today. And now I realize that you are surely going to be king, and that the kingdom of Israel will flourish under your rule. Now swear to me by the LORD that when that happens you will not kill my family and destroy my line of descendants!"

So David promised this to Saul with an oath. Then Saul went home, but David and his men went back to their stronghold.

Now Samuel died, and all Israel gathered for his funeral. They buried him at his house in Ramah.

Then David moved down to the wilderness of Maon. There was a wealthy man from Maon who owned property near the town of Carmel. He had 3,000 sheep and 1,000 goats, and it was sheep-shearing time. This man's name was Nabal, and his wife, Abigail, was a sensible and beautiful woman. But Nabal, a descendant of Caleb, was crude and mean in all his dealings.

When David heard that Nabal was shearing his sheep, he sent ten of his young men to Carmel with this message for Nabal: "Peace and prosperity to you, your family, and everything you own! I am told that it is sheep-shearing time. While your shepherds stayed among us near Carmel, we never harmed them, and nothing was ever stolen from them. Ask your own men, and they will tell you this is true. So would you be kind to us, since we have come at a time of celebration? Please share any provisions you might have on hand with us and with your friend David." David's young men gave this message to Nabal in David's name, and they waited for a reply.

"Who is this fellow David?" Nabal sneered to the young men. "Who does this son of Jesse think he is? There are lots of servants these days who run away from their masters. Should I take my bread and my water and my meat that I've slaughtered for my shearers and give it to a band of outlaws who come from who knows where?"

So David's young men returned and told him what Nabal had said. "Get your swords!" was David's reply as he strapped on his own. Then 400 men started off with David, and 200 remained behind to guard their equipment.

Meanwhile, one of Nabal's servants went to Abigail and told her, "David sent messengers from the wilderness to greet our master, but he screamed insults at them. These men have been very good to us, and we never suffered any harm from them. Nothing was stolen from us the whole time they were with us. In fact, day and night they were like a wall of protection to us and the sheep. You need to know this and figure out what to do, for there is going to be trouble for our master and his whole family. He's so ill-tempered that no one can even talk to him!"

Abigail wasted no time. She quickly gathered 200 loaves of bread, two wineskins full of wine, five sheep that had been slaughtered, nearly a bushel of roasted grain, 100 clusters of raisins, and 200 fig cakes. She packed them on donkeys and said to her servants, "Go on ahead. I will follow you shortly." But she didn't tell her husband Nabal what she was doing.

As she was riding her donkey into a mountain ravine, she saw David and his men coming toward her. David had just been saying, "A lot of good it did to help this fellow. We protected his flocks in the wilderness, and nothing he owned was lost or stolen. But he has repaid me evil for good. May God strike me and kill me if even one man of his household is still alive tomorrow morning!"

When Abigail saw David, she quickly got off her donkey and bowed low before him. She fell at his feet and said, "I accept all blame in this matter, my lord. Please listen to what I have to say. I know Nabal is a wicked and ill-tempered man; please don't pay any attention to him. He is a fool, just as his name suggests. But I never even saw the young men you sent.

"Now, my lord, as surely as the LORD lives and you yourself live, since the LORD has kept you from murdering and taking vengeance into your own hands, let all your enemies and those who try to harm you be as cursed as Nabal is. And here is a present that I, your servant, have brought to you and your young men. Please forgive me if I have offended you in any way. The LORD will surely reward you with a lasting dynasty, for you are fighting the LORD's battles. And you have not done wrong throughout your entire life.

"Even when you are chased by those who seek to kill you, your life is safe in the care of the LORD your God, secure in his treasure pouch! But the lives of your enemies will disappear like stones shot from a sling! When the LORD has done all he promised and has made you leader of Israel, don't let this be a blemish on your record. Then your conscience won't have to bear the staggering burden of needless bloodshed and vengeance. And when the LORD has done these great things for you, please remember me, your servant!"

David replied to Abigail, "Praise the LORD, the God of Israel, who has sent you to meet me today! Thank God for your good sense! Bless you for keeping me from murder and from carrying out vengeance with my own hands. For I swear by the LORD, the God of Israel, who has kept me from hurting you, that if you had not hurried out to meet me, not one of Nabal's men would still be alive tomorrow morning." Then David accepted her present and told her, "Return home in peace. I have heard what you said. We will not kill your husband."

When Abigail arrived home, she found that Nabal was throwing a big party and was celebrating like a king. He was very drunk, so she didn't tell him anything about her meeting with David until dawn the next day. In the morning when Nabal was sober, his wife told him what had happened. As a result he had a stroke, and he lay paralyzed on his bed like a stone. About ten days later, the LORD struck him, and he died.

When David heard that Nabal was dead, he said, "Praise the LORD, who has avenged the insult I received from Nabal and has kept me from doing it myself. Nabal has received the punishment for his sin." Then David sent messengers to Abigail to ask her to become his wife.

When the messengers arrived at Carmel, they told Abigail, "David has sent us to take you back to marry him."

She bowed low to the ground and responded, "I, your servant, would be happy to marry David. I would even be willing to become a slave, washing the feet of his servants!" Quickly getting ready, she took along five of her servant girls as attendants, mounted her donkey, and went with David's messengers. And so she became his wife. David also married Ahinoam from Jezreel, making both of them his wives. Saul, meanwhile, had given his daughter Michal, David's wife, to a man from Gallim named Palti son of Laish.

Now some men from Ziph came to Saul at Gibeah to tell him, "David is hiding on the hill of Hakilah, which overlooks Jeshimon."

So Saul took 3,000 of Israel's elite troops and went to hunt him down in the wilderness of Ziph. Saul camped along the road beside the hill of Hakilah, near Jeshimon, where David was hiding. When David learned that Saul had come after him into the wilderness, he sent out spies to verify the report of Saul's arrival.

David slipped over to Saul's camp one night to look around. Saul and Abner son of Ner, the commander of his army, were sleeping inside a ring formed by the slumbering warriors. "Who will volunteer to go in there with me?" David asked Ahimelech the Hittite and Abishai son of Zeruiah, Joab's brother.

"I'll go with you," Abishai replied. So David and Abishai went right into Saul's camp and found him asleep, with his spear stuck in the ground beside his head. Abner and the soldiers were lying asleep around him.

"God has surely handed your enemy over to you this time!" Abishai whispered to David. "Let me pin him to the ground with one thrust of the spear; I won't need to strike twice!"

"No!" David said. "Don't kill him. For who can remain innocent after attacking the LORD's anointed one? Surely the LORD will strike Saul down someday, or he will die of old age or in battle. The LORD forbid that I should kill the one he has anointed! But take his spear and that jug of water beside his head, and then let's get out of here!"

So David took the spear and jug of water that were near Saul's head. Then he and Abishai got away without anyone seeing them or even waking up, because the LORD had put Saul's men into a deep sleep.

David climbed the hill opposite the camp until he was at a safe distance. Then he shouted down to the soldiers and to Abner son of Ner, "Wake up, Abner!"

"Who is it?" Abner demanded.

"Well, Abner, you're a great man, aren't you?" David taunted. "Where in all Israel is there anyone as mighty? So why haven't you guarded your master the king when someone came to kill him? This isn't good at all! I swear by the LORD that you and your men deserve to die, because you failed to protect your master, the LORD's anointed! Look around! Where are the king's spear and the jug of water that were beside his head?"

Saul recognized David's voice and called out, "Is that you, my son David?"

And David replied, "Yes, my lord the king. Why are you chasing me? What have I done? What is my crime? But now let my lord the king listen to his servant. If the LORD has stirred you up against me, then let him accept my offering. But if this is simply a human scheme, then may those involved be cursed by the LORD. For they have driven me from my home, so I can no longer live among the LORD's people, and they have said, 'Go, worship pagan gods.' Must I die on foreign soil, far from the presence of the LORD? Why has the king of Israel come out to search for a single flea? Why does he hunt me down like a partridge on the mountains?"

Then Saul confessed, "I have sinned. Come back home, my son, and I will no longer try to harm you, for you valued my life today. I have been a fool and very, very wrong."

"Here is your spear, O king," David replied. "Let one of your young men come over and get it. The LORD gives his own reward for doing good and for being loyal, and I refused to kill you even when the LORD placed you in my power, for you are the LORD's anointed one. Now may the LORD value my life, even as I have valued yours today. May he rescue me from all my troubles."

And Saul said to David, "Blessings on you, my son David. You will do many heroic deeds, and you will surely succeed." Then David went away, and Saul returned home.

+

But David kept thinking to himself, "Someday Saul is going to get me. The best thing I can do is escape to the Philistines. Then Saul will stop hunting for me in Israelite territory, and I will finally be safe."

So David took his 600 men and went over and joined Achish son of Maoch, the king of Gath. David and his men and their families settled there with Achish at Gath. David brought his two wives along with him—Ahinoam from Jezreel and Abigail, Nabal's widow from Carmel. Word soon reached Saul that David had fled to Gath, so he stopped hunting for him.

One day David said to Achish, "If it is all right with you, we would rather live in one of the country towns instead of here in the royal city."

So Achish gave him the town of Ziklag (which still belongs to the kings of Judah to this day), and they lived there among the Philistines for a year and four months.

David and his men spent their time raiding the Geshurites, the Girzites, and the Amalekites—people who had lived near Shur, toward the land of Egypt, since ancient times. David did not leave one person alive in the villages he attacked. He took the sheep, goats, cattle, donkeys, camels, and clothing before returning home to see King Achish.

"Where did you make your raid today?" Achish would ask.

And David would reply, "Against the south of Judah, the Jerahmeelites, and the Kenites."

No one was left alive to come to Gath and tell where he had really been. This happened again and again while he was living among the Philistines. Achish believed David and thought to himself, "By now the people of Israel must hate him bitterly. Now he will have to stay here and serve me forever!"

About that time the Philistines mustered their armies for another war with Israel. King Achish told David, "You and your men will be expected to join me in battle."

"Very well!" David agreed. "Now you will see for yourself what we can do."

Then Achish told David, "I will make you my personal bodyguard for life."

Meanwhile, Samuel had died, and all Israel had mourned for him. He was buried in Ramah, his hometown. And Saul had banned from the land of Israel all mediums and those who consult the spirits of the dead.

The Philistines set up their camp at Shunem, and Saul gathered all the army of Israel and camped at Gilboa. When Saul saw the vast Philistine army, he became frantic with fear. He asked the LORD what he should do, but the LORD refused to answer him, either by dreams or by sacred lots or by the prophets. Saul then said to his advisers, "Find a woman who is a medium, so I can go and ask her what to do."

His advisers replied, "There is a medium at Endor."

So Saul disguised himself by wearing ordinary clothing instead of his royal robes. Then he went to the woman's home at night, accompanied by two of his men.

"I have to talk to a man who has died," he said. "Will you call up his spirit for me?"

"Are you trying to get me killed?" the woman demanded. "You know that Saul has outlawed all the mediums and all who consult the spirits of the dead. Why are you setting a trap for me?"

But Saul took an oath in the name of the LORD and promised, "As surely as the LORD lives, nothing bad will happen to you for doing this."

Finally, the woman said, "Well, whose spirit do you want me to call up?"

"Call up Samuel," Saul replied.

When the woman saw Samuel, she screamed, "You've deceived me! You are Saul!"

"Don't be afraid!" the king told her. "What do you see?"

"I see a god coming up out of the earth," she said.

"What does he look like?" Saul asked.

"He is an old man wrapped in a robe," she replied. Saul realized it was Samuel, and he fell to the ground before him.

"Why have you disturbed me by calling me back?" Samuel asked Saul.

"Because I am in deep trouble," Saul replied. "The Philistines are at war with me, and God has left me and won't reply by prophets or dreams. So I have called for you to tell me what to do."

But Samuel replied, "Why ask me, since the LORD has left you and has become your enemy? The LORD has done just as he said he would. He has torn the kingdom from you and given it to your rival, David. The LORD has done this to you today because you refused to carry out his fierce anger against the Amalekites. What's more, the LORD will hand you and the army of Israel over to the Philistines tomorrow, and you and your sons will be here with me. The LORD will bring down the entire army of Israel in defeat."

Saul fell full length on the ground, paralyzed with fright because of Samuel's words. He was also faint with hunger, for he had eaten nothing all day and all night.

When the woman saw how distraught he was, she said, "Sir, I obeyed your command at the risk of my life. Now do what I say, and let me give you a little something to eat so you can regain your strength for the trip back."

But Saul refused to eat anything. Then his advisers joined the woman in urging him to eat, so he finally yielded and got up from the ground and sat on the couch.

The woman had been fattening a calf, so she hurried out and killed it. She took some flour, kneaded it into dough and baked unleavened bread. She brought the meal to Saul and his advisers, and they ate it. Then they went out into the night.

The entire Philistine army now mobilized at Aphek, and the Israelites camped at the spring in Jezreel. As the Philistine rulers were leading out their troops in groups of hundreds and thousands, David and his men marched at the rear with King Achish. But the Philistine commanders demanded, "What are these Hebrews doing here?"

And Achish told them, "This is David, the servant of King Saul of Israel. He's been with me for years, and I've never found a single fault in him from the day he arrived until today."

But the Philistine commanders were angry. "Send him back to the town you've given him!" they demanded. "He can't go into the battle with us. What if he turns against us in battle and becomes our adversary? Is there any better way for him to reconcile himself with his master than by handing our heads over to him? Isn't this the same David about whom the women of Israel sing in their dances,

'Saul has killed his thousands,
    and David his ten thousands'?"

So Achish finally summoned David and said to him, "I swear by the LORD that you have been a trustworthy ally. I think you should go with me into battle, for I've never found a single flaw in you from the day you arrived until today. But the other Philistine rulers won't hear of it. Please don't upset them, but go back quietly."

"What have I done to deserve this treatment?" David demanded. "What have you ever found in your servant, that I can't go and fight the enemies of my lord the king?"

But Achish insisted, "As far as I'm concerned, you're as perfect as an angel of God. But the Philistine commanders are afraid to have you with them in the battle. Now get up early in the morning, and leave with your men as soon as it gets light."

So David and his men headed back into the land of the Philistines, while the Philistine army went on to Jezreel.

Three days later, when David and his men arrived home at their town of Ziklag, they found that the Amalekites had made a raid into the Negev and Ziklag; they had crushed Ziklag and burned it to the ground. They had carried off the women and children and everyone else but without killing anyone.

When David and his men saw the ruins and realized what had happened to their families, they wept until they could weep no more. David's two wives, Ahinoam from Jezreel and Abigail, the widow of Nabal from Carmel, were among those captured. David was now in great danger because all his men were very bitter about losing their sons and daughters, and they began to talk of stoning him. But David found strength in the LORD his God.

Then he said to Abiathar the priest, "Bring me the ephod!" So Abiathar brought it. Then David asked the LORD, "Should I chase after this band of raiders? Will I catch them?"

And the LORD told him, "Yes, go after them. You will surely recover everything that was taken from you!"

So David and his 600 men set out, and they came to the brook Besor. But 200 of the men were too exhausted to cross the brook, so David continued the pursuit with 400 men.

Along the way they found an Egyptian man in a field and brought him to David. They gave him some bread to eat and water to drink. They also gave him part of a fig cake and two clusters of raisins, for he hadn't had anything to eat or drink for three days and nights. Before long his strength returned.

"To whom do you belong, and where do you come from?" David asked him.

"I am an Egyptian—the slave of an Amalekite," he replied. "My master abandoned me three days ago because I was sick. We were on our way back from raiding the Kerethites in the Negev, the territory of Judah, and the land of Caleb, and we had just burned Ziklag."

"Will you lead me to this band of raiders?" David asked.

The young man replied, "If you take an oath in God's name that you will not kill me or give me back to my master, then I will guide you to them."

So he led David to them, and they found the Amalekites spread out across the fields, eating and drinking and dancing with joy because of the vast amount of plunder they had taken from the Philistines and the land of Judah. David and his men rushed in among them and slaughtered them throughout that night and the entire next day until evening. None of the Amalekites escaped except 400 young men who fled on camels. David got back everything the Amalekites had taken, and he rescued his two wives. Nothing was missing: small or great, son or daughter, nor anything else that had been taken. David brought everything back. He also recovered all the flocks and herds, and his men drove them ahead of the other livestock. "This plunder belongs to David!" they said.

Then David returned to the brook Besor and met up with the 200 men who had been left behind because they were too exhausted to go with him. They went out to meet David and his men, and David greeted them joyfully. But some evil troublemakers among David's men said, "They didn't go with us, so they can't have any of the plunder we recovered. Give them their wives and children, and tell them to be gone."

But David said, "No, my brothers! Don't be selfish with what the LORD has given us. He has kept us safe and helped us defeat the band of raiders that attacked us. Who will listen when you talk like this? We share and share alike—those who go to battle and those who guard the equipment." From then on David made this a decree and regulation for Israel, and it is still followed today.

When he arrived at Ziklag, David sent part of the plunder to the elders of Judah, who were his friends. "Here is a present for you, taken from the LORD's enemies," he said.

The gifts were sent to the people of the following towns David had visited: Bethel, Ramoth-negev, Jattir, Aroer, Siphmoth, Eshtemoa, Racal, the towns of the Jerahmeelites, the towns of the Kenites, Hormah, Bor-ashan, Athach, Hebron, and all the other places David and his men had visited.

Now the Philistines attacked Israel, and the men of Israel fled before them. Many were slaughtered on the slopes of Mount Gilboa. The Philistines closed in on Saul and his sons, and they killed three of his sons—Jonathan, Abinadab, and Malkishua. The fighting grew very fierce around Saul, and the Philistine archers caught up with him and wounded him severely.

Saul groaned to his armor bearer, "Take your sword and kill me before these pagan Philistines come to run me through and taunt and torture me."

But his armor bearer was afraid and would not do it. So Saul took his own sword and fell on it. When his armor bearer realized that Saul was dead, he fell on his own sword and died beside the king. So Saul, his three sons, his armor bearer, and his troops all died together that same day.

When the Israelites on the other side of the Jezreel Valley and beyond the Jordan saw that the Israelite army had fled and that Saul and his sons were dead, they abandoned their towns and fled. So the Philistines moved in and occupied their towns.

The next day, when the Philistines went out to strip the dead, they found the bodies of Saul and his three sons on Mount Gilboa. So they cut off Saul's head and stripped off his armor. Then they proclaimed the good news of Saul's death in their pagan temple and to the people throughout the land of Philistia. They placed his armor in the temple of the Ashto-reths, and they fastened his body to the wall of the city of Beth-shan.

But when the people of Jabesh-gilead heard what the Philistines had done to Saul, all their mighty warriors traveled through the night to Beth-shan and took the bodies of Saul and his sons down from the wall. They brought them to Jabesh, where they burned the bodies. Then they took their bones and buried them beneath the tamarisk tree at Jabesh, and they fasted for seven days.

After the death of Saul, David returned from his victory over the Ama-lekites and spent two days in Ziklag. On the third day a man arrived from Saul's army camp. He had torn his clothes and put dirt on his head to show that he was in mourning. He fell to the ground before David in deep respect.

"Where have you come from?" David asked.

"I escaped from the Israelite camp," the man replied.

"What happened?" David demanded. "Tell me how the battle went."

The man replied, "Our entire army fled from the battle. Many of the men are dead, and Saul and his son Jonathan are also dead."

"How do you know Saul and Jonathan are dead?" David demanded of the young man.

The man answered, "I happened to be on Mount Gilboa, and there was Saul leaning on his spear with the enemy chariots and charioteers closing in on him. When he turned and saw me, he cried out for me to come to him. 'How can I help?' I asked him.

"He responded, 'Who are you?'

"'I am an Amalekite,' I told him.

"Then he begged me, 'Come over here and put me out of my misery, for I am in terrible pain and want to die.'

"So I killed him," the Amalekite told David, "for I knew he couldn't live. Then I took his crown and his armband, and I have brought them here to you, my lord."

David and his men tore their clothes in sorrow when they heard the news. They mourned and wept and fasted all day for Saul and his son Jon-athan, and for the LORD's army and the nation of Israel, because they had died by the sword that day.

Then David said to the young man who had brought the news, "Where are you from?"

And he replied, "I am a foreigner, an Amalekite, who lives in your land."

"Why were you not afraid to kill the LORD's anointed one?" David asked.

Then David said to one of his men, "Kill him!" So the man thrust his sword into the Amalekite and killed him. "You have condemned yourself," David said, "for you yourself confessed that you killed the Lord's anointed one."

Then David composed a funeral song for Saul and Jonathan, and he commanded that it be taught to the people of Judah. It is known as the Song of the Bow, and it is recorded in *The Book of Jashar.*

Your pride and joy, O Israel, lies dead on the hills!
    Oh, how the mighty heroes have fallen!
Don't announce the news in Gath,
    don't proclaim it in the streets of Ashkelon,
or the daughters of the Philistines will rejoice
    and the pagans will laugh in triumph.

O mountains of Gilboa,
    let there be no dew or rain upon you,
    nor fruitful fields producing offerings of grain.
For there the shield of the mighty heroes was defiled;
    the shield of Saul will no longer be anointed with oil.
The bow of Jonathan was powerful,
    and the sword of Saul did its mighty work.
They shed the blood of their enemies
    and pierced the bodies of mighty heroes.

How beloved and gracious were Saul and Jonathan!
    They were together in life and in death.
They were swifter than eagles,
    stronger than lions.
O women of Israel, weep for Saul,
for he dressed you in luxurious scarlet clothing,
    in garments decorated with gold.

Oh, how the mighty heroes have fallen in battle!
    Jonathan lies dead on the hills.
How I weep for you, my brother Jonathan!
    Oh, how much I loved you!
And your love for me was deep,
    deeper than the love of women!

Oh, how the mighty heroes have fallen!
    Stripped of their weapons, they lie dead.

After this, David asked the Lord, "Should I move back to one of the towns of Judah?"

"Yes," the LORD replied.

Then David asked, "Which town should I go to?"

"To Hebron," the LORD answered.

David's two wives were Ahinoam from Jezreel and Abigail, the widow of Nabal from Carmel. So David and his wives and his men and their families all moved to Judah, and they settled in the villages near Hebron. Then the men of Judah came to David and anointed him king over the people of Judah.

When David heard that the men of Jabesh-gilead had buried Saul, he sent them this message: "May the LORD bless you for being so loyal to your master Saul and giving him a decent burial. May the LORD be loyal to you in return and reward you with his unfailing love! And I, too, will reward you for what you have done. Now that Saul is dead, I ask you to be my strong and loyal subjects like the people of Judah, who have anointed me as their new king."

But Abner son of Ner, the commander of Saul's army, had already gone to Mahanaim with Saul's son Ishbosheth. There he proclaimed Ishbosheth king over Gilead, Jezreel, Ephraim, Benjamin, the land of the Ashurites, and all the rest of Israel.

+ + +

Ishbosheth, Saul's son, was forty years old when he became king, and he ruled from Mahanaim for two years. Meanwhile, the people of Judah remained loyal to David. David made Hebron his capital, and he ruled as king of Judah for seven and a half years.

One day Abner led Ishbosheth's troops from Mahanaim to Gibeon. About the same time, Joab son of Zeruiah led David's troops out and met them at the pool of Gibeon. The two groups sat down there, facing each other from opposite sides of the pool.

Then Abner suggested to Joab, "Let's have a few of our warriors fight hand to hand here in front of us."

"All right," Joab agreed. So twelve men were chosen to fight from each side—twelve men of Benjamin representing Ishbosheth son of Saul, and twelve representing David. Each one grabbed his opponent by the hair and thrust his sword into the other's side so that all of them died. So this place at Gibeon has been known ever since as the Field of Swords.

A fierce battle followed that day, and Abner and the men of Israel were defeated by the forces of David.

Joab, Abishai, and Asahel—the three sons of Zeruiah—were among David's forces that day. Asahel could run like a gazelle, and he began chasing Abner. He pursued him relentlessly, not stopping for anything.

When Abner looked back and saw him coming, he called out, "Is that you, Asahel?"

"Yes, it is," he replied.

"Go fight someone else!" Abner warned. "Take on one of the younger men, and strip him of his weapons." But Asahel kept right on chasing Abner.

Again Abner shouted to him, "Get away from here! I don't want to kill you. How could I ever face your brother Joab again?"

But Asahel refused to turn back, so Abner thrust the butt end of his spear through Asahel's stomach, and the spear came out through his back. He stumbled to the ground and died there. And everyone who came by that spot stopped and stood still when they saw Asahel lying there.

When Joab and Abishai found out what had happened, they set out after Abner. The sun was just going down as they arrived at the hill of Ammah near Giah, along the road to the wilderness of Gibeon. Abner's troops from the tribe of Benjamin regrouped there at the top of the hill to take a stand.

Abner shouted down to Joab, "Must we always be killing each other? Don't you realize that bitterness is the only result? When will you call off your men from chasing their Israelite brothers?"

Then Joab said, "God only knows what would have happened if you hadn't spoken, for we would have chased you all night if necessary." So Joab blew the ram's horn, and his men stopped chasing the troops of Israel.

All that night Abner and his men retreated through the Jordan Valley. They crossed the Jordan River, traveling all through the morning, and didn't stop until they arrived at Mahanaim.

Meanwhile, Joab and his men also returned home. When Joab counted his casualties, he discovered that only 19 men were missing in addition to Asahel. But 360 of Abner's men had been killed, all from the tribe of Benjamin. Joab and his men took Asahel's body to Bethlehem and buried him there in his father's tomb. Then they traveled all night and reached Hebron at daybreak.

That was the beginning of a long war between those who were loyal to Saul and those loyal to David. As time passed David became stronger and stronger, while Saul's dynasty became weaker and weaker.

These are the sons who were born to David in Hebron:

The oldest was Amnon, whose mother was Ahinoam from Jezreel.
The second was Daniel, whose mother was Abigail, the widow of Nabal from Carmel.
The third was Absalom, whose mother was Maacah, the daughter of Talmai, king of Geshur.

The fourth was Adonijah, whose mother was Haggith.
The fifth was Shephatiah, whose mother was Abital.
The sixth was Ithream, whose mother was Eglah, David's wife.

These sons were all born to David in Hebron.

As the war between the house of Saul and the house of David went on, Abner became a powerful leader among those loyal to Saul. One day Ishbosheth, Saul's son, accused Abner of sleeping with one of his father's concubines, a woman named Rizpah, daughter of Aiah.

Abner was furious. "Am I some Judean dog to be kicked around like this?" he shouted. "After all I have done for your father, Saul, and his family and friends by not handing you over to David, is this my reward—that you find fault with me about this woman? May God strike me and even kill me if I don't do everything I can to help David get what the LORD has promised him! I'm going to take Saul's kingdom and give it to David. I will establish the throne of David over Israel as well as Judah, all the way from Dan in the north to Beersheba in the south." Ishbosheth didn't dare say another word because he was afraid of what Abner might do.

Then Abner sent messengers to David, saying, "Doesn't the entire land belong to you? Make a solemn pact with me, and I will help turn over all of Israel to you."

"All right," David replied, "but I will not negotiate with you unless you bring back my wife Michal, Saul's daughter, when you come."

David then sent this message to Ishbosheth, Saul's son: "Give me back my wife Michal, for I bought her with the lives of 100 Philistines."

So Ishbosheth took Michal away from her husband, Palti son of Laish. Palti followed along behind her as far as Bahurim, weeping as he went. Then Abner told him, "Go back home!" So Palti returned.

Meanwhile, Abner had consulted with the elders of Israel. "For some time now," he told them, "you have wanted to make David your king. Now is the time! For the LORD has said, 'I have chosen David to save my people Israel from the hands of the Philistines and from all their other enemies.'" Abner also spoke with the men of Benjamin. Then he went to Hebron to tell David that all the people of Israel and Benjamin had agreed to support him.

When Abner and twenty of his men came to Hebron, David entertained them with a great feast. Then Abner said to David, "Let me go and call an assembly of all Israel to support my lord the king. They will make a covenant with you to make you their king, and you will rule over everything your heart desires." So David sent Abner safely on his way.

But just after David had sent Abner away in safety, Joab and some of

David's troops returned from a raid, bringing much plunder with them. When Joab arrived, he was told that Abner had just been there visiting the king and had been sent away in safety.

Joab rushed to the king and demanded, "What have you done? What do you mean by letting Abner get away? You know perfectly well that he came to spy on you and find out everything you're doing!"

Joab then left David and sent messengers to catch up with Abner, asking him to return. They found him at the well of Sirah and brought him back, though David knew nothing about it. When Abner arrived back at Hebron, Joab took him aside at the gateway as if to speak with him privately. But then he stabbed Abner in the stomach and killed him in revenge for killing his brother Asahel.

When David heard about it, he declared, "I vow by the LORD that I and my kingdom are forever innocent of this crime against Abner son of Ner. Joab and his family are the guilty ones. May the family of Joab be cursed in every generation with a man who has open sores or leprosy or who walks on crutches or dies by the sword or begs for food!"

So Joab and his brother Abishai killed Abner because Abner had killed their brother Asahel at the battle of Gibeon.

Then David said to Joab and all those who were with him, "Tear your clothes and put on burlap. Mourn for Abner." And King David himself walked behind the procession to the grave. They buried Abner in Hebron, and the king and all the people wept at his graveside. Then the king sang this funeral song for Abner:

"Should Abner have died as fools die?
Your hands were not bound;
    your feet were not chained.
No, you were murdered—
    the victim of a wicked plot."

All the people wept again for Abner. David had refused to eat anything on the day of the funeral, and now everyone begged him to eat. But David had made a vow, saying, "May God strike me and even kill me if I eat anything before sundown."

This pleased the people very much. In fact, everything the king did pleased them! So everyone in Judah and all Israel understood that David was not responsible for Abner's murder.

Then King David said to his officials, "Don't you realize that a great commander has fallen today in Israel? And even though I am the anointed king, these two sons of Zeruiah—Joab and Abishai—are too strong for me to control. So may the LORD repay these evil men for their evil deeds."

When Ishbosheth, Saul's son, heard about Abner's death at Hebron, he lost all courage, and all Israel became paralyzed with fear. Now there were two brothers, Baanah and Recab, who were captains of Ishbosheth's raiding parties. They were sons of Rimmon, a member of the tribe of Benjamin who lived in Beeroth. The town of Beeroth is now part of Benjamin's territory because the original people of Beeroth fled to Gittaim, where they still live as foreigners.

(Saul's son Jonathan had a son named Mephibosheth, who was crippled as a child. He was five years old when the report came from Jezreel that Saul and Jonathan had been killed in battle. When the child's nurse heard the news, she picked him up and fled. But as she hurried away, she dropped him, and he became crippled.)

One day Recab and Baanah, the sons of Rimmon from Beeroth, went to Ishbosheth's house around noon as he was taking his midday rest. The doorkeeper, who had been sifting wheat, became drowsy and fell asleep. So Recab and Baanah slipped past her. They went into the house and found Ishbosheth sleeping on his bed. They struck and killed him and cut off his head. Then, taking his head with them, they fled across the Jordan Valley through the night. When they arrived at Hebron, they presented Ishbosheth's head to David. "Look!" they exclaimed to the king. "Here is the head of Ishbosheth, the son of your enemy Saul who tried to kill you. Today the LORD has given my lord the king revenge on Saul and his entire family!"

But David said to Recab and Baanah, "The LORD, who saves me from all my enemies, is my witness. Someone once told me, 'Saul is dead,' thinking he was bringing me good news. But I seized him and killed him at Ziklag. That's the reward I gave him for his news! How much more should I reward evil men who have killed an innocent man in his own house and on his own bed? Shouldn't I hold you responsible for his blood and rid the earth of you?"

So David ordered his young men to kill them, and they did. They cut off their hands and feet and hung their bodies beside the pool in Hebron. Then they took Ishbosheth's head and buried it in Abner's tomb in Hebron.

Then all the tribes of Israel went to David at Hebron and told him, "We are your own flesh and blood. In the past, when Saul was our king, you were the one who really led the forces of Israel. And the LORD told you, 'You will be the shepherd of my people Israel. You will be Israel's leader.'"

So there at Hebron, King David made a covenant before the LORD with all the elders of Israel. And they anointed him king of Israel.

+ + +

David was thirty years old when he began to reign, and he reigned forty years in all. He had reigned over Judah from Hebron for seven years and six months, and from Jerusalem he reigned over all Israel and Judah for thirty-three years.

David then led his men to Jerusalem to fight against the Jebusites, the original inhabitants of the land who were living there. The Jebusites taunted David, saying, "You'll never get in here! Even the blind and lame could keep you out!" For the Jebusites thought they were safe. But David captured the fortress of Zion, which is now called the City of David.

On the day of the attack, David said to his troops, "I hate those 'lame' and 'blind' Jebusites. Whoever attacks them should strike by going into the city through the water tunnel." That is the origin of the saying, "The blind and the lame may not enter the house."

So David made the fortress his home, and he called it the City of David. He extended the city, starting at the supporting terraces and working inward. And David became more and more powerful, because the LORD God of Heaven's Armies was with him.

Then King Hiram of Tyre sent messengers to David, along with cedar timber and carpenters and stonemasons, and they built David a palace. And David realized that the LORD had confirmed him as king over Israel and had blessed his kingdom for the sake of his people Israel.

After moving from Hebron to Jerusalem, David married more concubines and wives, and they had more sons and daughters. These are the names of David's sons who were born in Jerusalem: Shammua, Shobab, Nathan, Solomon, Ibhar, Elishua, Nepheg, Japhia, Elishama, Eliada, and Eliphelet.

When the Philistines heard that David had been anointed king of Israel, they mobilized all their forces to capture him. But David was told they were coming, so he went into the stronghold. The Philistines arrived and spread out across the valley of Rephaim. So David asked the LORD, "Should I go out to fight the Philistines? Will you hand them over to me?"

The LORD replied to David, "Yes, go ahead. I will certainly hand them over to you."

So David went to Baal-perazim and defeated the Philistines there. "The LORD did it!" David exclaimed. "He burst through my enemies like a raging flood!" So he named that place Baal-perazim (which means "the Lord who bursts through"). The Philistines had abandoned their idols there, so David and his men confiscated them.

But after a while the Philistines returned and again spread out across the valley of Rephaim. And again David asked the LORD what to do. "Do not attack them straight on," the LORD replied. "Instead, circle around behind and attack them near the poplar trees. When you hear a sound like marching feet in the tops of the poplar trees, be on the alert! That will be the signal that the LORD is moving ahead of you to strike down the Philistine army." So David did what the LORD commanded, and he struck down the Philistines all the way from Gibeon to Gezer.

+

Then David again gathered all the elite troops in Israel, 30,000 in all. He led them to Baalah of Judah to bring back the Ark of God, which bears the name of the LORD of Heaven's Armies, who is enthroned between the cherubim. They placed the Ark of God on a new cart and brought it from Abinadab's house, which was on a hill. Uzzah and Ahio, Abinadab's sons, were guiding the cart that carried the Ark of God. Ahio walked in front of the Ark. David and all the people of Israel were celebrating before the LORD, singing songs and playing all kinds of musical instruments—lyres, harps, tambourines, castanets, and cymbals.

But when they arrived at the threshing floor of Nacon, the oxen stumbled, and Uzzah reached out his hand and steadied the Ark of God. Then the LORD's anger was aroused against Uzzah, and God struck him dead because of this. So Uzzah died right there beside the Ark of God.

David was angry because the LORD's anger had burst out against Uzzah. He named that place Perez-uzzah (which means "to burst out against Uzzah"), as it is still called today.

David was now afraid of the LORD, and he asked, "How can I ever bring the Ark of the LORD back into my care?" So David decided not to move the Ark of the LORD into the City of David. Instead, he took it to the house of Obed-edom of Gath. The Ark of the LORD remained there in Obed-edom's house for three months, and the LORD blessed Obed-edom and his entire household.

Then King David was told, "The LORD has blessed Obed-edom's household and everything he has because of the Ark of God." So David went there and brought the Ark of God from the house of Obed-edom to the City of David with a great celebration. After the men who were carrying the Ark of the LORD had gone six steps, David sacrificed a bull and a fattened calf. And David danced before the LORD with all his might, wearing a priestly garment. So David and all the people of Israel brought up the Ark of the LORD with shouts of joy and the blowing of rams' horns.

But as the Ark of the LORD entered the City of David, Michal, the daughter of Saul, looked down from her window. When she saw King David leaping and dancing before the LORD, she was filled with contempt for him.

They brought the Ark of the LORD and set it in its place inside the special tent David had prepared for it. And David sacrificed burnt offerings and peace offerings to the LORD. When he had finished his sacrifices, David blessed the people in the name of the LORD of Heaven's Armies. Then he gave to every Israelite man and woman in the crowd a loaf of bread, a cake of dates, and a cake of raisins. Then all the people returned to their homes.

When David returned home to bless his own family, Michal, the daughter of Saul, came out to meet him. She said in disgust, "How distinguished the king of Israel looked today, shamelessly exposing himself to the servant girls like any vulgar person might do!"

David retorted to Michal, "I was dancing before the LORD, who chose me above your father and all his family! He appointed me as the leader of Israel, the people of the LORD, so I celebrate before the LORD. Yes, and I am willing to look even more foolish than this, even to be humiliated in my own eyes! But those servant girls you mentioned will indeed think I am distinguished!" So Michal, the daughter of Saul, remained childless throughout her entire life.

When King David was settled in his palace and the LORD had given him rest from all the surrounding enemies, the king summoned Nathan the prophet. "Look," David said, "I am living in a beautiful cedar palace, but the Ark of God is out there in a tent!"

Nathan replied to the king, "Go ahead and do whatever you have in mind, for the LORD is with you."

But that same night the LORD said to Nathan,

"Go and tell my servant David, 'This is what the LORD has declared: Are you the one to build a house for me to live in? I have never lived in a house, from the day I brought the Israelites out of Egypt until this very day. I have always moved from one place to another with a tent and a Tabernacle as my dwelling. Yet no matter where I have gone with the Israelites, I have never once complained to Israel's tribal leaders, the shepherds of my people Israel. I have never asked them, "Why haven't you built me a beautiful cedar house?"'

"Now go and say to my servant David, 'This is what the LORD of Heaven's Armies has declared: I took you from tending sheep in the pasture and selected you to be the leader of my people Israel. I have been with you wherever you have gone, and I have destroyed

all your enemies before your eyes. Now I will make your name
as famous as anyone who has ever lived on the earth! And I will
provide a homeland for my people Israel, planting them in a secure
place where they will never be disturbed. Evil nations won't oppress
them as they've done in the past, starting from the time I appointed
judges to rule my people Israel. And I will give you rest from all your
enemies.

"'Furthermore, the LORD declares that he will make a house for
you—a dynasty of kings! For when you die and are buried with your
ancestors, I will raise up one of your descendants, your own offspring,
and I will make his kingdom strong. He is the one who will build a
house—a temple—for my name. And I will secure his royal throne
forever. I will be his father, and he will be my son. If he sins, I will
correct and discipline him with the rod, like any father would do. But
my favor will not be taken from him as I took it from Saul, whom I
removed from your sight. Your house and your kingdom will continue
before me for all time, and your throne will be secure forever.'"

So Nathan went back to David and told him everything the LORD had said
in this vision.

Then King David went in and sat before the LORD and prayed,

"Who am I, O Sovereign LORD, and what is my family, that you
have brought me this far? And now, Sovereign LORD, in addition to
everything else, you speak of giving your servant a lasting dynasty! Do
you deal with everyone this way, O Sovereign LORD?

"What more can I say to you? You know what your servant is really
like, Sovereign LORD. Because of your promise and according to your
will, you have done all these great things and have made them known
to your servant.

"How great you are, O Sovereign LORD! There is no one like you.
We have never even heard of another God like you! What other nation
on earth is like your people Israel? What other nation, O God, have
you redeemed from slavery to be your own people? You made a great
name for yourself when you redeemed your people from Egypt. You
performed awesome miracles and drove out the nations and gods that
stood in their way. You made Israel your very own people forever, and
you, O LORD, became their God.

"And now, O LORD God, I am your servant; do as you have
promised concerning me and my family. Confirm it as a promise
that will last forever. And may your name be honored forever so that
everyone will say, 'The LORD of Heaven's Armies is God over Israel!'
And may the house of your servant David continue before you forever.

"O LORD of Heaven's Armies, God of Israel, I have been bold
enough to pray this prayer to you because you have revealed all this to
your servant, saying, 'I will build a house for you—a dynasty of kings!'
For you are God, O Sovereign LORD. Your words are truth, and you
have promised these good things to your servant. And now, may it
please you to bless the house of your servant, so that it may continue
forever before you. For you have spoken, and when you grant a
blessing to your servant, O Sovereign LORD, it is an eternal blessing!"

+

After this, David defeated and subdued the Philistines by conquering
Gath, their largest town. David also conquered the land of Moab. He made
the people lie down on the ground in a row, and he measured them off in
groups with a length of rope. He measured off two groups to be executed
for every one group to be spared. The Moabites who were spared became
David's subjects and paid him tribute money.

David also destroyed the forces of Hadadezer son of Rehob, king of
Zobah, when Hadadezer marched out to strengthen his control along the
Euphrates River. David captured 1,000 chariots, 7,000 charioteers, and
20,000 foot soldiers. He crippled all the chariot horses except enough for
100 chariots.

When Arameans from Damascus arrived to help King Hadadezer, David
killed 22,000 of them. Then he placed several army garrisons in Damascus,
the Aramean capital, and the Arameans became David's subjects and paid
him tribute money. So the LORD made David victorious wherever he went.

David brought the gold shields of Hadadezer's officers to Jerusalem,
along with a large amount of bronze from Hadadezer's towns of Tebah
and Berothai.

When King Toi of Hamath heard that David had destroyed the entire
army of Hadadezer, he sent his son Joram to congratulate King David for
his successful campaign. Hadadezer and Toi had been enemies and were
often at war. Joram presented David with many gifts of silver, gold, and
bronze.

King David dedicated all these gifts to the LORD, as he did with the silver
and gold from the other nations he had defeated—from Edom, Moab,
Ammon, Philistia, and Amalek—and from Hadadezer son of Rehob, king
of Zobah.

So David became even more famous when he returned from destroying
18,000 Edomites in the Valley of Salt. He placed army garrisons throughout Edom, and all the Edomites became David's subjects. In fact, the LORD
made David victorious wherever he went.

So David reigned over all Israel and did what was just and right for all his people. Joab son of Zeruiah was commander of the army. Jehoshaphat son of Ahilud was the royal historian. Zadok son of Ahitub and Ahimelech son of Abiathar were the priests. Seraiah was the court secretary. Benaiah son of Jehoiada was captain of the king's bodyguard. And David's sons served as priestly leaders.

One day David asked, "Is anyone in Saul's family still alive—anyone to whom I can show kindness for Jonathan's sake?" He summoned a man named Ziba, who had been one of Saul's servants. "Are you Ziba?" the king asked.

"Yes sir, I am," Ziba replied.

The king then asked him, "Is anyone still alive from Saul's family? If so, I want to show God's kindness to them."

Ziba replied, "Yes, one of Jonathan's sons is still alive. He is crippled in both feet."

"Where is he?" the king asked.

"In Lo-debar," Ziba told him, "at the home of Makir son of Ammiel."

So David sent for him and brought him from Makir's home. His name was Mephibosheth; he was Jonathan's son and Saul's grandson. When he came to David, he bowed low to the ground in deep respect. David said, "Greetings, Mephibosheth."

Mephibosheth replied, "I am your servant."

"Don't be afraid!" David said. "I intend to show kindness to you because of my promise to your father, Jonathan. I will give you all the property that once belonged to your grandfather Saul, and you will eat here with me at the king's table!"

Mephibosheth bowed respectfully and exclaimed, "Who is your servant, that you should show such kindness to a dead dog like me?"

Then the king summoned Saul's servant Ziba and said, "I have given your master's grandson everything that belonged to Saul and his family. You and your sons and servants are to farm the land for him to produce food for your master's household. But Mephibosheth, your master's grandson, will eat here at my table." (Ziba had fifteen sons and twenty servants.)

Ziba replied, "Yes, my lord the king; I am your servant, and I will do all that you have commanded." And from that time on, Mephibosheth ate regularly at David's table, like one of the king's own sons.

Mephibosheth had a young son named Mica. From then on, all the members of Ziba's household were Mephibosheth's servants. And Mephibosheth, who was crippled in both feet, lived in Jerusalem and ate regularly at the king's table.

Some time after this, King Nahash of the Ammonites died, and his son Hanun became king. David said, "I am going to show loyalty to Hanun just as his father, Nahash, was always loyal to me." So David sent ambassadors to express sympathy to Hanun about his father's death.

But when David's ambassadors arrived in the land of Ammon, the Ammonite commanders said to Hanun, their master, "Do you really think these men are coming here to honor your father? No! David has sent them to spy out the city so they can come in and conquer it!" So Hanun seized David's ambassadors and shaved off half of each man's beard, cut off their robes at the buttocks, and sent them back to David in shame.

When David heard what had happened, he sent messengers to tell the men, "Stay at Jericho until your beards grow out, and then come back." For they felt deep shame because of their appearance.

When the people of Ammon realized how seriously they had angered David, they sent and hired 20,000 Aramean foot soldiers from the lands of Beth-rehob and Zobah, 1,000 from the king of Maacah, and 12,000 from the land of Tob. When David heard about this, he sent Joab and all his warriors to fight them. The Ammonite troops came out and drew up their battle lines at the entrance of the city gate, while the Arameans from Zobah and Rehob and the men from Tob and Maacah positioned themselves to fight in the open fields.

When Joab saw that he would have to fight on both the front and the rear, he chose some of Israel's elite troops and placed them under his personal command to fight the Arameans in the fields. He left the rest of the army under the command of his brother Abishai, who was to attack the Ammonites. "If the Arameans are too strong for me, then come over and help me," Joab told his brother. "And if the Ammonites are too strong for you, I will come and help you. Be courageous! Let us fight bravely for our people and the cities of our God. May the LORD's will be done."

When Joab and his troops attacked, the Arameans began to run away. And when the Ammonites saw the Arameans running, they ran from Abishai and retreated into the city. After the battle was over, Joab returned to Jerusalem.

The Arameans now realized that they were no match for Israel. So when they regrouped, they were joined by additional Aramean troops summoned by Hadadezer from the other side of the Euphrates River. These troops arrived at Helam under the command of Shobach, the commander of Hadadezer's forces.

When David heard what was happening, he mobilized all Israel, crossed the Jordan River, and led the army to Helam. The Arameans positioned themselves in battle formation and fought against David. But again the Arameans fled from the Israelites. This time David's forces killed 700 charioteers and 40,000 foot soldiers, including Shobach, the commander of their army. When all the kings allied with Hadadezer saw that they had been defeated by Israel, they surrendered to Israel and became their subjects. After that, the Arameans were afraid to help the Ammonites.

+

In the spring of the year, when kings normally go out to war, David sent Joab and the Israelite army to fight the Ammonites. They destroyed the Ammonite army and laid siege to the city of Rabbah. However, David stayed behind in Jerusalem.

Late one afternoon, after his midday rest, David got out of bed and was walking on the roof of the palace. As he looked out over the city, he noticed a woman of unusual beauty taking a bath. He sent someone to find out who she was, and he was told, "She is Bathsheba, the daughter of Eliam and the wife of Uriah the Hittite." Then David sent messengers to get her; and when she came to the palace, he slept with her. She had just completed the purification rites after having her menstrual period. Then she returned home. Later, when Bathsheba discovered that she was pregnant, she sent David a message, saying, "I'm pregnant."

Then David sent word to Joab: "Send me Uriah the Hittite." So Joab sent him to David. When Uriah arrived, David asked him how Joab and the army were getting along and how the war was progressing. Then he told Uriah, "Go on home and relax." David even sent a gift to Uriah after he had left the palace. But Uriah didn't go home. He slept that night at the palace entrance with the king's palace guard.

When David heard that Uriah had not gone home, he summoned him and asked, "What's the matter? Why didn't you go home last night after being away for so long?"

Uriah replied, "The Ark and the armies of Israel and Judah are living in tents, and Joab and my master's men are camping in the open fields. How could I go home to wine and dine and sleep with my wife? I swear that I would never do such a thing."

"Well, stay here today," David told him, "and tomorrow you may return to the army." So Uriah stayed in Jerusalem that day and the next. Then David invited him to dinner and got him drunk. But even then he couldn't get Uriah to go home to his wife. Again he slept at the palace entrance with the king's palace guard.

So the next morning David wrote a letter to Joab and gave it to Uriah to deliver. The letter instructed Joab, "Station Uriah on the front lines where the battle is fiercest. Then pull back so that he will be killed." So Joab assigned Uriah to a spot close to the city wall where he knew the enemy's strongest men were fighting. And when the enemy soldiers came out of the city to fight, Uriah the Hittite was killed along with several other Israelite soldiers.

Then Joab sent a battle report to David. He told his messenger, "Report all the news of the battle to the king. But he might get angry and ask, 'Why did the troops go so close to the city? Didn't they know there would be shooting from the walls? Wasn't Abimelech son of Gideon killed at Thebez by a woman who threw a millstone down on him from the wall? Why would you get so close to the wall?' Then tell him, 'Uriah the Hittite was killed, too.'"

So the messenger went to Jerusalem and gave a complete report to David. "The enemy came out against us in the open fields," he said. "And as we chased them back to the city gate, the archers on the wall shot arrows at us. Some of the king's men were killed, including Uriah the Hittite."

"Well, tell Joab not to be discouraged," David said. "The sword devours this one today and that one tomorrow! Fight harder next time, and conquer the city!"

When Uriah's wife heard that her husband was dead, she mourned for him. When the period of mourning was over, David sent for her and brought her to the palace, and she became one of his wives. Then she gave birth to a son. But the LORD was displeased with what David had done.

So the LORD sent Nathan the prophet to tell David this story: "There were two men in a certain town. One was rich, and one was poor. The rich man owned a great many sheep and cattle. The poor man owned nothing but one little lamb he had bought. He raised that little lamb, and it grew up with his children. It ate from the man's own plate and drank from his cup. He cuddled it in his arms like a baby daughter. One day a guest arrived at the home of the rich man. But instead of killing an animal from his own flock or herd, he took the poor man's lamb and killed it and prepared it for his guest."

David was furious. "As surely as the LORD lives," he vowed, "any man who would do such a thing deserves to die! He must repay four lambs to the poor man for the one he stole and for having no pity."

Then Nathan said to David, "You are that man! The LORD, the God of Israel, says: I anointed you king of Israel and saved you from the power of Saul. I gave you your master's house and his wives and the kingdoms of Israel and Judah. And if that had not been enough, I would have given you much, much more. Why, then, have you despised the word of the LORD and done this horrible deed? For you have murdered Uriah the Hittite with the sword of the Ammonites and stolen his wife. From this time on, your family will live by the sword because you have despised me by taking Uriah's wife to be your own.

"This is what the LORD says: Because of what you have done, I will cause your own household to rebel against you. I will give your wives to another man before your very eyes, and he will go to bed with them in public view. You did it secretly, but I will make this happen to you openly in the sight of all Israel."

Then David confessed to Nathan, "I have sinned against the LORD."

Nathan replied, "Yes, but the LORD has forgiven you, and you won't die for this sin. Nevertheless, because you have shown utter contempt for the word of the LORD by doing this, your child will die."

After Nathan returned to his home, the LORD sent a deadly illness to the child of David and Uriah's wife. David begged God to spare the child. He went without food and lay all night on the bare ground. The elders of his household pleaded with him to get up and eat with them, but he refused.

Then on the seventh day the child died. David's advisers were afraid to tell him. "He wouldn't listen to reason while the child was ill," they said. "What drastic thing will he do when we tell him the child is dead?"

When David saw them whispering, he realized what had happened. "Is the child dead?" he asked.

"Yes," they replied, "he is dead."

Then David got up from the ground, washed himself, put on lotions, and changed his clothes. He went to the Tabernacle and worshiped the LORD. After that, he returned to the palace and was served food and ate.

His advisers were amazed. "We don't understand you," they told him. "While the child was still living, you wept and refused to eat. But now that the child is dead, you have stopped your mourning and are eating again."

David replied, "I fasted and wept while the child was alive, for I said, 'Perhaps the LORD will be gracious to me and let the child live.' But why should I fast when he is dead? Can I bring him back again? I will go to him one day, but he cannot return to me."

Then David comforted Bathsheba, his wife, and slept with her. She became pregnant and gave birth to a son, and David named him Solomon. The LORD loved the child and sent word through Nathan the prophet that they should name him Jedidiah (which means "beloved of the LORD"), as the LORD had commanded.

Meanwhile, Joab was fighting against Rabbah, the capital of Ammon, and he captured the royal fortifications. Joab sent messengers to tell David, "I have fought against Rabbah and captured its water supply. Now bring the rest of the army and capture the city. Otherwise, I will capture it and get credit for the victory."

So David gathered the rest of the army and went to Rabbah, and he fought against it and captured it. David removed the crown from the king's head, and it was placed on his own head. The crown was made of gold and set with gems, and it weighed seventy-five pounds. David took a vast amount of plunder from the city. He also made slaves of the people of Rabbah and forced them to labor with saws, iron picks, and iron axes, and to work in the brick kilns. That is how he dealt with the people of all the Ammonite towns. Then David and all the army returned to Jerusalem.

✛

Now David's son Absalom had a beautiful sister named Tamar. And Amnon, her half brother, fell desperately in love with her. Amnon became so obsessed with Tamar that he became ill. She was a virgin, and Amnon thought he could never have her.

But Amnon had a very crafty friend—his cousin Jonadab. He was the son of David's brother Shimea. One day Jonadab said to Amnon, "What's the trouble? Why should the son of a king look so dejected morning after morning?"

So Amnon told him, "I am in love with Tamar, my brother Absalom's sister."

"Well," Jonadab said, "I'll tell you what to do. Go back to bed and pretend you are ill. When your father comes to see you, ask him to let Tamar come and prepare some food for you. Tell him you'll feel better if she prepares it as you watch and feeds you with her own hands."

So Amnon lay down and pretended to be sick. And when the king came to see him, Amnon asked him, "Please let my sister Tamar come and cook my favorite dish as I watch. Then I can eat it from her own hands." So David agreed and sent Tamar to Amnon's house to prepare some food for him.

When Tamar arrived at Amnon's house, she went to the place where he was lying down so he could watch her mix some dough. Then she baked his favorite dish for him. But when she set the serving tray before him, he refused to eat. "Everyone get out of here," Amnon told his servants. So they all left.

Then he said to Tamar, "Now bring the food into my bedroom and feed it to me here." So Tamar took his favorite dish to him. But as she was feeding him, he grabbed her and demanded, "Come to bed with me, my darling sister."

"No, my brother!" she cried. "Don't be foolish! Don't do this to me! Such wicked things aren't done in Israel. Where could I go in my shame?

And you would be called one of the greatest fools in Israel. Please, just speak to the king about it, and he will let you marry me."

But Amnon wouldn't listen to her, and since he was stronger than she was, he raped her. Then suddenly Amnon's love turned to hate, and he hated her even more than he had loved her. "Get out of here!" he snarled at her.

"No, no!" Tamar cried. "Sending me away now is worse than what you've already done to me."

But Amnon wouldn't listen to her. He shouted for his servant and demanded, "Throw this woman out, and lock the door behind her!"

So the servant put her out and locked the door behind her. She was wearing a long, beautiful robe, as was the custom in those days for the king's virgin daughters. But now Tamar tore her robe and put ashes on her head. And then, with her face in her hands, she went away crying.

Her brother Absalom saw her and asked, "Is it true that Amnon has been with you? Well, my sister, keep quiet for now, since he's your brother. Don't you worry about it." So Tamar lived as a desolate woman in her brother Absalom's house.

When King David heard what had happened, he was very angry. And though Absalom never spoke to Amnon about this, he hated Amnon deeply because of what he had done to his sister.

Two years later, when Absalom's sheep were being sheared at Baal-hazor near Ephraim, Absalom invited all the king's sons to come to a feast. He went to the king and said, "My sheep-shearers are now at work. Would the king and his servants please come to celebrate the occasion with me?"

The king replied, "No, my son. If we all came, we would be too much of a burden on you." Absalom pressed him, but the king would not come, though he gave Absalom his blessing.

"Well, then," Absalom said, "if you can't come, how about sending my brother Amnon with us?"

"Why Amnon?" the king asked. But Absalom kept on pressing the king until he finally agreed to let all his sons attend, including Amnon. So Absalom prepared a feast fit for a king.

Absalom told his men, "Wait until Amnon gets drunk; then at my signal, kill him! Don't be afraid. I'm the one who has given the command. Take courage and do it!" So at Absalom's signal they murdered Amnon. Then the other sons of the king jumped on their mules and fled.

As they were on the way back to Jerusalem, this report reached David: "Absalom has killed all the king's sons; not one is left alive!" The king got up, tore his robe, and threw himself on the ground. His advisers also tore their clothes in horror and sorrow.

But just then Jonadab, the son of David's brother Shimea, arrived and said, "No, don't believe that all the king's sons have been killed! It was only Amnon! Absalom has been plotting this ever since Amnon raped his sister Tamar. No, my lord the king, your sons aren't all dead! It was only Amnon." Meanwhile Absalom escaped.

Then the watchman on the Jerusalem wall saw a great crowd coming down the hill on the road from the west. He ran to tell the king, "I see a crowd of people coming from the Horonaim road along the side of the hill."

"Look!" Jonadab told the king. "There they are now! The king's sons are coming, just as I said."

They soon arrived, weeping and sobbing, and the king and all his servants wept bitterly with them. And David mourned many days for his son Amnon.

Absalom fled to his grandfather, Talmai son of Ammihud, the king of Geshur. He stayed there in Geshur for three years. And King David, now reconciled to Amnon's death, longed to be reunited with his son Absalom.

Joab realized how much the king longed to see Absalom. So he sent for a woman from Tekoa who had a reputation for great wisdom. He said to her, "Pretend you are in mourning; wear mourning clothes and don't put on lotions. Act like a woman who has been mourning for the dead for a long time. Then go to the king and tell him the story I am about to tell you." Then Joab told her what to say.

When the woman from Tekoa approached the king, she bowed with her face to the ground in deep respect and cried out, "O king! Help me!"

"What's the trouble?" the king asked.

"Alas, I am a widow!" she replied. "My husband is dead. My two sons had a fight out in the field. And since no one was there to stop it, one of them was killed. Now the rest of the family is demanding, 'Let us have your son. We will execute him for murdering his brother. He doesn't deserve to inherit his family's property.' They want to extinguish the only coal I have left, and my husband's name and family will disappear from the face of the earth."

"Leave it to me," the king told her. "Go home, and I'll see to it that no one touches him."

"Oh, thank you, my lord the king," the woman from Tekoa replied. "If you are criticized for helping me, let the blame fall on me and on my father's house, and let the king and his throne be innocent."

"If anyone objects," the king said, "bring him to me. I can assure you he will never harm you again!"

Then she said, "Please swear to me by the LORD your God that you won't let anyone take vengeance against my son. I want no more bloodshed."

"As surely as the LORD lives," he replied, "not a hair on your son's head will be disturbed!"

"Please allow me to ask one more thing of my lord the king," she said.

"Go ahead and speak," he responded.

She replied, "Why don't you do as much for the people of God as you have promised to do for me? You have convicted yourself in making this decision, because you have refused to bring home your own banished son. All of us must die eventually. Our lives are like water spilled out on the ground, which cannot be gathered up again. But God does not just sweep life away; instead, he devises ways to bring us back when we have been separated from him.

"I have come to plead with my lord the king because people have threatened me. I said to myself, 'Perhaps the king will listen to me and rescue us from those who would cut us off from the inheritance God has given us. Yes, my lord the king will give us peace of mind again.' I know that you are like an angel of God in discerning good from evil. May the LORD your God be with you."

"I must know one thing," the king replied, "and tell me the truth."

"Yes, my lord the king," she responded.

"Did Joab put you up to this?"

And the woman replied, "My lord the king, how can I deny it? Nobody can hide anything from you. Yes, Joab sent me and told me what to say. He did it to place the matter before you in a different light. But you are as wise as an angel of God, and you understand everything that happens among us!"

So the king sent for Joab and told him, "All right, go and bring back the young man Absalom."

Joab bowed with his face to the ground in deep respect and said, "At last I know that I have gained your approval, my lord the king, for you have granted me this request!"

Then Joab went to Geshur and brought Absalom back to Jerusalem. But the king gave this order: "Absalom may go to his own house, but he must never come into my presence." So Absalom did not see the king.

Now Absalom was praised as the most handsome man in all Israel. He was flawless from head to foot. He cut his hair only once a year, and then only because it was so heavy. When he weighed it out, it came to five pounds! He had three sons and one daughter. His daughter's name was Tamar, and she was very beautiful.

Absalom lived in Jerusalem for two years, but he never got to see the king. Then Absalom sent for Joab to ask him to intercede for him, but Joab refused to come. Absalom sent for him a second time, but again Joab refused to come. So Absalom said to his servants, "Go and set fire to Joab's barley field, the field next to mine." So they set his field on fire, as Absalom had commanded.

Then Joab came to Absalom at his house and demanded, "Why did your servants set my field on fire?"

And Absalom replied, "Because I wanted you to ask the king why he brought me back from Geshur if he didn't intend to see me. I might as well have stayed there. Let me see the king; if he finds me guilty of anything, then let him kill me."

So Joab told the king what Absalom had said. Then at last David summoned Absalom, who came and bowed low before the king, and the king kissed him.

After this, Absalom bought a chariot and horses, and he hired fifty bodyguards to run ahead of him. He got up early every morning and went out to the gate of the city. When people brought a case to the king for judgment, Absalom would ask where in Israel they were from, and they would tell him their tribe. Then Absalom would say, "You've really got a strong case here! It's too bad the king doesn't have anyone to hear it. I wish I were the judge. Then everyone could bring their cases to me for judgment, and I would give them justice!"

When people tried to bow before him, Absalom wouldn't let them. Instead, he took them by the hand and kissed them. Absalom did this with everyone who came to the king for judgment, and so he stole the hearts of all the people of Israel.

After four years, Absalom said to the king, "Let me go to Hebron to offer a sacrifice to the LORD and fulfill a vow I made to him. For while your servant was at Geshur in Aram, I promised to sacrifice to the LORD in Hebron if he would bring me back to Jerusalem."

"All right," the king told him. "Go and fulfill your vow."

So Absalom went to Hebron. But while he was there, he sent secret messengers to all the tribes of Israel to stir up a rebellion against the king. "As soon as you hear the ram's horn," his message read, "you are to say, 'Absalom has been crowned king in Hebron.'" He took 200 men from Jerusalem with him as guests, but they knew nothing of his intentions. While Absalom was offering the sacrifices, he sent for Ahithophel, one of David's counselors who lived in Giloh. Soon many others also joined Absalom, and the conspiracy gained momentum.

A messenger soon arrived in Jerusalem to tell David, "All Israel has joined Absalom in a conspiracy against you!"

"Then we must flee at once, or it will be too late!" David urged his men.

"Hurry! If we get out of the city before Absalom arrives, both we and the city of Jerusalem will be spared from disaster."

"We are with you," his advisers replied. "Do what you think is best."

So the king and all his household set out at once. He left no one behind except ten of his concubines to look after the palace. The king and all his people set out on foot, pausing at the last house to let all the king's men move past to lead the way. There were 600 men from Gath who had come with David, along with the king's bodyguard.

Then the king turned and said to Ittai, a leader of the men from Gath, "Why are you coming with us? Go on back to King Absalom, for you are a guest in Israel, a foreigner in exile. You arrived only recently, and should I force you today to wander with us? I don't even know where we will go. Go on back and take your kinsmen with you, and may the LORD show you his unfailing love and faithfulness."

But Ittai said to the king, "I vow by the LORD and by your own life that I will go wherever my lord the king goes, no matter what happens—whether it means life or death."

David replied, "All right, come with us." So Ittai and all his men and their families went along.

Everyone cried loudly as the king and his followers passed by. They crossed the Kidron Valley and then went out toward the wilderness.

Zadok and all the Levites also came along, carrying the Ark of the Covenant of God. They set down the Ark of God, and Abiathar offered sacrifices until everyone had passed out of the city.

Then the king instructed Zadok to take the Ark of God back into the city. "If the LORD sees fit," David said, "he will bring me back to see the Ark and the Tabernacle again. But if he is through with me, then let him do what seems best to him."

The king also told Zadok the priest, "Look, here is my plan. You and Abiathar should return quietly to the city with your son Ahimaaz and Abiathar's son Jonathan. I will stop at the shallows of the Jordan River and wait there for a report from you." So Zadok and Abiathar took the Ark of God back to the city and stayed there.

David walked up the road to the Mount of Olives, weeping as he went. His head was covered and his feet were bare as a sign of mourning. And the people who were with him covered their heads and wept as they climbed the hill. When someone told David that his adviser Ahithophel was now backing Absalom, David prayed, "O LORD, let Ahithophel give Absalom foolish advice!"

When David reached the summit of the Mount of Olives where people worshiped God, Hushai the Arkite was waiting there for him. Hushai had torn his clothing and put dirt on his head as a sign of mourning. But David told him, "If you go with me, you will only be a burden. Return to Jerusalem and tell Absalom, 'I will now be your adviser, O king, just as I was your father's adviser in the past.' Then you can frustrate and counter Ahithophel's advice. Zadok and Abiathar, the priests, will be there. Tell them about the plans being made in the king's palace, and they will send their sons Ahimaaz and Jonathan to tell me what is going on."

So David's friend Hushai returned to Jerusalem, getting there just as Absalom arrived.

When David had gone a little beyond the summit of the Mount of Olives, Ziba, the servant of Mephibosheth, was waiting there for him. He had two donkeys loaded with 200 loaves of bread, 100 clusters of raisins, 100 bunches of summer fruit, and a wineskin full of wine.

"What are these for?" the king asked Ziba.

Ziba replied, "The donkeys are for the king's people to ride on, and the bread and summer fruit are for the young men to eat. The wine is for those who become exhausted in the wilderness."

"And where is Mephibosheth, Saul's grandson?" the king asked him.

"He stayed in Jerusalem," Ziba replied. "He said, 'Today I will get back the kingdom of my grandfather Saul.'"

"In that case," the king told Ziba, "I give you everything Mephibosheth owns."

"I bow before you," Ziba replied. "May I always be pleasing to you, my lord the king."

As King David came to Bahurim, a man came out of the village cursing them. It was Shimei son of Gera, from the same clan as Saul's family. He threw stones at the king and the king's officers and all the mighty warriors who surrounded him. "Get out of here, you murderer, you scoundrel!" he shouted at David. "The LORD is paying you back for all the bloodshed in Saul's clan. You stole his throne, and now the LORD has given it to your son Absalom. At last you will taste some of your own medicine, for you are a murderer!"

"Why should this dead dog curse my lord the king?" Abishai son of Zeruiah demanded. "Let me go over and cut off his head!"

"No!" the king said. "Who asked your opinion, you sons of Zeruiah! If the LORD has told him to curse me, who are you to stop him?"

Then David said to Abishai and to all his servants, "My own son is trying to kill me. Doesn't this relative of Saul have even more reason to do so? Leave him alone and let him curse, for the LORD has told him to do it. And perhaps the LORD will see that I am being wronged and will bless me because of these curses today." So David and his men continued down the road, and Shimei kept pace with them on a nearby hillside, cursing and throwing stones and dirt at David.

The king and all who were with him grew weary along the way, so they rested when they reached the Jordan River.

Meanwhile, Absalom and all the army of Israel arrived at Jerusalem, accompanied by Ahithophel. When David's friend Hushai the Arkite arrived, he went immediately to see Absalom. "Long live the king!" he exclaimed. "Long live the king!"

"Is this the way you treat your friend David?" Absalom asked him. "Why aren't you with him?"

"I'm here because I belong to the man who is chosen by the LORD and by all the men of Israel," Hushai replied. "And anyway, why shouldn't I serve you? Just as I was your father's adviser, now I will be your adviser!"

Then Absalom turned to Ahithophel and asked him, "What should I do next?"

Ahithophel told him, "Go and sleep with your father's concubines, for he has left them here to look after the palace. Then all Israel will know that you have insulted your father beyond hope of reconciliation, and they will throw their support to you." So they set up a tent on the palace roof where everyone could see it, and Absalom went in and had sex with his father's concubines.

Absalom followed Ahithophel's advice, just as David had done. For every word Ahithophel spoke seemed as wise as though it had come directly from the mouth of God.

Now Ahithophel urged Absalom, "Let me choose 12,000 men to start out after David tonight. I will catch up with him while he is weary and discouraged. He and his troops will panic, and everyone will run away. Then I will kill only the king, and I will bring all the people back to you as a bride returns to her husband. After all, it is only one man's life that you seek. Then you will be at peace with all the people." This plan seemed good to Absalom and to all the elders of Israel.

But then Absalom said, "Bring in Hushai the Arkite. Let's see what he thinks about this." When Hushai arrived, Absalom told him what Ahithophel had said. Then he asked, "What is your opinion? Should we follow Ahithophel's advice? If not, what do you suggest?"

"Well," Hushai replied to Absalom, "this time Ahithophel has made a mistake. You know your father and his men; they are mighty warriors. Right now they are as enraged as a mother bear who has been robbed of her cubs. And remember that your father is an experienced man of war. He won't be spending the night among the troops. He has probably already hidden in some pit or cave. And when he comes out and attacks and a few of your men fall, there will be panic among your troops, and the word will spread that Absalom's men are being slaughtered. Then even the bravest soldiers, though they have the heart of a lion, will be paralyzed with fear. For all Israel knows what a mighty warrior your father is and how courageous his men are.

"I recommend that you mobilize the entire army of Israel, bringing them from as far away as Dan in the north and Beersheba in the south. That way you will have an army as numerous as the sand on the seashore. And I advise that you personally lead the troops. When we find David, we'll fall on him like dew that falls on the ground. Then neither he nor any of his men will be left alive. And if David were to escape into some town, you will have all Israel there at your command. Then we can take ropes and drag the walls of the town into the nearest valley until every stone is torn down."

Then Absalom and all the men of Israel said, "Hushai's advice is better than Ahithophel's." For the LORD had determined to defeat the counsel of Ahithophel, which really was the better plan, so that he could bring disaster on Absalom!

Hushai told Zadok and Abiathar, the priests, what Ahithophel had said to Absalom and the elders of Israel and what he himself had advised instead. "Quick!" he told them. "Find David and urge him not to stay at the shallows of the Jordan River tonight. He must go across at once into the wilderness beyond. Otherwise he will die and his entire army with him."

Jonathan and Ahimaaz had been staying at En-rogel so as not to be seen entering and leaving the city. Arrangements had been made for a servant girl to bring them the message they were to take to King David. But a boy spotted them at En-rogel, and he told Absalom about it. So they quickly escaped to Bahurim, where a man hid them down inside a well in his courtyard. The man's wife put a cloth over the top of the well and scattered grain on it to dry in the sun; so no one suspected they were there.

When Absalom's men arrived, they asked her, "Have you seen Ahimaaz and Jonathan?"

The woman replied, "They were here, but they crossed over the brook." Absalom's men looked for them without success and returned to Jerusalem.

Then the two men crawled out of the well and hurried on to King David. "Quick!" they told him, "cross the Jordan tonight!" And they told him how Ahithophel had advised that he be captured and killed. So David and all the people with him went across the Jordan River during the night, and they were all on the other bank before dawn.

When Ahithophel realized that his advice had not been followed, he saddled his donkey, went to his hometown, set his affairs in order, and hanged himself. He died there and was buried in the family tomb.

David soon arrived at Mahanaim. By now, Absalom had mobilized the entire army of Israel and was leading his troops across the Jordan River. Absalom had appointed Amasa as commander of his army, replacing Joab, who had been commander under David. (Amasa was Joab's cousin. His father was Jether, an Ishmaelite. His mother, Abigail daughter of Nahash, was the sister of Joab's mother, Zeruiah.) Absalom and the Israelite army set up camp in the land of Gilead.

When David arrived at Mahanaim, he was warmly greeted by Shobi son of Nahash, who came from Rabbah of the Ammonites, and by Makir son of Ammiel from Lo-debar, and by Barzillai of Gilead from Rogelim. They brought sleeping mats, cooking pots, serving bowls, wheat and barley, flour and roasted grain, beans, lentils, honey, butter, sheep, goats, and cheese for David and those who were with him. For they said, "You must all be very hungry and tired and thirsty after your long march through the wilderness."

David now mustered the men who were with him and appointed generals and captains to lead them. He sent the troops out in three groups, placing one group under Joab, one under Joab's brother Abishai son of Zeruiah, and one under Ittai, the man from Gath. The king told his troops, "I am going out with you."

But his men objected strongly. "You must not go," they urged. "If we have to turn and run—and even if half of us die—it will make no difference to Absalom's troops; they will be looking only for you. You are worth 10,000 of us, and it is better that you stay here in the town and send help if we need it."

"If you think that's the best plan, I'll do it," the king answered. So he stood alongside the gate of the town as all the troops marched out in groups of hundreds and of thousands.

And the king gave this command to Joab, Abishai, and Ittai: "For my sake, deal gently with young Absalom." And all the troops heard the king give this order to his commanders.

So the battle began in the forest of Ephraim, and the Israelite troops were beaten back by David's men. There was a great slaughter that day, and 20,000 men laid down their lives. The battle raged all across the countryside, and more men died because of the forest than were killed by the sword.

During the battle, Absalom happened to come upon some of David's men. He tried to escape on his mule, but as he rode beneath the thick branches of a great tree, his hair got caught in the tree. His mule kept going and left him dangling in the air. One of David's men saw what had happened and told Joab, "I saw Absalom dangling from a great tree."

"What?" Joab demanded. "You saw him there and didn't kill him? I would have rewarded you with ten pieces of silver and a hero's belt!"

"I would not kill the king's son for even a thousand pieces of silver," the man replied to Joab. "We all heard the king say to you and Abishai and Ittai, 'For my sake, please spare young Absalom.' And if I had betrayed the king by killing his son—and the king would certainly find out who did it—you yourself would be the first to abandon me."

"Enough of this nonsense," Joab said. Then he took three daggers and plunged them into Absalom's heart as he dangled, still alive, in the great tree. Ten of Joab's young armor bearers then surrounded Absalom and killed him.

Then Joab blew the ram's horn, and his men returned from chasing the army of Israel. They threw Absalom's body into a deep pit in the forest and piled a great heap of stones over it. And all Israel fled to their homes.

During his lifetime, Absalom had built a monument to himself in the King's Valley, for he said, "I have no son to carry on my name." He named the monument after himself, and it is known as Absalom's Monument to this day.

Then Zadok's son Ahimaaz said, "Let me run to the king with the good news that the LORD has rescued him from his enemies."

"No," Joab told him, "it wouldn't be good news to the king that his son is dead. You can be my messenger another time, but not today."

Then Joab said to a man from Ethiopia, "Go tell the king what you have seen." The man bowed and ran off.

But Ahimaaz continued to plead with Joab, "Whatever happens, please let me go, too."

"Why should you go, my son?" Joab replied. "There will be no reward for your news."

"Yes, but let me go anyway," he begged.

Joab finally said, "All right, go ahead." So Ahimaaz took the less demanding route by way of the plain and ran to Mahanaim ahead of the Ethiopian.

While David was sitting between the inner and outer gates of the town, the watchman climbed to the roof of the gateway by the wall. As he looked, he saw a lone man running toward them. He shouted the news down to David, and the king replied, "If he is alone, he has news."

As the messenger came closer, the watchman saw another man running toward them. He shouted down, "Here comes another one!"

The king replied, "He also will have news."

"The first man runs like Ahimaaz son of Zadok," the watchman said.

"He is a good man and comes with good news," the king replied.

Then Ahimaaz cried out to the king, "Everything is all right!" He bowed before the king with his face to the ground and said, "Praise to the LORD your God, who has handed over the rebels who dared to stand against my lord the king."

"What about young Absalom?" the king demanded. "Is he all right?"

Ahimaaz replied, "When Joab told me to come, there was a lot of commotion. But I didn't know what was happening."

"Wait here," the king told him. So Ahimaaz stepped aside.

Then the man from Ethiopia arrived and said, "I have good news for my lord the king. Today the LORD has rescued you from all those who rebelled against you."

"What about young Absalom?" the king demanded. "Is he all right?"

And the Ethiopian replied, "May all of your enemies, my lord the king, both now and in the future, share the fate of that young man!"

The king was overcome with emotion. He went up to the room over the gateway and burst into tears. And as he went, he cried, "O my son Absalom! My son, my son Absalom! If only I had died instead of you! O Absalom, my son, my son."

Word soon reached Joab that the king was weeping and mourning for Absalom. As all the people heard of the king's deep grief for his son, the joy of that day's victory was turned into deep sadness. They crept back into the town that day as though they were ashamed and had deserted in battle. The king covered his face with his hands and kept on crying, "O my son Absalom! O Absalom, my son, my son!"

Then Joab went to the king's room and said to him, "We saved your life today and the lives of your sons, your daughters, and your wives and concubines. Yet you act like this, making us feel ashamed of ourselves. You seem to love those who hate you and hate those who love you. You have made it clear today that your commanders and troops mean nothing to you. It seems that if Absalom had lived and all of us had died, you would be pleased. Now go out there and congratulate your troops, for I swear by the LORD that if you don't go out, not a single one of them will remain here tonight. Then you will be worse off than ever before."

So the king went out and took his seat at the town gate, and as the news spread throughout the town that he was there, everyone went to him.

Meanwhile, the Israelites who had supported Absalom fled to their homes. And throughout all the tribes of Israel there was much discussion and argument going on. The people were saying, "The king rescued us from our enemies and saved us from the Philistines, but Absalom chased him out of the country. Now Absalom, whom we anointed to rule over us, is dead. Why not ask David to come back and be our king again?"

Then King David sent Zadok and Abiathar, the priests, to say to the elders of Judah, "Why are you the last ones to welcome back the king into his palace? For I have heard that all Israel is ready. You are my relatives, my own tribe, my own flesh and blood! So why are you the last ones to welcome back the king?" And David told them to tell Amasa, "Since you are my own flesh and blood, like Joab, may God strike me and even kill me if I do not appoint you as commander of my army in his place."

Then Amasa convinced all the men of Judah, and they responded unanimously. They sent word to the king, "Return to us, and bring back all who are with you."

So the king started back to Jerusalem. And when he arrived at the Jordan River, the people of Judah came to Gilgal to meet him and escort him across the river. Shimei son of Gera, the man from Bahurim in Benjamin, hurried across with the men of Judah to welcome King David. A thousand other men from the tribe of Benjamin were with him, including Ziba, the chief servant of the house of Saul, and Ziba's fifteen sons and twenty servants. They rushed down to the Jordan to meet the king. They crossed the shallows of the Jordan to bring the king's household across the river, helping him in every way they could.

As the king was about to cross the river, Shimei fell down before him. "My lord the king, please forgive me," he pleaded. "Forget the terrible thing your servant did when you left Jerusalem. May the king put it out of his mind. I know how much I sinned. That is why I have come here today, the very first person in all Israel to greet my lord the king."

Then Abishai son of Zeruiah said, "Shimei should die, for he cursed the LORD's anointed king!"

"Who asked your opinion, you sons of Zeruiah!" David exclaimed. "Why have you become my adversary today? This is not a day for execution, for today I am once again the king of Israel!" Then, turning to Shimei, David vowed, "Your life will be spared."

Now Mephibosheth, Saul's grandson, came down from Jerusalem to meet the king. He had not cared for his feet, trimmed his beard, or washed his clothes since the day the king left Jerusalem. "Why didn't you come with me, Mephibosheth?" the king asked him.

Mephibosheth replied, "My lord the king, my servant Ziba deceived me. I told him, 'Saddle my donkey so I can go with the king.' For as you know I am crippled. Ziba has slandered me by saying that I refused to come. But I know that my lord the king is like an angel of God, so do what you think is best. All my relatives and I could expect only death from you, my lord, but instead you have honored me by allowing me to eat at your own table! What more can I ask?"

"You've said enough," David replied. "I've decided that you and Ziba will divide your land equally between you."

"Give him all of it," Mephibosheth said. "I am content just to have you safely back again, my lord the king!"

Barzillai of Gilead had come down from Rogelim to escort the king across the Jordan. He was very old—eighty years of age—and very wealthy. He was the one who had provided food for the king during his stay in Mahanaim. "Come across with me and live in Jerusalem," the king said to Barzillai. "I will take care of you there."

"No," he replied, "I am far too old to go with the king to Jerusalem. I am eighty years old today, and I can no longer enjoy anything. Food and wine are no longer tasty, and I cannot hear the singers as they sing. I would only be a burden to my lord the king. Just to go across the Jordan River with the king is all the honor I need! Then let me return again to die in my own town, where my father and mother are buried. But here is your servant, my son Kimham. Let him go with my lord the king and receive whatever you want to give him."

"Good," the king agreed. "Kimham will go with me, and I will help him in any way you would like. And I will do for you anything you want." So all the people crossed the Jordan with the king. After David had blessed Barzillai and kissed him, Barzillai returned to his own home.

The king then crossed over to Gilgal, taking Kimham with him. All the troops of Judah and half the troops of Israel escorted the king on his way.

But all the men of Israel complained to the king, "The men of Judah stole the king and didn't give us the honor of helping take you, your household, and all your men across the Jordan."

The men of Judah replied, "The king is one of our own kinsmen. Why should this make you angry? We haven't eaten any of the king's food or received any special favors!"

"But there are ten tribes in Israel," the others replied. "So we have ten times as much right to the king as you do. What right do you have to treat us with such contempt? Weren't we the first to speak of bringing him back to be our king again?" The argument continued back and forth, and the men of Judah spoke even more harshly than the men of Israel.

There happened to be a troublemaker there named Sheba son of Bicri, a man from the tribe of Benjamin. Sheba blew a ram's horn and began to chant:

"Down with the dynasty of David!
   We have no interest in the son of Jesse.

Come on, you men of Israel,
  back to your homes!"

So all the men of Israel deserted David and followed Sheba son of Bicri.
But the men of Judah stayed with their king and escorted him from the
Jordan River to Jerusalem.

When David came to his palace in Jerusalem, he took the ten concubines he had left to look after the palace and placed them in seclusion.
Their needs were provided for, but he no longer slept with them. So each
of them lived like a widow until she died.

Then the king told Amasa, "Mobilize the army of Judah within three
days, and report back at that time." So Amasa went out to notify Judah,
but it took him longer than the time he had been given.

Then David said to Abishai, "Sheba son of Bicri is going to hurt us more
than Absalom did. Quick, take my troops and chase after him before he
gets into a fortified town where we can't reach him."

So Abishai and Joab, together with the king's bodyguard and all the
mighty warriors, set out from Jerusalem to go after Sheba. As they arrived
at the great stone in Gibeon, Amasa met them. Joab was wearing his military tunic with a dagger strapped to his belt. As he stepped forward to greet
Amasa, he slipped the dagger from its sheath.

"How are you, my cousin?" Joab said and took him by the beard with
his right hand as though to kiss him. Amasa didn't notice the dagger in his
left hand, and Joab stabbed him in the stomach with it so that his insides
gushed out onto the ground. Joab did not need to strike again, and Amasa
soon died. Joab and his brother Abishai left him lying there and continued
after Sheba.

One of Joab's young men shouted to Amasa's troops, "If you are for
Joab and David, come and follow Joab." But Amasa lay in his blood in the
middle of the road, and Joab's man saw that everyone was stopping to stare
at him. So he pulled him off the road into a field and threw a cloak over
him. With Amasa's body out of the way, everyone went on with Joab to
capture Sheba son of Bicri.

Meanwhile, Sheba traveled through all the tribes of Israel and eventually came to the town of Abel-beth-maacah. All the members of his own
clan, the Bicrites, assembled for battle and followed him into the town.
When Joab's forces arrived, they attacked Abel-beth-maacah. They built
a siege ramp against the town's fortifications and began battering down
the wall. But a wise woman in the town called out to Joab, "Listen to me,
Joab. Come over here so I can talk to you." As he approached, the woman
asked, "Are you Joab?"

"I am," he replied.

So she said, "Listen carefully to your servant."

"I'm listening," he said.

Then she continued, "There used to be a saying, 'If you want to settle an argument, ask advice at the town of Abel.' I am one who is peace loving and faithful in Israel. But you are destroying an important town in Israel. Why do you want to devour what belongs to the LORD?"

And Joab replied, "Believe me, I don't want to devour or destroy your town! That's not my purpose. All I want is a man named Sheba son of Bicri from the hill country of Ephraim, who has revolted against King David. If you hand over this one man to me, I will leave the town in peace."

"All right," the woman replied, "we will throw his head over the wall to you." Then the woman went to all the people with her wise advice, and they cut off Sheba's head and threw it out to Joab. So he blew the ram's horn and called his troops back from the attack. They all returned to their homes, and Joab returned to the king at Jerusalem.

Now Joab was the commander of the army of Israel. Benaiah son of Jehoiada was captain of the king's bodyguard. Adoniram was in charge of forced labor. Jehoshaphat son of Ahilud was the royal historian. Sheva was the court secretary. Zadok and Abiathar were the priests. And Ira, a descendant of Jair, was David's personal priest.

+

There was a famine during David's reign that lasted for three years, so David asked the LORD about it. And the LORD said, "The famine has come because Saul and his family are guilty of murdering the Gibeonites."

So the king summoned the Gibeonites. They were not part of Israel but were all that was left of the nation of the Amorites. The people of Israel had sworn not to kill them, but Saul, in his zeal for Israel and Judah, had tried to wipe them out. David asked them, "What can I do for you? How can I make amends so that you will bless the LORD's people again?"

"Well, money can't settle this matter between us and the family of Saul," the Gibeonites replied. "Neither can we demand the life of anyone in Israel."

"What can I do then?" David asked. "Just tell me and I will do it for you."

Then they replied, "It was Saul who planned to destroy us, to keep us from having any place at all in the territory of Israel. So let seven of Saul's sons be handed over to us, and we will execute them before the LORD at Gibeon, on the mountain of the LORD."

"All right," the king said, "I will do it." The king spared Jonathan's son Mephibosheth, who was Saul's grandson, because of the oath David and Jonathan had sworn before the LORD. But he gave them Saul's two sons Armoni and Mephibosheth, whose mother was Rizpah daughter of Aiah. He also gave them the five sons of Saul's daughter Merab, the wife of Adriel son of Barzillai from Meholah. The men of Gibeon executed them on the mountain before the LORD. So all seven of them died together at the beginning of the barley harvest.

Then Rizpah daughter of Aiah, the mother of two of the men, spread burlap on a rock and stayed there the entire harvest season. She prevented the scavenger birds from tearing at their bodies during the day and stopped wild animals from eating them at night. When David learned what Rizpah, Saul's concubine, had done, he went to the people of Jabesh-gilead and retrieved the bones of Saul and his son Jonathan. (When the Philistines had killed Saul and Jonathan on Mount Gilboa, the people of Jabesh-gilead stole their bodies from the public square of Beth-shan, where the Philistines had hung them.) So David obtained the bones of Saul and Jonathan, as well as the bones of the men the Gibeonites had executed.

Then the king ordered that they bury the bones in the tomb of Kish, Saul's father, at the town of Zela in the land of Benjamin. After that, God ended the famine in the land.

Once again the Philistines were at war with Israel. And when David and his men were in the thick of battle, David became weak and exhausted. Ishbi-benob was a descendant of the giants; his bronze spearhead weighed more than seven pounds, and he was armed with a new sword. He had cornered David and was about to kill him. But Abishai son of Zeruiah came to David's rescue and killed the Philistine. Then David's men declared, "You are not going out to battle with us again! Why risk snuffing out the light of Israel?"

After this, there was another battle against the Philistines at Gob. As they fought, Sibbecai from Hushah killed Saph, another descendant of the giants.

During another battle at Gob, Elhanan son of Jair from Bethlehem killed the brother of Goliath of Gath. The handle of his spear was as thick as a weaver's beam!

In another battle with the Philistines at Gath, they encountered a huge man with six fingers on each hand and six toes on each foot, twenty-four in all, who was also a descendant of the giants. But when he defied and taunted Israel, he was killed by Jonathan, the son of David's brother Shimea.

These four Philistines were descendants of the giants of Gath, but David and his warriors killed them.

David sang this song to the Lord on the day the Lord rescued him from all his enemies and from Saul. He sang:

"The Lord is my rock, my fortress, and my savior;
  my God is my rock, in whom I find protection.
He is my shield, the power that saves me,
  and my place of safety.
He is my refuge, my savior,
  the one who saves me from violence.
I called on the Lord, who is worthy of praise,
  and he saved me from my enemies.

"The waves of death overwhelmed me;
  floods of destruction swept over me.
The grave wrapped its ropes around me;
  death laid a trap in my path.
But in my distress I cried out to the Lord;
  yes, I cried to my God for help.
He heard me from his sanctuary;
  my cry reached his ears.

"Then the earth quaked and trembled.
  The foundations of the heavens shook;
  they quaked because of his anger.
Smoke poured from his nostrils;
  fierce flames leaped from his mouth.
  Glowing coals blazed forth from him.
He opened the heavens and came down;
  dark storm clouds were beneath his feet.
Mounted on a mighty angelic being, he flew,
  soaring on the wings of the wind.
He shrouded himself in darkness,
  veiling his approach with dense rain clouds.
A great brightness shone around him,
  and burning coals blazed forth.
The Lord thundered from heaven;
  the voice of the Most High resounded.
He shot arrows and scattered his enemies;
  his lightning flashed, and they were confused.
Then at the command of the Lord,
  at the blast of his breath,
the bottom of the sea could be seen,
  and the foundations of the earth were laid bare.

"He reached down from heaven and rescued me;
  he drew me out of deep waters.
He rescued me from my powerful enemies,
  from those who hated me and were too strong for me.
They attacked me at a moment when I was in distress,
  but the LORD supported me.
He led me to a place of safety;
  he rescued me because he delights in me.
The LORD rewarded me for doing right;
  he restored me because of my innocence.
For I have kept the ways of the LORD;
  I have not turned from my God to follow evil.
I have followed all his regulations;
  I have never abandoned his decrees.
I am blameless before God;
  I have kept myself from sin.
The LORD rewarded me for doing right.
  He has seen my innocence.

"To the faithful you show yourself faithful;
  to those with integrity you show integrity.
To the pure you show yourself pure,
  but to the crooked you show yourself shrewd.
You rescue the humble,
  but your eyes watch the proud and humiliate them.
O LORD, you are my lamp.
  The LORD lights up my darkness.
In your strength I can crush an army;
  with my God I can scale any wall.

"God's way is perfect.
  All the LORD's promises prove true.
  He is a shield for all who look to him for protection.
For who is God except the LORD?
  Who but our God is a solid rock?
God is my strong fortress,
  and he makes my way perfect.
He makes me as surefooted as a deer,
  enabling me to stand on mountain heights.
He trains my hands for battle;
  he strengthens my arm to draw a bronze bow.
You have given me your shield of victory;
  your help has made me great.

You have made a wide path for my feet
   to keep them from slipping.

"I chased my enemies and destroyed them;
   I did not stop until they were conquered.
I consumed them;
   I struck them down so they did not get up;
   they fell beneath my feet.
You have armed me with strength for the battle;
   you have subdued my enemies under my feet.
You placed my foot on their necks.
   I have destroyed all who hated me.
They looked for help, but no one came to their rescue.
   They even cried to the LORD, but he refused to answer.
I ground them as fine as the dust of the earth;
   I trampled them in the gutter like dirt.

"You gave me victory over my accusers.
   You preserved me as the ruler over nations;
   people I don't even know now serve me.
Foreign nations cringe before me;
   as soon as they hear of me, they submit.
They all lose their courage
   and come trembling from their strongholds.

"The LORD lives! Praise to my Rock!
   May God, the Rock of my salvation, be exalted!
He is the God who pays back those who harm me;
   he brings down the nations under me
   and delivers me from my enemies.
You hold me safe beyond the reach of my enemies;
   you save me from violent opponents.
For this, O LORD, I will praise you among the nations;
   I will sing praises to your name.
You give great victories to your king;
   you show unfailing love to your anointed,
   to David and all his descendants forever."

These are the last words of David:

"David, the son of Jesse, speaks—
   David, the man who was raised up so high,
David, the man anointed by the God of Jacob,
   David, the sweet psalmist of Israel.

"The Spirit of the LORD speaks through me;
　his words are upon my tongue.
The God of Israel spoke.
　The Rock of Israel said to me:
'The one who rules righteously,
　who rules in the fear of God,
is like the light of morning at sunrise,
　like a morning without clouds,
like the gleaming of the sun
　on new grass after rain.'

"Is it not my family God has chosen?
　Yes, he has made an everlasting covenant with me.
His agreement is arranged and guaranteed in every detail.
　He will ensure my safety and success.
But the godless are like thorns to be thrown away,
　for they tear the hand that touches them.
One must use iron tools to chop them down;
　they will be totally consumed by fire."

These are the names of David's mightiest warriors. The first was Jasho-beam the Hacmonite, who was leader of the Three—the three mightiest warriors among David's men. He once used his spear to kill 800 enemy warriors in a single battle.

Next in rank among the Three was Eleazar son of Dodai, a descendant of Ahoah. Once Eleazar and David stood together against the Philistines when the entire Israelite army had fled. He killed Philistines until his hand was too tired to lift his sword, and the LORD gave him a great victory that day. The rest of the army did not return until it was time to collect the plunder!

Next in rank was Shammah son of Agee from Harar. One time the Philistines gathered at Lehi and attacked the Israelites in a field full of lentils. The Israelite army fled, but Shammah held his ground in the middle of the field and beat back the Philistines. So the LORD brought about a great victory.

Once during the harvest, when David was at the cave of Adullam, the Philistine army was camped in the valley of Rephaim. The Three (who were among the Thirty—an elite group among David's fighting men) went down to meet him there. David was staying in the stronghold at the time, and a Philistine detachment had occupied the town of Bethlehem.

David remarked longingly to his men, "Oh, how I would love some of that good water from the well by the gate in Bethlehem." So the Three broke through the Philistine lines, drew some water from the well by the gate in Bethlehem, and brought it back to David. But he refused to drink it. Instead, he poured it out as an offering to the LORD. "The LORD forbid that I should drink this!" he exclaimed. "This water is as precious as the blood of these men who risked their lives to bring it to me." So David did not drink it. These are examples of the exploits of the Three.

Abishai son of Zeruiah, the brother of Joab, was the leader of the Thirty. He once used his spear to kill 300 enemy warriors in a single battle. It was by such feats that he became as famous as the Three. Abishai was the most famous of the Thirty and was their commander, though he was not one of the Three.

There was also Benaiah son of Jehoiada, a valiant warrior from Kab-zeel. He did many heroic deeds, which included killing two champions of Moab. Another time, on a snowy day, he chased a lion down into a pit and killed it. Once, armed only with a club, he killed an imposing Egyptian warrior who was armed with a spear. Benaiah wrenched the spear from the Egyptian's hand and killed him with it. Deeds like these made Benaiah as famous as the Three mightiest warriors. He was more honored than the other members of the Thirty, though he was not one of the Three. And David made him captain of his bodyguard.

Other members of the Thirty included:

Asahel, Joab's brother;
Elhanan son of Dodo from Bethlehem;
Shammah from Harod;
Elika from Harod;
Helez from Pelon;
Ira son of Ikkesh from Tekoa;
Abiezer from Anathoth;
Sibbecai from Hushah;
Zalmon from Ahoah;
Maharai from Netophah;
Heled son of Baanah from Netophah;
Ithai son of Ribai from Gibeah (in the land of Benjamin);
Benaiah from Pirathon;
Hurai from Nahale-gaash;
Abi-albon from Arabah;
Azmaveth from Bahurim;
Eliahba from Shaalbon;
the sons of Jashen;
Jonathan son of Shagee from Harar;
Ahiam son of Sharar from Harar;

Eliphelet son of Ahasbai from Maacah;
Eliam son of Ahithophel from Giloh;
Hezro from Carmel;
Paarai from Arba;
Igal son of Nathan from Zobah;
Bani from Gad;
Zelek from Ammon;
Naharai from Beeroth, the armor bearer of Joab son of Zeruiah;
Ira from Jattir;
Gareb from Jattir;
Uriah the Hittite.

There were thirty-seven in all.

Once again the anger of the LORD burned against Israel, and he caused David to harm them by taking a census. "Go and count the people of Israel and Judah," the LORD told him.

So the king said to Joab and the commanders of the army, "Take a census of all the tribes of Israel—from Dan in the north to Beersheba in the south—so I may know how many people there are."

But Joab replied to the king, "May the LORD your God let you live to see a hundred times as many people as there are now! But why, my lord the king, do you want to do this?"

But the king insisted that they take the census, so Joab and the commanders of the army went out to count the people of Israel. First they crossed the Jordan and camped at Aroer, south of the town in the valley, in the direction of Gad. Then they went on to Jazer, then to Gilead in the land of Tahtim-hodshi and to Dan-jaan and around to Sidon. Then they came to the fortress of Tyre, and all the towns of the Hivites and Canaanites. Finally, they went south to Judah as far as Beersheba.

Having gone through the entire land for nine months and twenty days, they returned to Jerusalem. Joab reported the number of people to the king. There were 800,000 capable warriors in Israel who could handle a sword, and 500,000 in Judah.

But after he had taken the census, David's conscience began to bother him. And he said to the LORD, "I have sinned greatly by taking this census. Please forgive my guilt, LORD, for doing this foolish thing."

The next morning the word of the LORD came to the prophet Gad, who was David's seer. This was the message: "Go and say to David, 'This is what the LORD says: I will give you three choices. Choose one of these punishments, and I will inflict it on you.'"

So Gad came to David and asked him, "Will you choose three years of famine throughout your land, three months of fleeing from your enemies, or three days of severe plague throughout your land? Think this over and decide what answer I should give the LORD who sent me."

"I'm in a desperate situation!" David replied to Gad. "But let us fall into the hands of the LORD, for his mercy is great. Do not let me fall into human hands."

So the LORD sent a plague upon Israel that morning, and it lasted for three days. A total of 70,000 people died throughout the nation, from Dan in the north to Beersheba in the south. But as the angel was preparing to destroy Jerusalem, the LORD relented and said to the death angel, "Stop! That is enough!" At that moment the angel of the LORD was by the threshing floor of Araunah the Jebusite.

When David saw the angel, he said to the LORD, "I am the one who has sinned and done wrong! But these people are as innocent as sheep—what have they done? Let your anger fall against me and my family."

That day Gad came to David and said to him, "Go up and build an altar to the LORD on the threshing floor of Araunah the Jebusite."

So David went up to do what the LORD had commanded him. When Araunah saw the king and his men coming toward him, he came and bowed before the king with his face to the ground. "Why have you come, my lord the king?" Araunah asked.

David replied, "I have come to buy your threshing floor and to build an altar to the LORD there, so that he will stop the plague."

"Take it, my lord the king, and use it as you wish," Araunah said to David. "Here are oxen for the burnt offering, and you can use the threshing boards and ox yokes for wood to build a fire on the altar. I will give it all to you, Your Majesty, and may the LORD your God accept your sacrifice."

But the king replied to Araunah, "No, I insist on buying it, for I will not present burnt offerings to the LORD my God that have cost me nothing." So David paid him fifty pieces of silver for the threshing floor and the oxen.

David built an altar there to the LORD and sacrificed burnt offerings and peace offerings. And the LORD answered his prayer for the land, and the plague on Israel was stopped.

+

King David was now very old, and no matter how many blankets covered him, he could not keep warm. So his advisers told him, "Let us find a young virgin to wait on you and look after you, my lord. She will lie in your arms and keep you warm."

So they searched throughout the land of Israel for a beautiful girl, and they found Abishag from Shunem and brought her to the king. The girl was very beautiful, and she looked after the king and took care of him. But the king had no sexual relations with her.

About that time David's son Adonijah, whose mother was Haggith, began boasting, "I will make myself king." So he provided himself with chariots and charioteers and recruited fifty men to run in front of him. Now his father, King David, had never disciplined him at any time, even by asking, "Why are you doing that?" Adonijah had been born next after Absalom, and he was very handsome.

Adonijah took Joab son of Zeruiah and Abiathar the priest into his confidence, and they agreed to help him become king. But Zadok the priest, Benaiah son of Jehoiada, Nathan the prophet, Shimei, Rei, and David's personal bodyguard refused to support Adonijah.

Adonijah went to the Stone of Zoheleth near the spring of En-rogel, where he sacrificed sheep, cattle, and fattened calves. He invited all his brothers—the other sons of King David—and all the royal officials of Judah. But he did not invite Nathan the prophet or Benaiah or the king's bodyguard or his brother Solomon.

Then Nathan went to Bathsheba, Solomon's mother, and asked her, "Haven't you heard that Haggith's son, Adonijah, has made himself king, and our lord David doesn't even know about it? If you want to save your own life and the life of your son Solomon, follow my advice. Go at once to King David and say to him, 'My lord the king, didn't you make a vow and say to me, "Your son Solomon will surely be the next king and will sit on my throne"? Why then has Adonijah become king?' And while you are still talking with him, I will come and confirm everything you have said."

So Bathsheba went into the king's bedroom. (He was very old now, and Abishag was taking care of him.) Bathsheba bowed down before the king.

"What can I do for you?" he asked her.

She replied, "My lord, you made a vow before the LORD your God when you said to me, 'Your son Solomon will surely be the next king and will sit on my throne.' But instead, Adonijah has made himself king, and my lord the king does not even know about it. He has sacrificed many cattle, fattened calves, and sheep, and he has invited all the king's sons to attend the celebration. He also invited Abiathar the priest and Joab, the commander of the army. But he did not invite your servant Solomon. And now, my lord the king, all Israel is waiting for you to announce who will become king after you. If you do not act, my son Solomon and I will be treated as criminals as soon as my lord the king has died."

While she was still speaking with the king, Nathan the prophet arrived. The king's officials told him, "Nathan the prophet is here to see you."

Nathan went in and bowed before the king with his face to the ground. Nathan asked, "My lord the king, have you decided that Adonijah will be the next king and that he will sit on your throne? Today he has sacrificed many cattle, fattened calves, and sheep, and he has invited all the king's sons to attend the celebration. He also invited the commanders of the army and Abiathar the priest. They are feasting and drinking with him and shouting, 'Long live King Adonijah!' But he did not invite me or Zadok the priest or Benaiah or your servant Solomon. Has my lord the king really done this without letting any of his officials know who should be the next king?"

King David responded, "Call Bathsheba!" So she came back in and stood before the king. And the king repeated his vow: "As surely as the LORD lives, who has rescued me from every danger, your son Solomon will be the next king and will sit on my throne this very day, just as I vowed to you before the LORD, the God of Israel."

Then Bathsheba bowed down with her face to the ground before the king and exclaimed, "May my lord King David live forever!"

Then King David ordered, "Call Zadok the priest, Nathan the prophet, and Benaiah son of Jehoiada." When they came into the king's presence, the king said to them, "Take Solomon and my officials down to Gihon Spring. Solomon is to ride on my own mule. There Zadok the priest and Nathan the prophet are to anoint him king over Israel. Blow the ram's horn and shout, 'Long live King Solomon!' Then escort him back here, and he will sit on my throne. He will succeed me as king, for I have appointed him to be ruler over Israel and Judah."

"Amen!" Benaiah son of Jehoiada replied. "May the LORD, the God of my lord the king, decree that it happen. And may the LORD be with Solomon as he has been with you, my lord the king, and may he make Solomon's reign even greater than yours!"

So Zadok the priest, Nathan the prophet, Benaiah son of Jehoiada, and the king's bodyguard took Solomon down to Gihon Spring, with Solomon riding on King David's own mule. There Zadok the priest took the flask of olive oil from the sacred tent and anointed Solomon with the oil. Then they sounded the ram's horn and all the people shouted, "Long live King Solomon!" And all the people followed Solomon into Jerusalem, playing flutes and shouting for joy. The celebration was so joyous and noisy that the earth shook with the sound.

Adonijah and his guests heard the celebrating and shouting just as they were finishing their banquet. When Joab heard the sound of the ram's horn, he asked, "What's going on? Why is the city in such an uproar?"

And while he was still speaking, Jonathan son of Abiathar the priest arrived. "Come in," Adonijah said to him, "for you are a good man. You must have good news."

"Not at all!" Jonathan replied. "Our lord King David has just declared Solomon king! The king sent him down to Gihon Spring with Zadok the priest, Nathan the prophet, and Benaiah son of Jehoiada, protected by the king's bodyguard. They had him ride on the king's own mule, and Zadok and Nathan have anointed him at Gihon Spring as the new king. They have just returned, and the whole city is celebrating and rejoicing. That's what all the noise is about. What's more, Solomon is now sitting on the royal throne as king. And all the royal officials have gone to King David and congratulated him, saying, 'May your God make Solomon's fame even greater than your own, and may Solomon's reign be even greater than yours!' Then the king bowed his head in worship as he lay in his bed, and he said, 'Praise the LORD, the God of Israel, who today has chosen a successor to sit on my throne while I am still alive to see it.'"

Then all of Adonijah's guests jumped up in panic from the banquet table and quickly scattered. Adonijah was afraid of Solomon, so he rushed to the sacred tent and grabbed on to the horns of the altar. Word soon reached Solomon that Adonijah had seized the horns of the altar in fear, and that he was pleading, "Let King Solomon swear today that he will not kill me!"

Solomon replied, "If he proves himself to be loyal, not a hair on his head will be touched. But if he makes trouble, he will die." So King Solomon summoned Adonijah, and they brought him down from the altar. He came and bowed respectfully before King Solomon, who dismissed him, saying, "Go on home."

As the time of King David's death approached, he gave this charge to his son Solomon:

"I am going where everyone on earth must someday go. Take courage and be a man. Observe the requirements of the LORD your God, and follow all his ways. Keep the decrees, commands, regulations, and laws written in the Law of Moses so that you will be successful in all you do and wherever you go. If you do this, then the LORD will keep the promise he made to me. He told me, 'If your descendants live as they should and follow me faithfully with all their heart and soul, one of them will always sit on the throne of Israel.'

"And there is something else. You know what Joab son of Zeruiah did to me when he murdered my two army commanders, Abner son of Ner and Amasa son of Jether. He pretended that it was an act of war, but it was done in a time of peace, staining his belt and sandals with innocent blood. Do with him what you think best, but don't let him grow old and go to his grave in peace.

"Be kind to the sons of Barzillai of Gilead. Make them permanent guests at your table, for they took care of me when I fled from your brother Absalom.

"And remember Shimei son of Gera, the man from Bahurim in Benjamin. He cursed me with a terrible curse as I was fleeing to Mahanaim. When he came down to meet me at the Jordan River, I swore by the LORD that I would not kill him. But that oath does not make him innocent. You are a wise man, and you will know how to arrange a bloody death for him."

Then David died and was buried with his ancestors in the City of David. David had reigned over Israel for forty years, seven of them in Hebron and thirty-three in Jerusalem.

+ + +

Solomon became king and sat on the throne of David his father, and his kingdom was firmly established.

One day Adonijah, whose mother was Haggith, came to see Bathsheba, Solomon's mother. "Have you come with peaceful intentions?" she asked him.

"Yes," he said, "I come in peace. In fact, I have a favor to ask of you."

"What is it?" she asked.

He replied, "As you know, the kingdom was rightfully mine; all Israel wanted me to be the next king. But the tables were turned, and the kingdom went to my brother instead; for that is the way the LORD wanted it. So now I have just one favor to ask of you. Please don't turn me down."

"What is it?" she asked.

He replied, "Speak to King Solomon on my behalf, for I know he will do anything you request. Ask him to let me marry Abishag, the girl from Shunem."

"All right," Bathsheba replied. "I will speak to the king for you."

So Bathsheba went to King Solomon to speak on Adonijah's behalf. The king rose from his throne to meet her, and he bowed down before her. When he sat down on his throne again, the king ordered that a throne be brought for his mother, and she sat at his right hand.

"I have one small request to make of you," she said. "I hope you won't turn me down."

"What is it, my mother?" he asked. "You know I won't refuse you."

"Then let your brother Adonijah marry Abishag, the girl from Shunem," she replied.

"How can you possibly ask me to give Abishag to Adonijah?" King Solomon demanded. "You might as well ask me to give him the kingdom! You know that he is my older brother, and that he has Abiathar the priest and Joab son of Zeruiah on his side."

Then King Solomon made a vow before the LORD: "May God strike me and even kill me if Adonijah has not sealed his fate with this request. The LORD has confirmed me and placed me on the throne of my father, David; he has established my dynasty as he promised. So as surely as the LORD lives, Adonijah will die this very day!" So King Solomon ordered Benaiah son of Jehoiada to execute him, and Adonijah was put to death.

Then the king said to Abiathar the priest, "Go back to your home in Anathoth. You deserve to die, but I will not kill you now, because you carried the Ark of the Sovereign LORD for David my father and you shared all his hardships." So Solomon deposed Abiathar from his position as priest of the LORD, thereby fulfilling the prophecy the LORD had given at Shiloh concerning the descendants of Eli.

Joab had not joined Absalom's earlier rebellion, but he had joined Adonijah's rebellion. So when Joab heard about Adonijah's death, he ran to the sacred tent of the LORD and grabbed on to the horns of the altar. When this was reported to King Solomon, he sent Benaiah son of Jehoiada to execute him.

Benaiah went to the sacred tent of the LORD and said to Joab, "The king orders you to come out!"

But Joab answered, "No, I will die here."

So Benaiah returned to the king and told him what Joab had said.

"Do as he said," the king replied. "Kill him there beside the altar and bury him. This will remove the guilt of Joab's senseless murders from me and from my father's family. The LORD will repay him for the murders of two men who were more righteous and better than he. For my father knew nothing about the deaths of Abner son of Ner, commander of the army of Israel, and of Amasa son of Jether, commander of the army of Judah. May their blood be on Joab and his descendants forever, and may the LORD grant peace forever to David, his descendants, his dynasty, and his throne."

So Benaiah son of Jehoiada returned to the sacred tent and killed Joab, and he was buried at his home in the wilderness. Then the king appointed Benaiah to command the army in place of Joab, and he installed Zadok the priest to take the place of Abiathar.

The king then sent for Shimei and told him, "Build a house here in Jerusalem and live there. But don't step outside the city to go anywhere else. On the day you so much as cross the Kidron Valley, you will surely die; and your blood will be on your own head."

Shimei replied, "Your sentence is fair; I will do whatever my lord the king commands." So Shimei lived in Jerusalem for a long time.

But three years later two of Shimei's slaves ran away to King Achish son of Maacah of Gath. When Shimei learned where they were, he saddled his donkey and went to Gath to search for them. When he found them, he brought them back to Jerusalem.

Solomon heard that Shimei had left Jerusalem and had gone to Gath and returned. So the king sent for Shimei and demanded, "Didn't I make you swear by the LORD and warn you not to go anywhere else or you would surely die? And you replied, 'The sentence is fair; I will do as you say.' Then why haven't you kept your oath to the LORD and obeyed my command?"

The king also said to Shimei, "You certainly remember all the wicked things you did to my father, David. May the LORD now bring that evil on your own head. But may I, King Solomon, receive the LORD's blessings, and may one of David's descendants always sit on this throne in the presence of the LORD." Then, at the king's command, Benaiah son of Jehoiada took Shimei outside and killed him.

So the kingdom was now firmly in Solomon's grip.

Solomon made an alliance with Pharaoh, the king of Egypt, and married one of his daughters. He brought her to live in the City of David until he could finish building his palace and the Temple of the LORD and the wall around the city. At that time the people of Israel sacrificed their offerings at local places of worship, for a temple honoring the name of the LORD had not yet been built.

Solomon loved the LORD and followed all the decrees of his father, David, except that Solomon, too, offered sacrifices and burned incense at the local places of worship. The most important of these places of worship was at Gibeon, so the king went there and sacrificed 1,000 burnt offerings. That night the LORD appeared to Solomon in a dream, and God said, "What do you want? Ask, and I will give it to you!"

Solomon replied, "You showed great and faithful love to your servant my father, David, because he was honest and true and faithful to you. And you have continued to show this great and faithful love to him today by giving him a son to sit on his throne.

"Now, O LORD my God, you have made me king instead of my father, David, but I am like a little child who doesn't know his way around. And here I am in the midst of your own chosen people, a nation so great and numerous they cannot be counted! Give me an understanding heart so that I can govern your people well and know the difference between right and wrong. For who by himself is able to govern this great people of yours?"

The Lord was pleased that Solomon had asked for wisdom. So God replied, "Because you have asked for wisdom in governing my people with justice and have not asked for a long life or wealth or the death of your enemies—I will give you what you asked for! I will give you a wise and understanding heart such as no one else has had or ever will have! And I will also give you what you did not ask for—riches and fame! No other king in all the world will be compared to you for the rest of your life! And if you follow me and obey my decrees and my commands as your father, David, did, I will give you a long life."

Then Solomon woke up and realized it had been a dream. He returned to Jerusalem and stood before the Ark of the Lord's Covenant, where he sacrificed burnt offerings and peace offerings. Then he invited all his officials to a great banquet.

Some time later two prostitutes came to the king to have an argument settled. "Please, my lord," one of them began, "this woman and I live in the same house. I gave birth to a baby while she was with me in the house. Three days later this woman also had a baby. We were alone; there were only two of us in the house.

"But her baby died during the night when she rolled over on it. Then she got up in the night and took my son from beside me while I was asleep. She laid her dead child in my arms and took mine to sleep beside her. And in the morning when I tried to nurse my son, he was dead! But when I looked more closely in the morning light, I saw that it wasn't my son at all."

Then the other woman interrupted, "It certainly was your son, and the living child is mine."

"No," the first woman said, "the living child is mine, and the dead one is yours." And so they argued back and forth before the king.

Then the king said, "Let's get the facts straight. Both of you claim the living child is yours, and each says that the dead one belongs to the other. All right, bring me a sword." So a sword was brought to the king.

Then he said, "Cut the living child in two, and give half to one woman and half to the other!"

Then the woman who was the real mother of the living child, and who loved him very much, cried out, "Oh no, my lord! Give her the child— please do not kill him!"

But the other woman said, "All right, he will be neither yours nor mine; divide him between us!"

Then the king said, "Do not kill the child, but give him to the woman who wants him to live, for she is his mother!"

When all Israel heard the king's decision, the people were in awe of the king, for they saw the wisdom God had given him for rendering justice.

+

King Solomon now ruled over all Israel, and these were his high officials:

Azariah son of Zadok was the priest.

Elihoreph and Ahijah, the sons of Shisha, were court secretaries.

Jehoshaphat son of Ahilud was the royal historian.

Benaiah son of Jehoiada was commander of the army.

Zadok and Abiathar were priests.

Azariah son of Nathan was in charge of the district governors.

Zabud son of Nathan, a priest, was a trusted adviser to the king.

Ahishar was manager of the palace property.

Adoniram son of Abda was in charge of forced labor.

Solomon also had twelve district governors who were over all Israel. They were responsible for providing food for the king's household. Each of them arranged provisions for one month of the year. These are the names of the twelve governors:

Ben-hur, in the hill country of Ephraim.

Ben-deker, in Makaz, Shaalbim, Beth-shemesh, and Elon-bethhanan.

Ben-hesed, in Arubboth, including Socoh and all the land of Hepher.

Ben-abinadab, in all of Naphoth-dor. (He was married to Taphath, one of Solomon's daughters.)

Baana son of Ahilud, in Taanach and Megiddo, all of Beth-shan near Zarethan below Jezreel, and all the territory from Beth-shan to Abel-meholah and over to Jokmeam.

Ben-geber, in Ramoth-gilead, including the Towns of Jair (named for Jair of the tribe of Manasseh) in Gilead, and in the Argob region of Bashan, including sixty large fortified towns with bronze bars on their gates.

Ahinadab son of Iddo, in Mahanaim.

Ahimaaz, in Naphtali. (He was married to Basemath, another of Solomon's daughters.)

Baana son of Hushai, in Asher and in Aloth.

Jehoshaphat son of Paruah, in Issachar.

Shimei son of Ela, in Benjamin.

Geber son of Uri, in the land of Gilead, including the territories of King Sihon of the Amorites and King Og of Bashan.

There was also one governor over the land of Judah.

The people of Judah and Israel were as numerous as the sand on the seashore. They were very contented, with plenty to eat and drink. Solomon ruled over all the kingdoms from the Euphrates River in the north to the land of the Philistines and the border of Egypt in the south. The conquered peoples of those lands sent tribute money to Solomon and continued to serve him throughout his lifetime.

The daily food requirements for Solomon's palace were 150 bushels of choice flour and 300 bushels of meal; also 10 oxen from the fattening pens, 20 pasture-fed cattle, 100 sheep or goats, as well as deer, gazelles, roe deer, and choice poultry.

Solomon's dominion extended over all the kingdoms west of the Euphrates River, from Tiphsah to Gaza. And there was peace on all his borders. During the lifetime of Solomon, all of Judah and Israel lived in peace and safety. And from Dan in the north to Beersheba in the south, each family had its own home and garden.

Solomon had 4,000 stalls for his chariot horses, and he had 12,000 horses.

The district governors faithfully provided food for King Solomon and his court; each made sure nothing was lacking during the month assigned to him. They also brought the necessary barley and straw for the royal horses in the stables.

God gave Solomon very great wisdom and understanding, and knowledge as vast as the sands of the seashore. In fact, his wisdom exceeded that of all the wise men of the East and the wise men of Egypt. He was wiser than anyone else, including Ethan the Ezrahite and the sons of Mahol—Heman, Calcol, and Darda. His fame spread throughout all the surrounding nations. He composed some 3,000 proverbs and wrote 1,005 songs. He could speak with authority about all kinds of plants, from the great cedar of Lebanon to the tiny hyssop that grows from cracks in a wall. He could also speak about animals, birds, small creatures, and fish. And kings from every nation sent their ambassadors to listen to the wisdom of Solomon.

King Hiram of Tyre had always been a loyal friend of David. When Hiram learned that David's son Solomon was the new king of Israel, he sent ambassadors to congratulate him.

Then Solomon sent this message back to Hiram:

"You know that my father, David, was not able to build a Temple to honor the name of the LORD his God because of the many wars waged against him by surrounding nations. He could not build until the LORD gave him victory over all his enemies. But now the LORD my God has given me peace on every side; I have no enemies, and all is well. So I am planning to build a Temple to honor the name of the LORD my God, just as he had instructed my father, David. For the LORD told him, 'Your son, whom I will place on your throne, will build the Temple to honor my name.'

"Therefore, please command that cedars from Lebanon be cut for me. Let my men work alongside yours, and I will pay your men whatever wages you ask. As you know, there is no one among us who can cut timber like you Sidonians!"

When Hiram received Solomon's message, he was very pleased and said, "Praise the LORD today for giving David a wise son to be king of the great nation of Israel." Then he sent this reply to Solomon:

"I have received your message, and I will supply all the cedar and cypress timber you need. My servants will bring the logs from the Lebanon mountains to the Mediterranean Sea and make them into rafts and float them along the coast to whatever place you choose. Then we will break the rafts apart so you can carry the logs away. You can pay me by supplying me with food for my household."

So Hiram supplied as much cedar and cypress timber as Solomon desired. In return, Solomon sent him an annual payment of 100,000 bushels of wheat for his household and 110,000 gallons of pure olive oil. So the LORD gave wisdom to Solomon, just as he had promised. And Hiram and Solomon made a formal alliance of peace.

Then King Solomon conscripted a labor force of 30,000 men from all Israel. He sent them to Lebanon in shifts, 10,000 every month, so that each man would be one month in Lebanon and two months at home. Adoniram was in charge of this labor force. Solomon also had 70,000 common laborers, 80,000 quarry workers in the hill country, and 3,600 foremen to supervise the work. At the king's command, they quarried large blocks of high-quality stone and shaped them to make the foundation of the Temple. Men from the city of Gebal helped Solomon's and Hiram's builders prepare the timber and stone for the Temple.

+

It was in midspring, in the month of Ziv, during the fourth year of Solomon's reign, that he began to construct the Temple of the LORD. This was 480 years after the people of Israel were rescued from their slavery in the land of Egypt.

The Temple that King Solomon built for the LORD was 90 feet long, 30 feet wide, and 45 feet high. The entry room at the front of the Temple was 30 feet wide, running across the entire width of the Temple. It projected outward 15 feet from the front of the Temple. Solomon also made narrow recessed windows throughout the Temple.

He built a complex of rooms against the outer walls of the Temple, all the way around the sides and rear of the building. The complex was three stories high, the bottom floor being 7½ feet wide, the second floor 9 feet wide, and the top floor 10½ feet wide. The rooms were connected to the walls of the Temple by beams resting on ledges built out from the wall. So the beams were not inserted into the walls themselves.

The stones used in the construction of the Temple were finished at the quarry, so there was no sound of hammer, ax, or any other iron tool at the building site.

The entrance to the bottom floor was on the south side of the Temple. There were winding stairs going up to the second floor, and another flight of stairs between the second and third floors. After completing the Temple structure, Solomon put in a ceiling made of cedar beams and planks. As already stated, he built a complex of rooms along the sides of the building, attached to the Temple walls by cedar timbers. Each story of the complex was 7½ feet high.

Then the Lord gave this message to Solomon: "Concerning this Temple you are building, if you keep all my decrees and regulations and obey all my commands, I will fulfill through you the promise I made to your father, David. I will live among the Israelites and will never abandon my people Israel."

So Solomon finished building the Temple. The entire inside, from floor to ceiling, was paneled with wood. He paneled the walls and ceilings with cedar, and he used planks of cypress for the floors. He partitioned off an inner sanctuary—the Most Holy Place—at the far end of the Temple. It was 30 feet deep and was paneled with cedar from floor to ceiling. The main room of the Temple, outside the Most Holy Place, was 60 feet long. Cedar paneling completely covered the stone walls throughout the Temple, and the paneling was decorated with carvings of gourds and open flowers.

He prepared the inner sanctuary at the far end of the Temple, where the Ark of the Lord's Covenant would be placed. This inner sanctuary was 30 feet long, 30 feet wide, and 30 feet high. He overlaid the inside with solid gold. He also overlaid the altar made of cedar. Then Solomon overlaid the rest of the Temple's interior with solid gold, and he made gold chains to protect the entrance to the Most Holy Place. So he finished overlaying the entire Temple with gold, including the altar that belonged to the Most Holy Place.

He made two cherubim of wild olive wood, each 15 feet tall, and placed them in the inner sanctuary. The wingspan of each of the cherubim was 15 feet, each wing being 7½ feet long. The two cherubim were identical in shape and size; each was 15 feet tall. He placed them side by side in the inner sanctuary of the Temple. Their outspread wings reached from wall to wall, while their inner wings touched at the center of the room. He overlaid the two cherubim with gold.

He decorated all the walls of the inner sanctuary and the main room with carvings of cherubim, palm trees, and open flowers. He overlaid the floor in both rooms with gold.

For the entrance to the inner sanctuary, he made double doors of wild olive wood with five-sided doorposts. These double doors were decorated with carvings of cherubim, palm trees, and open flowers. The doors, including the decorations of cherubim and palm trees, were overlaid with gold.

Then he made four-sided doorposts of wild olive wood for the entrance to the Temple. There were two folding doors of cypress wood, and each door was hinged to fold back upon itself. These doors were decorated with carvings of cherubim, palm trees, and open flowers—all overlaid evenly with gold.

The walls of the inner courtyard were built so that there was one layer of cedar beams between every three layers of finished stone.

The foundation of the LORD's Temple was laid in midspring, in the month of Ziv, during the fourth year of Solomon's reign. The entire building was completed in every detail by midautumn, in the month of Bul, during the eleventh year of his reign. So it took seven years to build the Temple.

Solomon also built a palace for himself, and it took him thirteen years to complete the construction.

One of Solomon's buildings was called the Palace of the Forest of Lebanon. It was 150 feet long, 75 feet wide, and 45 feet high. There were four rows of cedar pillars, and great cedar beams rested on the pillars. The hall had a cedar roof. Above the beams on the pillars were forty-five side rooms, arranged in three tiers of fifteen each. On each end of the long hall were three rows of windows facing each other. All the doorways and doorposts had rectangular frames and were arranged in sets of three, facing each other.

Solomon also built the Hall of Pillars, which was 75 feet long and 45 feet wide. There was a porch in front, along with a canopy supported by pillars.

Solomon also built the throne room, known as the Hall of Justice, where he sat to hear legal matters. It was paneled with cedar from floor to ceiling. Solomon's living quarters surrounded a courtyard behind this hall, and they were constructed the same way. He also built similar living quarters for Pharaoh's daughter, whom he had married.

From foundation to eaves, all these buildings were built from huge blocks of high-quality stone, cut with saws and trimmed to exact measure on all sides. Some of the huge foundation stones were 15 feet long, and some were 12 feet long. The blocks of high-quality stone used in the walls were also cut to measure, and cedar beams were also used. The walls of the great courtyard were built so that there was one layer of cedar beams between every three layers of finished stone, just like the walls of the inner courtyard of the Lord's Temple with its entry room.

King Solomon then asked for a man named Huram to come from Tyre. He was half Israelite, since his mother was a widow from the tribe of Naphtali, and his father had been a craftsman in bronze from Tyre. Huram was extremely skillful and talented in any work in bronze, and he came to do all the metal work for King Solomon.

Huram cast two bronze pillars, each 27 feet tall and 18 feet in circumference. For the tops of the pillars he cast bronze capitals, each 7½ feet tall. Each capital was decorated with seven sets of latticework and interwoven chains. He also encircled the latticework with two rows of pomegranates to decorate the capitals over the pillars. The capitals on the columns inside the entry room were shaped like water lilies, and they were six feet tall. The capitals on the two pillars had 200 pomegranates in two rows around them, beside the rounded surface next to the latticework. Huram set the pillars at the entrance of the Temple, one toward the south and one toward the north. He named the one on the south Jakin, and the one on the north Boaz. The capitals on the pillars were shaped like water lilies. And so the work on the pillars was finished.

Then Huram cast a great round basin, 15 feet across from rim to rim, called the Sea. It was 7½ feet deep and about 45 feet in circumference. It was encircled just below its rim by two rows of decorative gourds. There were about six gourds per foot all the way around, and they were cast as part of the basin.

The Sea was placed on a base of twelve bronze oxen, all facing outward. Three faced north, three faced west, three faced south, and three faced east, and the Sea rested on them. The walls of the Sea were about three inches thick, and its rim flared out like a cup and resembled a water lily blossom. It could hold about 11,000 gallons of water.

Huram also made ten bronze water carts, each 6 feet long, 6 feet wide, and 4½ feet tall. They were constructed with side panels braced with crossbars. Both the panels and the crossbars were decorated with carved lions, oxen, and cherubim. Above and below the lions and oxen were wreath decorations. Each of these carts had four bronze wheels and bronze axles. There were supporting posts for the bronze basins at the corners of the carts; these supports were decorated on each side with carvings of wreaths. The top of each cart had a rounded frame for the basin. It projected 1½ feet above the cart's top like a round pedestal, and its opening was 2¼ feet across; it was decorated on the outside with carvings of wreaths. The panels of the carts were square, not round. Under the panels were four wheels that were connected to axles that had been cast as one unit with the cart. The wheels were 2¼ feet in diameter and were similar to chariot wheels. The axles, spokes, rims, and hubs were all cast from molten bronze.

There were handles at each of the four corners of the carts, and these, too, were cast as one unit with the cart. Around the top of each cart was a rim nine inches wide. The corner supports and side panels were cast as one unit with the cart. Carvings of cherubim, lions, and palm trees decorated the panels and corner supports wherever there was room, and there were wreaths all around. All ten water carts were the same size and were made alike, for each was cast from the same mold.

Huram also made ten smaller bronze basins, one for each cart. Each basin was six feet across and could hold 220 gallons of water. He set five water carts on the south side of the Temple and five on the north side. The great bronze basin called the Sea was placed near the southeast corner of the Temple. He also made the necessary washbasins, shovels, and bowls.

So at last Huram completed everything King Solomon had assigned him to make for the Temple of the LORD:

the two pillars;
the two bowl-shaped capitals on top of the pillars;
the two networks of interwoven chains that decorated the capitals;
the 400 pomegranates that hung from the chains on the capitals (two
    rows of pomegranates for each of the chain networks that decorated
    the capitals on top of the pillars);
the ten water carts holding the ten basins;
the Sea and the twelve oxen under it;
the ash buckets, the shovels, and the bowls.

Huram made all these things of burnished bronze for the Temple of the LORD, just as King Solomon had directed. The king had them cast in clay molds in the Jordan Valley between Succoth and Zarethan. Solomon did not weigh all these things because there were so many; the weight of the bronze could not be measured.

Solomon also made all the furnishings of the Temple of the LORD:

the gold altar;
the gold table for the Bread of the Presence;
the lampstands of solid gold, five on the south and five on the north,
    in front of the Most Holy Place;

the flower decorations, lamps, and tongs—all of gold;

the small bowls, lamp snuffers, bowls, ladles, and incense burners—all of solid gold;

the doors for the entrances to the Most Holy Place and the main room of the Temple, with their fronts overlaid with gold.

So King Solomon finished all his work on the Temple of the LORD. Then he brought all the gifts his father, David, had dedicated—the silver, the gold, and the various articles—and he stored them in the treasuries of the LORD's Temple.

+

Solomon then summoned to Jerusalem the elders of Israel and all the heads of the tribes—the leaders of the ancestral families of the Israelites. They were to bring the Ark of the LORD's Covenant to the Temple from its location in the City of David, also known as Zion. So all the men of Israel assembled before King Solomon at the annual Festival of Shelters, which is held in early autumn in the month of Ethanim.

When all the elders of Israel arrived, the priests picked up the Ark. The priests and Levites brought up the Ark of the LORD along with the special tent and all the sacred items that had been in it. There, before the Ark, King Solomon and the entire community of Israel sacrificed so many sheep, goats, and cattle that no one could keep count!

Then the priests carried the Ark of the LORD's Covenant into the inner sanctuary of the Temple—the Most Holy Place—and placed it beneath the wings of the cherubim. The cherubim spread their wings over the Ark, forming a canopy over the Ark and its carrying poles. These poles were so long that their ends could be seen from the Holy Place, which is in front of the Most Holy Place, but not from the outside. They are still there to this day. Nothing was in the Ark except the two stone tablets that Moses had placed in it at Mount Sinai, where the LORD made a covenant with the people of Israel when they left the land of Egypt.

When the priests came out of the Holy Place, a thick cloud filled the Temple of the LORD. The priests could not continue their service because of the cloud, for the glorious presence of the LORD filled the Temple of the LORD.

Then Solomon prayed, "O LORD, you have said that you would live in a thick cloud of darkness. Now I have built a glorious Temple for you, a place where you can live forever!"

Then the king turned around to the entire community of Israel standing before him and gave this blessing: "Praise the LORD, the God of Israel, who has kept the promise he made to my father, David. For he told my father, 'From the day I brought my people Israel out of Egypt, I have never chosen a city among any of the tribes of Israel as the place where a Temple should be built to honor my name. But I have chosen David to be king over my people Israel.'"

Then Solomon said, "My father, David, wanted to build this Temple to honor the name of the LORD, the God of Israel. But the LORD told him, 'You wanted to build the Temple to honor my name. Your intention is good, but you are not the one to do it. One of your own sons will build the Temple to honor me.'

"And now the LORD has fulfilled the promise he made, for I have become king in my father's place, and now I sit on the throne of Israel, just as the LORD promised. I have built this Temple to honor the name of the LORD, the God of Israel. And I have prepared a place there for the Ark, which contains the covenant that the LORD made with our ancestors when he brought them out of Egypt."

Then Solomon stood before the altar of the LORD in front of the entire community of Israel. He lifted his hands toward heaven, and he prayed,

"O LORD, God of Israel, there is no God like you in all of heaven above or on the earth below. You keep your covenant and show unfailing love to all who walk before you in wholehearted devotion. You have kept your promise to your servant David, my father. You made that promise with your own mouth, and with your own hands you have fulfilled it today.

"And now, O LORD, God of Israel, carry out the additional promise you made to your servant David, my father. For you said to him, 'If your descendants guard their behavior and faithfully follow me as you have done, one of them will always sit on the throne of Israel.' Now, O God of Israel, fulfill this promise to your servant David, my father.

"But will God really live on earth? Why, even the highest heavens cannot contain you. How much less this Temple I have built! Nevertheless, listen to my prayer and my plea, O LORD my God. Hear the cry and the prayer that your servant is making to you today. May you watch over this Temple night and day, this place where you have said, 'My name will be there.' May you always hear the prayers I make toward this place. May you hear the humble and earnest requests from me and your people Israel when we pray toward this place. Yes, hear us from heaven where you live, and when you hear, forgive.

"If someone wrongs another person and is required to take an oath of innocence in front of your altar in this Temple, then hear from heaven and judge between your servants—the accuser and the accused. Punish the guilty as they deserve. Acquit the innocent because of their innocence.

"If your people Israel are defeated by their enemies because they have sinned against you, and if they turn to you and acknowledge your name and pray to you here in this Temple, then hear from heaven and forgive the sin of your people Israel and return them to this land you gave their ancestors.

"If the skies are shut up and there is no rain because your people have sinned against you, and if they pray toward this Temple and acknowledge your name and turn from their sins because you have punished them, then hear from heaven and forgive the sins of your servants, your people Israel. Teach them to follow the right path, and send rain on your land that you have given to your people as their special possession.

"If there is a famine in the land or a plague or crop disease or attacks of locusts or caterpillars, or if your people's enemies are in the land besieging their towns—whatever disaster or disease there is—and if your people Israel pray about their troubles, raising their hands toward this Temple, then hear from heaven where you live, and forgive. Give your people what their actions deserve, for you alone know each human heart. Then they will fear you as long as they live in the land you gave to our ancestors.

"In the future, foreigners who do not belong to your people Israel will hear of you. They will come from distant lands because of your name, for they will hear of your great name and your strong hand and your powerful arm. And when they pray toward this Temple, then hear from heaven where you live, and grant what they ask of you. In this way, all the people of the earth will come to know and fear you, just as your own people Israel do. They, too, will know that this Temple I have built honors your name.

"If your people go out where you send them to fight their enemies, and if they pray to the LORD by turning toward this city you have chosen and toward this Temple I have built to honor your name, then hear their prayers from heaven and uphold their cause.

"If they sin against you—and who has never sinned?—you might become angry with them and let their enemies conquer them and take them captive to their land far away or near. But in that land of exile, they might turn to you in repentance and pray, 'We have sinned, done evil, and acted wickedly.' If they turn to you with their whole heart and soul in the land of their enemies and pray toward the land you gave to their ancestors—toward this city you have chosen, and toward this Temple I have built to honor your name—then hear their prayers and their petition from heaven where you live, and uphold their cause. Forgive your people who have sinned against you. Forgive all the offenses they have committed against you. Make their captors merciful to them, for they are your people—your special possession— whom you brought out of the iron-smelting furnace of Egypt.

"May your eyes be open to my requests and to the requests of your people Israel. May you hear and answer them whenever they cry out to you. For when you brought our ancestors out of Egypt, O Sovereign LORD, you told your servant Moses that you had set Israel apart from all the nations of the earth to be your own special possession."

When Solomon finished making these prayers and petitions to the LORD, he stood up in front of the altar of the LORD, where he had been kneeling with his hands raised toward heaven. He stood and in a loud voice blessed the entire congregation of Israel:

"Praise the LORD who has given rest to his people Israel, just as he promised. Not one word has failed of all the wonderful promises he gave through his servant Moses. May the LORD our God be with us as he was with our ancestors; may he never leave us or abandon us. May he give us the desire to do his will in everything and to obey all the commands, decrees, and regulations that he gave our ancestors. And may these words that I have prayed in the presence of the LORD be before him constantly, day and night, so that the LORD our God may give justice to me and to his people Israel, according to each day's needs. Then people all over the earth will know that the LORD alone is God and there is no other. And may you be completely faithful to the LORD our God. May you always obey his decrees and commands, just as you are doing today."

Then the king and all Israel with him offered sacrifices to the LORD. Solomon offered to the LORD a peace offering of 22,000 cattle and 120,000 sheep and goats. And so the king and all the people of Israel dedicated the Temple of the LORD.

That same day the king consecrated the central area of the courtyard in front of the LORD's Temple. He offered burnt offerings, grain offerings, and the fat of peace offerings there, because the bronze altar in the LORD's presence was too small to hold all the burnt offerings, grain offerings, and the fat of the peace offerings.

Then Solomon and all Israel celebrated the Festival of Shelters in the presence of the LORD our God. A large congregation had gathered from as far away as Lebo-hamath in the north and the Brook of Egypt in the south. The celebration went on for fourteen days in all—seven days for the dedication of the altar and seven days for the Festival of Shelters. After the festival was over, Solomon sent the people home. They blessed the king and went to their homes joyful and glad because the LORD had been good to his servant David and to his people Israel.

So Solomon finished building the Temple of the LORD, as well as the royal palace. He completed everything he had planned to do. Then the LORD appeared to Solomon a second time, as he had done before at Gibeon. The LORD said to him,

> "I have heard your prayer and your petition. I have set this Temple apart to be holy—this place you have built where my name will be honored forever. I will always watch over it, for it is dear to my heart.
>
> "As for you, if you will follow me with integrity and godliness, as David your father did, obeying all my commands, decrees, and regulations, then I will establish the throne of your dynasty over Israel forever. For I made this promise to your father, David: 'One of your descendants will always sit on the throne of Israel.'
>
> "But if you or your descendants abandon me and disobey the commands and decrees I have given you, and if you serve and worship other gods, then I will uproot Israel from this land that I have given them. I will reject this Temple that I have made holy to honor my name. I will make Israel an object of mockery and ridicule among the nations. And though this Temple is impressive now, all who pass by will be appalled and will gasp in horror. They will ask, 'Why did the LORD do such terrible things to this land and to this Temple?'
>
> "And the answer will be, 'Because his people abandoned the LORD their God, who brought their ancestors out of Egypt, and they worshiped other gods instead and bowed down to them. That is why the LORD has brought all these disasters on them.'"

+

It took Solomon twenty years to build the LORD's Temple and his own royal palace. At the end of that time, he gave twenty towns in the land of Galilee to King Hiram of Tyre. (Hiram had previously provided all the cedar and cypress timber and gold that Solomon had requested.) But when Hiram came from Tyre to see the towns Solomon had given him, he was not at all pleased with them. "What kind of towns are these, my brother?" he asked. So Hiram called that area Cabul (which means "worthless"), as it is still known today. Nevertheless, Hiram paid Solomon 9,000 pounds of gold.

This is the account of the forced labor that King Solomon conscripted to build the LORD's Temple, the royal palace, the supporting terraces, the wall of Jerusalem, and the cities of Hazor, Megiddo, and Gezer. (Pharaoh, the king of Egypt, had attacked and captured Gezer, killing the Canaanite population and burning it down. He gave the city to his daughter as a wedding gift when she married Solomon. So Solomon rebuilt the city of Gezer.) He also built up the towns of Lower Beth-horon, Baalath, and Tamar in the wilderness within his land. He built towns as supply centers and constructed towns where his chariots and horses could be stationed. He built everything he desired in Jerusalem and Lebanon and throughout his entire realm.

There were still some people living in the land who were not Israelites, including Amorites, Hittites, Perizzites, Hivites, and Jebusites. These were descendants of the nations whom the people of Israel had not completely destroyed. So Solomon conscripted them as slaves, and they serve as forced laborers to this day. But Solomon did not conscript any of the Israelites for forced labor. Instead, he assigned them to serve as fighting men, government officials, officers and captains in his army, commanders of his chariots, and charioteers. Solomon appointed 550 of them to supervise the people working on his various projects.

Solomon moved his wife, Pharaoh's daughter, from the City of David to the new palace he had built for her. Then he constructed the supporting terraces.

Three times each year Solomon presented burnt offerings and peace offerings on the altar he had built for the LORD. He also burned incense to the LORD. And so he finished the work of building the Temple.

King Solomon also built a fleet of ships at Ezion-geber, a port near Elath in the land of Edom, along the shore of the Red Sea. Hiram sent experienced crews of sailors to sail the ships with Solomon's men. They sailed to Ophir and brought back to Solomon some sixteen tons of gold.

When the queen of Sheba heard of Solomon's fame, which brought honor to the name of the LORD, she came to test him with hard questions. She arrived in Jerusalem with a large group of attendants and a great caravan of camels loaded with spices, large quantities of gold, and precious jewels. When she met with Solomon, she talked with him about everything she had on her mind. Solomon had answers for all her questions; nothing was too hard for the king to explain to her. When the queen of Sheba realized how very wise Solomon was, and when she saw the palace he had built, she was overwhelmed. She was also amazed at the food on his tables, the organization of his officials and their splendid clothing, the cup-bearers, and the burnt offerings Solomon made at the Temple of the LORD.

She exclaimed to the king, "Everything I heard in my country about your achievements and wisdom is true! I didn't believe what was said until I arrived here and saw it with my own eyes. In fact, I had not heard the half of it! Your wisdom and prosperity are far beyond what I was told. How happy your people must be! What a privilege for your officials to stand here day after day, listening to your wisdom! Praise the LORD your God, who delights in you and has placed you on the throne of Israel. Because of the LORD's eternal love for Israel, he has made you king so you can rule with justice and righteousness."

Then she gave the king a gift of 9,000 pounds of gold, great quantities of spices, and precious jewels. Never again were so many spices brought in as those the queen of Sheba gave to King Solomon.

(In addition, Hiram's ships brought gold from Ophir, and they also brought rich cargoes of red sandalwood and precious jewels. The king used the sandalwood to make railings for the Temple of the LORD and the royal palace, and to construct lyres and harps for the musicians. Never before or since has there been such a supply of sandalwood.)

King Solomon gave the queen of Sheba whatever she asked for, besides all the customary gifts he had so generously given. Then she and all her attendants returned to their own land.

Each year Solomon received about 25 tons of gold. This did not include the additional revenue he received from merchants and traders, all the kings of Arabia, and the governors of the land.

King Solomon made 200 large shields of hammered gold, each weighing more than fifteen pounds. He also made 300 smaller shields of hammered gold, each weighing nearly four pounds. The king placed these shields in the Palace of the Forest of Lebanon.

Then the king made a huge throne, decorated with ivory and overlaid with fine gold. The throne had six steps and a rounded back. There were armrests on both sides of the seat, and the figure of a lion stood on each side of the throne. There were also twelve other lions, one standing on each end of the six steps. No other throne in all the world could be compared with it!

All of King Solomon's drinking cups were solid gold, as were all the utensils in the Palace of the Forest of Lebanon. They were not made of silver, for silver was considered worthless in Solomon's day!

The king had a fleet of trading ships of Tarshish that sailed with Hiram's fleet. Once every three years the ships returned, loaded with gold, silver, ivory, apes, and peacocks.

So King Solomon became richer and wiser than any other king on earth. People from every nation came to consult him and to hear the wisdom

God had given him. Year after year everyone who visited brought him gifts of silver and gold, clothing, weapons, spices, horses, and mules.

Solomon built up a huge force of chariots and horses. He had 1,400 chariots and 12,000 horses. He stationed some of them in the chariot cities and some near him in Jerusalem. The king made silver as plentiful in Jerusalem as stone. And valuable cedar timber was as common as the sycamore-fig trees that grow in the foothills of Judah. Solomon's horses were imported from Egypt and from Cilicia; the king's traders acquired them from Cilicia at the standard price. At that time chariots from Egypt could be purchased for 600 pieces of silver, and horses for 150 pieces of silver. They were then exported to the kings of the Hittites and the kings of Aram.

+

Now King Solomon loved many foreign women. Besides Pharaoh's daughter, he married women from Moab, Ammon, Edom, Sidon, and from among the Hittites. The LORD had clearly instructed the people of Israel, "You must not marry them, because they will turn your hearts to their gods." Yet Solomon insisted on loving them anyway. He had 700 wives of royal birth and 300 concubines. And in fact, they did turn his heart away from the LORD.

In Solomon's old age, they turned his heart to worship other gods instead of being completely faithful to the LORD his God, as his father, David, had been. Solomon worshiped Ashtoreth, the goddess of the Sidonians, and Molech, the detestable god of the Ammonites. In this way, Solomon did what was evil in the LORD's sight; he refused to follow the LORD completely, as his father, David, had done.

On the Mount of Olives, east of Jerusalem, he even built a pagan shrine for Chemosh, the detestable god of Moab, and another for Molech, the detestable god of the Ammonites. Solomon built such shrines for all his foreign wives to use for burning incense and sacrificing to their gods.

The LORD was very angry with Solomon, for his heart had turned away from the LORD, the God of Israel, who had appeared to him twice. He had warned Solomon specifically about worshiping other gods, but Solomon did not listen to the LORD's command. So now the LORD said to him, "Since you have not kept my covenant and have disobeyed my decrees, I will surely tear the kingdom away from you and give it to one of your servants. But for the sake of your father, David, I will not do this while you are still alive. I will take the kingdom away from your son. And even so, I will not take away the entire kingdom; I will let him be king of one tribe, for the sake of my servant David and for the sake of Jerusalem, my chosen city."

Then the LORD raised up Hadad the Edomite, a member of Edom's royal family, to be Solomon's adversary. Years before, David had defeated Edom. Joab, his army commander, had stayed to bury some of the Israelite soldiers who had died in battle. While there, they killed every male in Edom. Joab and the army of Israel had stayed there for six months, killing them.

But Hadad and a few of his father's royal officials escaped and headed for Egypt. (Hadad was just a boy at the time.) They set out from Midian and went to Paran, where others joined them. Then they traveled to Egypt and went to Pharaoh, who gave them a home, food, and some land. Pharaoh grew very fond of Hadad, and he gave him his wife's sister in marriage— the sister of Queen Tahpenes. She bore him a son named Genubath. Tahpenes raised him in Pharaoh's palace among Pharaoh's own sons.

When the news reached Hadad in Egypt that David and his commander Joab were both dead, he said to Pharaoh, "Let me return to my own country."

"Why?" Pharaoh asked him. "What do you lack here that makes you want to go home?"

"Nothing," he replied. "But even so, please let me return home."

God also raised up Rezon son of Eliada as Solomon's adversary. Rezon had fled from his master, King Hadadezer of Zobah, and had become the leader of a gang of rebels. After David conquered Hadadezer, Rezon and his men fled to Damascus, where he became king. Rezon was Israel's bitter adversary for the rest of Solomon's reign, and he made trouble, just as Hadad did. Rezon hated Israel intensely and continued to reign in Aram.

Another rebel leader was Jeroboam son of Nebat, one of Solomon's own officials. He came from the town of Zeredah in Ephraim, and his mother was Zeruah, a widow.

This is the story behind his rebellion. Solomon was rebuilding the supporting terraces and repairing the walls of the city of his father, David. Jeroboam was a very capable young man, and when Solomon saw how industrious he was, he put him in charge of the labor force from the tribes of Ephraim and Manasseh, the descendants of Joseph.

One day as Jeroboam was leaving Jerusalem, the prophet Ahijah from Shiloh met him along the way. Ahijah was wearing a new cloak. The two of them were alone in a field, and Ahijah took hold of the new cloak he was wearing and tore it into twelve pieces. Then he said to Jeroboam, "Take ten of these pieces, for this is what the LORD, the God of Israel, says: 'I am about to tear the kingdom from the hand of Solomon, and I will give ten of the tribes to you! But I will leave him one tribe for the sake of my servant David and for the sake of Jerusalem, which I have chosen out of all the tribes of Israel. For Solomon has abandoned me and worshiped Ashtoreth, the goddess of the Sidonians; Chemosh, the god of Moab; and Molech, the god of the Ammonites. He has not followed my ways and done what is pleasing in my sight. He has not obeyed my decrees and regulations as David his father did.

"'But I will not take the entire kingdom from Solomon at this time. For the sake of my servant David, the one whom I chose and who obeyed my commands and decrees, I will keep Solomon as leader for the rest of his life. But I will take the kingdom away from his son and give ten of the tribes to you. His son will have one tribe so that the descendants of David my servant will continue to reign, shining like a lamp in Jerusalem, the city I have chosen to be the place for my name. And I will place you on the throne of Israel, and you will rule over all that your heart desires. If you listen to what I tell you and follow my ways and do whatever I consider to be right, and if you obey my decrees and commands, as my servant David did, then I will always be with you. I will establish an enduring dynasty for you as I did for David, and I will give Israel to you. Because of Solomon's sin I will punish the descendants of David—though not forever.'"

Solomon tried to kill Jeroboam, but he fled to King Shishak of Egypt and stayed there until Solomon died.

The rest of the events in Solomon's reign, including all his deeds and his wisdom, are recorded in *The Book of the Acts of Solomon*. Solomon ruled in Jerusalem over all Israel for forty years. When he died, he was buried in the City of David, named for his father. Then his son Rehoboam became the next king.

+ + +

Rehoboam went to Shechem, where all Israel had gathered to make him king. When Jeroboam son of Nebat heard of this, he returned from Egypt, for he had fled to Egypt to escape from King Solomon. The leaders of Israel summoned him, and Jeroboam and the whole assembly of Israel went to speak with Rehoboam. "Your father was a hard master," they said. "Lighten the harsh labor demands and heavy taxes that your father imposed on us. Then we will be your loyal subjects."

Rehoboam replied, "Give me three days to think this over. Then come back for my answer." So the people went away.

Then King Rehoboam discussed the matter with the older men who had counseled his father, Solomon. "What is your advice?" he asked. "How should I answer these people?"

The older counselors replied, "If you are willing to be a servant to these people today and give them a favorable answer, they will always be your loyal subjects."

But Rehoboam rejected the advice of the older men and instead asked the opinion of the young men who had grown up with him and were now his advisers. "What is your advice?" he asked them. "How should I answer these people who want me to lighten the burdens imposed by my father?"

The young men replied, "This is what you should tell those complainers who want a lighter burden: 'My little finger is thicker than my father's waist! Yes, my father laid heavy burdens on you, but I'm going to make them even heavier! My father beat you with whips, but I will beat you with scorpions!'"

Three days later Jeroboam and all the people returned to hear Rehoboam's decision, just as the king had ordered. But Rehoboam spoke harshly to the people, for he rejected the advice of the older counselors and followed the counsel of his younger advisers. He told the people, "My father laid heavy burdens on you, but I'm going to make them even heavier! My father beat you with whips, but I will beat you with scorpions!"

So the king paid no attention to the people. This turn of events was the will of the LORD, for it fulfilled the LORD's message to Jeroboam son of Nebat through the prophet Ahijah from Shiloh.

When all Israel realized that the king had refused to listen to them, they responded,

"Down with the dynasty of David!
    We have no interest in the son of Jesse.
Back to your homes, O Israel!
    Look out for your own house, O David!"

So the people of Israel returned home. But Rehoboam continued to rule over the Israelites who lived in the towns of Judah.

King Rehoboam sent Adoniram, who was in charge of forced labor, to restore order, but the people of Israel stoned him to death. When this news reached King Rehoboam, he quickly jumped into his chariot and fled to Jerusalem. And to this day the northern tribes of Israel have refused to be ruled by a descendant of David.

When the people of Israel learned of Jeroboam's return from Egypt, they called an assembly and made him king over all Israel. So only the tribe of Judah remained loyal to the family of David.

When Rehoboam arrived at Jerusalem, he mobilized the men of Judah and the tribe of Benjamin—180,000 select troops—to fight against the men of Israel and to restore the kingdom to himself.

But God said to Shemaiah, the man of God, "Say to Rehoboam son of Solomon, king of Judah, and to all the people of Judah and Benjamin, and to the rest of the people, 'This is what the LORD says: Do not fight against your relatives, the Israelites. Go back home, for what has happened is my doing!'" So they obeyed the message of the LORD and went home, as the LORD had commanded.

Jeroboam then built up the city of Shechem in the hill country of Ephraim, and it became his capital. Later he went and built up the town of Peniel.

Jeroboam thought to himself, "Unless I am careful, the kingdom will return to the dynasty of David. When these people go to Jerusalem to offer sacrifices at the Temple of the LORD, they will again give their allegiance to King Rehoboam of Judah. They will kill me and make him their king instead."

So on the advice of his counselors, the king made two gold calves. He said to the people, "It is too much trouble for you to worship in Jerusalem. Look, Israel, these are the gods who brought you out of Egypt!"

He placed these calf idols in Bethel and in Dan—at either end of his kingdom. But this became a great sin, for the people worshiped the idols, traveling as far north as Dan to worship the one there.

Jeroboam also erected buildings at the pagan shrines and ordained priests from the common people—those who were not from the priestly tribe of Levi. And Jeroboam instituted a religious festival in Bethel, held on the fifteenth day of the eighth month, in imitation of the annual Festival of Shelters in Judah. There at Bethel he himself offered sacrifices to the calves he had made, and he appointed priests for the pagan shrines he had made. So on the fifteenth day of the eighth month, a day that he himself had designated, Jeroboam offered sacrifices on the altar at Bethel. He instituted a religious festival for Israel, and he went up to the altar to burn incense.

At the LORD's command, a man of God from Judah went to Bethel, arriving there just as Jeroboam was approaching the altar to burn incense. Then at the LORD's command, he shouted, "O altar, altar! This is what the LORD says: A child named Josiah will be born into the dynasty of David. On you he will sacrifice the priests from the pagan shrines who come here to burn incense, and human bones will be burned on you." That same day the man of God gave a sign to prove his message. He said, "The LORD has promised to give this sign: This altar will split apart, and its ashes will be poured out on the ground."

When King Jeroboam heard the man of God speaking against the altar at Bethel, he pointed at him and shouted, "Seize that man!" But instantly the king's hand became paralyzed in that position, and he couldn't pull it back. At the same time a wide crack appeared in the altar, and the ashes poured out, just as the man of God had predicted in his message from the LORD.

The king cried out to the man of God, "Please ask the LORD your God to restore my hand again!" So the man of God prayed to the LORD, and the king's hand was restored and he could move it again.

Then the king said to the man of God, "Come to the palace with me and have something to eat, and I will give you a gift."

But the man of God said to the king, "Even if you gave me half of everything you own, I would not go with you. I would not eat or drink anything in this place. For the LORD gave me this command: 'You must not eat or drink anything while you are there, and do not return to Judah by the same way you came.'" So he left Bethel and went home another way.

As it happened, there was an old prophet living in Bethel, and his sons came home and told him what the man of God had done in Bethel that day. They also told their father what the man had said to the king. The old prophet asked them, "Which way did he go?" So they showed their father which road the man of God had taken. "Quick, saddle the donkey," the old man said. So they saddled the donkey for him, and he mounted it.

Then he rode after the man of God and found him sitting under a great tree. The old prophet asked him, "Are you the man of God who came from Judah?"

"Yes, I am," he replied.

Then he said to the man of God, "Come home with me and eat some food."

"No, I cannot," he replied. "I am not allowed to eat or drink anything here in this place. For the LORD gave me this command: 'You must not eat or drink anything while you are there, and do not return to Judah by the same way you came.'"

But the old prophet answered, "I am a prophet, too, just as you are. And an angel gave me this command from the LORD: 'Bring him home with you so he can have something to eat and drink.'" But the old man was lying to him. So they went back together, and the man of God ate and drank at the prophet's home.

Then while they were sitting at the table, a command from the LORD came to the old prophet. He cried out to the man of God from Judah, "This is what the LORD says: You have defied the word of the LORD and have disobeyed the command the LORD your God gave you. You came back to this place and ate and drank where he told you not to eat or drink. Because of this, your body will not be buried in the grave of your ancestors."

After the man of God had finished eating and drinking, the old prophet saddled his own donkey for him, and the man of God started off again. But as he was traveling along, a lion came out and killed him. His body lay there on the road, with the donkey and the lion standing beside it. People who passed by saw the body lying in the road and the lion standing beside it, and they went and reported it in Bethel, where the old prophet lived.

When the prophet heard the report, he said, "It is the man of God who disobeyed the LORD's command. The LORD has fulfilled his word by caus-ing the lion to attack and kill him."

Then the prophet said to his sons, "Saddle a donkey for me." So they saddled a donkey, and he went out and found the body lying in the road. The donkey and lion were still standing there beside it, for the lion had not eaten the body nor attacked the donkey. So the prophet laid the body of the man of God on the donkey and took it back to the town to mourn over him and bury him. He laid the body in his own grave, crying out in grief, "Oh, my brother!"

Afterward the prophet said to his sons, "When I die, bury me in the grave where the man of God is buried. Lay my bones beside his bones. For the message the LORD told him to proclaim against the altar in Bethel and against the pagan shrines in the towns of Samaria will certainly come true."

But even after this, Jeroboam did not turn from his evil ways. He con-tinued to choose priests from the common people. He appointed anyone who wanted to become a priest for the pagan shrines. This became a great sin and resulted in the utter destruction of Jeroboam's dynasty from the face of the earth.

At that time Jeroboam's son Abijah became very sick. So Jeroboam told his wife, "Disguise yourself so that no one will recognize you as my wife. Then go to the prophet Ahijah at Shiloh—the man who told me I would become king. Take him a gift of ten loaves of bread, some cakes, and a jar of honey, and ask him what will happen to the boy."

So Jeroboam's wife went to Ahijah's home at Shiloh. He was an old man now and could no longer see. But the LORD had told Ahijah, "Jeroboam's wife will come here, pretending to be someone else. She will ask you about her son, for he is very sick. Give her the answer I give you."

So when Ahijah heard her footsteps at the door, he called out, "Come in, wife of Jeroboam! Why are you pretending to be someone else?" Then he told her, "I have bad news for you. Give your husband, Jeroboam, this message from the LORD, the God of Israel: 'I promoted you from the ranks of the common people and made you ruler over my people Israel. I ripped the kingdom away from the family of David and gave it to you. But you have not been like my servant David, who obeyed my commands and fol-lowed me with all his heart and always did whatever I wanted. You have done more evil than all who lived before you. You have made other gods for yourself and have made me furious with your gold calves. And since you have turned your back on me, I will bring disaster on your dynasty and will destroy every one of your male descendants, slave and free alike, anywhere in Israel. I will burn up your royal dynasty as one burns up trash until it is all gone. The members of Jeroboam's family who die in the city will be eaten by dogs, and those who die in the field will be eaten by vultures. I, the LORD, have spoken.'"

Then Ahijah said to Jeroboam's wife, "Go on home, and when you enter the city, the child will die. All Israel will mourn for him and bury him. He is the only member of your family who will have a proper burial, for this child is the only good thing that the LORD, the God of Israel, sees in the entire family of Jeroboam.

"In addition, the LORD will raise up a king over Israel who will destroy the family of Jeroboam. This will happen today, even now! Then the LORD will shake Israel like a reed whipped about in a stream. He will uproot the people of Israel from this good land that he gave their ancestors and will scatter them beyond the Euphrates River, for they have angered the LORD with the Asherah poles they have set up for worship. He will abandon Israel because Jeroboam sinned and made Israel sin along with him."

So Jeroboam's wife returned to Tirzah, and the child died just as she walked through the door of her home. And all Israel buried him and mourned for him, as the LORD had promised through the prophet Ahijah.

The rest of the events in Jeroboam's reign, including all his wars and how he ruled, are recorded in *The Book of the History of the Kings of Israel*. Jeroboam reigned in Israel twenty-two years. When Jeroboam died, his son Nadab became the next king.

+ + +

Meanwhile, Rehoboam son of Solomon was king in Judah. He was forty-one years old when he became king, and he reigned seventeen years in Jerusalem, the city the LORD had chosen from among all the tribes of Israel as the place to honor his name. Rehoboam's mother was Naamah, an Ammonite woman.

During Rehoboam's reign, the people of Judah did what was evil in the LORD's sight, provoking his anger with their sin, for it was even worse than that of their ancestors. For they also built for themselves pagan shrines and set up sacred pillars and Asherah poles on every high hill and under every green tree. There were even male and female shrine prostitutes throughout the land. The people imitated the detestable practices of the pagan nations the LORD had driven from the land ahead of the Israelites.

In the fifth year of King Rehoboam's reign, King Shishak of Egypt came up and attacked Jerusalem. He ransacked the treasuries of the LORD's Temple and the royal palace; he stole everything, including all the gold shields Solomon had made. King Rehoboam later replaced them with bronze shields as substitutes, and he entrusted them to the care of the commanders of the guard who protected the entrance to the royal palace. Whenever the king went to the Temple of the LORD, the guards would also take the shields and then return them to the guardroom.

The rest of the events in Rehoboam's reign and everything he did are recorded in *The Book of the History of the Kings of Judah*. There was constant war between Rehoboam and Jeroboam. When Rehoboam died, he was buried among his ancestors in the City of David. His mother was Naamah, an Ammonite woman. Then his son Abijam became the next king.

+ + +

Abijam began to rule over Judah in the eighteenth year of Jeroboam's reign in Israel. He reigned in Jerusalem three years. His mother was Maacah, the granddaughter of Absalom.

He committed the same sins as his father before him, and he was not faithful to the LORD his God, as his ancestor David had been. But for David's sake, the LORD his God allowed his descendants to continue ruling, shining like a lamp, and he gave Abijam a son to rule after him in Jerusalem. For David had done what was pleasing in the LORD's sight and had obeyed the LORD's commands throughout his life, except in the affair concerning Uriah the Hittite.

There was war between Abijam and Jeroboam throughout Abijam's reign.

The rest of the events in Abijam's reign and everything he did are recorded in *The Book of the History of the Kings of Judah*. There was constant war between Abijam and Jeroboam. When Abijam died, he was buried in the City of David. Then his son Asa became the next king.

+ + +

Asa began to rule over Judah in the twentieth year of Jeroboam's reign in Israel. He reigned in Jerusalem forty-one years. His grandmother was Maacah, the granddaughter of Absalom.

Asa did what was pleasing in the LORD's sight, as his ancestor David had done. He banished the male and female shrine prostitutes from the land and got rid of all the idols his ancestors had made. He even deposed his grandmother Maacah from her position as queen mother because she had made an obscene Asherah pole. He cut down her obscene pole and burned it in the Kidron Valley. Although the pagan shrines were not removed, Asa's heart remained completely faithful to the LORD throughout his life. He brought into the Temple of the LORD the silver and gold and the various items that he and his father had dedicated.

There was constant war between King Asa of Judah and King Baasha of Israel. King Baasha of Israel invaded Judah and fortified Ramah in order to prevent anyone from entering or leaving King Asa's territory in Judah.

Asa responded by removing all the silver and gold that was left in the treasuries of the Temple of the LORD and the royal palace. He sent it with some of his officials to Ben-hadad son of Tabrimmon, son of Hezion, the king of Aram, who was ruling in Damascus, along with this message:

> "Let there be a treaty between you and me like the one between your father and my father. See, I am sending you a gift of silver and gold. Break your treaty with King Baasha of Israel so that he will leave me alone."

Ben-hadad agreed to King Asa's request and sent the commanders of his army to attack the towns of Israel. They conquered the towns of Ijon, Dan, Abel-beth-maacah, and all Kinnereth, and all the land of Naphtali. As soon as Baasha of Israel heard what was happening, he abandoned his project of fortifying Ramah and withdrew to Tirzah. Then King Asa sent an order throughout Judah, requiring that everyone, without exception, help to carry away the building stones and timbers that Baasha had been using to fortify Ramah. Asa used these materials to fortify the town of Geba in Benjamin and the town of Mizpah.

The rest of the events in Asa's reign—the extent of his power, everything he did, and the names of the cities he built—are recorded in *The Book of the History of the Kings of Judah.* In his old age his feet became diseased. When Asa died, he was buried with his ancestors in the City of David.

Then Jehoshaphat, Asa's son, became the next king.

✛ ✛ ✛

Nadab son of Jeroboam began to rule over Israel in the second year of King Asa's reign in Judah. He reigned in Israel two years. But he did what was evil in the LORD's sight and followed the example of his father, continuing the sins that Jeroboam had led Israel to commit.

Then Baasha son of Ahijah, from the tribe of Issachar, plotted against Nadab and assassinated him while he and the Israelite army were laying siege to the Philistine town of Gibbethon. Baasha killed Nadab in the third year of King Asa's reign in Judah, and he became the next king of Israel.

He immediately slaughtered all the descendants of King Jeroboam, so that not one of the royal family was left, just as the LORD had promised concerning Jeroboam by the prophet Ahijah from Shiloh. This was done because Jeroboam had provoked the anger of the LORD, the God of Israel, by the sins he had committed and the sins he had led Israel to commit.

The rest of the events in Nadab's reign and everything he did are recorded in *The Book of the History of the Kings of Israel.*

+ + +

There was constant war between King Asa of Judah and King Baasha of Israel. Baasha son of Ahijah began to rule over all Israel in the third year of King Asa's reign in Judah. Baasha reigned in Tirzah twenty-four years. But he did what was evil in the LORD's sight and followed the example of Jeroboam, continuing the sins that Jeroboam had led Israel to commit.

This message from the LORD was delivered to King Baasha by the prophet Jehu son of Hanani: "I lifted you out of the dust to make you ruler of my people Israel, but you have followed the evil example of Jeroboam. You have provoked my anger by causing my people Israel to sin. So now I will destroy you and your family, just as I destroyed the descendants of Jeroboam son of Nebat. The members of Baasha's family who die in the city will be eaten by dogs, and those who die in the field will be eaten by vultures."

The rest of the events in Baasha's reign and the extent of his power are recorded in *The Book of the History of the Kings of Israel.* When Baasha died, he was buried in Tirzah. Then his son Elah became the next king.

The message from the LORD against Baasha and his family came through the prophet Jehu son of Hanani. It was delivered because Baasha had done what was evil in the LORD's sight (just as the family of Jeroboam had done), and also because Baasha had destroyed the family of Jeroboam. The LORD's anger was provoked by Baasha's sins.

+ + +

Elah son of Baasha began to rule over Israel in the twenty-sixth year of King Asa's reign in Judah. He reigned in the city of Tirzah for two years.

Then Zimri, who commanded half of the royal chariots, made plans to kill him. One day in Tirzah, Elah was getting drunk at the home of Arza, the supervisor of the palace. Zimri walked in and struck him down and killed him. This happened in the twenty-seventh year of King Asa's reign in Judah. Then Zimri became the next king.

Zimri immediately killed the entire royal family of Baasha, leaving him not even a single male child. He even destroyed distant relatives and friends. So Zimri destroyed the dynasty of Baasha as the LORD had promised through the prophet Jehu. This happened because of all the sins Baasha and his son Elah had committed, and because of the sins they led Israel to commit. They provoked the anger of the LORD, the God of Israel, with their worthless idols.

The rest of the events in Elah's reign and everything he did are recorded in *The Book of the History of the Kings of Israel.*

+ + +

Zimri began to rule over Israel in the twenty-seventh year of King Asa's reign in Judah, but his reign in Tirzah lasted only seven days.

The army of Israel was then attacking the Philistine town of Gibbethon. When they heard that Zimri had committed treason and had assassinated the king, that very day they chose Omri, commander of the army, as the new king of Israel. So Omri led the entire army of Israel up from Gibbethon to attack Tirzah, Israel's capital. When Zimri saw that the city had been taken, he went into the citadel of the palace and burned it down over himself and died in the flames. For he, too, had done what was evil in the LORD's sight. He followed the example of Jeroboam in all the sins he had committed and led Israel to commit.

The rest of the events in Zimri's reign and his conspiracy are recorded in *The Book of the History of the Kings of Israel.*

+ + +

But now the people of Israel were split into two factions. Half the people tried to make Tibni son of Ginath their king, while the other half supported Omri. But Omri's supporters defeated the supporters of Tibni. So Tibni was killed, and Omri became the next king.

Omri began to rule over Israel in the thirty-first year of King Asa's reign in Judah. He reigned twelve years in all, six of them in Tirzah.

Then Omri bought the hill now known as Samaria from its owner, Shemer, for 150 pounds of silver. He built a city on it and called the city Samaria in honor of Shemer.

But Omri did what was evil in the LORD's sight, even more than any of the kings before him. He followed the example of Jeroboam son of Nebat in all the sins he had committed and led Israel to commit. The people provoked the anger of the LORD, the God of Israel, with their worthless idols.

The rest of the events in Omri's reign, the extent of his power, and everything he did are recorded in *The Book of the History of the Kings of Israel*. When Omri died, he was buried in Samaria. Then his son Ahab became the next king.

+ + +

Ahab son of Omri began to rule over Israel in the thirty-eighth year of King Asa's reign in Judah. He reigned in Samaria twenty-two years. But Ahab son of Omri did what was evil in the LORD's sight, even more than any of the kings before him. And as though it were not enough to follow the sinful example of Jeroboam, he married Jezebel, the daughter of King Ethbaal of the Sidonians, and he began to bow down in worship of Baal. First Ahab built a temple and an altar for Baal in Samaria. Then he set up an Asherah pole. He did more to provoke the anger of the LORD, the God of Israel, than any of the other kings of Israel before him.

It was during his reign that Hiel, a man from Bethel, rebuilt Jericho. When he laid its foundations, it cost him the life of his oldest son, Abiram. And when he completed it and set up its gates, it cost him the life of his youngest son, Segub. This all happened according to the message from the LORD concerning Jericho spoken by Joshua son of Nun.

+

Now Elijah, who was from Tishbe in Gilead, told King Ahab, "As surely as the LORD, the God of Israel, lives—the God I serve—there will be no dew or rain during the next few years until I give the word!"

Then the LORD said to Elijah, "Go to the east and hide by Kerith Brook, near where it enters the Jordan River. Drink from the brook and eat what the ravens bring you, for I have commanded them to bring you food."

So Elijah did as the LORD told him and camped beside Kerith Brook, east of the Jordan. The ravens brought him bread and meat each morning and evening, and he drank from the brook. But after a while the brook dried up, for there was no rainfall anywhere in the land.

Then the LORD said to Elijah, "Go and live in the village of Zarephath, near the city of Sidon. I have instructed a widow there to feed you."

So he went to Zarephath. As he arrived at the gates of the village, he saw a widow gathering sticks, and he asked her, "Would you please bring me a little water in a cup?" As she was going to get it, he called to her, "Bring me a bite of bread, too."

But she said, "I swear by the LORD your God that I don't have a single piece of bread in the house. And I have only a handful of flour left in the jar and a little cooking oil in the bottom of the jug. I was just gathering a few sticks to cook this last meal, and then my son and I will die."

But Elijah said to her, "Don't be afraid! Go ahead and do just what you've said, but make a little bread for me first. Then use what's left to prepare a meal for yourself and your son. For this is what the LORD, the God of Israel, says: There will always be flour and olive oil left in your containers until the time when the LORD sends rain and the crops grow again!"

So she did as Elijah said, and she and Elijah and her family continued to eat for many days. There was always enough flour and olive oil left in the containers, just as the LORD had promised through Elijah.

Some time later the woman's son became sick. He grew worse and worse, and finally he died. Then she said to Elijah, "O man of God, what have you done to me? Have you come here to point out my sins and kill my son?"

But Elijah replied, "Give me your son." And he took the child's body from her arms, carried him up the stairs to the room where he was staying, and laid the body on his bed. Then Elijah cried out to the LORD, "O LORD my God, why have you brought tragedy to this widow who has opened her home to me, causing her son to die?"

And he stretched himself out over the child three times and cried out to the LORD, "O LORD my God, please let this child's life return to him." The LORD heard Elijah's prayer, and the life of the child returned, and he revived! Then Elijah brought him down from the upper room and gave him to his mother. "Look!" he said. "Your son is alive!"

Then the woman told Elijah, "Now I know for sure that you are a man of God, and that the LORD truly speaks through you."

Later on, in the third year of the drought, the LORD said to Elijah, "Go and present yourself to King Ahab. Tell him that I will soon send rain!" So Elijah went to appear before Ahab.

Meanwhile, the famine had become very severe in Samaria. So Ahab summoned Obadiah, who was in charge of the palace. (Obadiah was a devoted follower of the LORD. Once when Jezebel had tried to kill all the LORD's prophets, Obadiah had hidden 100 of them in two caves. He put fifty prophets in each cave and supplied them with food and water.) Ahab said to Obadiah, "We must check every spring and valley in the land to see if we can find enough grass to save at least some of my horses and mules." So they divided the land between them. Ahab went one way by himself, and Obadiah went another way by himself.

As Obadiah was walking along, he suddenly saw Elijah coming toward him. Obadiah recognized him at once and bowed low to the ground before him. "Is it really you, my lord Elijah?" he asked.

"Yes, it is," Elijah replied. "Now go and tell your master, 'Elijah is here.'"

"Oh, sir," Obadiah protested, "what harm have I done to you that you are sending me to my death at the hands of Ahab? For I swear by the LORD your God that the king has searched every nation and kingdom on earth from end to end to find you. And each time he was told, 'Elijah isn't here,' King Ahab forced the king of that nation to swear to the truth of his claim. And now you say, 'Go and tell your master, "Elijah is here."' But as soon as I leave you, the Spirit of the LORD will carry you away to who knows where. When Ahab comes and cannot find you, he will kill me. Yet I have been a true servant of the LORD all my life. Has no one told you, my lord, about the time when Jezebel was trying to kill the LORD's prophets? I hid 100 of them in two caves and supplied them with food and water. And now you say, 'Go and tell your master, "Elijah is here."' Sir, if I do that, Ahab will certainly kill me."

But Elijah said, "I swear by the LORD Almighty, in whose presence I stand, that I will present myself to Ahab this very day."

So Obadiah went to tell Ahab that Elijah had come, and Ahab went out to meet Elijah. When Ahab saw him, he exclaimed, "So, is it really you, you troublemaker of Israel?"

"I have made no trouble for Israel," Elijah replied. "You and your family are the troublemakers, for you have refused to obey the commands of the LORD and have worshiped the images of Baal instead. Now summon all Israel to join me at Mount Carmel, along with the 450 prophets of Baal and the 400 prophets of Asherah who are supported by Jezebel."

So Ahab summoned all the people of Israel and the prophets to Mount Carmel. Then Elijah stood in front of them and said, "How much longer will you waver, hobbling between two opinions? If the LORD is God, follow him! But if Baal is God, then follow him!" But the people were completely silent.

Then Elijah said to them, "I am the only prophet of the LORD who is left, but Baal has 450 prophets. Now bring two bulls. The prophets of Baal may choose whichever one they wish and cut it into pieces and lay it on the wood of their altar, but without setting fire to it. I will prepare the other bull and lay it on the wood on the altar, but not set fire to it. Then call on the name of your god, and I will call on the name of the LORD. The god who answers by setting fire to the wood is the true God!" And all the people agreed.

Then Elijah said to the prophets of Baal, "You go first, for there are many of you. Choose one of the bulls, and prepare it and call on the name of your god. But do not set fire to the wood."

So they prepared one of the bulls and placed it on the altar. Then they called on the name of Baal from morning until noontime, shouting, "O Baal, answer us!" But there was no reply of any kind. Then they danced, hobbling around the altar they had made.

About noontime Elijah began mocking them. "You'll have to shout louder," he scoffed, "for surely he is a god! Perhaps he is daydreaming, or is relieving himself. Or maybe he is away on a trip, or is asleep and needs to be wakened!"

So they shouted louder, and following their normal custom, they cut themselves with knives and swords until the blood gushed out. They raved all afternoon until the time of the evening sacrifice, but still there was no sound, no reply, no response.

Then Elijah called to the people, "Come over here!" They all crowded around him as he repaired the altar of the LORD that had been torn down. He took twelve stones, one to represent each of the tribes of Israel, and he used the stones to rebuild the altar in the name of the LORD. Then he dug a trench around the altar large enough to hold about three gallons. He piled wood on the altar, cut the bull into pieces, and laid the pieces on the wood.

Then he said, "Fill four large jars with water, and pour the water over the offering and the wood."

After they had done this, he said, "Do the same thing again!" And when they were finished, he said, "Now do it a third time!" So they did as he said, and the water ran around the altar and even filled the trench.

At the usual time for offering the evening sacrifice, Elijah the prophet walked up to the altar and prayed, "O LORD, God of Abraham, Isaac, and Jacob, prove today that you are God in Israel and that I am your servant. Prove that I have done all this at your command. O LORD, answer me! Answer me so these people will know that you, O LORD, are God and that you have brought them back to yourself."

Immediately the fire of the LORD flashed down from heaven and burned up the young bull, the wood, the stones, and the dust. It even licked up all the water in the trench! And when all the people saw it, they fell face down on the ground and cried out, "The LORD—he is God! Yes, the LORD is God!"

Then Elijah commanded, "Seize all the prophets of Baal. Don't let a single one escape!" So the people seized them all, and Elijah took them down to the Kishon Valley and killed them there.

Then Elijah said to Ahab, "Go get something to eat and drink, for I hear a mighty rainstorm coming!"

So Ahab went to eat and drink. But Elijah climbed to the top of Mount Carmel and bowed low to the ground and prayed with his face between his knees.

Then he said to his servant, "Go and look out toward the sea."

The servant went and looked, then returned to Elijah and said, "I didn't see anything."

Seven times Elijah told him to go and look. Finally the seventh time, his servant told him, "I saw a little cloud about the size of a man's hand rising from the sea."

Then Elijah shouted, "Hurry to Ahab and tell him, 'Climb into your chariot and go back home. If you don't hurry, the rain will stop you!'"

And soon the sky was black with clouds. A heavy wind brought a terrific rainstorm, and Ahab left quickly for Jezreel. Then the LORD gave special strength to Elijah. He tucked his cloak into his belt and ran ahead of Ahab's chariot all the way to the entrance of Jezreel.

When Ahab got home, he told Jezebel everything Elijah had done, including the way he had killed all the prophets of Baal. So Jezebel sent this message to Elijah: "May the gods strike me and even kill me if by this time tomorrow I have not killed you just as you killed them."

Elijah was afraid and fled for his life. He went to Beersheba, a town in Judah, and he left his servant there. Then he went on alone into the wilderness, traveling all day. He sat down under a solitary broom tree and prayed that he might die. "I have had enough, LORD," he said. "Take my life, for I am no better than my ancestors who have already died."

Then he lay down and slept under the broom tree. But as he was sleeping, an angel touched him and told him, "Get up and eat!" He looked around and there beside his head was some bread baked on hot stones and a jar of water! So he ate and drank and lay down again.

Then the angel of the LORD came again and touched him and said, "Get up and eat some more, or the journey ahead will be too much for you."

So he got up and ate and drank, and the food gave him enough strength to travel forty days and forty nights to Mount Sinai, the mountain of God. There he came to a cave, where he spent the night.

But the LORD said to him, "What are you doing here, Elijah?"

Elijah replied, "I have zealously served the LORD God Almighty. But the people of Israel have broken their covenant with you, torn down your altars, and killed every one of your prophets. I am the only one left, and now they are trying to kill me, too."

"Go out and stand before me on the mountain," the LORD told him. And as Elijah stood there, the LORD passed by, and a mighty windstorm hit the mountain. It was such a terrible blast that the rocks were torn loose, but the LORD was not in the wind. After the wind there was an earthquake, but the LORD was not in the earthquake. And after the earthquake there was a fire, but the LORD was not in the fire. And after the fire there was the sound of a gentle whisper. When Elijah heard it, he wrapped his face in his cloak and went out and stood at the entrance of the cave.

And a voice said, "What are you doing here, Elijah?"

He replied again, "I have zealously served the LORD God Almighty. But the people of Israel have broken their covenant with you, torn down your altars, and killed every one of your prophets. I am the only one left, and now they are trying to kill me, too."

Then the LORD told him, "Go back the same way you came, and travel to the wilderness of Damascus. When you arrive there, anoint Hazael to be king of Aram. Then anoint Jehu grandson of Nimshi to be king of Israel, and anoint Elisha son of Shaphat from the town of Abel-meholah to replace you as my prophet. Anyone who escapes from Hazael will be killed by Jehu, and those who escape Jehu will be killed by Elisha! Yet I will preserve 7,000 others in Israel who have never bowed down to Baal or kissed him!"

So Elijah went and found Elisha son of Shaphat plowing a field. There were twelve teams of oxen in the field, and Elisha was plowing with the twelfth team. Elijah went over to him and threw his cloak across his shoulders and then walked away. Elisha left the oxen standing there, ran after Elijah, and said to him, "First let me go and kiss my father and mother good-bye, and then I will go with you!"

Elijah replied, "Go on back, but think about what I have done to you."

So Elisha returned to his oxen and slaughtered them. He used the wood from the plow to build a fire to roast their flesh. He passed around the meat to the townspeople, and they all ate. Then he went with Elijah as his assistant.

+

About that time King Ben-hadad of Aram mobilized his army, supported by the chariots and horses of thirty-two allied kings. They went to besiege Samaria, the capital of Israel, and launched attacks against it. Ben-hadad sent messengers into the city to relay this message to King Ahab of Israel: "This is what Ben-hadad says: 'Your silver and gold are mine, and so are your wives and the best of your children!'"

"All right, my lord the king," Israel's king replied. "All that I have is yours!"

Soon Ben-hadad's messengers returned again and said, "This is what Ben-hadad says: 'I have already demanded that you give me your silver, gold, wives, and children. But about this time tomorrow I will send my officials to search your palace and the homes of your officials. They will take away everything you consider valuable!'"

Then Ahab summoned all the elders of the land and said to them, "Look how this man is stirring up trouble! I already agreed with his demand that I give him my wives and children and silver and gold."

"Don't give in to any more demands," all the elders and the people advised.

So Ahab told the messengers from Ben-hadad, "Say this to my lord the king: 'I will give you everything you asked for the first time, but I cannot accept this last demand of yours.'" So the messengers returned to Ben-hadad with that response.

Then Ben-hadad sent this message to Ahab: "May the gods strike me and even kill me if there remains enough dust from Samaria to provide even a handful for each of my soldiers."

The king of Israel sent back this answer: "A warrior putting on his sword for battle should not boast like a warrior who has already won."

Ahab's reply reached Ben-hadad and the other kings as they were drinking in their tents. "Prepare to attack!" Ben-hadad commanded his officers. So they prepared to attack the city.

Then a certain prophet came to see King Ahab of Israel and told him, "This is what the LORD says: Do you see all these enemy forces? Today I will hand them all over to you. Then you will know that I am the LORD."

Ahab asked, "How will he do it?"

And the prophet replied, "This is what the LORD says: The troops of the provincial commanders will do it."

"Should we attack first?" Ahab asked.

"Yes," the prophet answered.

So Ahab mustered the troops of the 232 provincial commanders. Then he called out the rest of the army of Israel, some 7,000 men. About noontime, as Ben-hadad and the thirty-two allied kings were still in their tents drinking themselves into a stupor, the troops of the provincial commanders marched out of the city as the first contingent.

As they approached, Ben-hadad's scouts reported to him, "Some troops are coming from Samaria."

"Take them alive," Ben-hadad commanded, "whether they have come for peace or for war."

But Ahab's provincial commanders and the entire army had now come out to fight. Each Israelite soldier killed his Aramean opponent, and suddenly the entire Aramean army panicked and fled. The Israelites chased them, but King Ben-hadad and a few of his charioteers escaped on horses. However, the king of Israel destroyed the other horses and chariots and slaughtered the Arameans.

Afterward the prophet said to King Ahab, "Get ready for another attack. Begin making plans now, for the king of Aram will come back next spring."

After their defeat, Ben-hadad's officers said to him, "The Israelite gods are gods of the hills; that is why they won. But we can beat them easily on the plains. Only this time replace the kings with field commanders! Recruit another army like the one you lost. Give us the same number of horses, chariots, and men, and we will fight against them on the plains. There's no doubt that we will beat them." So King Ben-hadad did as they suggested.

The following spring he called up the Aramean army and marched out against Israel, this time at Aphek. Israel then mustered its army, set up supply lines, and marched out for battle. But the Israelite army looked like two little flocks of goats in comparison to the vast Aramean forces that filled the countryside!

Then the man of God went to the king of Israel and said, "This is what the LORD says: The Arameans have said, 'The LORD is a god of the hills and not of the plains.' So I will defeat this vast army for you. Then you will know that I am the LORD."

The two armies camped opposite each other for seven days, and on the seventh day the battle began. The Israelites killed 100,000 Aramean foot soldiers in one day. The rest fled into the town of Aphek, but the wall fell on them and killed another 27,000. Ben-hadad fled into the town and hid in a secret room.

Ben-hadad's officers said to him, "Sir, we have heard that the kings of Israel are merciful. So let's humble ourselves by wearing burlap around our waists and putting ropes on our heads, and surrender to the king of Israel. Then perhaps he will let you live."

So they put on burlap and ropes, and they went to the king of Israel and begged, "Your servant Ben-hadad says, 'Please let me live!'"

The king of Israel responded, "Is he still alive? He is my brother!"

The men took this as a good sign and quickly picked up on his words. "Yes," they said, "your brother Ben-hadad!"

"Go and get him," the king of Israel told them. And when Ben-hadad arrived, Ahab invited him up into his chariot.

Ben-hadad told him, "I will give back the towns my father took from your father, and you may establish places of trade in Damascus, as my father did in Samaria."

Then Ahab said, "I will release you under these conditions." So they made a new treaty, and Ben-hadad was set free.

Meanwhile, the Lord instructed one of the group of prophets to say to another man, "Hit me!" But the man refused to hit the prophet. Then the prophet told him, "Because you have not obeyed the voice of the Lord, a lion will kill you as soon as you leave me." And when he had gone, a lion did attack and kill him.

Then the prophet turned to another man and said, "Hit me!" So he struck the prophet and wounded him.

The prophet placed a bandage over his eyes to disguise himself and then waited beside the road for the king. As the king passed by, the prophet called out to him, "Sir, I was in the thick of battle, and suddenly a man brought me a prisoner. He said, 'Guard this man; if for any reason he gets away, you will either die or pay a fine of seventy-five pounds of silver!' But while I was busy doing something else, the prisoner disappeared!"

"Well, it's your own fault," the king replied. "You have brought the judgment on yourself."

Then the prophet quickly pulled the bandage from his eyes, and the king of Israel recognized him as one of the prophets. The prophet said to him, "This is what the Lord says: Because you have spared the man I said must be destroyed, now you must die in his place, and your people will die instead of his people." So the king of Israel went home to Samaria angry and sullen.

+

Now there was a man named Naboth, from Jezreel, who owned a vineyard in Jezreel beside the palace of King Ahab of Samaria. One day Ahab said to Naboth, "Since your vineyard is so convenient to my palace, I would like to buy it to use as a vegetable garden. I will give you a better vineyard in exchange, or if you prefer, I will pay you for it."

But Naboth replied, "The Lord forbid that I should give you the inheritance that was passed down by my ancestors."

So Ahab went home angry and sullen because of Naboth's answer. The king went to bed with his face to the wall and refused to eat!

"What's the matter?" his wife Jezebel asked him. "What's made you so upset that you're not eating?"

"I asked Naboth to sell me his vineyard or trade it, but he refused!" Ahab told her.

"Are you the king of Israel or not?" Jezebel demanded. "Get up and eat something, and don't worry about it. I'll get you Naboth's vineyard!"

So she wrote letters in Ahab's name, sealed them with his seal, and sent them to the elders and other leaders of the town where Naboth lived. In her letters she commanded: "Call the citizens together for a time of fasting, and give Naboth a place of honor. And then seat two scoundrels across from him who will accuse him of cursing God and the king. Then take him out and stone him to death."

So the elders and other town leaders followed the instructions Jezebel had written in the letters. They called for a fast and put Naboth at a prominent place before the people. Then the two scoundrels came and sat down across from him. And they accused Naboth before all the people, saying, "He cursed God and the king." So he was dragged outside the town and stoned to death. The town leaders then sent word to Jezebel, "Naboth has been stoned to death."

When Jezebel heard the news, she said to Ahab, "You know the vineyard Naboth wouldn't sell you? Well, you can have it now! He's dead!" So Ahab immediately went down to the vineyard of Naboth to claim it.

But the LORD said to Elijah, "Go down to meet King Ahab of Israel, who rules in Samaria. He will be at Naboth's vineyard in Jezreel, claiming it for himself. Give him this message: 'This is what the LORD says: Wasn't it enough that you killed Naboth? Must you rob him, too? Because you have done this, dogs will lick your blood at the very place where they licked the blood of Naboth!'"

"So, my enemy, you have found me!" Ahab exclaimed to Elijah.

"Yes," Elijah answered, "I have come because you have sold yourself to what is evil in the LORD's sight. So now the LORD says, 'I will bring disaster on you and consume you. I will destroy every one of your male descendants, slave and free alike, anywhere in Israel! I am going to destroy your family as I did the family of Jeroboam son of Nebat and the family of Baasha son of Ahijah, for you have made me very angry and have led Israel into sin.'

"And regarding Jezebel, the LORD says, 'Dogs will eat Jezebel's body at the plot of land in Jezreel.'

"The members of Ahab's family who die in the city will be eaten by dogs, and those who die in the field will be eaten by vultures."

(No one else so completely sold himself to what was evil in the LORD's sight as Ahab did under the influence of his wife Jezebel. His worst outrage was worshiping idols just as the Amorites had done—the people whom the LORD had driven out from the land ahead of the Israelites.)

But when Ahab heard this message, he tore his clothing, dressed in burlap, and fasted. He even slept in burlap and went about in deep mourning.

Then another message from the LORD came to Elijah: "Do you see how Ahab has humbled himself before me? Because he has done this, I will not do what I promised during his lifetime. It will happen to his sons; I will destroy his dynasty."

+

For three years there was no war between Aram and Israel. Then during the third year, King Jehoshaphat of Judah went to visit King Ahab of Israel. During the visit, the king of Israel said to his officials, "Do you realize that the town of Ramoth-gilead belongs to us? And yet we've done nothing to recapture it from the king of Aram!"

Then he turned to Jehoshaphat and asked, "Will you join me in battle to recover Ramoth-gilead?"

Jehoshaphat replied to the king of Israel, "Why, of course! You and I are as one. My troops are your troops, and my horses are your horses." Then Jehoshaphat added, "But first let's find out what the LORD says."

So the king of Israel summoned the prophets, about 400 of them, and asked them, "Should I go to war against Ramoth-gilead, or should I hold back?"

They all replied, "Yes, go right ahead! The Lord will give the king victory."

But Jehoshaphat asked, "Is there not also a prophet of the LORD here? We should ask him the same question."

The king of Israel replied to Jehoshaphat, "There is one more man who could consult the LORD for us, but I hate him. He never prophesies anything but trouble for me! His name is Micaiah son of Imlah."

Jehoshaphat replied, "That's not the way a king should talk! Let's hear what he has to say."

So the king of Israel called one of his officials and said, "Quick! Bring Micaiah son of Imlah."

King Ahab of Israel and King Jehoshaphat of Judah, dressed in their royal robes, were sitting on thrones at the threshing floor near the gate of Samaria. All of Ahab's prophets were prophesying there in front of them. One of them, Zedekiah son of Kenaanah, made some iron horns and proclaimed, "This is what the LORD says: With these horns you will gore the Arameans to death!"

All the other prophets agreed. "Yes," they said, "go up to Ramoth-gilead and be victorious, for the LORD will give the king victory!"

Meanwhile, the messenger who went to get Micaiah said to him, "Look, all the prophets are promising victory for the king. Be sure that you agree with them and promise success."

But Micaiah replied, "As surely as the LORD lives, I will say only what the LORD tells me to say."

When Micaiah arrived before the king, Ahab asked him, "Micaiah, should we go to war against Ramoth-gilead, or should we hold back?"

Micaiah replied sarcastically, "Yes, go up and be victorious, for the LORD will give the king victory!"

But the king replied sharply, "How many times must I demand that you speak only the truth to me when you speak for the LORD?"

Then Micaiah told him, "In a vision I saw all Israel scattered on the mountains, like sheep without a shepherd. And the LORD said, 'Their master has been killed. Send them home in peace.'"

"Didn't I tell you?" the king of Israel exclaimed to Jehoshaphat. "He never prophesies anything but trouble for me."

Then Micaiah continued, "Listen to what the LORD says! I saw the LORD sitting on his throne with all the armies of heaven around him, on his right and on his left. And the LORD said, 'Who can entice Ahab to go into battle against Ramoth-gilead so he can be killed?'

"There were many suggestions, and finally a spirit approached the LORD and said, 'I can do it!'

"'How will you do this?' the LORD asked.

"And the spirit replied, 'I will go out and inspire all of Ahab's prophets to speak lies.'

"'You will succeed,' said the LORD. 'Go ahead and do it.'

"So you see, the LORD has put a lying spirit in the mouths of all your prophets. For the LORD has pronounced your doom."

Then Zedekiah son of Kenaanah walked up to Micaiah and slapped him across the face. "Since when did the Spirit of the LORD leave me to speak to you?" he demanded.

And Micaiah replied, "You will find out soon enough when you are trying to hide in some secret room!"

"Arrest him!" the king of Israel ordered. "Take him back to Amon, the governor of the city, and to my son Joash. Give them this order from the king: 'Put this man in prison, and feed him nothing but bread and water until I return safely from the battle!'"

But Micaiah replied, "If you return safely, it will mean that the LORD has not spoken through me!" Then he added to those standing around, "Everyone mark my words!"

So King Ahab of Israel and King Jehoshaphat of Judah led their armies against Ramoth-gilead. The king of Israel said to Jehoshaphat, "As we go into battle, I will disguise myself so no one will recognize me, but you wear your royal robes." So the king of Israel disguised himself, and they went into battle.

Meanwhile, the king of Aram had issued these orders to his thirty-two chariot commanders: "Attack only the king of Israel. Don't bother with anyone else!" So when the Aramean chariot commanders saw Jehoshaphat in his royal robes, they went after him. "There is the king of Israel!" they shouted. But when Jehoshaphat called out, the chariot commanders realized he was not the king of Israel, and they stopped chasing him.

An Aramean soldier, however, randomly shot an arrow at the Israelite troops and hit the king of Israel between the joints of his armor. "Turn the horses and get me out of here!" Ahab groaned to the driver of his chariot. "I'm badly wounded!"

The battle raged all that day, and the king remained propped up in his chariot facing the Arameans. The blood from his wound ran down to the floor of his chariot, and as evening arrived he died. Just as the sun was setting, the cry ran through his troops: "We're done for! Run for your lives!"

So the king died, and his body was taken to Samaria and buried there. Then his chariot was washed beside the pool of Samaria, and dogs came and licked his blood at the place where the prostitutes bathed, just as the LORD had promised.

The rest of the events in Ahab's reign and everything he did, including the story of the ivory palace and the towns he built, are recorded in *The Book of the History of the Kings of Israel*. So Ahab died, and his son Ahaziah became the next king.

✦ ✦ ✦

Jehoshaphat son of Asa began to rule over Judah in the fourth year of King Ahab's reign in Israel. Jehoshaphat was thirty-five years old when he became king, and he reigned in Jerusalem twenty-five years. His mother was Azubah, the daughter of Shilhi.

Jehoshaphat was a good king, following the example of his father, Asa. He did what was pleasing in the LORD's sight. During his reign, however, he failed to remove all the pagan shrines, and the people still offered sacrifices and burned incense there. Jehoshaphat also made peace with the king of Israel.

The rest of the events in Jehoshaphat's reign, the extent of his power, and the wars he waged are recorded in *The Book of the History of the Kings of Judah*. He banished from the land the rest of the male and female shrine prostitutes, who still continued their practices from the days of his father, Asa.

(There was no king in Edom at that time, only a deputy.)

Jehoshaphat also built a fleet of trading ships to sail to Ophir for gold. But the ships never set sail, for they met with disaster in their home port of Ezion-geber. At one time Ahaziah son of Ahab had proposed to Jehoshaphat, "Let my men sail with your men in the ships." But Jehoshaphat refused the request.

When Jehoshaphat died, he was buried with his ancestors in the City of David. Then his son Jehoram became the next king.

+ + +

Ahaziah son of Ahab began to rule over Israel in the seventeenth year of King Jehoshaphat's reign in Judah. He reigned in Samaria two years. But he did what was evil in the LORD's sight, following the example of his father and mother and the example of Jeroboam son of Nebat, who had led Israel to sin. He served Baal and worshiped him, provoking the anger of the LORD, the God of Israel, just as his father had done.

After King Ahab's death, the land of Moab rebelled against Israel.

One day Israel's new king, Ahaziah, fell through the latticework of an upper room at his palace in Samaria and was seriously injured. So he sent messengers to the temple of Baal-zebub, the god of Ekron, to ask whether he would recover.

But the angel of the LORD told Elijah, who was from Tishbe, "Go and confront the messengers of the king of Samaria and ask them, 'Is there no God in Israel? Why are you going to Baal-zebub, the god of Ekron, to ask whether the king will recover? Now, therefore, this is what the LORD says: You will never leave the bed you are lying on; you will surely die.'" So Elijah went to deliver the message.

When the messengers returned to the king, he asked them, "Why have you returned so soon?"

They replied, "A man came up to us and told us to go back to the king and give him this message. 'This is what the LORD says: Is there no God in Israel? Why are you sending men to Baal-zebub, the god of Ekron, to ask whether you will recover? Therefore, because you have done this, you will never leave the bed you are lying on; you will surely die.'"

"What sort of man was he?" the king demanded. "What did he look like?"

They replied, "He was a hairy man, and he wore a leather belt around his waist."

"Elijah from Tishbe!" the king exclaimed.

Then he sent an army captain with fifty soldiers to arrest him. They found him sitting on top of a hill. The captain said to him, "Man of God, the king has commanded you to come down with us."

But Elijah replied to the captain, "If I am a man of God, let fire come down from heaven and destroy you and your fifty men!" Then fire fell from heaven and killed them all.

So the king sent another captain with fifty men. The captain said to him, "Man of God, the king demands that you come down at once."

Elijah replied, "If I am a man of God, let fire come down from heaven and destroy you and your fifty men!" And again the fire of God fell from heaven and killed them all.

Once more the king sent a third captain with fifty men. But this time the captain went up the hill and fell to his knees before Elijah. He pleaded with him, "O man of God, please spare my life and the lives of these, your fifty servants. See how the fire from heaven came down and destroyed the first two groups. But now please spare my life!"

Then the angel of the LORD said to Elijah, "Go down with him, and don't be afraid of him." So Elijah got up and went with him to the king.

And Elijah said to the king, "This is what the LORD says: Why did you send messengers to Baal-zebub, the god of Ekron, to ask whether you will recover? Is there no God in Israel to answer your question? Therefore, because you have done this, you will never leave the bed you are lying on; you will surely die."

So Ahaziah died, just as the LORD had promised through Elijah. Since Ahaziah did not have a son to succeed him, his brother Joram became the next king. This took place in the second year of the reign of Jehoram son of Jehoshaphat, king of Judah.

The rest of the events in Ahaziah's reign and everything he did are recorded in *The Book of the History of the Kings of Israel.*

+ + +

When the LORD was about to take Elijah up to heaven in a whirlwind, Elijah and Elisha were traveling from Gilgal. And Elijah said to Elisha, "Stay here, for the LORD has told me to go to Bethel."

But Elisha replied, "As surely as the LORD lives and you yourself live, I will never leave you!" So they went down together to Bethel.

The group of prophets from Bethel came to Elisha and asked him, "Did you know that the LORD is going to take your master away from you today?"

"Of course I know," Elisha answered. "But be quiet about it."

Then Elijah said to Elisha, "Stay here, for the LORD has told me to go to Jericho."

But Elisha replied again, "As surely as the LORD lives and you yourself live, I will never leave you." So they went on together to Jericho.

Then the group of prophets from Jericho came to Elisha and asked him, "Did you know that the LORD is going to take your master away from you today?"

"Of course I know," Elisha answered. "But be quiet about it."

Then Elijah said to Elisha, "Stay here, for the LORD has told me to go to the Jordan River."

But again Elisha replied, "As surely as the LORD lives and you yourself live, I will never leave you." So they went on together.

Fifty men from the group of prophets also went and watched from a distance as Elijah and Elisha stopped beside the Jordan River. Then Elijah folded his cloak together and struck the water with it. The river divided, and the two of them went across on dry ground!

When they came to the other side, Elijah said to Elisha, "Tell me what I can do for you before I am taken away."

And Elisha replied, "Please let me inherit a double share of your spirit and become your successor."

"You have asked a difficult thing," Elijah replied. "If you see me when I am taken from you, then you will get your request. But if not, then you won't."

As they were walking along and talking, suddenly a chariot of fire appeared, drawn by horses of fire. It drove between the two men, separating them, and Elijah was carried by a whirlwind into heaven. Elisha saw it and cried out, "My father! My father! I see the chariots and charioteers of Israel!" And as they disappeared from sight, Elisha tore his clothes in distress.

Elisha picked up Elijah's cloak, which had fallen when he was taken up. Then Elisha returned to the bank of the Jordan River. He struck the water with Elijah's cloak and cried out, "Where is the LORD, the God of Elijah?" Then the river divided, and Elisha went across.

When the group of prophets from Jericho saw from a distance what happened, they exclaimed, "Elijah's spirit rests upon Elisha!" And they went to meet him and bowed to the ground before him. "Sir," they said, "just say the word and fifty of our strongest men will search the wilderness for your master. Perhaps the Spirit of the LORD has left him on some mountain or in some valley."

"No," Elisha said, "don't send them." But they kept urging him until they shamed him into agreeing, and he finally said, "All right, send them." So fifty men searched for three days but did not find Elijah. Elisha was still at Jericho when they returned. "Didn't I tell you not to go?" he asked.

One day the leaders of the town of Jericho visited Elisha. "We have a problem, my lord," they told him. "This town is located in pleasant surroundings, as you can see. But the water is bad, and the land is unproductive."

Elisha said, "Bring me a new bowl with salt in it." So they brought it to him. Then he went out to the spring that supplied the town with water and threw the salt into it. And he said, "This is what the Lord says: I have purified this water. It will no longer cause death or infertility." And the water has remained pure ever since, just as Elisha said.

Elisha left Jericho and went up to Bethel. As he was walking along the road, a group of boys from the town began mocking and making fun of him. "Go away, baldy!" they chanted. "Go away, baldy!" Elisha turned around and looked at them, and he cursed them in the name of the Lord. Then two bears came out of the woods and mauled forty-two of them. From there Elisha went to Mount Carmel and finally returned to Samaria.

+ + +

Ahab's son Joram began to rule over Israel in the eighteenth year of King Jehoshaphat's reign in Judah. He reigned in Samaria twelve years. He did what was evil in the Lord's sight, but not to the same extent as his father and mother. He at least tore down the sacred pillar of Baal that his father had set up. Nevertheless, he continued in the sins that Jeroboam son of Nebat had committed and led the people of Israel to commit.

+

King Mesha of Moab was a sheep breeder. He used to pay the king of Israel an annual tribute of 100,000 lambs and the wool of 100,000 rams. But after Ahab's death, the king of Moab rebelled against the king of Israel. So King Joram promptly mustered the army of Israel and marched from Samaria. On the way, he sent this message to King Jehoshaphat of Judah: "The king of Moab has rebelled against me. Will you join me in battle against him?"

And Jehoshaphat replied, "Why, of course! You and I are as one. My troops are your troops, and my horses are your horses." Then Jehoshaphat asked, "What route will we take?"

"We will attack from the wilderness of Edom," Joram replied.

The king of Edom and his troops joined them, and all three armies traveled along a roundabout route through the wilderness for seven days. But there was no water for the men or their animals.

"What should we do?" the king of Israel cried out. "The Lord has brought the three of us here to let the king of Moab defeat us."

But King Jehoshaphat of Judah asked, "Is there no prophet of the Lord with us? If there is, we can ask the Lord what to do through him."

One of King Joram's officers replied, "Elisha son of Shaphat is here. He used to be Elijah's personal assistant."

Jehoshaphat said, "Yes, the LORD speaks through him." So the king of Israel, King Jehoshaphat of Judah, and the king of Edom went to consult with Elisha.

"Why are you coming to me?" Elisha asked the king of Israel. "Go to the pagan prophets of your father and mother!"

But King Joram of Israel said, "No! For it was the LORD who called us three kings here—only to be defeated by the king of Moab!"

Elisha replied, "As surely as the LORD Almighty lives, whom I serve, I wouldn't even bother with you except for my respect for King Jehoshaphat of Judah. Now bring me someone who can play the harp."

While the harp was being played, the power of the LORD came upon Elisha, and he said, "This is what the LORD says: This dry valley will be filled with pools of water! You will see neither wind nor rain, says the LORD, but this valley will be filled with water. You will have plenty for yourselves and your cattle and other animals. But this is only a simple thing for the LORD, for he will make you victorious over the army of Moab! You will conquer the best of their towns, even the fortified ones. You will cut down all their good trees, stop up all their springs, and ruin all their good land with stones."

The next day at about the time when the morning sacrifice was offered, water suddenly appeared! It was flowing from the direction of Edom, and soon there was water everywhere.

Meanwhile, when the people of Moab heard about the three armies marching against them, they mobilized every man who was old enough to strap on a sword, and they stationed themselves along their border. But when they got up the next morning, the sun was shining across the water, making it appear red to the Moabites—like blood. "It's blood!" the Moabites exclaimed. "The three armies must have attacked and killed each other! Let's go, men of Moab, and collect the plunder!"

But when the Moabites arrived at the Israelite camp, the army of Israel rushed out and attacked them until they turned and ran. The army of Israel chased them into the land of Moab, destroying everything as they went. They destroyed the towns, covered their good land with stones, stopped up all the springs, and cut down all the good trees. Finally, only Kir-hareseth and its stone walls were left, but men with slings surrounded and attacked it.

When the king of Moab saw that he was losing the battle, he led 700 of his swordsmen in a desperate attempt to break through the enemy lines near the king of Edom, but they failed. Then the king of Moab took his oldest son, who would have been the next king, and sacrificed him as a burnt offering on the wall. So there was great anger against Israel, and the Israelites withdrew and returned to their own land.

+

One day the widow of a member of the group of prophets came to Elisha and cried out, "My husband who served you is dead, and you know how he feared the LORD. But now a creditor has come, threatening to take my two sons as slaves."

"What can I do to help you?" Elisha asked. "Tell me, what do you have in the house?"

"Nothing at all, except a flask of olive oil," she replied.

And Elisha said, "Borrow as many empty jars as you can from your friends and neighbors. Then go into your house with your sons and shut the door behind you. Pour olive oil from your flask into the jars, setting each one aside when it is filled."

So she did as she was told. Her sons kept bringing jars to her, and she filled one after another. Soon every container was full to the brim!

"Bring me another jar," she said to one of her sons.

"There aren't any more!" he told her. And then the olive oil stopped flowing.

When she told the man of God what had happened, he said to her, "Now sell the olive oil and pay your debts, and you and your sons can live on what is left over."

One day Elisha went to the town of Shunem. A wealthy woman lived there, and she urged him to come to her home for a meal. After that, whenever he passed that way, he would stop there for something to eat.

She said to her husband, "I am sure this man who stops in from time to time is a holy man of God. Let's build a small room for him on the roof and furnish it with a bed, a table, a chair, and a lamp. Then he will have a place to stay whenever he comes by."

One day Elisha returned to Shunem, and he went up to this upper room to rest. He said to his servant Gehazi, "Tell the woman from Shunem I want to speak to her." When she appeared, Elisha said to Gehazi, "Tell her, 'We appreciate the kind concern you have shown us. What can we do for you? Can we put in a good word for you to the king or to the commander of the army?'"

"No," she replied, "my family takes good care of me."

Later Elisha asked Gehazi, "What can we do for her?"

Gehazi replied, "She doesn't have a son, and her husband is an old man."

"Call her back again," Elisha told him. When the woman returned, Elisha said to her as she stood in the doorway, "Next year at this time you will be holding a son in your arms!"

"No, my lord!" she cried. "O man of God, don't deceive me and get my hopes up like that."

But sure enough, the woman soon became pregnant. And at that time the following year she had a son, just as Elisha had said.

One day when her child was older, he went out to help his father, who was working with the harvesters. Suddenly he cried out, "My head hurts! My head hurts!"

His father said to one of the servants, "Carry him home to his mother."

So the servant took him home, and his mother held him on her lap. But around noontime he died. She carried him up and laid him on the bed of the man of God, then shut the door and left him there. She sent a message to her husband: "Send one of the servants and a donkey so that I can hurry to the man of God and come right back."

"Why go today?" he asked. "It is neither a new moon festival nor a Sabbath."

But she said, "It will be all right."

So she saddled the donkey and said to the servant, "Hurry! Don't slow down unless I tell you to."

As she approached the man of God at Mount Carmel, Elisha saw her in the distance. He said to Gehazi, "Look, the woman from Shunem is coming. Run out to meet her and ask her, 'Is everything all right with you, your husband, and your child?'"

"Yes," the woman told Gehazi, "everything is fine."

But when she came to the man of God at the mountain, she fell to the ground before him and caught hold of his feet. Gehazi began to push her away, but the man of God said, "Leave her alone. She is deeply troubled, but the LORD has not told me what it is."

Then she said, "Did I ask you for a son, my lord? And didn't I say, 'Don't deceive me and get my hopes up'?"

Then Elisha said to Gehazi, "Get ready to travel; take my staff and go! Don't talk to anyone along the way. Go quickly and lay the staff on the child's face."

But the boy's mother said, "As surely as the LORD lives and you yourself live, I won't go home unless you go with me." So Elisha returned with her.

Gehazi hurried on ahead and laid the staff on the child's face, but nothing happened. There was no sign of life. He returned to meet Elisha and told him, "The child is still dead."

When Elisha arrived, the child was indeed dead, lying there on the prophet's bed. He went in alone and shut the door behind him and prayed to the LORD. Then he lay down on the child's body, placing his mouth on the child's mouth, his eyes on the child's eyes, and his hands on the child's hands. And as he stretched out on him, the child's body began to grow warm again! Elisha got up, walked back and forth across the room once, and then stretched himself out again on the child. This time the boy sneezed seven times and opened his eyes!

Then Elisha summoned Gehazi. "Call the child's mother!" he said. And when she came in, Elisha said, "Here, take your son!" She fell at his feet and bowed before him, overwhelmed with gratitude. Then she took her son in her arms and carried him downstairs.

Elisha now returned to Gilgal, and there was a famine in the land. One day as the group of prophets was seated before him, he said to his servant, "Put a large pot on the fire, and make some stew for the rest of the group."

One of the young men went out into the field to gather herbs and came back with a pocketful of wild gourds. He shredded them and put them into the pot without realizing they were poisonous. Some of the stew was served to the men. But after they had eaten a bite or two they cried out, "Man of God, there's poison in this stew!" So they would not eat it.

Elisha said, "Bring me some flour." Then he threw it into the pot and said, "Now it's all right; go ahead and eat." And then it did not harm them.

One day a man from Baal-shalishah brought the man of God a sack of fresh grain and twenty loaves of barley bread made from the first grain of his harvest. Elisha said, "Give it to the people so they can eat."

"What?" his servant exclaimed. "Feed a hundred people with only this?"

But Elisha repeated, "Give it to the people so they can eat, for this is what the LORD says: Everyone will eat, and there will even be some left over!" And when they gave it to the people, there was plenty for all and some left over, just as the LORD had promised.

The king of Aram had great admiration for Naaman, the commander of his army, because through him the LORD had given Aram great victories. But though Naaman was a mighty warrior, he suffered from leprosy.

At this time Aramean raiders had invaded the land of Israel, and among their captives was a young girl who had been given to Naaman's wife as a maid. One day the girl said to her mistress, "I wish my master would go to see the prophet in Samaria. He would heal him of his leprosy."

So Naaman told the king what the young girl from Israel had said. "Go and visit the prophet," the king of Aram told him. "I will send a letter of introduction for you to take to the king of Israel." So Naaman started out, carrying as gifts 750 pounds of silver, 150 pounds of gold, and ten sets of clothing. The letter to the king of Israel said: "With this letter I present my servant Naaman. I want you to heal him of his leprosy."

When the king of Israel read the letter, he tore his clothes in dismay and said, "Am I God, that I can give life and take it away? Why is this man asking me to heal someone with leprosy? I can see that he's just trying to pick a fight with me."

But when Elisha, the man of God, heard that the king of Israel had torn his clothes in dismay, he sent this message to him: "Why are you so upset? Send Naaman to me, and he will learn that there is a true prophet here in Israel."

So Naaman went with his horses and chariots and waited at the door of Elisha's house. But Elisha sent a messenger out to him with this message: "Go and wash yourself seven times in the Jordan River. Then your skin will be restored, and you will be healed of your leprosy."

But Naaman became angry and stalked away. "I thought he would certainly come out to meet me!" he said. "I expected him to wave his hand over the leprosy and call on the name of the LORD his God and heal me! Aren't the rivers of Damascus, the Abana and the Pharpar, better than any of the rivers of Israel? Why shouldn't I wash in them and be healed?" So Naaman turned and went away in a rage.

But his officers tried to reason with him and said, "Sir, if the prophet had told you to do something very difficult, wouldn't you have done it? So you should certainly obey him when he says simply, 'Go and wash and be cured!'" So Naaman went down to the Jordan River and dipped himself seven times, as the man of God had instructed him. And his skin became as healthy as the skin of a young child, and he was healed!

Then Naaman and his entire party went back to find the man of God. They stood before him, and Naaman said, "Now I know that there is no God in all the world except in Israel. So please accept a gift from your servant."

But Elisha replied, "As surely as the LORD lives, whom I serve, I will not accept any gifts." And though Naaman urged him to take the gift, Elisha refused.

Then Naaman said, "All right, but please allow me to load two of my mules with earth from this place, and I will take it back home with me. From now on I will never again offer burnt offerings or sacrifices to any other god except the LORD. However, may the LORD pardon me in this one thing: When my master the king goes into the temple of the god Rimmon to worship there and leans on my arm, may the LORD pardon me when I bow, too."

"Go in peace," Elisha said. So Naaman started home again.

But Gehazi, the servant of Elisha, the man of God, said to himself, "My master should not have let this Aramean get away without accepting any of his gifts. As surely as the LORD lives, I will chase after him and get something from him." So Gehazi set off after Naaman.

When Naaman saw Gehazi running after him, he climbed down from his chariot and went to meet him. "Is everything all right?" Naaman asked.

"Yes," Gehazi said, "but my master has sent me to tell you that two young prophets from the hill country of Ephraim have just arrived. He would like 75 pounds of silver and two sets of clothing to give to them."

"By all means, take twice as much silver," Naaman insisted. He gave him two sets of clothing, tied up the money in two bags, and sent two of his servants to carry the gifts for Gehazi. But when they arrived at the citadel, Gehazi took the gifts from the servants and sent the men back. Then he went and hid the gifts inside the house.

When he went in to his master, Elisha asked him, "Where have you been, Gehazi?"

"I haven't been anywhere," he replied.

But Elisha asked him, "Don't you realize that I was there in spirit when Naaman stepped down from his chariot to meet you? Is this the time to receive money and clothing, olive groves and vineyards, sheep and cattle, and male and female servants? Because you have done this, you and your descendants will suffer from Naaman's leprosy forever." When Gehazi left the room, he was covered with leprosy; his skin was white as snow.

One day the group of prophets came to Elisha and told him, "As you can see, this place where we meet with you is too small. Let's go down to the Jordan River, where there are plenty of logs. There we can build a new place for us to meet."

"All right," he told them, "go ahead."

"Please come with us," someone suggested.

"I will," he said. So he went with them.

When they arrived at the Jordan, they began cutting down trees. But as one of them was cutting a tree, his ax head fell into the river. "Oh, sir!" he cried. "It was a borrowed ax!"

"Where did it fall?" the man of God asked. When he showed him the place, Elisha cut a stick and threw it into the water at that spot. Then the ax head floated to the surface. "Grab it," Elisha said. And the man reached out and grabbed it.

+

When the king of Aram was at war with Israel, he would confer with his officers and say, "We will mobilize our forces at such and such a place."

But immediately Elisha, the man of God, would warn the king of Israel,

"Do not go near that place, for the Arameans are planning to mobilize their troops there." So the king of Israel would send word to the place indicated by the man of God. Time and again Elisha warned the king, so that he would be on the alert there.

The king of Aram became very upset over this. He called his officers together and demanded, "Which of you is the traitor? Who has been informing the king of Israel of my plans?"

"It's not us, my lord the king," one of the officers replied. "Elisha, the prophet in Israel, tells the king of Israel even the words you speak in the privacy of your bedroom!"

"Go and find out where he is," the king commanded, "so I can send troops to seize him."

And the report came back: "Elisha is at Dothan." So one night the king of Aram sent a great army with many chariots and horses to surround the city.

When the servant of the man of God got up early the next morning and went outside, there were troops, horses, and chariots everywhere. "Oh, sir, what will we do now?" the young man cried to Elisha.

"Don't be afraid!" Elisha told him. "For there are more on our side than on theirs!" Then Elisha prayed, "O Lord, open his eyes and let him see!" The Lord opened the young man's eyes, and when he looked up, he saw that the hillside around Elisha was filled with horses and chariots of fire.

As the Aramean army advanced toward him, Elisha prayed, "O Lord, please make them blind." So the Lord struck them with blindness as Elisha had asked.

Then Elisha went out and told them, "You have come the wrong way! This isn't the right city! Follow me, and I will take you to the man you are looking for." And he led them to the city of Samaria.

As soon as they had entered Samaria, Elisha prayed, "O Lord, now open their eyes and let them see." So the Lord opened their eyes, and they discovered that they were in the middle of Samaria.

When the king of Israel saw them, he shouted to Elisha, "My father, should I kill them? Should I kill them?"

"Of course not!" Elisha replied. "Do we kill prisoners of war? Give them food and drink and send them home again to their master."

So the king made a great feast for them and then sent them home to their master. After that, the Aramean raiders stayed away from the land of Israel.

Some time later, however, King Ben-hadad of Aram mustered his entire army and besieged Samaria. As a result, there was a great famine in the city. The siege lasted so long that a donkey's head sold for eighty pieces of silver, and a cup of dove's dung sold for five pieces of silver.

One day as the king of Israel was walking along the wall of the city, a woman called to him, "Please help me, my lord the king!"

He answered, "If the LORD doesn't help you, what can I do? I have neither food from the threshing floor nor wine from the press to give you." But then the king asked, "What is the matter?"

She replied, "This woman said to me: 'Come on, let's eat your son today, then we will eat my son tomorrow.' So we cooked my son and ate him. Then the next day I said to her, 'Kill your son so we can eat him,' but she has hidden her son."

When the king heard this, he tore his clothes in despair. And as the king walked along the wall, the people could see that he was wearing burlap under his robe next to his skin. "May God strike me and even kill me if I don't separate Elisha's head from his shoulders this very day," the king vowed.

Elisha was sitting in his house with the elders of Israel when the king sent a messenger to summon him. But before the messenger arrived, Elisha said to the elders, "A murderer has sent a man to cut off my head. When he arrives, shut the door and keep him out. We will soon hear his master's steps following him."

While Elisha was still saying this, the messenger arrived. And the king said, "All this misery is from the LORD! Why should I wait for the LORD any longer?"

Elisha replied, "Listen to this message from the LORD! This is what the LORD says: By this time tomorrow in the markets of Samaria, six quarts of choice flour will cost only one piece of silver, and twelve quarts of barley grain will cost only one piece of silver."

The officer assisting the king said to the man of God, "That couldn't happen even if the LORD opened the windows of heaven!"

But Elisha replied, "You will see it happen with your own eyes, but you won't be able to eat any of it!"

Now there were four men with leprosy sitting at the entrance of the city gates. "Why should we sit here waiting to die?" they asked each other. "We will starve if we stay here, but with the famine in the city, we will starve if we go back there. So we might as well go out and surrender to the Aramean army. If they let us live, so much the better. But if they kill us, we would have died anyway."

So at twilight they set out for the camp of the Arameans. But when they came to the edge of the camp, no one was there! For the Lord had caused the Aramean army to hear the clatter of speeding chariots and the galloping of horses and the sounds of a great army approaching. "The king of Israel has hired the Hittites and Egyptians to attack us!" they cried to one another. So they panicked and ran into the night, abandoning their tents, horses, donkeys, and everything else, as they fled for their lives.

When the men with leprosy arrived at the edge of the camp, they went into one tent after another, eating and drinking wine; and they carried off silver and gold and clothing and hid it. Finally, they said to each other, "This is not right. This is a day of good news, and we aren't sharing it with anyone! If we wait until morning, some calamity will certainly fall upon us. Come on, let's go back and tell the people at the palace."

So they went back to the city and told the gatekeepers what had happened. "We went out to the Aramean camp," they said, "and no one was there! The horses and donkeys were tethered and the tents were all in order, but there wasn't a single person around!" Then the gatekeepers shouted the news to the people in the palace.

The king got out of bed in the middle of the night and told his officers, "I know what has happened. The Arameans know we are starving, so they have left their camp and have hidden in the fields. They are expecting us to leave the city, and then they will take us alive and capture the city."

One of his officers replied, "We had better send out scouts to check into this. Let them take five of the remaining horses. If something happens to them, it will be no worse than if they stay here and die with the rest of us."

So two chariots with horses were prepared, and the king sent scouts to see what had happened to the Aramean army. They went all the way to the Jordan River, following a trail of clothing and equipment that the Arameans had thrown away in their mad rush to escape. The scouts returned and told the king about it. Then the people of Samaria rushed out and plundered the Aramean camp. So it was true that six quarts of choice flour were sold that day for one piece of silver, and twelve quarts of barley grain were sold for one piece of silver, just as the LORD had promised. The king appointed his officer to control the traffic at the gate, but he was knocked down and trampled to death as the people rushed out.

So everything happened exactly as the man of God had predicted when the king came to his house. The man of God had said to the king, "By this time tomorrow in the markets of Samaria, six quarts of choice flour will cost one piece of silver, and twelve quarts of barley grain will cost one piece of silver."

The king's officer had replied, "That couldn't happen even if the LORD opened the windows of heaven!" And the man of God had said, "You will see it happen with your own eyes, but you won't be able to eat any of it!" And so it was, for the people trampled him to death at the gate!

Elisha had told the woman whose son he had brought back to life, "Take your family and move to some other place, for the LORD has called for a famine on Israel that will last for seven years." So the woman did as the man of God instructed. She took her family and settled in the land of the Philistines for seven years.

After the famine ended she returned from the land of the Philistines, and she went to see the king about getting back her house and land. As she came in, the king was talking with Gehazi, the servant of the man of God. The king had just said, "Tell me some stories about the great things Elisha has done." And Gehazi was telling the king about the time Elisha had brought a boy back to life. At that very moment, the mother of the boy walked in to make her appeal to the king about her house and land.

"Look, my lord the king!" Gehazi exclaimed. "Here is the woman now, and this is her son—the very one Elisha brought back to life!"

"Is this true?" the king asked her. And she told him the story. So he directed one of his officials to see that everything she had lost was restored to her, including the value of any crops that had been harvested during her absence.

Elisha went to Damascus, the capital of Aram, where King Ben-hadad lay sick. When someone told the king that the man of God had come, the king said to Hazael, "Take a gift to the man of God. Then tell him to ask the LORD, 'Will I recover from this illness?'"

So Hazael loaded down forty camels with the finest products of Damascus as a gift for Elisha. He went to him and said, "Your servant Ben-hadad, the king of Aram, has sent me to ask, 'Will I recover from this illness?'"

And Elisha replied, "Go and tell him, 'You will surely recover.' But actually the LORD has shown me that he will surely die!" Elisha stared at Hazael with a fixed gaze until Hazael became uneasy. Then the man of God started weeping.

"What's the matter, my lord?" Hazael asked him.

Elisha replied, "I know the terrible things you will do to the people of Israel. You will burn their fortified cities, kill their young men with the sword, dash their little children to the ground, and rip open their pregnant women!"

Hazael responded, "How could a nobody like me ever accomplish such great things?"

Elisha answered, "The LORD has shown me that you are going to be the king of Aram."

When Hazael left Elisha and went back, the king asked him, "What did Elisha tell you?"

And Hazael replied, "He told me that you will surely recover."

But the next day Hazael took a blanket, soaked it in water, and held it over the king's face until he died. Then Hazael became the next king of Aram.

+ + +

Jehoram son of King Jehoshaphat of Judah began to rule over Judah in the fifth year of the reign of Joram son of Ahab, king of Israel. Jehoram was thirty-two years old when he became king, and he reigned in Jerusalem eight years. But Jehoram followed the example of the kings of Israel and was as wicked as King Ahab, for he had married one of Ahab's daughters. So Jehoram did what was evil in the LORD's sight. But the LORD did not want to destroy Judah, for he had promised his servant David that his descendants would continue to rule, shining like a lamp forever.

During Jehoram's reign, the Edomites revolted against Judah and crowned their own king. So Jehoram went with all his chariots to attack the town of Zair. The Edomites surrounded him and his chariot commanders, but he went out at night and attacked them under cover of darkness. But Jehoram's army deserted him and fled to their homes. So Edom has been independent from Judah to this day. The town of Libnah also revolted about that same time.

The rest of the events in Jehoram's reign and everything he did are recorded in *The Book of the History of the Kings of Judah*. When Jehoram died, he was buried with his ancestors in the City of David. Then his son Ahaziah became the next king.

+ + +

Ahaziah son of Jehoram began to rule over Judah in the twelfth year of the reign of Joram son of Ahab, king of Israel.

Ahaziah was twenty-two years old when he became king, and he reigned in Jerusalem one year. His mother was Athaliah, a granddaughter of King Omri of Israel. Ahaziah followed the evil example of King Ahab's family. He did what was evil in the LORD's sight, just as Ahab's family had done, for he was related by marriage to the family of Ahab.

Ahaziah joined Joram son of Ahab in his war against King Hazael of Aram at Ramoth-gilead. When the Arameans wounded King Joram in the battle, he returned to Jezreel to recover from the wounds he had received at Ramoth. Because Joram was wounded, King Ahaziah of Judah went to Jezreel to visit him.

Meanwhile, Elisha the prophet had summoned a member of the group of prophets. "Get ready to travel," he told him, "and take this flask of olive oil with you. Go to Ramoth-gilead, and find Jehu son of Jehoshaphat, son of Nimshi. Call him into a private room away from his friends, and pour the oil over his head. Say to him, 'This is what the LORD says: I anoint you to be the king over Israel.' Then open the door and run for your life!"

So the young prophet did as he was told and went to Ramoth-gilead. When he arrived there, he found Jehu sitting around with the other army officers. "I have a message for you, Commander," he said.

"For which one of us?" Jehu asked.

"For you, Commander," he replied.

So Jehu left the others and went into the house. Then the young prophet poured the oil over Jehu's head and said, "This is what the LORD, the God of Israel, says: I anoint you king over the LORD's people, Israel. You are to destroy the family of Ahab, your master. In this way, I will avenge the murder of my prophets and all the LORD's servants who were killed by Jezebel. The entire family of Ahab must be wiped out. I will destroy every one of his male descendants, slave and free alike, anywhere in Israel. I will destroy the family of Ahab as I destroyed the families of Jeroboam son of Nebat and of Baasha son of Ahijah. Dogs will eat Ahab's wife Jezebel at the plot of land in Jezreel, and no one will bury her." Then the young prophet opened the door and ran.

Jehu went back to his fellow officers, and one of them asked him, "What did that madman want? Is everything all right?"

"You know how a man like that babbles on," Jehu replied.

"You're hiding something," they said. "Tell us."

So Jehu told them, "He said to me, 'This is what the LORD says: I have anointed you to be king over Israel.'"

Then they quickly spread out their cloaks on the bare steps and blew the ram's horn, shouting, "Jehu is king!"

So Jehu son of Jehoshaphat, son of Nimshi, led a conspiracy against King Joram. (Now Joram had been with the army at Ramoth-gilead, defending Israel against the forces of King Hazael of Aram. But King Joram was wounded in the fighting and returned to Jezreel to recover from his wounds.) So Jehu told the men with him, "If you want me to be king, don't let anyone leave town and go to Jezreel to report what we have done."

Then Jehu got into a chariot and rode to Jezreel to find King Joram, who was lying there wounded. King Ahaziah of Judah was there, too, for he had gone to visit him. The watchman on the tower of Jezreel saw Jehu and his company approaching, so he shouted to Joram, "I see a company of troops coming!"

"Send out a rider to ask if they are coming in peace," King Joram ordered.

So a horseman went out to meet Jehu and said, "The king wants to know if you are coming in peace."

Jehu replied, "What do you know about peace? Fall in behind me!"

The watchman called out to the king, "The messenger has met them, but he's not returning."

So the king sent out a second horseman. He rode up to them and said, "The king wants to know if you come in peace."

Again Jehu answered, "What do you know about peace? Fall in behind me!"

The watchman exclaimed, "The messenger has met them, but he isn't returning either! It must be Jehu son of Nimshi, for he's driving like a madman."

"Quick! Get my chariot ready!" King Joram commanded.

Then King Joram of Israel and King Ahaziah of Judah rode out in their chariots to meet Jehu. They met him at the plot of land that had belonged to Naboth of Jezreel. King Joram demanded, "Do you come in peace, Jehu?"

Jehu replied, "How can there be peace as long as the idolatry and witchcraft of your mother, Jezebel, are all around us?"

Then King Joram turned the horses around and fled, shouting to King Ahaziah, "Treason, Ahaziah!" But Jehu drew his bow and shot Joram between the shoulders. The arrow pierced his heart, and he sank down dead in his chariot.

Jehu said to Bidkar, his officer, "Throw him into the plot of land that belonged to Naboth of Jezreel. Do you remember when you and I were riding along behind his father, Ahab? The LORD pronounced this message against him: 'I solemnly swear that I will repay him here on this plot of land, says the LORD, for the murder of Naboth and his sons that I saw yesterday.' So throw him out on Naboth's property, just as the LORD said."

When King Ahaziah of Judah saw what was happening, he fled along the road to Beth-haggan. Jehu rode after him, shouting, "Shoot him, too!" So they shot Ahaziah in his chariot at the Ascent of Gur, near Ibleam. He was able to go on as far as Megiddo, but he died there. His servants took him by chariot to Jerusalem, where they buried him with his ancestors in the City of David. Ahaziah had become king over Judah in the eleventh year of the reign of Joram son of Ahab.

When Jezebel, the queen mother, heard that Jehu had come to Jezreel, she painted her eyelids and fixed her hair and sat at a window. When Jehu entered the gate of the palace, she shouted at him, "Have you come in peace, you murderer? You're just like Zimri, who murdered his master!"

Jehu looked up and saw her at the window and shouted, "Who is on my side?" And two or three eunuchs looked out at him. "Throw her down!" Jehu yelled. So they threw her out the window, and her blood spattered against the wall and on the horses. And Jehu trampled her body under his horses' hooves.

Then Jehu went into the palace and ate and drank. Afterward he said, "Someone go and bury this cursed woman, for she is the daughter of a king." But when they went out to bury her, they found only her skull, her feet, and her hands.

When they returned and told Jehu, he stated, "This fulfills the message from the LORD, which he spoke through his servant Elijah from Tishbe: 'At the plot of land in Jezreel, dogs will eat Jezebel's body. Her remains will be scattered like dung on the plot of land in Jezreel, so that no one will be able to recognize her.'"

Ahab had seventy sons living in the city of Samaria. So Jehu wrote letters and sent them to Samaria, to the elders and officials of the city, and to the guardians of King Ahab's sons. He said, "The king's sons are with you, and you have at your disposal chariots, horses, a fortified city, and weapons. As soon as you receive this letter, select the best qualified of your master's sons to be your king, and prepare to fight for Ahab's dynasty."

But they were paralyzed with fear and said, "We've seen that two kings couldn't stand against this man! What can we do?"

So the palace and city administrators, together with the elders and the guardians of the king's sons, sent this message to Jehu: "We are your servants and will do anything you tell us. We will not make anyone king; do whatever you think is best."

Jehu responded with a second letter: "If you are on my side and are going to obey me, bring the heads of your master's sons to me at Jezreel by this time tomorrow." Now the seventy sons of the king were being cared for by the leaders of Samaria, where they had been raised since childhood. When the letter arrived, the leaders killed all seventy of the king's sons. They placed their heads in baskets and presented them to Jehu at Jezreel.

A messenger went to Jehu and said, "They have brought the heads of the king's sons."

So Jehu ordered, "Pile them in two heaps at the entrance of the city gate, and leave them there until morning."

In the morning he went out and spoke to the crowd that had gathered around them. "You are not to blame," he told them. "I am the one who conspired against my master and killed him. But who killed all these? You can be sure that the message of the LORD that was spoken concerning Ahab's family will not fail. The LORD declared through his servant Elijah that this would happen." Then Jehu killed all who were left of Ahab's relatives living in Jezreel and all his important officials, his personal friends, and his priests. So Ahab was left without a single survivor.

Then Jehu set out for Samaria. Along the way, while he was at Beth-eked of the Shepherds, he met some relatives of King Ahaziah of Judah. "Who are you?" he asked them.

And they replied, "We are relatives of King Ahaziah. We are going to visit the sons of King Ahab and the sons of the queen mother."

"Take them alive!" Jehu shouted to his men. And they captured all forty-two of them and killed them at the well of Beth-eked. None of them escaped.

When Jehu left there, he met Jehonadab son of Recab, who was coming to meet him. After they had greeted each other, Jehu said to him, "Are you as loyal to me as I am to you?"

"Yes, I am," Jehonadab replied.

"If you are," Jehu said, "then give me your hand." So Jehonadab put out his hand, and Jehu helped him into the chariot. Then Jehu said, "Now come with me, and see how devoted I am to the LORD." So Jehonadab rode along with him.

When Jehu arrived in Samaria, he killed everyone who was left there from Ahab's family, just as the LORD had promised through Elijah.

Then Jehu called a meeting of all the people of the city and said to them, "Ahab's worship of Baal was nothing compared to the way I will worship him! Therefore, summon all the prophets and worshipers of Baal, and call together all his priests. See to it that every one of them comes, for I am going to offer a great sacrifice to Baal. Anyone who fails to come will be put to death." But Jehu's cunning plan was to destroy all the worshipers of Baal.

Then Jehu ordered, "Prepare a solemn assembly to worship Baal!" So they did. He sent messengers throughout all Israel summoning those who worshiped Baal. They all came—not a single one remained behind—and they filled the temple of Baal from one end to the other. And Jehu instructed the keeper of the wardrobe, "Be sure that every worshiper of Baal wears one of these robes." So robes were given to them.

Then Jehu went into the temple of Baal with Jehonadab son of Recab. Jehu said to the worshipers of Baal, "Make sure no one who worships the LORD is here—only those who worship Baal." So they were all inside the temple to offer sacrifices and burnt offerings. Now Jehu had stationed eighty of his men outside the building and had warned them, "If you let anyone escape, you will pay for it with your own life."

As soon as Jehu had finished sacrificing the burnt offering, he commanded his guards and officers, "Go in and kill all of them. Don't let a single one escape!" So they killed them all with their swords, and the guards and officers dragged their bodies outside. Then Jehu's men went into the innermost fortress of the temple of Baal. They dragged out the sacred pillar used in the worship of Baal and burned it. They smashed the sacred pillar and wrecked the temple of Baal, converting it into a public toilet, as it remains to this day.

In this way, Jehu destroyed every trace of Baal worship from Israel. He did not, however, destroy the gold calves at Bethel and Dan, with which Jeroboam son of Nebat had caused Israel to sin.

Nonetheless the LORD said to Jehu, "You have done well in following my instructions to destroy the family of Ahab. Therefore, your descendants will be kings of Israel down to the fourth generation." But Jehu did not obey the Law of the LORD, the God of Israel, with all his heart. He refused to turn from the sins that Jeroboam had led Israel to commit.

At about that time the LORD began to cut down the size of Israel's territory. King Hazael conquered several sections of the country east of the Jordan River, including all of Gilead, Gad, Reuben, and Manasseh. He conquered the area from the town of Aroer by the Arnon Gorge to as far north as Gilead and Bashan.

The rest of the events in Jehu's reign—everything he did and all his achievements—are recorded in *The Book of the History of the Kings of Israel.* When Jehu died, he was buried in Samaria. Then his son Jehoahaz became the next king. In all, Jehu reigned over Israel from Samaria for twenty-eight years.

✛ ✛ ✛

When Athaliah, the mother of King Ahaziah of Judah, learned that her son was dead, she began to destroy the rest of the royal family. But Ahaziah's sister Jehosheba, the daughter of King Jehoram, took Ahaziah's infant son, Joash, and stole him away from among the rest of the king's children, who were about to be killed. She put Joash and his nurse in a bedroom, and they hid him from Athaliah, so the child was not murdered. Joash remained hidden in the Temple of the LORD for six years while Athaliah ruled over the land.

In the seventh year of Athaliah's reign, Jehoiada the priest summoned the commanders, the Carite mercenaries, and the palace guards to come to the Temple of the LORD. He made a solemn pact with them and made them swear an oath of loyalty there in the LORD's Temple; then he showed them the king's son.

Jehoiada told them, "This is what you must do. A third of you who are on duty on the Sabbath are to guard the royal palace itself. Another third of you are to stand guard at the Sur Gate. And the final third must stand guard behind the palace guard. These three groups will all guard the palace. The other two units who are off duty on the Sabbath must stand guard for the king at the LORD's Temple. Form a bodyguard around the king and keep your weapons in hand. Kill anyone who tries to break through. Stay with the king wherever he goes."

So the commanders did everything as Jehoiada the priest ordered. The commanders took charge of the men reporting for duty that Sabbath, as well as those who were going off duty. They brought them all to Jehoiada the priest, and he supplied them with the spears and small shields that had once belonged to King David and were stored in the Temple of the LORD. The palace guards stationed themselves around the king, with their weapons ready. They formed a line from the south side of the Temple around to the north side and all around the altar.

Then Jehoiada brought out Joash, the king's son, placed the crown on his head, and presented him with a copy of God's laws. They anointed him and proclaimed him king, and everyone clapped their hands and shouted, "Long live the king!"

When Athaliah heard the noise made by the palace guards and the people, she hurried to the LORD's Temple to see what was happening. When she arrived, she saw the newly crowned king standing in his place of authority by the pillar, as was the custom at times of coronation. The commanders and trumpeters were surrounding him, and people from all over the land were rejoicing and blowing trumpets. When Athaliah saw all this, she tore her clothes in despair and shouted, "Treason! Treason!"

Then Jehoiada the priest ordered the commanders who were in charge of the troops, "Take her to the soldiers in front of the Temple, and kill anyone who tries to rescue her." For the priest had said, "She must not be killed in the Temple of the LORD." So they seized her and led her out to the gate where horses enter the palace grounds, and she was killed there.

Then Jehoiada made a covenant between the LORD and the king and the people that they would be the LORD's people. He also made a covenant between the king and the people. And all the people of the land went over to the temple of Baal and tore it down. They demolished the altars and smashed the idols to pieces, and they killed Mattan the priest of Baal in front of the altars.

Jehoiada the priest stationed guards at the Temple of the LORD. Then the commanders, the Carite mercenaries, the palace guards, and all the people of the land escorted the king from the Temple of the LORD. They went through the gate of the guards and into the palace, and the king took his seat on the royal throne. So all the people of the land rejoiced, and the city was peaceful because Athaliah had been killed at the king's palace.

+ + +

Joash was seven years old when he became king.

Joash began to rule over Judah in the seventh year of King Jehu's reign in Israel. He reigned in Jerusalem forty years. His mother was Zibiah from Beersheba. All his life Joash did what was pleasing in the LORD's sight because Jehoiada the priest instructed him. Yet even so, he did not destroy the pagan shrines, and the people still offered sacrifices and burned incense there.

One day King Joash said to the priests, "Collect all the money brought as a sacred offering to the LORD's Temple, whether it is a regular assessment, a payment of vows, or a voluntary gift. Let the priests take some of that money to pay for whatever repairs are needed at the Temple."

But by the twenty-third year of Joash's reign, the priests still had not repaired the Temple. So King Joash called for Jehoiada and the other priests and asked them, "Why haven't you repaired the Temple? Don't use any more money for your own needs. From now on, it must all be spent on Temple repairs." So the priests agreed not to accept any more money from the people, and they also agreed to let others take responsibility for repairing the Temple.

Then Jehoiada the priest bored a hole in the lid of a large chest and set it on the right-hand side of the altar at the entrance of the Temple of the LORD. The priests guarding the entrance put all of the people's contributions into the chest. Whenever the chest became full, the court secretary and the high priest counted the money that had been brought to the LORD's Temple and put it into bags. Then they gave the money to the construction supervisors, who used it to pay the people working on the LORD's Temple—the carpenters, the builders, the masons, and the stonecutters. They also used the money to buy the timber and the finished stone needed for repairing the LORD's Temple, and they paid any other expenses related to the Temple's restoration.

The money brought to the Temple was not used for making silver bowls, lamp snuffers, basins, trumpets, or other articles of gold or silver for the Temple of the LORD. It was paid to the workmen, who used it for the Temple repairs. No accounting of this money was required from the construction supervisors, because they were honest and trustworthy men. However, the money that was contributed for guilt offerings and sin offerings was not brought into the LORD's Temple. It was given to the priests for their own use.

About this time King Hazael of Aram went to war against Gath and captured it. Then he turned to attack Jerusalem. King Joash collected all the sacred objects that Jehoshaphat, Jehoram, and Ahaziah, the previous kings of Judah, had dedicated, along with what he himself had dedicated. He sent them all to Hazael, along with all the gold in the treasuries of the LORD's Temple and the royal palace. So Hazael called off his attack on Jerusalem.

The rest of the events in Joash's reign and everything he did are recorded in *The Book of the History of the Kings of Judah.*

Joash's officers plotted against him and assassinated him at Beth-millo on the road to Silla. The assassins were Jozacar son of Shimeath and Jehozabad son of Shomer—both trusted advisers. Joash was buried with his ancestors in the City of David. Then his son Amaziah became the next king.

+ + +

Jehoahaz son of Jehu began to rule over Israel in the twenty-third year of King Joash's reign in Judah. He reigned in Samaria seventeen years. But he did what was evil in the LORD's sight. He followed the example of Jeroboam son of Nebat, continuing the sins that Jeroboam had led Israel to commit. So the LORD was very angry with Israel, and he allowed King Hazael of Aram and his son Ben-hadad to defeat them repeatedly.

Then Jehoahaz prayed for the LORD's help, and the LORD heard his prayer, for he could see how severely the king of Aram was oppressing Israel. So the LORD provided someone to rescue the Israelites from the tyranny of the Arameans. Then Israel lived in safety again as they had in former days.

But they continued to sin, following the evil example of Jeroboam. They also allowed the Asherah pole in Samaria to remain standing. Finally, Jehoahaz's army was reduced to 50 charioteers, 10 chariots, and 10,000 foot soldiers. The king of Aram had killed the others, trampling them like dust under his feet.

The rest of the events in Jehoahaz's reign—everything he did and the extent of his power—are recorded in *The Book of the History of the Kings of Israel.* When Jehoahaz died, he was buried in Samaria. Then his son Jehoash became the next king.

+ + +

Jehoash son of Jehoahaz began to rule over Israel in the thirty-seventh year of King Joash's reign in Judah. He reigned in Samaria sixteen years. But he did what was evil in the LORD's sight. He refused to turn from the sins that Jeroboam son of Nebat had led Israel to commit.

The rest of the events in Jehoash's reign and everything he did, including the extent of his power and his war with King Amaziah of Judah, are recorded in *The Book of the History of the Kings of Israel*. When Jehoash died, he was buried in Samaria with the kings of Israel. Then his son Jeroboam II became the next king.

✦ ✦ ✦

When Elisha was in his last illness, King Jehoash of Israel visited him and wept over him. "My father! My father! I see the chariots and charioteers of Israel!" he cried.

Elisha told him, "Get a bow and some arrows." And the king did as he was told. Elisha told him, "Put your hand on the bow," and Elisha laid his own hands on the king's hands.

Then he commanded, "Open that eastern window," and he opened it. Then he said, "Shoot!" So he shot an arrow. Elisha proclaimed, "This is the LORD's arrow, an arrow of victory over Aram, for you will completely conquer the Arameans at Aphek."

Then he said, "Now pick up the other arrows and strike them against the ground." So the king picked them up and struck the ground three times. But the man of God was angry with him. "You should have struck the ground five or six times!" he exclaimed. "Then you would have beaten Aram until it was entirely destroyed. Now you will be victorious only three times."

Then Elisha died and was buried.

Groups of Moabite raiders used to invade the land each spring. Once when some Israelites were burying a man, they spied a band of these raiders. So they hastily threw the corpse into the tomb of Elisha and fled. But as soon as the body touched Elisha's bones, the dead man revived and jumped to his feet!

King Hazael of Aram had oppressed Israel during the entire reign of King Jehoahaz. But the LORD was gracious and merciful to the people of Israel, and they were not totally destroyed. He pitied them because of his covenant with Abraham, Isaac, and Jacob. And to this day he still has not completely destroyed them or banished them from his presence.

King Hazael of Aram died, and his son Ben-hadad became the next king. Then Jehoash son of Jehoahaz recaptured from Ben-hadad son of Hazael the towns that had been taken from Jehoash's father, Jehoahaz. Jehoash defeated Ben-hadad on three occasions, and he recovered the Israelite towns.

+ + +

Amaziah son of Joash began to rule over Judah in the second year of the reign of King Jehoash of Israel. Amaziah was twenty-five years old when he became king, and he reigned in Jerusalem twenty-nine years. His mother was Jehoaddin from Jerusalem. Amaziah did what was pleasing in the LORD's sight, but not like his ancestor David. Instead, he followed the example of his father, Joash. Amaziah did not destroy the pagan shrines, and the people still offered sacrifices and burned incense there.

When Amaziah was well established as king, he executed the officials who had assassinated his father. However, he did not kill the children of the assassins, for he obeyed the command of the LORD as written by Moses in the Book of the Law: "Parents must not be put to death for the sins of their children, nor children for the sins of their parents. Those deserving to die must be put to death for their own crimes."

Amaziah also killed 10,000 Edomites in the Valley of Salt. He also conquered Sela and changed its name to Joktheel, as it is called to this day.

One day Amaziah sent messengers with this challenge to Israel's king Jehoash, the son of Jehoahaz and grandson of Jehu: "Come and meet me in battle!"

But King Jehoash of Israel replied to King Amaziah of Judah with this story: "Out in the Lebanon mountains, a thistle sent a message to a mighty cedar tree: 'Give your daughter in marriage to my son.' But just then a wild animal of Lebanon came by and stepped on the thistle, crushing it!

"You have indeed defeated Edom, and you are proud of it. But be content with your victory and stay at home! Why stir up trouble that will only bring disaster on you and the people of Judah?"

But Amaziah refused to listen, so King Jehoash of Israel mobilized his army against King Amaziah of Judah. The two armies drew up their battle lines at Beth-shemesh in Judah. Judah was routed by the army of Israel, and its army scattered and fled for home. King Jehoash of Israel captured Judah's king, Amaziah son of Joash and grandson of Ahaziah, at Beth-shemesh. Then he marched to Jerusalem, where he demolished 600 feet of Jerusalem's wall, from the Ephraim Gate to the Corner Gate. He carried off all the gold and silver and all the articles from the Temple of the LORD. He also seized the treasures from the royal palace, along with hostages, and then returned to Samaria.

The rest of the events in Jehoash's reign and everything he did, including the extent of his power and his war with King Amaziah of Judah, are recorded in *The Book of the History of the Kings of Israel.* When Jehoash died, he was buried in Samaria with the kings of Israel. And his son Jeroboam II became the next king.

King Amaziah of Judah lived for fifteen years after the death of King Jehoash of Israel. The rest of the events in Amaziah's reign are recorded in *The Book of the History of the Kings of Judah.*

There was a conspiracy against Amaziah's life in Jerusalem, and he fled to Lachish. But his enemies sent assassins after him, and they killed him there. They brought his body back to Jerusalem on a horse, and he was buried with his ancestors in the City of David.

All the people of Judah had crowned Amaziah's sixteen-year-old son, Uzziah, as king in place of his father, Amaziah. After his father's death, Uzziah rebuilt the town of Elath and restored it to Judah.

+ + +

Jeroboam II, the son of Jehoash, began to rule over Israel in the fifteenth year of King Amaziah's reign in Judah. He reigned in Samaria forty-one years. He did what was evil in the LORD's sight. He refused to turn from the sins that Jeroboam son of Nebat had led Israel to commit. Jeroboam II recovered the territories of Israel between Lebo-hamath and the Dead Sea, just as the LORD, the God of Israel, had promised through Jonah son of Amittai, the prophet from Gath-hepher.

For the LORD saw the bitter suffering of everyone in Israel, and that there was no one in Israel, slave or free, to help them. And because the LORD had not said he would blot out the name of Israel completely, he used Jeroboam II, the son of Jehoash, to save them.

The rest of the events in the reign of Jeroboam II and everything he did—including the extent of his power, his wars, and how he recovered for Israel both Damascus and Hamath, which had belonged to Judah—are recorded in *The Book of the History of the Kings of Israel.* When Jeroboam II died, he was buried in Samaria with the kings of Israel. Then his son Zechariah became the next king.

+ + +

Uzziah son of Amaziah began to rule over Judah in the twenty-seventh year of the reign of King Jeroboam II of Israel. He was sixteen years old when he became king, and he reigned in Jerusalem fifty-two years. His mother was Jecoliah from Jerusalem.

He did what was pleasing in the LORD's sight, just as his father, Amaziah, had done. But he did not destroy the pagan shrines, and the people still offered sacrifices and burned incense there. The LORD struck the king with leprosy, which lasted until the day he died. He lived in isolation in a separate house. The king's son Jotham was put in charge of the royal palace, and he governed the people of the land.

The rest of the events in Uzziah's reign and everything he did are recorded in *The Book of the History of the Kings of Judah*. When Uzziah died, he was buried with his ancestors in the City of David. And his son Jotham became the next king.

+ + +

Zechariah son of Jeroboam II began to rule over Israel in the thirty-eighth year of King Uzziah's reign in Judah. He reigned in Samaria six months. Zechariah did what was evil in the LORD's sight, as his ancestors had done. He refused to turn from the sins that Jeroboam son of Nebat had led Israel to commit. Then Shallum son of Jabesh conspired against Zechariah, assassinated him in public, and became the next king.

The rest of the events in Zechariah's reign are recorded in *The Book of the History of the Kings of Israel*. So the LORD's message to Jehu came true: "Your descendants will be kings of Israel down to the fourth generation."

+ + +

Shallum son of Jabesh began to rule over Israel in the thirty-ninth year of King Uzziah's reign in Judah. Shallum reigned in Samaria only one month. Then Menahem son of Gadi went to Samaria from Tirzah and assassinated him, and he became the next king.

The rest of the events in Shallum's reign, including his conspiracy, are recorded in *The Book of the History of the Kings of Israel*.

+ + +

At that time Menahem destroyed the town of Tappuah and all the surrounding countryside as far as Tirzah, because its citizens refused to surrender the town. He killed the entire population and ripped open the pregnant women.

Menahem son of Gadi began to rule over Israel in the thirty-ninth year of King Uzziah's reign in Judah. He reigned in Samaria ten years. But

Menahem did what was evil in the LORD's sight. During his entire reign, he refused to turn from the sins that Jeroboam son of Nebat had led Israel to commit.

Then King Tiglath-pileser of Assyria invaded the land. But Menahem paid him thirty-seven tons of silver to gain his support in tightening his grip on royal power. Menahem extorted the money from the rich of Israel, demanding that each of them pay fifty pieces of silver to the king of Assyria. So the king of Assyria turned from attacking Israel and did not stay in the land.

The rest of the events in Menahem's reign and everything he did are recorded in *The Book of the History of the Kings of Israel*. When Menahem died, his son Pekahiah became the next king.

+ + +

Pekahiah son of Menahem began to rule over Israel in the fiftieth year of King Uzziah's reign in Judah. He reigned in Samaria two years. But Pekahiah did what was evil in the LORD's sight. He refused to turn from the sins that Jeroboam son of Nebat had led Israel to commit.

Then Pekah son of Remaliah, the commander of Pekahiah's army, conspired against him. With fifty men from Gilead, Pekah assassinated the king, along with Argob and Arieh, in the citadel of the palace at Samaria. And Pekah reigned in his place.

The rest of the events in Pekahiah's reign and everything he did are recorded in *The Book of the History of the Kings of Israel*.

+ + +

Pekah son of Remaliah began to rule over Israel in the fifty-second year of King Uzziah's reign in Judah. He reigned in Samaria twenty years. But Pekah did what was evil in the LORD's sight. He refused to turn from the sins that Jeroboam son of Nebat had led Israel to commit.

During Pekah's reign, King Tiglath-pileser of Assyria attacked Israel again, and he captured the towns of Ijon, Abel-beth-maacah, Janoah, Kedesh, and Hazor. He also conquered the regions of Gilead, Galilee, and all of Naphtali, and he took the people to Assyria as captives. Then Hoshea son of Elah conspired against Pekah and assassinated him. He began to rule over Israel in the twentieth year of Jotham son of Uzziah.

The rest of the events in Pekah's reign and everything he did are recorded in *The Book of the History of the Kings of Israel.*

+ + +

Jotham son of Uzziah began to rule over Judah in the second year of King Pekah's reign in Israel. He was twenty-five years old when he became king, and he reigned in Jerusalem sixteen years. His mother was Jerusha, the daughter of Zadok.

Jotham did what was pleasing in the LORD's sight. He did everything his father, Uzziah, had done. But he did not destroy the pagan shrines, and the people still offered sacrifices and burned incense there. He rebuilt the upper gate of the Temple of the LORD.

The rest of the events in Jotham's reign and everything he did are recorded in *The Book of the History of the Kings of Judah.* In those days the LORD began to send King Rezin of Aram and King Pekah of Israel to attack Judah. When Jotham died, he was buried with his ancestors in the City of David. And his son Ahaz became the next king.

+ + +

Ahaz son of Jotham began to rule over Judah in the seventeenth year of King Pekah's reign in Israel. Ahaz was twenty years old when he became king, and he reigned in Jerusalem sixteen years. He did not do what was pleasing in the sight of the LORD his God, as his ancestor David had done. Instead, he followed the example of the kings of Israel, even sacrificing his own son in the fire. In this way, he followed the detestable practices of the pagan nations the LORD had driven from the land ahead of the Israelites. He offered sacrifices and burned incense at the pagan shrines and on the hills and under every green tree.

Then King Rezin of Aram and King Pekah of Israel came up to attack Jerusalem. They besieged Ahaz but could not conquer him. At that time the king of Edom recovered the town of Elath for Edom. He drove out the people of Judah and sent Edomites to live there, as they do to this day.

King Ahaz sent messengers to King Tiglath-pileser of Assyria with this message: "I am your servant and your vassal. Come up and rescue me from the attacking armies of Aram and Israel." Then Ahaz took the silver and gold from the Temple of the LORD and the palace treasury and sent it as a payment to the Assyrian king. So the king of Assyria attacked the

Aramean capital of Damascus and led its population away as captives, re-settling them in Kir. He also killed King Rezin.

King Ahaz then went to Damascus to meet with King Tiglath-pileser of Assyria. While he was there, he took special note of the altar. Then he sent a model of the altar to Uriah the priest, along with its design in full detail. Uriah followed the king's instructions and built an altar just like it, and it was ready before the king returned from Damascus. When the king returned, he inspected the altar and made offerings on it. He presented a burnt offering and a grain offering, he poured out a liquid offering, and he sprinkled the blood of peace offerings on the altar.

Then King Ahaz removed the old bronze altar from its place in front of the LORD's Temple, between the entrance and the new altar, and placed it on the north side of the new altar. He told Uriah the priest, "Use the new altar for the morning sacrifices of burnt offering, the evening grain offer-ing, the king's burnt offering and grain offering, and the burnt offerings of all the people, as well as their grain offerings and liquid offerings. Sprinkle the blood from all the burnt offerings and sacrifices on the new altar. The bronze altar will be for my personal use only." Uriah the priest did just as King Ahaz commanded him.

Then the king removed the side panels and basins from the portable water carts. He also removed the great bronze basin called the Sea from the backs of the bronze oxen and placed it on the stone pavement. In def-erence to the king of Assyria, he also removed the canopy that had been constructed inside the palace for use on the Sabbath day, as well as the king's outer entrance to the Temple of the LORD.

The rest of the events in Ahaz's reign and everything he did are recorded in *The Book of the History of the Kings of Judah.* When Ahaz died, he was buried with his ancestors in the City of David. Then his son Hezekiah became the next king.

✦ ✦ ✦

Hoshea son of Elah began to rule over Israel in the twelfth year of King Ahaz's reign in Judah. He reigned in Samaria nine years. He did what was evil in the LORD's sight, but not to the same extent as the kings of Israel who ruled before him.

King Shalmaneser of Assyria attacked King Hoshea, so Hoshea was forced to pay heavy tribute to Assyria. But Hoshea stopped paying the annual tribute and conspired against the king of Assyria by asking King So of Egypt to help him shake free of Assyria's power. When the king of Assyria discovered this treachery, he seized Hoshea and put him in prison.

Then the king of Assyria invaded the entire land, and for three years he besieged the city of Samaria. Finally, in the ninth year of King Hoshea's reign, Samaria fell, and the people of Israel were exiled to Assyria. They were settled in colonies in Halah, along the banks of the Habor River in Gozan, and in the cities of the Medes.

This disaster came upon the people of Israel because they worshiped other gods. They sinned against the LORD their God, who had brought them safely out of Egypt and had rescued them from the power of Pharaoh, the king of Egypt. They had followed the practices of the pagan nations the LORD had driven from the land ahead of them, as well as the practices the kings of Israel had introduced. The people of Israel had also secretly done many things that were not pleasing to the LORD their God. They built pagan shrines for themselves in all their towns, from the smallest outpost to the largest walled city. They set up sacred pillars and Asherah poles at the top of every hill and under every green tree. They offered sacrifices on all the hilltops, just like the nations the LORD had driven from the land ahead of them. So the people of Israel had done many evil things, arousing the LORD's anger. Yes, they worshiped idols, despite the LORD's specific and repeated warnings.

Again and again the LORD had sent his prophets and seers to warn both Israel and Judah: "Turn from all your evil ways. Obey my commands and decrees—the entire law that I commanded your ancestors to obey, and that I gave you through my servants the prophets."

But the Israelites would not listen. They were as stubborn as their ancestors who had refused to believe in the LORD their God. They rejected his decrees and the covenant he had made with their ancestors, and they despised all his warnings. They worshiped worthless idols, so they became worthless themselves. They followed the example of the nations around them, disobeying the LORD's command not to imitate them.

They rejected all the commands of the LORD their God and made two calves from metal. They set up an Asherah pole and worshiped Baal and all the forces of heaven. They even sacrificed their own sons and daughters in the fire. They consulted fortune-tellers and practiced sorcery and sold themselves to evil, arousing the LORD's anger.

Because the LORD was very angry with Israel, he swept them away from his presence. Only the tribe of Judah remained in the land. But even the people of Judah refused to obey the commands of the LORD their God, for they followed the evil practices that Israel had introduced. The LORD rejected all the descendants of Israel. He punished them by handing them over to their attackers until he had banished Israel from his presence.

For when the LORD tore Israel away from the kingdom of David, they chose Jeroboam son of Nebat as their king. But Jeroboam drew Israel away from following the LORD and made them commit a great sin. And the people of Israel persisted in all the evil ways of Jeroboam. They did not turn from these sins until the LORD finally swept them away from his presence, just as all his prophets had warned. So Israel was exiled from their land to Assyria, where they remain to this day.

The king of Assyria transported groups of people from Babylon, Cuthah, Avva, Hamath, and Sepharvaim and resettled them in the towns of Samaria, replacing the people of Israel. They took possession of Samaria and lived in its towns. But since these foreign settlers did not worship the LORD when they first arrived, the LORD sent lions among them, which killed some of them.

So a message was sent to the king of Assyria: "The people you have sent to live in the towns of Samaria do not know the religious customs of the God of the land. He has sent lions among them to destroy them because they have not worshiped him correctly."

The king of Assyria then commanded, "Send one of the exiled priests back to Samaria. Let him live there and teach the new residents the religious customs of the God of the land." So one of the priests who had been exiled from Samaria returned to Bethel and taught the new residents how to worship the LORD.

But these various groups of foreigners also continued to worship their own gods. In town after town where they lived, they placed their idols at the pagan shrines that the people of Samaria had built. Those from Babylon worshiped idols of their god Succoth-benoth. Those from Cuthah worshiped their god Nergal. And those from Hamath worshiped Ashima. The Avvites worshiped their gods Nibhaz and Tartak. And the people from Sepharvaim even burned their own children as sacrifices to their gods Adrammelech and Anammelech.

These new residents worshiped the LORD, but they also appointed from among themselves all sorts of people as priests to offer sacrifices at their places of worship. And though they worshiped the LORD, they continued to follow their own gods according to the religious customs of the nations from which they came. And this is still going on today. They continue to follow their former practices instead of truly worshiping the LORD and obeying the decrees, regulations, instructions, and commands he gave the descendants of Jacob, whose name he changed to Israel.

For the LORD had made a covenant with the descendants of Jacob and commanded them: "Do not worship any other gods or bow before them or serve them or offer sacrifices to them. But worship only the LORD, who brought you out of Egypt with great strength and a powerful arm. Bow down to him alone, and offer sacrifices only to him. Be careful at all times to obey the decrees, regulations, instructions, and commands that he wrote for you. You must not worship other gods. Do not forget the covenant I made with you, and do not worship other gods. You must worship only the LORD your God. He is the one who will rescue you from all your enemies."

But the people would not listen and continued to follow their former practices. So while these new residents worshiped the LORD, they also worshiped their idols. And to this day their descendants do the same.

+ + +

Hezekiah son of Ahaz began to rule over Judah in the third year of King Hoshea's reign in Israel. He was twenty-five years old when he became king, and he reigned in Jerusalem twenty-nine years. His mother was Abijah, the daughter of Zechariah. He did what was pleasing in the LORD's sight, just as his ancestor David had done. He removed the pagan shrines, smashed the sacred pillars, and cut down the Asherah poles. He broke up the bronze serpent that Moses had made, because the people of Israel had been offering sacrifices to it. The bronze serpent was called Nehushtan.

Hezekiah trusted in the LORD, the God of Israel. There was no one like him among all the kings of Judah, either before or after his time. He remained faithful to the LORD in everything, and he carefully obeyed all the commands the LORD had given Moses. So the LORD was with him, and Hezekiah was successful in everything he did. He revolted against the king of Assyria and refused to pay him tribute. He also conquered the Philistines as far distant as Gaza and its territory, from their smallest outpost to their largest walled city.

During the fourth year of Hezekiah's reign, which was the seventh year of King Hoshea's reign in Israel, King Shalmaneser of Assyria attacked the city of Samaria and began a siege against it. Three years later, during the sixth year of King Hezekiah's reign and the ninth year of King Hoshea's reign in Israel, Samaria fell. At that time the king of Assyria exiled the Israelites to Assyria and placed them in colonies in Halah, along the banks of the Habor River in Gozan, and in the cities of the Medes. For they refused to listen to the LORD their God and obey him. Instead, they violated his covenant—all the laws that Moses the LORD's servant had commanded them to obey.

In the fourteenth year of King Hezekiah's reign, King Sennacherib of

Assyria came to attack the fortified towns of Judah and conquered them. King Hezekiah sent this message to the king of Assyria at Lachish: "I have done wrong. I will pay whatever tribute money you demand if you will only withdraw." The king of Assyria then demanded a settlement of more than eleven tons of silver and one ton of gold. To gather this amount, King Hezekiah used all the silver stored in the Temple of the LORD and in the palace treasury. Hezekiah even stripped the gold from the doors of the LORD's Temple and from the doorposts he had overlaid with gold, and he gave it all to the Assyrian king.

Nevertheless, the king of Assyria sent his commander in chief, his field commander, and his chief of staff from Lachish with a huge army to confront King Hezekiah in Jerusalem. The Assyrians took up a position beside the aqueduct that feeds water into the upper pool, near the road leading to the field where cloth is washed. They summoned King Hezekiah, but the king sent these officials to meet with them: Eliakim son of Hilkiah, the palace administrator; Shebna the court secretary; and Joah son of Asaph, the royal historian.

Then the Assyrian king's chief of staff told them to give this message to Hezekiah:

"This is what the great king of Assyria says: What are you trusting in that makes you so confident? Do you think that mere words can substitute for military skill and strength? Who are you counting on, that you have rebelled against me? On Egypt? If you lean on Egypt, it will be like a reed that splinters beneath your weight and pierces your hand. Pharaoh, the king of Egypt, is completely unreliable!

"But perhaps you will say to me, 'We are trusting in the LORD our God!' But isn't he the one who was insulted by Hezekiah? Didn't Hezekiah tear down his shrines and altars and make everyone in Judah and Jerusalem worship only at the altar here in Jerusalem?

"I'll tell you what! Strike a bargain with my master, the king of Assyria. I will give you 2,000 horses if you can find that many men to ride on them! With your tiny army, how can you think of challenging even the weakest contingent of my master's troops, even with the help of Egypt's chariots and charioteers? What's more, do you think we have invaded your land without the LORD's direction? The LORD himself told us, 'Attack this land and destroy it!'"

Then Eliakim son of Hilkiah, Shebna, and Joah said to the Assyrian chief of staff, "Please speak to us in Aramaic, for we understand it well. Don't speak in Hebrew, for the people on the wall will hear."

But Sennacherib's chief of staff replied, "Do you think my master sent this message only to you and your master? He wants all the people to hear it, for when we put this city under siege, they will suffer along with you. They will be so hungry and thirsty that they will eat their own dung and drink their own urine."

Then the chief of staff stood and shouted in Hebrew to the people on the wall, "Listen to this message from the great king of Assyria! This is what the king says: Don't let Hezekiah deceive you. He will never be able to rescue you from my power. Don't let him fool you into trusting in the LORD by saying, 'The LORD will surely rescue us. This city will never fall into the hands of the Assyrian king!'

"Don't listen to Hezekiah! These are the terms the king of Assyria is offering: Make peace with me—open the gates and come out. Then each of you can continue eating from your own grapevine and fig tree and drinking from your own well. Then I will arrange to take you to another land like this one—a land of grain and new wine, bread and vineyards, olive groves and honey. Choose life instead of death!

"Don't listen to Hezekiah when he tries to mislead you by saying, 'The LORD will rescue us!' Have the gods of any other nations ever saved their people from the king of Assyria? What happened to the gods of Hamath and Arpad? And what about the gods of Sepharvaim, Hena, and Ivvah? Did any god rescue Samaria from my power? What god of any nation has ever been able to save its people from my power? So what makes you think that the LORD can rescue Jerusalem from me?"

But the people were silent and did not utter a word because Hezekiah had commanded them, "Do not answer him."

Then Eliakim son of Hilkiah, the palace administrator; Shebna the court secretary; and Joah son of Asaph, the royal historian, went back to Hezekiah. They tore their clothes in despair, and they went in to see the king and told him what the Assyrian chief of staff had said.

When King Hezekiah heard their report, he tore his clothes and put on burlap and went into the Temple of the LORD. And he sent Eliakim the palace administrator, Shebna the court secretary, and the leading priests, all dressed in burlap, to the prophet Isaiah son of Amoz. They told him, "This is what King Hezekiah says: Today is a day of trouble, insults, and disgrace. It is like when a child is ready to be born, but the mother has no strength to deliver the baby. But perhaps the LORD your God has heard the Assyrian chief of staff, sent by the king to defy the living God, and will punish him for his words. Oh, pray for those of us who are left!"

After King Hezekiah's officials delivered the king's message to Isaiah, the prophet replied, "Say to your master, 'This is what the LORD says: Do not be disturbed by this blasphemous speech against me from the Assyrian king's messengers. Listen! I myself will move against him, and the king will receive a message that he is needed at home. So he will return to his land, where I will have him killed with a sword.'"

Meanwhile, the Assyrian chief of staff left Jerusalem and went to consult the king of Assyria, who had left Lachish and was attacking Libnah.

Soon afterward King Sennacherib received word that King Tirhakah of Ethiopia was leading an army to fight against him. Before leaving to meet the attack, he sent messengers back to Hezekiah in Jerusalem with this message:

"This message is for King Hezekiah of Judah. Don't let your God, in whom you trust, deceive you with promises that Jerusalem will not be captured by the king of Assyria. You know perfectly well what the kings of Assyria have done wherever they have gone. They have completely destroyed everyone who stood in their way! Why should you be any different? Have the gods of other nations rescued them—such nations as Gozan, Haran, Rezeph, and the people of Eden who were in Tel-assar? My predecessors destroyed them all! What happened to the king of Hamath and the king of Arpad? What happened to the kings of Sepharvaim, Hena, and Ivvah?"

After Hezekiah received the letter from the messengers and read it, he went up to the LORD's Temple and spread it out before the LORD. And Hezekiah prayed this prayer before the LORD: "O LORD, God of Israel, you are enthroned between the mighty cherubim! You alone are God of all the kingdoms of the earth. You alone created the heavens and the earth. Bend down, O LORD, and listen! Open your eyes, O LORD, and see! Listen to Sennacherib's words of defiance against the living God.

"It is true, LORD, that the kings of Assyria have destroyed all these nations. And they have thrown the gods of these nations into the fire and burned them. But of course the Assyrians could destroy them! They were not gods at all—only idols of wood and stone shaped by human hands. Now, O LORD our God, rescue us from his power; then all the kingdoms of the earth will know that you alone, O LORD, are God."

Then Isaiah son of Amoz sent this message to Hezekiah: "This is what the LORD, the God of Israel, says: I have heard your prayer about King Sennacherib of Assyria. And the LORD has spoken this word against him:

"The virgin daughter of Zion
    despises you and laughs at you.
The daughter of Jerusalem
    shakes her head in derision as you flee.

"Whom have you been defying and ridiculing?
   Against whom did you raise your voice?
At whom did you look with such haughty eyes?
   It was the Holy One of Israel!
By your messengers you have defied the Lord.
   You have said, 'With my many chariots
I have conquered the highest mountains—
   yes, the remotest peaks of Lebanon.
I have cut down its tallest cedars
   and its finest cypress trees.
I have reached its farthest corners
   and explored its deepest forests.
I have dug wells in many foreign lands
   and refreshed myself with their water.
With the sole of my foot
   I stopped up all the rivers of Egypt!'

"But have you not heard?
   I decided this long ago.
Long ago I planned it,
   and now I am making it happen.
I planned for you to crush fortified cities
   into heaps of rubble.
That is why their people have so little power
   and are so frightened and confused.
They are as weak as grass,
   as easily trampled as tender green shoots.
They are like grass sprouting on a housetop,
   scorched before it can grow lush and tall.

"But I know you well—
   where you stay
and when you come and go.
   I know the way you have raged against me.
And because of your raging against me
   and your arrogance, which I have heard for
      myself,
I will put my hook in your nose
   and my bit in your mouth.
I will make you return
   by the same road on which you came."

Then Isaiah said to Hezekiah, "Here is the proof that what I say is true:

"This year you will eat only what grows up by itself,
　　and next year you will eat what springs up from that.
But in the third year you will plant crops and harvest them;
　　you will tend vineyards and eat their fruit.
And you who are left in Judah,
　　who have escaped the ravages of the siege,
will put roots down in your own soil
　　and will grow up and flourish.
For a remnant of my people will spread out from Jerusalem,
　　a group of survivors from Mount Zion.
The passionate commitment of the LORD of Heaven's Armies
　　will make this happen!

"And this is what the LORD says about the king of Assyria:

"His armies will not enter Jerusalem.
　　They will not even shoot an arrow at it.
They will not march outside its gates with their shields
　　nor build banks of earth against its walls.
The king will return to his own country
　　by the same road on which he came.
He will not enter this city,
　　says the LORD.
For my own honor and for the sake of my servant David,
　　I will defend this city and protect it."

That night the angel of the LORD went out to the Assyrian camp and killed 185,000 Assyrian soldiers. When the surviving Assyrians woke up the next morning, they found corpses everywhere. Then King Sennacherib of Assyria broke camp and returned to his own land. He went home to his capital of Nineveh and stayed there.

One day while he was worshiping in the temple of his god Nisroch, his sons Adrammelech and Sharezer killed him with their swords. They then escaped to the land of Ararat, and another son, Esarhaddon, became the next king of Assyria.

✛

About that time Hezekiah became deathly ill, and the prophet Isaiah son of Amoz went to visit him. He gave the king this message: "This is what the LORD says: Set your affairs in order, for you are going to die. You will not recover from this illness."

When Hezekiah heard this, he turned his face to the wall and prayed to the LORD, "Remember, O LORD, how I have always been faithful to

you and have served you single-mindedly, always doing what pleases you."
Then he broke down and wept bitterly.

But before Isaiah had left the middle courtyard, this message came to
him from the LORD: "Go back to Hezekiah, the leader of my people. Tell
him, 'This is what the LORD, the God of your ancestor David, says: I have
heard your prayer and seen your tears. I will heal you, and three days from
now you will get out of bed and go to the Temple of the LORD. I will add
fifteen years to your life, and I will rescue you and this city from the king
of Assyria. I will defend this city for my own honor and for the sake of my
servant David.'"

Then Isaiah said, "Make an ointment from figs." So Hezekiah's servants
spread the ointment over the boil, and Hezekiah recovered!

Meanwhile, Hezekiah had said to Isaiah, "What sign will the LORD give
to prove that he will heal me and that I will go to the Temple of the LORD
three days from now?"

Isaiah replied, "This is the sign from the LORD to prove that he will do
as he promised. Would you like the shadow on the sundial to go forward
ten steps or backward ten steps?"

"The shadow always moves forward," Hezekiah replied, "so that would
be easy. Make it go ten steps backward instead." So Isaiah the prophet
asked the LORD to do this, and he caused the shadow to move ten steps
backward on the sundial of Ahaz!

Soon after this, Merodach-baladan son of Baladan, king of Babylon, sent
Hezekiah his best wishes and a gift, for he had heard that Hezekiah had
been very sick. Hezekiah received the Babylonian envoys and showed
them everything in his treasure-houses—the silver, the gold, the spices,
and the aromatic oils. He also took them to see his armory and showed
them everything in his royal treasuries! There was nothing in his palace or
kingdom that Hezekiah did not show them.

Then Isaiah the prophet went to King Hezekiah and asked him, "What
did those men want? Where were they from?"

Hezekiah replied, "They came from the distant land of Babylon."

"What did they see in your palace?" Isaiah asked.

"They saw everything," Hezekiah replied. "I showed them everything I
own—all my royal treasuries."

Then Isaiah said to Hezekiah, "Listen to this message from the LORD:
The time is coming when everything in your palace—all the treasures
stored up by your ancestors until now—will be carried off to Babylon.
Nothing will be left, says the LORD. Some of your very own sons will be
taken away into exile. They will become eunuchs who will serve in the
palace of Babylon's king."

Then Hezekiah said to Isaiah, "This message you have given me from the LORD is good." For the king was thinking, "At least there will be peace and security during my lifetime."

The rest of the events in Hezekiah's reign, including the extent of his power and how he built a pool and dug a tunnel to bring water into the city, are recorded in *The Book of the History of the Kings of Judah*. Hezekiah died, and his son Manasseh became the next king.

+ + +

Manasseh was twelve years old when he became king, and he reigned in Jerusalem fifty-five years. His mother was Hephzibah. He did what was evil in the LORD's sight, following the detestable practices of the pagan nations that the LORD had driven from the land ahead of the Israelites. He rebuilt the pagan shrines his father, Hezekiah, had destroyed. He constructed altars for Baal and set up an Asherah pole, just as King Ahab of Israel had done. He also bowed before all the powers of the heavens and worshiped them.

He built pagan altars in the Temple of the LORD, the place where the LORD had said, "My name will remain in Jerusalem forever." He built these altars for all the powers of the heavens in both courtyards of the LORD's Temple. Manasseh also sacrificed his own son in the fire. He practiced sorcery and divination, and he consulted with mediums and psychics. He did much that was evil in the LORD's sight, arousing his anger.

Manasseh even made a carved image of Asherah and set it up in the Temple, the very place where the LORD had told David and his son Solomon: "My name will be honored forever in this Temple and in Jerusalem—the city I have chosen from among all the tribes of Israel. If the Israelites will be careful to obey my commands—all the laws my servant Moses gave them—I will not send them into exile from this land that I gave their ancestors." But the people refused to listen, and Manasseh led them to do even more evil than the pagan nations that the LORD had destroyed when the people of Israel entered the land.

Then the LORD said through his servants the prophets: "King Manasseh of Judah has done many detestable things. He is even more wicked than the Amorites, who lived in this land before Israel. He has caused the people of Judah to sin with his idols. So this is what the LORD, the God of Israel, says: I will bring such disaster on Jerusalem and Judah that the ears of those who hear about it will tingle with horror. I will judge Jerusalem by the same standard I used for Samaria and the same measure I used for the family of Ahab. I will wipe away the people of Jerusalem as one wipes a dish and turns it upside down. Then I will reject even the remnant of my own people who are left, and I will hand them over as plunder for their enemies. For they have done great evil in my sight and have angered me ever since their ancestors came out of Egypt."

Manasseh also murdered many innocent people until Jerusalem was filled from one end to the other with innocent blood. This was in addition to the sin that he caused the people of Judah to commit, leading them to do evil in the LORD's sight.

The rest of the events in Manasseh's reign and everything he did, including the sins he committed, are recorded in *The Book of the History of the Kings of Judah*. When Manasseh died, he was buried in the palace garden, the garden of Uzza. Then his son Amon became the next king.

+ + +

Amon was twenty-two years old when he became king, and he reigned in Jerusalem two years. His mother was Meshullemeth, the daughter of Haruz from Jotbah. He did what was evil in the LORD's sight, just as his father, Manasseh, had done. He followed the example of his father, worshiping the same idols his father had worshiped. He abandoned the LORD, the God of his ancestors, and he refused to follow the LORD's ways.

Then Amon's own officials conspired against him and assassinated him in his palace. But the people of the land killed all those who had conspired against King Amon, and they made his son Josiah the next king.

The rest of the events in Amon's reign and what he did are recorded in *The Book of the History of the Kings of Judah*. He was buried in his tomb in the garden of Uzza. Then his son Josiah became the next king.

+ + +

Josiah was eight years old when he became king, and he reigned in Jerusalem thirty-one years. His mother was Jedidah, the daughter of Adaiah from Bozkath. He did what was pleasing in the LORD's sight and followed the example of his ancestor David. He did not turn away from doing what was right.

In the eighteenth year of his reign, King Josiah sent Shaphan son of Azaliah and grandson of Meshullam, the court secretary, to the Temple of the LORD. He told him, "Go to Hilkiah the high priest and have him count the money the gatekeepers have collected from the people at the LORD's Temple. Entrust this money to the men assigned to supervise the restoration of the LORD's Temple. Then they can use it to pay workers to repair the Temple. They will need to hire carpenters, builders, and masons. Also have them buy the timber and the finished stone needed to repair the Temple. But don't require the construction supervisors to keep account of the money they receive, for they are honest and trustworthy men."

Hilkiah the high priest said to Shaphan the court secretary, "I have found the Book of the Law in the LORD's Temple!" Then Hilkiah gave the scroll to Shaphan, and he read it.

Shaphan went to the king and reported, "Your officials have turned over the money collected at the Temple of the LORD to the workers and supervisors at the Temple." Shaphan also told the king, "Hilkiah the priest has given me a scroll." So Shaphan read it to the king.

When the king heard what was written in the Book of the Law, he tore his clothes in despair. Then he gave these orders to Hilkiah the priest, Ahikam son of Shaphan, Acbor son of Micaiah, Shaphan the court secretary, and Asaiah the king's personal adviser: "Go to the Temple and speak to the LORD for me and for the people and for all Judah. Inquire about the words written in this scroll that has been found. For the LORD's great anger is burning against us because our ancestors have not obeyed the words in this scroll. We have not been doing everything it says we must do."

So Hilkiah the priest, Ahikam, Acbor, Shaphan, and Asaiah went to the New Quarter of Jerusalem to consult with the prophet Huldah. She was the wife of Shallum son of Tikvah, son of Harhas, the keeper of the Temple wardrobe.

She said to them, "The LORD, the God of Israel, has spoken! Go back and tell the man who sent you, 'This is what the LORD says: I am going to bring disaster on this city and its people. All the words written in the scroll that the king of Judah has read will come true. For my people have abandoned me and offered sacrifices to pagan gods, and I am very angry with them for everything they have done. My anger will burn against this place, and it will not be quenched.'

"But go to the king of Judah who sent you to seek the LORD and tell him: 'This is what the LORD, the God of Israel, says concerning the message you have just heard: You were sorry and humbled yourself before the LORD when you heard what I said against this city and its people—that this land would be cursed and become desolate. You tore your clothing in despair and wept before me in repentance. And I have indeed heard you, says the LORD. So I will not send the promised disaster until after you have died and been buried in peace. You will not see the disaster I am going to bring on this city.'"

So they took her message back to the king.

Then the king summoned all the elders of Judah and Jerusalem. And the king went up to the Temple of the LORD with all the people of Judah and Jerusalem, along with the priests and the prophets—all the people from the least to the greatest. There the king read to them the entire Book of the Covenant that had been found in the LORD's Temple. The king took his place of authority beside the pillar and renewed the covenant in the LORD's presence. He pledged to obey the LORD by keeping all his commands, laws, and decrees with all his heart and soul. In this way, he confirmed all the terms of the covenant that were written in the scroll, and all the people pledged themselves to the covenant.

Then the king instructed Hilkiah the high priest and the priests of the second rank and the Temple gatekeepers to remove from the LORD's Temple all the articles that were used to worship Baal, Asherah, and all the powers of the heavens. The king had all these things burned outside Jerusalem on the terraces of the Kidron Valley, and he carried the ashes away to Bethel. He did away with the idolatrous priests, who had been appointed by the previous kings of Judah, for they had offered sacrifices at the pagan shrines throughout Judah and even in the vicinity of Jerusalem. They had also offered sacrifices to Baal, and to the sun, the moon, the constellations, and to all the powers of the heavens. The king removed the Asherah pole from the LORD's Temple and took it outside Jerusalem to the Kidron Valley, where he burned it. Then he ground the ashes of the pole to dust and threw the dust over the graves of the people. He also tore down the living quarters of the male and female shrine prostitutes that were inside the Temple of the LORD, where the women wove coverings for the Asherah pole.

Josiah brought to Jerusalem all the priests who were living in other towns of Judah. He also defiled the pagan shrines, where they had offered sacrifices—all the way from Geba to Beersheba. He destroyed the shrines at the entrance to the gate of Joshua, the governor of Jerusalem. This gate was located to the left of the city gate as one enters the city. The priests who had served at the pagan shrines were not allowed to serve at the LORD's altar in Jerusalem, but they were allowed to eat unleavened bread with the other priests.

Then the king defiled the altar of Topheth in the valley of Ben-Hinnom, so no one could ever again use it to sacrifice a son or daughter in the fire as an offering to Molech. He removed from the entrance of the LORD's Temple the horse statues that the former kings of Judah had dedicated to the sun. They were near the quarters of Nathan-melech the eunuch, an officer of the court. The king also burned the chariots dedicated to the sun.

Josiah tore down the altars that the kings of Judah had built on the palace roof above the upper room of Ahaz. The king destroyed the altars that Manasseh had built in the two courtyards of the LORD's Temple. He smashed them to bits and scattered the pieces in the Kidron Valley. The king also desecrated the pagan shrines east of Jerusalem, to the south of the Mount of Corruption, where King Solomon of Israel had built shrines for Ashtoreth, the detestable goddess of the Sidonians; and for Chemosh, the detestable god of the Moabites; and for Molech, the vile god of the Ammonites. He smashed the sacred pillars and cut down the Asherah poles. Then he desecrated these places by scattering human bones over them.

The king also tore down the altar at Bethel—the pagan shrine that Jeroboam son of Nebat had made when he caused Israel to sin. He burned down the shrine and ground it to dust, and he burned the Asherah pole. Then Josiah turned around and noticed several tombs in the side of the hill. He ordered that the bones be brought out, and he burned them on the altar at Bethel to desecrate it. (This happened just as the LORD had promised through the man of God when Jeroboam stood beside the altar at the festival.)

Then Josiah turned and looked up at the tomb of the man of God who had predicted these things. "What is that monument over there?" Josiah asked.

And the people of the town told him, "It is the tomb of the man of God who came from Judah and predicted the very things that you have just done to the altar at Bethel!"

Josiah replied, "Leave it alone. Don't disturb his bones." So they did not burn his bones or those of the old prophet from Samaria.

Then Josiah demolished all the buildings at the pagan shrines in the towns of Samaria, just as he had done at Bethel. They had been built by the various kings of Israel and had made the LORD very angry. He executed the priests of the pagan shrines on their own altars, and he burned human bones on the altars to desecrate them. Finally, he returned to Jerusalem.

King Josiah then issued this order to all the people: "You must celebrate the Passover to the LORD your God, as required in this Book of the Covenant." There had not been a Passover celebration like that since the time when the judges ruled in Israel, nor throughout all the years of the kings of Israel and Judah. But in the eighteenth year of King Josiah's reign, this Passover was celebrated to the LORD in Jerusalem.

Josiah also got rid of the mediums and psychics, the household gods, the idols, and every other kind of detestable practice, both in Jerusalem and throughout the land of Judah. He did this in obedience to the laws written in the scroll that Hilkiah the priest had found in the LORD's Temple. Never before had there been a king like Josiah, who turned to the LORD with all his heart and soul and strength, obeying all the laws of Moses. And there has never been a king like him since.

Even so, the LORD was very angry with Judah because of all the wicked things Manasseh had done to provoke him. For the LORD said, "I will also banish Judah from my presence just as I have banished Israel. And I will reject my chosen city of Jerusalem and the Temple where my name was to be honored."

The rest of the events in Josiah's reign and all his deeds are recorded in *The Book of the History of the Kings of Judah.*

While Josiah was king, Pharaoh Neco, king of Egypt, went to the Euphrates River to help the king of Assyria. King Josiah and his army marched out to fight him, but King Neco killed him when they met at Megiddo. Josiah's officers took his body back in a chariot from Megiddo to Jerusalem and buried him in his own tomb. Then the people of the land anointed Josiah's son Jehoahaz and made him the next king.

+ + +

Jehoahaz was twenty-three years old when he became king, and he reigned in Jerusalem three months. His mother was Hamutal, the daughter of Jeremiah from Libnah. He did what was evil in the LORD's sight, just as his ancestors had done.

Pharaoh Neco put Jehoahaz in prison at Riblah in the land of Hamath to prevent him from ruling in Jerusalem. He also demanded that Judah pay 7,500 pounds of silver and 75 pounds of gold as tribute.

+ + +

Pharaoh Neco then installed Eliakim, another of Josiah's sons, to reign in place of his father, and he changed Eliakim's name to Jehoiakim. Jehoahaz was taken to Egypt as a prisoner, where he died.

In order to get the silver and gold demanded as tribute by Pharaoh Neco, Jehoiakim collected a tax from the people of Judah, requiring them to pay in proportion to their wealth.

Jehoiakim was twenty-five years old when he became king, and he reigned in Jerusalem eleven years. His mother was Zebidah, the daughter of Pedaiah from Rumah. He did what was evil in the LORD's sight, just as his ancestors had done.

During Jehoiakim's reign, King Nebuchadnezzar of Babylon invaded the land of Judah. Jehoiakim surrendered and paid him tribute for three years but then rebelled. Then the LORD sent bands of Babylonian, Aramean, Moabite, and Ammonite raiders against Judah to destroy it, just as the LORD had promised through his prophets. These disasters happened to Judah because of the LORD's command. He had decided to banish Judah from his presence because of the many sins of Manasseh, who had filled Jerusalem with innocent blood. The LORD would not forgive this.

The rest of the events in Jehoiakim's reign and all his deeds are recorded in *The Book of the History of the Kings of Judah*. When Jehoiakim died, his son Jehoiachin became the next king.

The king of Egypt did not venture out of his country after that, for the king of Babylon captured the entire area formerly claimed by Egypt—from the Brook of Egypt to the Euphrates River.

+ + +

Jehoiachin was eighteen years old when he became king, and he reigned in Jerusalem three months. His mother was Nehushta, the daughter of El-nathan from Jerusalem. Jehoiachin did what was evil in the LORD's sight, just as his father had done.

During Jehoiachin's reign, the officers of King Nebuchadnezzar of Babylon came up against Jerusalem and besieged it. Nebuchadnezzar himself arrived at the city during the siege. Then King Jehoiachin, along with the queen mother, his advisers, his commanders, and his officials, surrendered to the Babylonians.

In the eighth year of Nebuchadnezzar's reign, he took Jehoiachin prisoner. As the LORD had said beforehand, Nebuchadnezzar carried away all the treasures from the LORD's Temple and the royal palace. He stripped away all the gold objects that King Solomon of Israel had placed in the Temple. King Nebuchadnezzar took all of Jerusalem captive, including all the commanders and the best of the soldiers, craftsmen, and artisans—10,000 in all. Only the poorest people were left in the land.

Nebuchadnezzar led King Jehoiachin away as a captive to Babylon, along with the queen mother, his wives and officials, and all Jerusalem's elite. He also exiled 7,000 of the best troops and 1,000 craftsmen and artisans, all of whom were strong and fit for war. Then the king of Babylon installed Mattaniah, Jehoiachin's uncle, as the next king, and he changed Mattaniah's name to Zedekiah.

+ + +

Zedekiah was twenty-one years old when he became king, and he reigned in Jerusalem eleven years. His mother was Hamutal, the daughter of Jeremiah from Libnah. But Zedekiah did what was evil in the LORD's sight, just as Jehoiakim had done. These things happened because of the LORD's anger against the people of Jerusalem and Judah, until he finally banished them from his presence and sent them into exile.

Zedekiah rebelled against the king of Babylon.

So on January 15, during the ninth year of Zedekiah's reign, King Nebuchadnezzar of Babylon led his entire army against Jerusalem. They surrounded the city and built siege ramps against its walls. Jerusalem was kept under siege until the eleventh year of King Zedekiah's reign.

By July 18 in the eleventh year of Zedekiah's reign, the famine in the city had become very severe, and the last of the food was entirely gone. Then a section of the city wall was broken down. Since the city was surrounded by the Babylonians, the soldiers waited for nightfall and escaped through the gate between the two walls behind the king's garden. Then they headed toward the Jordan Valley.

But the Babylonian troops chased the king and overtook him on the plains of Jericho, for his men had all deserted him and scattered. They captured the king and took him to the king of Babylon at Riblah, where they pronounced judgment upon Zedekiah. They made Zedekiah watch as they slaughtered his sons. Then they gouged out Zedekiah's eyes, bound him in bronze chains, and led him away to Babylon.

On August 14 of that year, which was the nineteenth year of King Nebuchadnezzar's reign, Nebuzaradan, the captain of the guard and an official of the Babylonian king, arrived in Jerusalem. He burned down the Temple of the LORD, the royal palace, and all the houses of Jerusalem. He destroyed all the important buildings in the city. Then he supervised the entire Babylonian army as they tore down the walls of Jerusalem on every side. Then Nebuzaradan, the captain of the guard, took as exiles the rest of the people who remained in the city, the defectors who had declared their allegiance to the king of Babylon, and the rest of the population. But the captain of the guard allowed some of the poorest people to stay behind to care for the vineyards and fields.

The Babylonians broke up the bronze pillars in front of the LORD's

Temple, the bronze water carts, and the great bronze basin called the Sea, and they carried all the bronze away to Babylon. They also took all the ash buckets, shovels, lamp snuffers, ladles, and all the other bronze articles used for making sacrifices at the Temple. The captain of the guard also took the incense burners and basins, and all the other articles made of pure gold or silver.

The weight of the bronze from the two pillars, the Sea, and the water carts was too great to be measured. These things had been made for the LORD's Temple in the days of Solomon. Each of the pillars was 27 feet tall. The bronze capital on top of each pillar was 7½ feet high and was decorated with a network of bronze pomegranates all the way around.

Nebuzaradan, the captain of the guard, took with him as prisoners Seraiah the high priest, Zephaniah the priest of the second rank, and the three chief gatekeepers. And from among the people still hiding in the city, he took an officer who had been in charge of the Judean army; five of the king's personal advisers; the army commander's chief secretary, who was in charge of recruitment; and sixty other citizens. Nebuzaradan, the captain of the guard, took them all to the king of Babylon at Riblah. And there at Riblah, in the land of Hamath, the king of Babylon had them all put to death. So the people of Judah were sent into exile from their land.

Then King Nebuchadnezzar appointed Gedaliah son of Ahikam and grandson of Shaphan as governor over the people he had left in Judah. When all the army commanders and their men learned that the king of Babylon had appointed Gedaliah as governor, they went to see him at Mizpah. These included Ishmael son of Nethaniah, Johanan son of Kareah, Seraiah son of Tanhumeth the Netophathite, Jezaniah son of the Maacathite, and all their men.

Gedaliah vowed to them that the Babylonian officials meant them no harm. "Don't be afraid of them. Live in the land and serve the king of Babylon, and all will go well for you," he promised.

But in midautumn of that year, Ishmael son of Nethaniah and grandson of Elishama, who was a member of the royal family, went to Mizpah with ten men and killed Gedaliah. He also killed all the Judeans and Babylonians who were with him at Mizpah.

Then all the people of Judah, from the least to the greatest, as well as the army commanders, fled in panic to Egypt, for they were afraid of what the Babylonians would do to them.

+ + +

In the thirty-seventh year of the exile of King Jehoiachin of Judah, Evil-merodach ascended to the Babylonian throne. He was kind to Jehoiachin and released him from prison on April 2 of that year. He spoke kindly to Jehoiachin and gave him a higher place than all the other exiled kings in Babylon. He supplied Jehoiachin with new clothes to replace his prison garb and allowed him to dine in the king's presence for the rest of his life. So the king gave him a regular food allowance as long as he lived.

THE STORIES AND THE STORY
———————— *How the Bible Works* ————————

The Bible is a gift. The Creator of all things has entered into our human story, and he has spoken. Working through all the authors of the Bible's various writings, God brings wisdom into our lives and light to our path. But his biggest intention for the Bible is to invite us into its Story. What God wants from us, more than anything else, is to make the Bible's great drama of restoration and new life the story of our lives too.

The appropriate way to receive a gift like this is to come to know the Bible deeply, to lose ourselves in it precisely so that we can find ourselves in it. In other words, the best thing we can do with the Bible is to immerse ourselves in it.

The first step on this journey of immersion is to become intimately familiar with the Bible's individual books—the songs and stories, the visions and letters. These books reflect different kinds of writing, and each book with its various parts must first be read and understood on its own terms. Your *Immerse Bible* is designed to help you easily see what kind of writing is found in each book. This will foster a better reading experience that leads to reading more and to reading in context.

But there is an even bigger goal than understanding the individual books. At its heart, the Bible is God's grand narrative of the world and his intentions for it. By reading whole books and then reading them as a collection of writings, we discover how the Bible presents God's big story—*the* Story. The true destination of Bible reading is for us to inhabit the Story. All the smaller parts of the Bible—Gospels and histories, proverbs and prophecies—take their rightful places in revealing the saving drama of God.

As we begin our journey deep into the heart of the Bible, we come across many stories. The plots and subplots of these stories fit together to tell the Bible's big Story. All the characters, communities, and covenants play a part in bringing the overall Story to its fitting conclusion. That is, they are related to each other and work together to reveal God's bigger purposes for the world.

But how are they related?

The following overview of the main stories that make up the Story will help you understand the overall flow of the Bible. It will reveal how the major stories in the Bible are really subplots of the big Story. As each new subplot is introduced, we will see how it serves the bigger narrative, particularly the story that immediately precedes it.

The Bible is a connected, multi-layered story, and Jesus the Messiah is directly at the center of it all. Sent by the Father and empowered by the Spirit, he is the One who ultimately brings resolution to all the stories. He is the thread—the beginning and the end—that ties the Scriptures together. Jesus the Messiah makes the Story's good ending possible, enabling the completion of God's one, big, saving purpose for all things.

1. The Story of God and His World

In the beginning God made everything and said it was all very good. It is evident from the rich variety of interconnected living things in his created order that God delights in flourishing life. This thriving, teeming world brings God glory and reveals his power.

When we read the Bible in its ancient Near Eastern context, something else also becomes clear. The opening song of creation shows us that God intends for the entire cosmos to be his temple, the place where he makes his home. When the Bible says God "rested" on the seventh day, it doesn't simply mean he stopped working. In the ancient world, a deity "rested" in order to take up residence within a temple. So the new world God made becomes his creation-temple, and he rules over it, bringing peace and life.

This is the Bible's first account, and it forms the frame for everything else that happens. God's creation is the stage for all the acts of the Story going forward. And the role of others in the drama will determine whether or not the Creator's plan for flourishing life will be realized.

2. The Story of Humanity

Humans come into the creation story in a special way. They are portrayed as being formed from the earth itself, establishing their permanent connection with the rest of the creation. Yet they are set apart from the beginning with a unique calling: stewardship. Out of all the creatures, only humans are made in the image of God himself and are to bring God's intentions for his creation to fruition. Their job is to rule over all things, helping life to flourish. Humanity is God's plan for managing his world. As priests in the temple of God's creation, humans—more than any other creature—will determine the success or failure of God's purposes for the world.

However, there are also other forces at work. Evil powers exist and are in a position to influence humans, drawing them away from God and interfering with his aims. God's people are lured into self-assertion and rebellion. This disrupts not only their relationship with God but also the way they function in the world. Because of humanity's bond with the rest of creation and their special vocation within it, great tragedy comes into the world. As their own humanity is twisted out of shape, guilt, pain, violence, and death begin to wreak havoc throughout God's good creation. Human beings are made for worship, created to bring glory to the Creator. But when humans direct their worship elsewhere, the damage reverberates throughout the world.

You'd think this would be enough to make God reject humans completely. But instead, God makes a promise to Adam and Eve that he will continue to work in and through human beings. In fact, it will be an offspring of the woman who will defeat the powers of evil. God will overcome the moral chaos of the world, and he will do it in partnership with humanity. In the Bible's Story, the fate of humanity and the rest of creation are irrevocably bound together.

But the question then becomes: How will God do this?

3. The Story of Abraham and His Family

The book of Genesis reveals a surprising answer: God is going to mend the world and bring his blessing to all the families on earth through one man and his descendants. God calls Abram (his name is later changed to Abraham) to leave his home and go to a new land and a new future. God narrows his focus to one family for a time as the means for bringing restoration to all the world's families.

From this point on, the big stories of humanity and of creation will hinge on what happens in the smaller story of Abraham's descendants. God intends for this family to be an agent for the renewal of the world. This plan begins with God's making promises to Abraham—to bless him, to make his family into a great nation, and to bring blessing to all nations. Over time, God makes a series of these promises, or covenantal agreements, with Abraham's family. Each new covenant moves the story forward and makes God's ultimate intentions more clear.

Early in the narrative, Abraham's descendants go down to Egypt and are eventually enslaved there. But God comes down to set them free and bring them into their own land, an event known as the Exodus. This great act of liberation becomes the template, or pattern, for all the acts of deliverance that God will bring in the future. (The nation that comes from Abraham's descendants becomes known as Israel, named after Abraham's grandson.)

As part of the Exodus, God gives his Law to the people through the great leader Moses, and this Law becomes an important part of his covenantal agreement with Israel. In revealing his mandates to Israel, God expects Israel to become a light to the nations. God wants his people to show the rest of the world what it looks like to live well under God's rule.

Another critical event in the Exodus occurs when God's personal presence comes down and inhabits the Tabernacle (a great tent set up at the center of Israel's camp). This Tabernacle becomes God's house in the midst of his people and is filled with symbols of the earth and sky. It is thus a miniature picture of the cosmos, revealing God's desire to cleanse and renew the whole creation and to make his home with us here once again.

God is present with his people in their new land, keeping the promises he made through Moses. But Israel struggles to honor its covenantal obligations. Throughout the story of Israel, the nation turns away from God again and again. This breakdown threatens the covenant itself. God is committed to working through his people. So if they fail, then his restoration project cannot move forward.

But this story is full of God's surprises. Along the way, God establishes a further covenant with Israel's king David. God assures David of a dynasty of kings on which the promises and hopes of Israel will be concentrated. The destiny of Israel as the beginning of God's new humanity is now focused here.

However, the people of Israel persist in rejecting God's covenant—worshiping idols, inflicting injustice on the poor, and looking out only for themselves. In anger and frustration, God finally intervenes. He exiles his people from their own land and withdraws his presence from them. Others now rule over Abraham's family, and Israel's role in the divine drama seems to have disappeared. A key biblical truth is revealed here: There can be no renewal, for Israel or the wider world, until evil and wrongdoing are dealt with. Judgment is part of setting things right.

The failure of Israel is critical for the overall Story. Israel was called to be the means by which God saves the world, but now the rescue party itself needs rescuing. Everything God intended for his people—indeed, for the entire creation—now seems in doubt.

God sees everything that has gone wrong. But wrongdoing, violence, and death will not get the last word—not in God's Story. He has another promise. Through his prophets, God brings a vision of a new future, one aligned with his founding purpose. He will establish a new covenant, one that completes and surpasses all the covenants that came before. God himself will return to his people and restore them. They will be the light they were always meant to be. So the people wait—praying, worshiping, longing—for one more promise to come true.

4. The Story of Messiah Jesus

By the first century AD, Israel had been suffering under foreign rule for centuries. Now subjugated by the Roman Empire, God's people are divided about what to do. Zealous factions advocate violent rebellion. Many teachers and other religious leaders are urging people to get more serious about following Israel's distinctive way of life under God's law. And those running the Temple in Jerusalem survive by making compromises with their Roman overlords.

Israel's ancient prophet Isaiah had foretold a time when a messenger would come to Jerusalem proclaiming the good news that God is returning at last, that his people are being saved. But Rome had its own version of the good news, and it wasn't about Israel's God. The empire's gospel was about the great blessings brought by their own powerful leader, Caesar Augustus. He is, they said, "a savior for us and those who come after us, to make war to cease, to create order everywhere. The birthday of the god Augustus was the beginning for the world of the good tidings that have come to men through him" (from the Priene Calendar Inscription in Asia Minor, ca. 9 BC).

Into this world a child is born in Israel. He is a descendant of King David, but he comes from a humble family. An angel speaks to his mother, Mary, before he is born. He tells her that this child will be the long-promised and long-awaited Messiah, Israel's King, the One who will fulfill their history. Remarkably, Scripture's account of the ministry of Jesus echoes particulars of Israel's history.

Before Israel's Exodus, Pharaoh killed many Israelite babies, but Israel's deliverer, Moses, escaped; King Herod also kills many Israelite babies in trying to kill Jesus, but Jesus also escapes. The family of Israel went to Egypt to survive a deadly famine; the family of Jesus also survives by going to Egypt. Israel passed through the Jordan River to enter the Promised Land; Jesus is baptized in the Jordan River before beginning his ministry in Israel. Israel spent forty years in the wilderness, where they struggled with temptation; Jesus spends forty days fasting in the wilderness and is tempted by the devil. And as Israel had twelve sons who fathered twelve tribes, Jesus chooses twelve men to be his closest followers. In all of this, Jesus is reliving aspects of the ancient narrative of Israel, but now with a different outcome. Jesus is refreshing Israel's story and renewing Israel itself—through himself.

In his opening message to the people of Israel, Jesus calls them to be the light they were always meant to be, announcing the Good News that something unprecedented is happening in Israel's story. He demonstrates in powerful words and miraculous deeds what it looks like when God comes as King—teaching, correcting, and healing. Jesus is widely recognized as a rabbi and a mighty prophet in Israel, but the current religious leaders see him as a dangerous new problem. Jesus critiques their leadership, thus threatening their positions of power.

This tension between Jesus and the Jewish religious leaders rises until Jesus travels to Jerusalem for a final confrontation. His twelve disciples now recognize him as the Son of David, the Messiah, but they still don't understand his mission. They assume Jesus is going to fight his enemies and claim the throne. But Jesus talks about fighting a different kind of battle. He says his struggle is against the powers of darkness and the spiritual ruler of this world.

Then during Israel's annual celebration of the Exodus, Jesus shares a final Passover meal with his disciples. He tells them that his death will inaugurate the new covenant promised by the prophets. He is arrested by the religious leaders and handed over to the Romans for execution. He is nailed to a cross, with a mocking sign posted above his head that reads "The King of the Jews." It certainly looks as though Jesus has lost, that he is no king after all. But three days later, Jesus is raised from the dead and appears to his disciples.

It turns out that Jesus willingly went to his death as a sacrifice for the sins of his people. Through his sacrifice, he wins a surprising victory over the spiritual powers of darkness. He takes on sin and death directly—ironically, through death—emptying them of their power over humanity, and he rises from the dead to confirm his triumph. This unexpected story of Israel's Messiah reveals God's long-term plan. All the earlier covenants were leading to this one. The life and ministry of Jesus brings all the narrative threads in the Scriptures together into a single, coherent Story.

5. All the Stories in One

So we see that the story of Jesus does not simply stand alone. The Bible presents his narrative as intimately tied to all the plots and subplots that came before him. Jesus, crucified and raised, is God's answer to Israel's previous failure, humanity's wrongdoing and death, and the curse on all creation.

Jesus fulfills Israel's story and successfully plays the role of rescuer given to Abraham's family. He is Abraham's faithful descendant and David's powerful son, the Messiah. He is the light the nations have been longing for. People from every tribe, nation, and community can now join Abraham's family through belief in Jesus the Messiah. As the true Israelite, Jesus is also a new Adam, a fresh start for the human race. He has defeated our archenemies sin and death, restoring our relationship with God and ushering us into the life that is truly life. The new covenant in Jesus introduces a new world.

Jesus opens the doorway to the true worship of God, and we recover our God-given vocation to be his image-bearers through our stewardship of the world. As the new Adam, Jesus brings flourishing life back into the world. He embodies the new creation in his resurrection, blazing a path of future renewal for everything in heaven and on earth.

Jesus also launches a new community of God's people—the church—creating the renewed humanity that God envisioned from the beginning. This community is the focus of God's work on the way to a completely restored and healed creation. The book of Acts and the letters of the New Testament record how the earliest churches continued the ministry of God's coming reign that Jesus had begun. The context of this ministry changes over time and in location, but the ministry itself remains the same for God's new family: to embody and proclaim the Good News of God's victory through the Messiah.

In the end, the discovery of the narrative unity we find in the Scriptures is not merely for the purpose of information. The Bible is an invitation. It calls us to join the Story and take up our own role in God's ongoing redemptive drama. We read the Bible deeply and well in order to learn the true story of our lives within God's bigger Story of the world. We read the Bible to grasp the cosmic scope and meaning of Jesus' victory. And we read the Bible to know what it means to follow Jesus ourselves. The path of the cross—selfless love and sacrifice—is the path for us, too. But that path also ends in our own resurrection when the Messiah returns.

> Yet what we suffer now is nothing compared to the glory he will reveal to us later. For all creation is waiting eagerly for that future day when God will reveal who his children really are. Against its will, all creation was subjected to God's curse. But with eager hope, the creation looks forward to the day when it will join God's children in glorious freedom from death and decay. For we know that all creation has been groaning as in the pains of childbirth right up to the present time. And we believers also groan, even though we have the Holy Spirit within us as a foretaste of future glory, for we long for our bodies to be released from sin and suffering. We, too, wait with eager hope for the day when God will give us our full rights as his adopted children, including the new bodies he has promised us. We were given this hope when we were saved.
>
> From Paul's letter to the Romans

The final theme of the biblical chronicle is life, the same theme that began the Story. Through the power of the Spirit and the action of the Son, the Father's intention will be realized in a new heaven and a new earth.

—— *Introducing* ——

I M M E R S E
The Reading Bible

Many people feel discouraged in their Bible reading. The size and scope (not to mention the tiny fonts and the thin pages) intimidate new and seasoned readers alike, keeping them from diving into and immersing themselves in the word of God. The Bible itself is not the problem; how the Bible has been presented to readers for generations is.

Our Bibles currently look like reference books—a resource to put on the shelf and consult only when needed. So we read it like a reference book: infrequently and in small pieces. But the Bible is a collection of good writings that invite us to good reading—and it's God's word! There is an urgent need today for Christians to know the word of God, and the best way to do so is by reading the Bible. However, we need to understand the Bible on its own terms. We need to become deeply acquainted with whole books by reading them at length. And we can learn how to read the Bible well by altering a few of our current Bible reading habits.

First, we need to think about the Bible as a collection of writings written in various literary forms known as *genres*. Each literary form, or genre, used in the Bible—such as a poem, story, or letter—was chosen because, along with the words, it works to communicate truths about God to real people. (See "The Literary Forms of the Bible," p. 285, for a further explanation of some of these genres.) A complete book can be composed in a single genre, or the author may use several genres to tell one story. And even when books of the Bible are made up of several different compositions, as in the book of Psalms, those components are drawn together in such a way as to give each book an overall unity as a distinct work in itself.

Second, recognizing that the Bible is made up of whole books that tell a complete story, we should seek to understand the Bible's teaching and live out its story. To help readers better understand and read the Bible as whole books, we've removed any additives from the Bible text. Those additions, while inserted with good intentions, have accumulated over the centuries,

281

changing how people view the Bible and, therefore, what they think they're supposed to do with it.

Chapters and verses aren't the original units of the Bible. The latest books of the Bible were written in the first century AD; however, chapter divisions were added in the thirteenth century, and the verse divisions we use today appeared in the middle of the sixteenth century. So for the majority of its history, the Bible had no chapters or verses. They were introduced so that reference works like commentaries and concordances could be created. But if we rely on these later additions to guide our reading of the Bible, we often miss the original, natural structure. This also puts us at risk of missing the message and meaning of the Bible. For this reason, we have removed the chapter and verse markers from the text. (We do, however, include a verse range at the top of each page, allowing for easy reference.)

This edition also removes the section headings that are found in most Bibles. These are also not original but the work of modern publishers. These headings create the impression that the Bible is made up of short, encyclopedic sections. So, like chapters and verses, they can encourage us to treat the Bible as a kind of reference work rather than a collection of good writings that invite good reading. Many headings may also spoil the suspense that the inspired storytellers sought to create and use to such good effect. (For example, a heading that often appears in the book of Acts announces in advance "Peter's Miraculous Escape from Prison.")

So, in place of section headings, *Immerse: The Reading Bible* uses line spacing and graphic markers to simply and elegantly reflect the natural structures of the Bible's books. For example, in the letter known as 1 Corinthians, Paul addresses twelve issues in the life of the community in Corinth. In this edition, double line breaks and a single cross mark off the teaching Paul offers for each issue. Single line breaks separate different phases of the longer arguments Paul makes to support his teaching. And triple line breaks with three crosses set off the opening and closing of the letter from the main body. By contrast, the section headings in a typical Bible divide 1 Corinthians into nearly thirty parts. These divisions give no indication of which parts speak together to the same issue or where the letter's main body begins and ends.

Modern Bibles also include hundreds of footnotes and often include cross-references throughout the text. While these features provide information that can be helpful in certain settings, there's a danger that they, too, can encourage us to treat the Bible as a reference work. Constantly going back and forth between the text and the notes doesn't really qualify as being immersed in reading the Bible.

Third, the order in which the books appear is another important factor in reading the Bible well and at length. For the majority of the Bible's history, its books were not arranged in any fixed order. Instead, they were placed in a great variety of orders, depending on the needs and goals of each presentation. In some cases, books from the same time period were put together. In other cases, similar kinds of writing were set side by side. And often the Bible's books were organized according to the way the community used them in worship.

The order of books that we know today didn't become fixed until near the time of the invention of the printing press in the fifteenth century. This ordering has many drawbacks. For example, it presents Paul's letters in order of length (longest to shortest) rather than in the order in which he wrote them. Also, in this order, the books of the prophets are divided into groups by size, and the smaller books are then organized based on phrases they share. This arrangement puts them out of historical order and sends the reader swinging back and forth between centuries. And there are many other similar concerns in what we know as the traditional order.

This edition returns to the church's longstanding tradition of arranging the Bible's books to best meet the goals of a given presentation. To help readers delve deeper into the Story of the Bible, it places Paul's letters in their likely historical order. The books of the prophets are arranged in similar fashion. Furthermore, the collection of prophetic books is placed immediately after the story of Israel because the prophets were God's messengers to the people during the unfolding of that story. The remaining books of the First Testament, known traditionally as the "Writings," are placed after the prophets and arranged by type of writing. The introductions to the various groups of books in this Bible will explain more about how they are arranged and why.

Finally, some complete books of the Bible were broken into parts over time. The books of Samuel and Kings originally made up one long book, but they were separated into four parts so they would fit conveniently on ancient papyrus scrolls. The books of Chronicles, Ezra, and Nehemiah are similarly the divided parts of an originally unified composition. In this edition, both of these two longer works are put back together as Samuel–Kings and Chronicles–Ezra–Nehemiah. Luke and Acts were written as a unified story of the life of Jesus and the birth of the community of his followers. These two volumes had been separated so that Luke could be placed with the other Gospels. But since the two parts were meant to be read together, they have been reunited here as Luke–Acts.

All of this is presented in a clean, single-column format, allowing each of the Bible's basic units to be read like the books they are. The lines of Hebrew poetry can easily be seen, and stories, proverbs, letters, and other genres can readily be identified. In short, *Immerse: The Reading Bible* takes full advantage of good visual design to provide a more authentic encounter with God's sacred words.

It is our prayer that the combined effect of these changes to the visual layout of the Bible will enhance your reading experience. We believe these changes serve the Scriptures well and will allow you to receive these books on their own terms. The goal, after all, is to let the Bible be the book that God inspired so it can do its powerful work in our lives.

THE LITERARY FORMS OF THE BIBLE

Just as God's word uses existing human language, the inspired authors also employ existing human literary forms that enable words to be arranged in meaningful ways. These different types of writing are called *genres*.

Today most of us are probably more familiar with the concept of genre from watching movies. By watching the opening scene, we can identify whether it's a Western, a science fiction thriller, a romantic comedy, or a documentary. Once we know what kind of film it is, we know what expectations we should have about what can or can't happen, how things are likely to develop, and how we should interpret what is being shown. These expectations, created by previous films and respected by filmmakers, are like an agreement with the audience about how its message will be communicated and should be interpreted.

Likewise, the Bible's authors and editors, through God's inspiration, used and respected the genres of their day. We may be able to recognize some of them as similar to genres we know today, but others may be less familiar.

Since understanding genres is critical to reading the Bible well, we will describe the key types below. The compositions that reflect these genres make up either whole Bible books or smaller sections of larger books, so some Bible books are written partly in one genre and partly in another. (Many of the genres introduced here will be further explained in the introductions to books or sections of the Bible.) As indicated below, the specific genres employed in the Bible can be divided into two general categories of writing: prose and poetry.

PROSE GENRES

- ***Stories.*** Narrative—or stories—weave together events in a way that shows they have a larger meaning. Typically, a story situates the reader in a place and time and then introduces a conflict. This conflict intensifies until it reaches a climax, which is followed by a resolution.

  Narrative is the most common genre used in the Bible, emphasizing that God primarily makes himself known through his words and actions in specific historical events. The Bible doesn't teach about God merely in the abstract; its historical narratives are intentionally shaped to highlight key points about God and how he relates to people and the world.

The Bible features two special types of stories-within-stories. Sometimes a person will tell a story to illustrate a point about the larger narrative that person is in. These stories are called *parables* and were a favorite teaching tool of Jesus. They usually describe real-life situations but sometimes can be fanciful, like Jotham's parable in the book of Judges, which uses talking trees as the characters. People in a story may also relate *dreams* and *visions* that they've had. In this case they're not making up a story but reporting one they've seen. This subset of narrative speaks in pictures and uses symbols to represent realities.

- *Apocalypse.* Meaning "unveiling," apocalypse is an ancient genre structured as a narrative but composed entirely of *visions* employing vivid symbols which a heavenly visitor reveals to a person. These visions disclose the secrets of the spiritual world and, often, the future. The book of Revelation is a complete apocalypse, while the book of Daniel is split between narrative and apocalypse. Elements of apocalypse also appear in Isaiah, Ezekiel, and Zechariah.

- *Letters.* About one-third of the Bible's books are letters that were originally written by one person to another person or to a group. Letters in the Bible, following the form of ancient letters, have three parts: the opening, the main body, and the closing. In the opening, writers typically give their name, say who they're writing to, and offer a word of thanksgiving or prayer. The main body deals with the business of the letter. In the closing, the writer extends greetings, shares prayer requests, and offers a prayer for God to bless the recipients. Letters in the Bible are typically used by leaders to present their authoritative teaching to a community when they aren't physically present.

- *Laws.* Also known as commands, these are instructions for what to do in specific situations in order to live as God intends. Less frequently, laws are statements of general principles to follow. Many biblical laws have been gathered into large collections, but sometimes they are placed within narratives as part of the resolution after a conflict. God's instructions are most often presented in the Bible as part of his covenantal agreements with his people, contributing to his larger saving purposes.

- *Sermons.* These are public addresses to groups that have gathered for worship or for the celebration of a special occasion. They typically explain the meaning of earlier parts of the Bible's story for people living in a later part of that story. Most sermons in the Bible are found within narratives, but the book of Hebrews comprises four sermons that were collected and then sent out in the same letter.

The book of Deuteronomy is a series of sermons by Moses to the people of Israel as they were about to enter the Promised Land. Parts of it take the form of a *treaty* that high kings would make with the kings who served them. The Ten Commandments are a miniature version of that kind of treaty.

- **Prayers.** These are addressed to God and are usually offered in a public setting in the Bible, though sometimes they are private. They can include praise, thanksgiving, confession, and requests.

- **Lists.** Many kinds of lists are found in the Bible. One of the most common types, *genealogy*, is a record of a person's ancestors or descendants. The Bible also includes lists of things like offerings, building materials, assigned territories, stops along journeys, court officials, population counts, and so on. Lists in the Bible are not merely informative but usually make a theological point or provide verification of someone's connection to God's people.

POETRY GENRES

Hebrew poetry is based not on the repetition of sound (rhyme) but on the repetition of meaning. Its essential unit, the couplet, features a form of parallelism. One line states something, and the next line repeats, contrasts, or elaborates on the first line, intensifying its meaning. This feature is sometimes expanded to a triplet (three-line unit) for greater emphasis.

Poetry frequently uses metaphors and other figurative language to communicate messages with greater strength and emotion.

- **Proverbs.** These are short sayings, typically two lines in length (though sometimes longer), that teach practical lessons for life in God's world. Proverbs are not necessarily promises about how things will work out; mainly they are descriptions of wise ways to live.

- **Songs.** Poetry set to music. In the Bible, songs are used primarily for celebration or for mourning (in which case they are called *laments*). They are often found within narratives, but some books of the Bible are whole collections of songs.

  Psalms are songs used by people gathered for worship. These songs are most often addressed to God as prayers set to music.

- **Oracles.** These are messages from God delivered by prophets. In the Bible, oracles are most often recorded in poetry; originally, they may have been sung. Some oracles are in prose, but even those often use symbolic language similar to dreams and visions. Most biblical oracles are found within larger collections from the same prophet; however, the book of Obadiah consists of a single oracle.

- *Poetic dialogue.* Utilized in a number of ancient writings, poetic dialogue is a conversation in which each participant speaks in a form of poetry. In the Bible, this genre is found only in the book of Job.

Reading the Bible well starts with recognizing and then honoring each book's genre. Following this practice will help prevent mistakes in interpretation and allow us to discover the meaning that the Bible's creators originally intended.

NLT: A NOTE TO READERS

The *Holy Bible,* New Living Translation, was first published in 1996. It quickly became one of the most popular Bible translations in the English-speaking world. While the NLT's influence was rapidly growing, the Bible Translation Committee determined that an additional investment in scholarly review and text refinement could make it even better. So shortly after its initial publication, the committee began an eight-year process with the purpose of increasing the level of the NLT's precision without sacrificing its easy-to-understand quality. This second-generation text was completed in 2004, with minor changes subsequently introduced in 2007, 2013, and 2015.

The goal of any Bible translation is to convey the meaning and content of the ancient Hebrew, Aramaic, and Greek texts as accurately as possible to contemporary readers. The challenge for our translators was to create a text that would communicate as clearly and powerfully to today's readers as the original texts did to readers and listeners in the ancient biblical world. The resulting translation is easy to read and understand, while also accurately communicating the meaning and content of the original biblical texts. The NLT is a general-purpose text especially good for study, devotional reading, and reading aloud in worship services.

We believe that the New Living Translation—which combines the latest biblical scholarship with a clear, dynamic writing style—will communicate God's word powerfully to all who read it. We publish it with the prayer that God will use it to speak his timeless truth to the church and the world in a fresh, new way.

The Publishers

A full introduction to the NLT can be found at tyndale.com/nlt/process.

A complete list of the translators can be found at tyndale.com/nlt/scholars.

TWELVE TRIBES OF ISRAEL
AND THE CONQUEST OF CANAAN

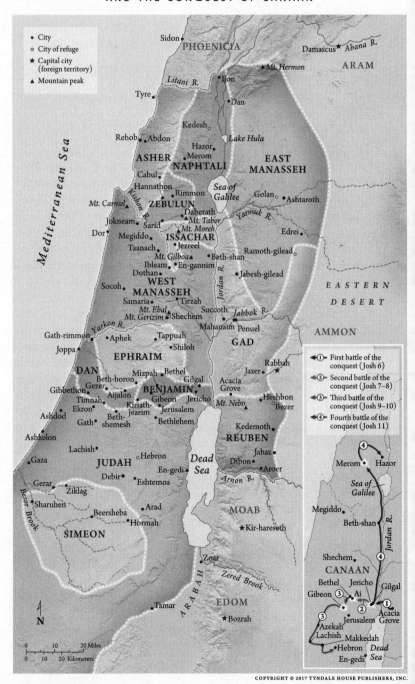

Legend:
- • City
- ◦ City of refuge
- ★ Capital city (foreign territory)
- ▲ Mountain peak

Map labels:

Sidon
PHOENICIA
Damascus ★ Abana R.
ARAM
Mt. Hermon
Litani R.
Ijon
Tyre
Dan
Kedesh
Rehob Abdon
ASHER
Hazor
Merom
Lake Hula
NAPHTALI
EAST MANASSEH
Cabul
Hannathon
Rimmon
Sea of Galilee
Golan Ashtaroth
Mt. Carmel
ZEBULUN
Daberath
Jokneam
Sarid
Mt. Tabor
Mt. Moreh
Yarmuk R.
Edrei
Dor
Megiddo
ISSACHAR
Jezreel
Taanach
Mt. Gilboa Beth-shan
Ramoth-gilead
Ibleam En-gannim
Dothan
Jabesh-gilead
WEST MANASSEH
Socoh
Jordan R.
Samaria Tirzah
Mt. Ebal
Mt. Gerizim Shechem
Succoth Jabbok R.
Mahanaim Penuel
EASTERN DESERT
Gath-rimmon Aphek
Tappuah
AMMON
Joppa
Shiloh
GAD
EPHRAIM
Mizpah Bethel
Jazer
Rabbah ★
DAN
Beth-horon
Gilgal
Acacia Grove
Gezer
Gibeon Jericho
Heshbon
Gibbethon
Aijalon
BENJAMIN
Mt. Nebo
Bezer
Timnah
Kiriath-jearim
Ekron
Jerusalem
Kedemoth
Ashdod
Beth-shemesh
Bethlehem
Gath
REUBEN
Ashkelon
Jahaz
Lachish
Hebron
Dead Sea
Dibon
Gaza
Debir En-gedi
Eshtemoa
Aroer
JUDAH
Arnon R.
Gerar Ziklag
Arad
MOAB
Sharuhen
Hormah
Besor Brook
Beersheba
Kir-hareseth
SIMEON
Zoar
Zered Brook
ARABAH
EDOM
Tamar
Bozrah
N

Scale:
0 10 20 Miles
0 10 20 Kilometers

Inset legend:
- ◀①▶ First battle of the conquest (Josh 6)
- ◀②▶ Second battle of the conquest (Josh 7–8)
- ◀③▶ Third battle of the conquest (Josh 9–10)
- ◀④▶ Fourth battle of the conquest (Josh 11)

Inset map labels:
④
Merom Hazor
Sea of Galilee
Megiddo
Beth-shan
Jordan R.
Shechem ④
CANAAN
Bethel Jericho
Gibeon ③ Ai Gilgal
①
Jerusalem ② Acacia Grove
③
Azekah
Lachish Makkedah
Hebron Dead Sea
En-gedi

UNITED AND DIVIDED KINGDOMS

UNITED KINGDOM OF ISRAEL

Aleppo

Euphrates R.

Tiphsah

N

Cyprus

Hamath

HAMATH

DIVIDED KINGDOM

Arvad

Tadmor

Lebo-hamath

Mediterranean Sea

PHOENICIA

Damascus

Tyre

Dan ARAM

Hazor

Sea of Galilee

Megiddo

Shechem

Joppa

Rabbah

PHILISTIA

Gezer

AMMON

Jerusalem

Gaza

Dead Sea

MOAB

Jordan R.

EASTERN DESERT

Beersheba

AMALEK

EDOM

Kadesh-barnea

SINAI

Ezion-geber

Gulf of Aqaba

① Kingdom of Saul
② David's Expansion
③ Solomon's Expansion

0 — 40 Miles
0 — 40 Kilometers

N

Orontes R.

HAMATH

Hamath

0 — 20 Miles
0 — 20 Kilometers

Arvad

Kadesh

Mediterranean Sea

Lebo-hamath

Berothai

PHOENICIA

Litani R.

Sidon

Damascus

ARAM

Tyre

Dan

Kedesh

Hazor

Sea of Galilee

Ashtaroth

Salecah

Beth-shan

Ramoth-gilead

Megiddo

ISRAEL

Jordan R.

Jabbok R.

Shechem

Joppa

AMMON

Bethel

Rabbah

Gezer

Gibeah

Ashdod

Gath

Jerusalem

Gaza

Lachish

Dead Sea

Aroer

Hebron

MOAB

Beersheba

Kir-hareseth

JUDAH

NEGEV

Brook of Egypt

PHILISTIA

Bozrah

Kadesh-barnea

EDOM

EASTERN DESERT

WILDERNESS OF ZIN

SINAI

Ezion-geber

Gulf of Aqaba

8-Week Reading Plan

Reading Plan Instructions: Always read to the largest break on the page where each reading ends. If there is more than one largest break, go to the last one. If no breaks appear on that page, read to the bottom of the page.

Week 1 Joshua
Day 1   p. A9-4
Day 2   p. 4-10
Day 3   p. 10-19
Day 4   p. 19-32
Day 5   p. 32-39

Week 2 Judges, Ruth
Day 6   p. 41-52
Day 7   p. 52-61
Day 8   p. 61-72
Day 9   p. 72-80
Day 10   p. 81-88

Week 3 Samuel–Kings
Day 11   p. 89-95
Day 12   p. 96-100
Day 13   p. 100-106
Day 14   p. 106-114
Day 15   p. 114-122

Week 4 Samuel–Kings
Day 16   p. 122-129
Day 17   p. 129-135
Day 18   p. 135-142
Day 19   p. 143-147
Day 20   p. 147-153

Week 5 Samuel–Kings
Day 21   p. 153-159
Day 22   p. 159-166
Day 23   p. 166-176
Day 24   p. 176-180
Day 25   p. 180-183

Week 6 Samuel–Kings
Day 26   p. 184-189
Day 27   p. 189-195
Day 28   p. 195-200
Day 29   p. 200-205
Day 30   p. 205-210

Week 7 Samuel–Kings
Day 31   p. 210-215
Day 32   p. 215-222
Day 33   p. 222-228
Day 34   p. 228-237
Day 35   p. 237-242

Week 8 Samuel–Kings
Day 36   p. 242-248
Day 37   p. 248-255
Day 38   p. 255-260
Day 39   p. 260-267
Day 40   p. 267-271

4 QUESTIONS TO GET YOUR CONVERSATION STARTED:

1. What stood out to you this week?
2. Was there anything confusing or troubling?
3. Did anything make you think differently about God?
4. How might this change the way we live?

More Immerse resources available at www.ImmerseBible.com/Kingdoms.

16-Week Reading Plan

Reading Plan Instructions: Always read to the largest break on the page where each reading ends. If there is more than one largest break, go to the last one. If no breaks appear on that page, read to the bottom of the page.

Week 1 Joshua
Day 1   pp. A9-2
Day 2   pp. 3-6
Day 3   pp. 6-10
Day 4   pp. 10-13
Day 5   pp. 13-17

Week 2 Joshua
Day 6   pp. 18-22
Day 7   pp. 22-28
Day 8   pp. 28-32
Day 9   pp. 32-36
Day 10   pp. 36-39

Week 3 Judges
Day 11   pp. 41-46
Day 12   pp. 46-52
Day 13   pp. 52-56
Day 14   pp. 56-61
Day 15   pp. 61-65

Week 4 Judges, Ruth
Day 16   pp. 65-72
Day 17   pp. 72-74
Day 18   pp. 74-80
Day 19   pp. 81-84
Day 20   pp. 84-88

Week 5 Samuel–Kings
Day 21   pp. 89-92
Day 22   pp. 92-95
Day 23   pp. 96-98
Day 24   pp. 98-100
Day 25   pp. 100-103

Week 6 Samuel–Kings
Day 26   pp. 103-106
Day 27   pp. 106-111
Day 28   pp. 111-114
Day 29   pp. 114-117
Day 30   pp. 117-122

Week 7 Samuel–Kings
Day 31   pp. 122-125
Day 32   pp. 125-129
Day 33   pp. 129-133
Day 34   pp. 133-135
Day 35   pp. 135-138

Week 8 Samuel–Kings
Day 36   pp. 138-142
Day 37   pp. 143-145
Day 38   pp. 145-147
Day 39   pp. 147-150
Day 40   pp. 150-153

Week 9 Samuel–Kings
Day 41   pp. 153-156
Day 42   pp. 156-159
Day 43   pp. 159-163
Day 44   pp. 163-166
Day 45   pp. 166-169

Week 10 Samuel–Kings
Day 46   pp. 169-173
Day 47   pp. 173-176
Day 48   pp. 176-180
Day 49   pp. 180-182
Day 50   pp. 182-183

Week 11 Samuel–Kings
Day 51   pp. 184-186
Day 52   pp. 186-189
Day 53   pp. 189-192
Day 54   pp. 192-195
Day 55   pp. 195-198

Week 12 Samuel–Kings
Day 56   pp. 198-200
Day 57   pp. 200-202
Day 58   pp. 202-205
Day 59   pp. 205-207
Day 60   pp. 207-210

Week 13 Samuel–Kings
Day 61   pp. 210-212
Day 62   pp. 212-215
Day 63   pp. 215-218
Day 64   pp. 218-222
Day 65   pp. 222-224

Week 14 Samuel–Kings
Day 66   pp. 224-228
Day 67   pp. 228-232
Day 68   pp. 232-237
Day 69   pp. 237-240
Day 70   pp. 240-242

Week 15 Samuel–Kings
Day 71   pp. 242-246
Day 72   pp. 246-248
Day 73   pp. 248-251
Day 74   pp. 251-255
Day 75   pp. 255-257

Week 16 Samuel–Kings
Day 76   pp. 257-260
Day 77   pp. 260-263
Day 78   pp. 263-267
Day 79   pp. 267-269
Day 80   pp. 269-271

THE IMMERSE BIBLE SERIES

IMMERSE: THE READING BIBLE comes in six volumes and presents each Bible book without the distractions of chapter and verse numbers, subject headers, or footnotes. It's designed for reading—especially for reading with others. By committing to just two eight-week sessions per year (spring and fall), you can read through the entire Bible in three years. And online video and audio support tools make it easy to read together in groups. Step into this three-year Immerse Bible reading cycle with your friends; then do it again—and again—for a lifetime of life-giving, life-changing Bible engagement!

Immerse: Beginnings includes the first five books of the Bible, known as the *Torah* (meaning "instruction"). These books describe the origins of God's creation, the human rebellion, and the family of Israel—the people God chose to be a light to all peoples. We follow the covenant community from its earliest ancestors to the time it is about to enter the Promised Land.

Immerse: Kingdoms tells the story of Israel from the time of its conquest of Canaan (Joshua) through its struggle to settle the land (Judges, Ruth) and the establishment of Israel's kingdom, which ends in a forced exile (Samuel–Kings). The nation of Israel, commissioned to be God's light to the nations, falls to division and then foreign conquest for rejecting God's rule.

Immerse: Prophets presents the First Testament prophets in groupings that generally represent four historical periods: before the fall of Israel's northern kingdom (Amos, Hosea, Micah, Isaiah), before the fall of the southern kingdom (Zephaniah, Nahum, Habakkuk), around the time of Jerusalem's destruction (Jeremiah, Obadiah, Ezekiel), and after the return from exile (Haggai, Zechariah, Malachi, Joel, Jonah).

Immerse: Poets presents the poetical books of the First Testament in two groupings, dividing the books between songs (Psalms, Lamentations, Song of Songs) and wisdom writings (Proverbs, Ecclesiastes, Job). These writings all reflect the daily, down-to-earth faith of God's people as they live out their covenant relationship with him in worship and wise living.

Immerse: Chronicles contains the remaining First Testament books: Chronicles–Ezra–Nehemiah, Esther, and Daniel. These works were all written after the Jewish people fell under the control of foreign empires and were scattered among the nations. They remind God's chastened people of their identity and calling to faithfully represent God to the nations and that there is still hope for the struggling dynasty of David.

Immerse: Messiah provides a unique guided journey through the entire New Testament. Each major section is anchored by one of the Gospels, highlighting the richness of Scripture's fourfold witness to Jesus the Messiah. This creates a fresh reading of the New Testament centered on Christ.